General John Fulton
Reynolds

His Biography, Words and Relations

Lawrence Knorr
Michael A Riley
Diane E Watson

General John Fulton Reynolds: His Biography, Words and Relations

SECOND SUNBURY PRESS EDITION
Printed in the United States of America
January 2013

ISBN 978-1-620061-81-7

Published by:
Sunbury Press, Inc.
50-A West Main Street
Mechanicsburg, PA 17055

ISBN# 9781-4528-261-3-4

www.sunburypress.com

Mechanicsburg, Pennsylvania USA

Thank You

Sincere 'thank yous' to both Diane E Watson and Michael A Riley for permission to use their booklets as chapters in this work. Some say 'the whole is better than its parts.' But, these are some 'very fine parts.'

Lawrence Knorr, 2010

Table of Contents

Part I:

"For God's Sake Forward!"

Gen. John F. Reynolds, USA

by

Michael A Riley

Afterword by:
Alan T Nolan

Introduction

In recent years historians have tended to slight the career of General John F. Reynolds and dismiss his sterling contributions to the Army of the Potomac during the early phases of the Gettysburg campaign. Such was not always the case. A generation ago, the foremost historian of the battle, Edwin Coddington, wrote that "if the fates had decreed other than they did, he (Reynolds) might have gone down as one of the greatest generals of the Civil War." Somewhat earlier, former President (and General) Eisenhower had referred to Reynolds as "the best general they (the Federals) had."

Eisenhower and Coddington were merely echoing the sentiments of a number of Reynolds' own contemporaries. On the Union side, his good friend George Meade characterized Reynolds as the "noblest ... bravest gentleman in the army. When he fell at Gettysburg the army lost its right arm." Confederate General Daniel Harvey Hill, a gentleman who seldom praised anyone, declared Reynolds to be "one of the noblest of mankind."

My own search for John Reynolds began in 1988, when, as a member of a local reenactment group, I became involved in a movement to rescue the general's boyhood home from the "adult bookstore" that occupied it. To better present John Reynolds to the public, I began to research the man in depth. Beginning with the standard Reynolds biography, Edward Nichols' *Toward Gettysburg,* I then moved into the family papers in an attempt to find the flesh and blood figure beneath the uniform.

Over time my research uncovered a very complex man with a three-sided personality. To staff officers and subordinates in proximity, Reynolds seemed perpetually reticent and aloof, in Meade's phrase: "A man of very few words." On the other hand, to his family and sisters, he was the warm correspondent, the protective brother who would write long affectionate letters pouring out his heart on all manner of subjects and persons. To his command level peers and the men in ranks there was a third, highly charismatic side best captured in a description by colonel Fred Hitchcock: "Reynolds was a superb looking man, dark complexioned, wearing full black whiskers, and sat on his horse like a Centaur, tall, straight and graceful, the ideal soldier."

All could feel the force behind those smoldering dark eyes, and in the words of a First Corps aide, " ... the love we had for him is beyond expression."

Given the crowded canvas and the full three-day fury of Gettysburg, it is easy to lose sight of John Reynolds, who was killed almost as soon as he arrived. My hope is to acquaint the general public with his early life and give some inkling of his importance to the Army of the Potomac. The fact is, by the late spring of 1863 a great many within the army, George Meade included, looked to John Reynolds for leadership. The measure of their trust in him was best expressed by General John Buford, the cavalry commander who preceded Reynolds to Gettysburg. Under siege from advancing Confederates, the harassed cavalryman looked round from the cupola of the Lutheran Seminary, spotted the reassuring figure of John Reynolds, and exclaimed: "Now we can hold this place."

I would like to express my thanks to all those who made a contribution to this project; in particular, Wayne E. Motts, who recommended that I write the Reynolds booklet for the Farnsworth commander series; also to John S. Peterson for helping me wrestle the ideas and words into better shape. My thanks as well to Tim Smith and the good people at the Adams County Historical Society, and to Scott Hartwig at the Gettysburg National Military Park. Thanks also to Terry Deal for her digital fortitude, and to Michael Kelly for his Pennsylvania Reserve expertise.

Many thanks to Ann Kenne and Janet Dotterer of the Archives & Special Collections Department of Franklin & Marshall College, for making the research a delightful experience. Blake Magner deserves thanks for his map-making talents, as does William Bitzer for his professional reproduction of the photographs in this book, including the original oil on the back cover. Along the way I've appreciated the support of Kalina Anderson, another Reynolds fan, and her packets of much-needed information.

I would also like to express gratitude to Ann Hoffman Cleaver, descendant of William Reynolds, for her patience with my question filled letters, and for sharing family history. My special thanks to the late Edward Nichols, whose Reynolds biography was of immeasurable assistance; and to Alan T. Nolan for his eloquent afterword.

Last but certainly not least, I would thank my wife Mary and children, Ethan and Megan, for their support and understanding as I sat trapped to a computer these past months. Having spent eight years listening to me speak of the general, their knowledge of John F. Reynolds probably exceeds my own.

Michael A. Riley Lancaster, PA

To the American men and women, on both sides, who served and sacrificed, for what they believed, **this book is respectfully dedicated.**

Fateful Orders

At 4:00 AM on the morning of July 1, 1863, Major William Riddle entered the back room of the Moritz Tavern, which was located on the Emmitsburg Road, six miles southeast of Gettysburg, Pennsylvania. The previous afternoon the tavern had become the headquarters of Major General John F. Reynolds, the acting Left Wing commander of the Army of the Potomac. Now, with the approach of dawn, Riddle carried orders from army commander, Major General George Gordon Meade, instructing Reynolds to concentrate his forces in the direction of Gettysburg.

Riddle found the general huddled in a blanket, asleep on the floor. The major felt a reluctance to wake him, which, in the circumstances, was understandable. The army had gotten little sleep in the past few days, and the general almost none. The weeks since Chancellorsville had been a time of wild uncertainty for the army, and for John Reynolds especially. Who knew what dreams might have come to him in this, his last living sleep? Perhaps his mind conjured scenes of the recent interview with Lincoln in which he had been sounded out on the command of the Army of the Potomac, a position he declined. Possibly he saw flashes of family and his boyhood home in Lancaster, Pennsylvania, now threatened by the Confederate invasion. Then again, he might have dreamed of a woman, the secret fiancée whose ring he wore in place of his West Point class ring. Quite likely, in his exhausted state, he dreamed of nothing at all.

Shaken awake, Reynolds lay on his back to stare at the ceiling while the major read the orders. His left wing consisted of the First, Third, and Eleventh Corps. General Meade directed the First Corps to Gettysburg, with the Eleventh to follow in close support, while the Third was to march to Emmitsburg, Maryland. Up ahead in Gettysburg, cavalry commander John Buford had posted his two brigades to the west and north of town in hopes of holding off the Rebels that he believed to be converging there in force. As John Reynolds arose to awaken his staff and put the infantry on the road, little did he know of the desperate race that he and his First Corps were about to run to help save the heights to the south of town. Nor could he have known that his own life would be included in the stakes.

Lancaster Youth

John Fulton Reynolds, born on September 21, 1820, in Lancaster, Pennsylvania, was one of thirteen children born to John and Lydia Reynolds, four of whom died at an early age. His father was a well-known Lancaster businessman and journalist, owning and editing a local Democratic newspaper, the *Lancaster Journal*. In addition, Reynolds, Sr. had served in the state legislature, had been captain of the local militia company, and was a personal friend and business associate of future President James Buchanan, whom the Reynolds children affectionately called "Mr. Buckwheat."

If young John had a predilection for military service, some of it could be traced to his maternal grandfather, Samuel Moore, who had been a captain of the Third

Pennsylvania Infantry of the Continental Line, and who had wintered at Valley Forge, as well as being wounded at Brandywine. Besides himself, John had three brothers who served in some capacity during the Civil War, the most noted of whom was his older brother, William, who had been appointed a midshipman in the navy in 1831, and who sailed around the world on the Wilkes Expedition, 1838-1842. This brother went on to serve with the South Atlantic Blockading Squadron during the war and retired as a rear admiral in 1877.

As a boy, young John was educated at a well-known public school run by Mr. John Beck in Lititz, Pennsylvania, where he was taught such subjects as "Franklin's Theory of Lightning." His letters home revealed an enthusiastic student: "I think I have improved very much since I am here ... " He later attended Long Green Academy of Baltimore, and then graduated from the Lancaster County Academy in 1835 at age fifteen.

John Reynolds, Sr. was not wealthy, and by 1836 he had begun looking for a means of furthering young John's education without straining family resources. Not surprisingly, he turned to his friend, James Buchanan, and requested his help in securing for his son a position at the United States Military Academy. John had at first leaned toward the navy, out of deference to his brother, William, but then came to accept the army.

Unfortunately, their first attempt came to naught. At fifteen, John was still a year shy of the regulation age, and a "mortified" Senator Buchanan apologized to the elder Reynolds for the oversight. He promised to obtain the appointment for the following term, and was as good as his word. On March 6, 1837, John Reynolds wrote the following letter of acceptance to Secretary of War, Lewis Casso:

> Yesterday I had the honor to receive from you a notice of my conditional appointment by the President as a Cadet in the service of the United States, requiring immediate information as to my acceptance or non acceptance of the same. I therefore hasten to assure you, that with great pleasure, I thankfully accept the appointment and shall report myself to the Superintendent of the Military Academy at West Point within the time specified.

John F. Reynolds was now to enter the United States Army and begin a career that would span twenty-six of the most turbulent years in the U.S. history.

West Point

When Reynolds arrived at the academy in June 1837, he was assigned a tent on the "Plain," where he and his fellow plebes would learn the rudiments of drill. He was known as "Josh" to his classmates, which included such future notables as Nathaniel Lyon, Israel B. Richardson, Horatio Wright, and the Garnett cousins, Robert and Richard. His friend, Henry Kendrick, remembered being "impressed" by Reynolds' "clear and independent thinking, even temperament and courtesy," as were most of his classmates. The next three months would be spent in drill, and though classes had yet to start, Reynolds wrote home in August that he was "very much pleased with my life here and think I shall continue to like it." With the beginning of class, life became hectic, as he explained to a sister who complained of his infrequent letters:

> *From 5 o'clock in the morning, or speaking "a la militate" from Reveille, until 10 o'clock at night we have only two hours to ourselves. Besides our military duties such as Guard, Drill, Parade, all the rest of the time we are obliged to be in our rooms studying Calculus, French, Ethics, etc. Cannot even visit our neighbors without getting 5 demerits.*

Reynolds was obviously feeling the sting of discipline, and he further noted that Commandant Charles F. Smith was a complete tyrant. Nonetheless, he encountered few serious problems in his first two years at the point, and by April 1839 was looking ahead to his summer furlough and "hoping to get home in time for strawberries ... "

In his third year Reynolds wrote that "we have commenced to ride and by the time I graduate I expect to be a great horseman." Later years would prove this to be no hollow boast. His remaining time at the Point was spent learning the duties of commissioned and junior officers, mixed with a bit of socializing. He wrote as follows on January 1, 1841:

> *New Years Day was spent, (that is the morning), in conforming to the established custom of the Point, of visiting all your acquaintances. It is I believe an old German custom, peculiarly northern, and I think a very good one.*

In this letter Reynolds asked the advice of his father as to the best branch of service, indicating that he himself was leaning toward the artillery or dragoons. At graduation, on July 1, 1841, Cadet John F. Reynolds stood 26th in a class of 52, and was commissioned brevet second lieutenant in Company E, Third United States Artillery Regiment.

Soldier's Life

Lieutenant Reynolds' first assignment was the garrison at Fort McHenry, Baltimore, from which he wrote on October 3, 1841, "I have at length made my way to the end of my journey and am now very comfortably situated in our Drawing Room at Ft. McH. in the capacity of Officer of the Day and in command of the fort." He seemed to be pleased with his first assignment, remarking that "the fort is situated on a beautiful spot and must be exceedingly pleasant in summer but a little too cold in winter ... " The sleeping arrangements also met with his approval: "Our quarters are excellent. We each have a sleeping room to ourselves and then a parlor and map room in common ... "

In November he wrote to his family concerning the possibility of promotion. "I have just seen the death of Capt. Garner of our Regt. in the papers, he died in Florida, which promotes me to a full 2nd. lieutenant..." In the pre-Civil War army promotions up to the rank of major came only within the regiment, so that a young officer could be forgiven if he saw the death of a fellow officer in terms of advancement. The following year, the concluding year of the Second Seminole War, Reynolds was posted to St. Augustine, Florida. From here he wrote that the "officers composing our garrison are Captain J.R. Vinton, Lt. Bragg, Hammond, and myself." Reynolds had always prided himself on his excellent health, but now, in the Florida summer heat, he became seriously ill.

> *On the evening of the 12th of July he (Reynolds) was taken with symptoms of fever and since the morning of the 13th has been confined to his bed by a pretty severe attack of bilious fever, and tho' he has at no time been considered dangerous, he has suffered a good deal. I am confident from having been in constant attendance on him that he is far better this morning than he has been since the first attack. .. You may rest assured that every attention has been and will be rendered him by myself and friends.*

The above letter and a later one, assuring the Reynolds family "of the continued improvement of my friend Lt. Reynolds," came from none other than Braxton Bragg, a man destined to become one of the more hated figures in the Confederacy. During his convalescence, Reynolds grew bored and referred to St. Augustine as "the dullest of all dull places." But by early March, much to his surprise, the regiment had been ordered to Fort Moultrie in Charleston, South Carolina. Remarking on the turn of events, he wrote that "we know not what changes a week of time make in this unsettled Life of a soldier ... "

Life in Charleston was much more to Reynolds' liking, as Charleston society and hospitality made this assignment perhaps the most coveted in the service. As for army companions, Reynolds now found himself in the company of William T. Sherman, George H. Thomas, and Erasmus Keys, who later stated that Reynolds was "as amiable as he is brave." "Cump" Sherman and Reynolds struck up a friendship and attended numerous balls and parties together, including one where their joint diplomacy possibly saved the life of Braxton Bragg. A local swain by the name of Stewart, in proposing a toast to the states of Virginia and South Carolina, referred to North Carolina as merely a strip of land between two great states. Bragg, a native Tar Heel, became enraged and as Sherman recalled the incident:

"High words and a challenge passed-pistols for two, coffee for one the next morning, but John F. Reynolds and I from remote and obscure regions like Pennsylvania and Ohio, were chosen peacemakers." Just possibly Reynolds was returning a favor to Bragg for having nursed him back to health in Florida.

In August 1843, Reynolds' mother became ill and eventually died. John was kept informed of her failing health but was unable to attend the funeral inasmuch as "Lt. Bragg is away and I am in command of my company ... " Almost two years would pass before he could obtain a furlough. March 1845 found him in Lancaster on a twenty-day leave which was eventually extended to three months. These were eventful times, as trouble was brewing in Mexico. When he made plans to return to his regiment he discovered that they had departed Charleston en route to New Orleans. Reynolds joined them on July 19, 1845, just in time to board ship for Texas.

John Fulton Reynolds - daguerreotype taken in Mexico (1846)

Collision With Mexico

When his regiment arrived in Corpus Christi, Texas, in August 1845, Reynolds was fully behind President Polk's policy towards Mexico and hoped, as a good Democrat, that this President would follow through as energetically as Andrew Jackson might have. The annexation of Texas and the ensuing dispute between Mexico and the United States over the location of the border had brought matters to a boiling point, and General Zachary Taylor worked feverishly to prepare his army as he awaited orders. In the meanwhile, junior officers such as Reynolds went about the task of training the army. His Company E was now converted to light artillery, which required complete conversion to horses. This meant extra work and, for an excellent horseman like Reynolds, extra exasperation: "I have been so much employed for the last two or three weeks, in imparting my knowledge of horsemanship to 20 to 30 stupid Germans, Irishmen, etc. ... " As the year drew to a close, the young lieutenant believed that Mexico was preparing to negotiate and that chances of war were slight.

It was mid-March by the time General Taylor was ready to move south of Corpus Christi, to a location known as Point Isabel. Here Taylor set up a base of supplies, and then marched further south to a point on the Rio Grande, across from the Mexican town of Matamoros. Reynolds received news of his promotion to first lieutenant on the march down. Unfortunately, his promotion involved a transfer to Company G, then stationed in Florida. Rather than leave the scene of war, Reynolds arranged to remain on detached service with Company E during the campaign. In the next month, as tensions escalated, he and his company busied themselves in building a fort.

On April 30, 1846, the commander of the Mexican forces ferried his men across the Rio Grande below Matamoros, with the object of threatening Taylor's base of supplies at Point Isabel. In response, Taylor immediately pulled the majority of his men out of the works, now christened Fort Texas, and moved to head him off. Left behind in the fort was a small force commanded by Major Jacob Brown, which included Reynolds' own battery and the Seventh Infantry, some 500 men in all. Taylor managed to beat the Mexicans to Point Isabel and when the latter caught up, their commander, General Arista, decided to send a column back to lay siege to Fort Texas, an engagement which was to last from May 3-9 and cost fifteen American casualties, including the life of Major Brown.

Meanwhile, fearing for the fort, Taylor decided to march to its relief. He collided with General Arista's force on May 8 and 9 at Palo Alto and Resaca de la Palma, where the Mexicans were trounced and sent flying back across the river.

Back at Fort Texas, renamed Fort Brown in honor of its dead commander, Reynolds wrote home as follows: "Of one thing I am certain, I can never again, I don't think, be placed in a more uncomfortable situation than the one we have just got out of.   "

He added that he preferred ten battlefields to a week's bombardment "such as we had in Fort Brown ... "

Later the young lieutenant had the chance to see the other side of war; visiting the Mexican hospitals and handing out money to the soldiers, who had no food or medicine. "How different would have been our fate if fortune had picked on the Mexican banner in these battles."

In early August, Taylor marched his 15,000-man force to Camargo, across the river on the Mexican side. Very quickly his army was plagued with sickness, and at least a third of the men fell ill, many to die. Leaving the majority of his volunteers behind, in late August Taylor marched south to Monterrey, leading a column of 6,000 men, which included Reynolds and his company of artillery. On September 19 they arrived opposite Monterrey where they were opposed by approximately 7,000 Mexicans under General Ampudia.

On the morning of the 21st, General William J. Worth led a force of 2,000 men in an attack from the north and west of town, while General Twiggs' Division and the remaining troops demonstrated against the eastern side. This demonstration ended at 10:00 AM, followed by an attack; after a severe day-long engagement, Reynolds' company assisted in securing a foothold east of town. Afterward, Lieutenant Joe Hooker remembered seeing Reynolds' battery crowded with wounded men and horses "down in the same spot, making the ground about the guns slippery with their gasped foam and blood." Reynolds himself wrote of this action:

> The attack commenced on the 21st, my birthday, and lasted the greater part of the day. I was amidst a continuous shower of grape and musketry, but escaped without a touch. Tho' I had my horse twice hit with a musket ball. How we all escaped I am unable to imagine, not an officer in the battery was wounded, but our battery suffered considerable.

Two more days of rugged fighting were required before the city surrendered. To avoid sniper fire, the advancing infantry cut holes through the walls of the house, while the artillery swept the narrow streets. It was, in Reynolds' description, a regular street fight. Finally, on the morning of the 25th, Ampudia surrendered, and, after difficult negotiations, his men were allowed to march out with their sidearms, flags, and personal property. Watching the Mexicans depart, Reynolds noted that " ... about 7,000 troops left for Sallito, as mean a looking rabble as a man ever set eyes upon ... "

We Are Pretty Well Used Up

In mid-December Taylor marched his 2,000-man column south to Victoria. During this trek, Reynolds and another company officer, Sam French, decided to celebrate New Year's Day, 1847 with a batch of eggnog. Having procured some eggs, they unfortunately came up short on liquor. This conundrum they solved by calling the company doctor to their quarters and placing him under arrest until he agreed to provide bottles of rum and brandy from company medical supplies. As a reward, he was allowed to share in the eggnog.

Two weeks later, Taylor's column would be back where it started, with little to show for the effort. Arriving in his old camp, Taylor discovered that General Winfield Scott had been there and gone, taking with him the bulk of Taylor's reserve infantry. Recently brevetted to lieutenant general and given command of the Mexico City expedition, Scott exercised his prerogative to commandeer a portion of Taylor's battle-tested "regulars." In a letter home, Reynolds vented the feelings of those left behind:

"General Taylor is perfectly disgusted with the part assigned to him here ... He certainly never expected the treatment he has now received at their hands, withdrawing all the regular troops and part of the volunteers ... " Meanwhile, Taylor had evidently become impressed with Reynolds. During this period one of the general's aides, William Bliss, wrote to a West Point acquaintance that "your young friend [Reynolds] has the general's high regard, and is the idol of his men."

By now, Santa Anna had assumed personal command of the Mexican army. In desperate need of a victory, he decided to march his 20,000-man force north to attack Taylor's 4,500 Americans at their camp near Aqua Nueva. Fully aware of the latter's intentions, Taylor pulled his own force north to a better defensive position on the heights of a valley overlooking the Buena Vista hacienda.

On February 22, 1847, Santa Anna attacked the American outposts and then offered Taylor a chance to surrender. In remembrance of George Washington's birthday, Taylor spurned the offer and the Mexicans attacked at 3:00 PM, fighting 'til dark, with minimal gain. The following morning Reynolds was able to grab a quick breakfast of ham and hard bread, and, before taking his post, wrote that "I never went into action in better spirits in my life ... "

The Mexicans resumed their attacks on the left and center of the American line, and Reynolds' company, now commanded by Captain Thomas Sherman, was brought to the front. Somewhat later, however, Reynolds' two-gun section was ordered to help repel a Mexican breakthrough near the hacienda. Here, in the words of one soldier, Reynolds' section fired "with astonishing accuracy and execution." Shortly after, when the American left flank was hit, Reynolds was pulled back to help Colonel Jefferson Davis and his regiment of Mississippi Rifles. Santa Anna made one more attempt to break the American lines, sending a 12,000-man assault against the American center, but this final attack sputtered in the face of stiff resistance, which included Reynolds' guns, and the Mexicans were forced to abandon the field.

Later that day Abner Doubleday found Reynolds leaning on a cannon near the spot of the attack, and asked him his thoughts when all of those Mexican soldiers began coming his way. Reynolds replied that he did "not allow myself to think on that subject, for I might have thought wrong." He later wrote that "this has been the greatest battle yet, I thought that at Monterrey I had been in a pretty tight place but it was nothing to this ... We are pretty well used up, both men and horses ... "

Little did Reynolds know that his own war was now over, even though he would spend another twenty months in Mexico. Taylor's army would now sit on the sidelines and watch as Scott moved to take Mexico City. During this stretch Reynolds grew quite weary of his surroundings and asked his father to try to use his influence to get him ordered to West Point as an instructor. "I am almost sick of the people of this country and everything in it..."

The twenty-seven year old bachelor also seemed to be experiencing pangs of another sort. Writing on New Year's Day, 1848, Reynolds informed his sister, Jane, that he was granting her full power to receive proposals from any of the female population at home. He had but three requirements: "the applicant must be good looking, amiable, and have a small portion of what is usually termed common sense," not that he would object to her having a bit of money. He ended by saying "enough of nonsense," but one can sense that the loneliness of army life was beginning to wear on John Reynolds.

Though Reynolds, Sr. was unable to obtain an appointment to West Point, he did write to his old friend, James Buchanan, now Secretary of State, asking him to look after John, referring obviously to brevets (commissions of honorary rank). Buchanan was more than willing to assist, replying that "I shall take good care of John when the proper time arrives. He richly deserves a brevet..." Reynolds professed himself indifferent, writing that: "All I care for and all the reward I expect is the good opinion of my brother officers in the Army and my friends at home ... " Of course Reynolds coveted them as much as any young officer in the regular army, but until he was awarded one, he remained a bit skeptical of their worth. Soon thereafter he received two brevets, one as captain and one as major for services at Monterrey and Buena Vista. In career terms, his Mexican adventure had been a success.

1850's Service

December 1848 found John Reynolds back in Lancaster on his first leave in over three years. The veteran of Mexico had changed dramatically since his last visit. The long locks of shoulder length hair were gone, cut off during the siege of Fort Brown when the heat had become unbearable. The slender six-footer was sporting a new mustache and beard, of which he was quite proud, and discerning family members could also detect a change within. In his time away, in the process of leading troops under fire, he had greatly matured.

The citizens of Lancaster were quite pleased to learn that the local "hero" of Buena Vista was amongst them, and decided to offer him a social dinner, " ... as a small token of their regard and admiration for your brave and meritorious conduct in the several battles, in which you were engaged ... " But, Reynolds surprisingly declined the honor, and in so doing undoubtedly passed on the chance to meet a number of eligible young ladies.

Your letter of today, offering me a "social dinner" was received with deep emotions, and I regret that my short stay among my fellow citizens of Lancaster compels me to decline the honor. Allow me to assure you that no feelings are more gratifying to the soldier than those excited by the approbation of his fellow countrymen; and that this testimony of your approval of my conduct in the service of my country will ever be most gratefully cherished by me.

17

In January 1849, Reynolds reported to Company G at Fort Preble, Maine, which was to be his home for the next four years. Once again he encountered garrison life with its interminable paperwork: " ...it is 1 o'clock and I have a pile of papers as high as my head on my table ..." A more critical complaint was the lack of good cigars, the local ones being but "trash," and he begged his sisters at home to send him the mildest smokes from Lancaster. To help him stave off the winter cold, his sister Harriet knitted a scarf that became the envy of the entire post, including his dog Milo, who "... seized it in his mouth and paws ..." and might have reduced it to its original condition had Reynolds not come to its rescue.

January 1853 found him transferred to General Twiggs' staff in New Orleans. An epidemic of yellow fever ravaged the city that year, and as the officers and men fled the city, Reynolds volunteered to stay, taking the place of his friend "Cump" Sherman, who with his family, was awaiting furlough. To Reynolds' shock and dismay, he himself came down with the fever, but was able to quickly recover.

By summer, he was again on leave when his father tragically succumbed to a massive stroke while visiting his daughter Jane in Baltimore. By the end of the year orders caught up with him, and in January 1854, Reynolds had comfortably settled in at Fort Lafayette, New York. During this winter the loneliness of garrison life seemed especially to lay heavy. "... I have been solitary and alone for one week, without seeing a soul that I could talk to ... "

The following spring, the two companies of the Third Artillery, of which Reynolds had temporary command, were ordered to prepare for an overland march to California. Their first stop was Fort Leavenworth, Kansas, where the expedition commander, Brevet Lt. Col. Edward Steptoe, was assembling his force. Their march commenced in early June and the column arrived at Salt Lake City on August 3. Here Reynolds had his first introduction to Brigham Young's Mormons, "made the acquaintance of several families, yet this did not give us entrée to their houses", and was highly irritated by their clannishness. His feelings toward them hardened after he had brought in a group of Indians charged with massacring a band of army engineers, only to see a Mormon court let them off with manslaughter ... "I cannot write the truth about these people here, but will sometime or other ... " In May 1855, he was off on the final leg of his journey to California, reaching Benicia Barracks in late July. He was also sporting a new rank, as word had come in March of his promotion to the regular rank of captain.

But there was another promotion that he wanted just as much.

Reynolds' old friend, Braxton Bragg, had been commissioned as a major in the cavalry arm, which meant that Bragg would be giving up his light artillery company, a unit that Reynolds wanted badly to command. Pulling out the stops, he wrote to his brother James, a lawyer with political clout and the ear of James Buchanan, soon to be elected President: " ... I wish you would use any and all the political influence you may have to get me that Co ... " Upon reaching California, he learned that Bragg had declined the cavalry commission, though there were rumors that he might resign from the army. Later came news that Bragg would indeed resign the following February, but that General Scott had recommended Robert Anderson for Bragg's position. In a letter to brother James that August, Reynolds' spirits were clearly sagging. "Merit is no recommendation and political influence everything ... I may say that I have never been so disgusted with this army as within the last twelve months." In recent years he had watched a number of northern-born officers resign to pursue more lucrative civilian careers. He might threaten to do so himself, but never did, though his letters would reflect a sense of frustration for months to come.

Reynolds was then ordered to Fort Orford, Oregon to assume command of Company H, Third Artillery. His trip north aboard the steamer *California* became one of the more perilous episodes of his life. As the ship entered the mouth of the Columbia River, a boiler burst, setting it on fire to drift toward the bar. The officers and soldiers assisted the crew in gaining control, but the ship was forced to return to San Francisco for repairs, and Reynolds was unable to report to his new post until January 1856.

In March the captain was caught up in his first Indian war, a campaign that required Reynolds' artillery and a regiment of infantry to chase a band of Rogue River Indians through some extremely rugged and mountainous country:

> *It is now three months since I left Ft. Orford, with my co., to take the field against the Indians who had committed the outrages on the settlers at this place ... and after a very laborious and fatiguing campaign with occasional skirmishing through the mountains, we have succeeded them all, or nearly all, to come in, give up their arms.*

He further noted that a band of hostiles still remained up in the mountains, and that he and Captain Edward Ord would have to go after them to bring them in. The two officers and their men must have done a credible job, for thirteen of the leading citizens of Fort Orford later joined in presenting Reynolds a gold watch.

> *Representing a portion of our fellow citizens who, desirous of manifesting the high esteem in which you are held by them, as an Officer, and for the interest shown by you for us, during our defenseless condition while you were in command of the Military Post, at this place. We ask your acceptance of the accompanying Gold Watch, as a small token of our high consideration and regard.*

Orders now reached Reynolds giving him the light artillery company he had coveted for the past year, but it was a hollow victory. The War Department had decided to replace the light artillery with long-range guns, thereby destroying the "finest battery" that Braxton Bragg had ever seen. Reynolds now commanded Company C, and was ordered to Fort Monroe, Virginia, where he arrived by the end of the year. This transfer to the east enabled him to take part in the accounting of his father's estate, a job that, in Reynolds' opinion, had been badly botched by his brother James. Reynolds' primary family concern was his two unmarried sisters, Harriet and Eleanor. He had always been the protective big brother to them, and he assured them that any deficiency caused by James' mishandling of the estate would be made up by himself. Lacking a family of his own while living the gypsy life of a soldier, Reynolds channeled his affection toward his siblings.

His impatience to clear up the estate was rooted in the knowledge that he would be off to Utah in the spring. Trouble was brewing with the Mormons; stories of three federal judges claiming to have been run out of the territory prompted President Buchanan to appoint a new governor, and in May 1857, Colonel Albert Sidney Johnston had been ordered to lead an expedition to Salt Lake City to reassert Federal authority. The Mormons mobilized their forces and harassed Johnston's column by stealing oxen, burning grazing lands, and destroying wagons. Short on supplies, Johnston and his force of 2,000 spent a bitter winter at Fort Bridger, Utah.

By the time Reynolds arrived at Camp Floyd, Utah Territory, in September 1858, President Buchanan's envoy had negotiated a settlement. The Federally appointed governor claimed his office, the grievances of the church were addressed, and the "Mormon War" was over. Nonetheless, Reynolds' old bitterness spilled in a letter home. The war in Utah had ended, "but I put no faith in anything of the kind, and will not believe it until the Mormons are out of our territory ... "

He spent the next twelve months at Camp Floyd near Salt Lake City before being ordered to Oregon in early September 1859. Though far to the west, Reynolds kept abreast of mounting tensions in the east and was clearly appalled by John Brown's raid on Harpers Ferry. Politically speaking, Reynolds was an old-line Democrat whose family had close ties with the Buchanan administration. Like most northern-born West Pointers, Reynolds was a social conservative for whom slavery was not an issue. In his opinion: "If they could hang, along with old Brown ... a few more of the abolitionist stripe, it would effectively stop this agitation for a time ... "

On the other hand, Reynolds was a strong unionist who felt equally betrayed by the secessionists. Later on, as commandant of West Point, he claimed that Jefferson Davis' "parricidal hand had filled it [the Academy] with poisonous weed of secession. The depth of his treachery has not been plumbed yet..."

As the country moved toward Civil War, an equally dramatic change was occurring in Reynolds' private life. The confirmed thirty-nine-year-old bachelor met and fell in love with Catherine Mary Hewitt, a twenty-year-old Catholic girl. The details of their courtship are few, but when Reynolds was ordered east in the next year, Kate was to follow and take up residence at a Catholic School near Philadelphia. Reynolds would presumably steal some time with her when visiting nearby family. Their relationship would remain a secret to the day he died.

Agonies of Dissolution

Reynolds obtained leave in the summer of 1860 and was able to visit his hometown before moving into his new post as Commandant of the Cadet Corps at West Point. Although he had regarded West Point as a choice duty post in 1845, by 1860 he was having his doubts: "I have not been on duty for a week trying to persuade myself that I shall like it." Given the high percentage of Southern cadets, and the high sectional tension, Reynolds had stepped into a hornet's nest, and he knew it.

Nonetheless, the duties of commandant had to be mastered, and Reynolds did his best. "These included the teaching of tactics for artillery, cavalry, and infantry; also equitation, strategy, grand tactics, and army administration." He was assisted in these chores by such future Civil War notables as Fitzhugh Lee, Charles Griffin, and Charles Field. One of his primary responsibilities while in command of the Cadet Corps was that of chief disciplinary officer, which was a difficult enough job during normal times.

Reynolds' discipline fell heavy on one cadet in particular, who watched his class leave for Washington in June 1861 from his quarters, placed there under arrest by the commandant. This young man was academically last in his class and three demerits short of expulsion, and after being brought before Reynolds for another offense, a court-martial was sought but never obtained. Reynolds would have liked to have kicked this rascal, George Armstrong Custer, out of the army, but hadn't the time to accomplish it. Nor was Custer the only cadet to feel the lash of discipline. Over the months Reynolds' cadets came to see him in the same tyrannical light that he had seen Commandant C. P. Smith during his own time at the Point. Not that he minded. Later, he was happy to note that, on his departure, there was "great rejoicing among the cadets at their being relieved of me."

Increasingly, Reynolds' attention was drawn to the developing national crisis. However badly his brother had managed the family estate, James was proving quite useful in bringing John's name to the attention of a fellow Pennsylvanian, Simon Cameron, the new Secretary of War. Reynolds himself was well aware that the current crisis meant fresh opportunities for promotion and advancement. He was willing to "serve in any position the government may call me to, with all the energy and power I possess." At the same time, Reynolds, the unionist, had lost all confidence in the administration of his benefactor, President James Buchanan. " ... a more disgraceful plot, on the part of our friend B's cabinet officers and the leading politicians of the South, to break up our Government, has never blackened the pages of history of any nation."

In early March, Reynolds received an offer to join the staff of commanding General Winfield Scott. In making the offer, Scott noted that "several years ago I said to you that I should offer you the first vacancy for an aide de camp that might occur on my staff," remarking further that Reynolds was the only officer he would consider for the post. Naturally, the West Point Commandant was flattered by the offer, but was also well aware that opportunities for wartime distinction lay not at headquarters, but in the field, and so he declined.

The attack on Fort Sumter, April 12, 1861, made the job of the academy commandant all but impossible. Reynolds assured the Southern cadets that they would be allowed the opportunity to complete their studies, at the same time speculating that by the end of April there would be no Southern cadets left at West Point. On May 2, orders came to graduate the first-class cadets at once, and, somewhat amazed at the turn of events, Reynolds wondered about his own future, writing as follows: " ... how long I will remain is uncertain. Much, everything, I may say depends on the turn events take, and Revolutionary events culminate rapidly ... One can hardly realize that this great nation is in the agonies of dissolution."

While stationed at Fort Trumbull, just outside New London, Reynolds received another promotion and a fresh batch of orders. He received a brigadier's appointment in mid-September, back-dated to August 20, and soon after was handed a telegram from Major General George B. McClellan, commander of the Army of the Potomac: "Do you accept your appointment of brig. general and if so when will you be here-answer." As Reynolds was deliberating his promotion, another set of orders arrived assigning him to Hatteras Inlet, North Carolina, under the command of General John Wool, who was delighted to obtain the services of "such an able and experienced officer." When McClellan got wind of this he complained directly to the Secretary of War. As a consequence, on September 12, Reynolds was directed to report to Washington, D.C., to the headquarters of the Army of the Potomac.

Here he was assigned the First Brigade of the Pennsylvania Reserve Division, which was commanded by General George McCall, and which consisted of the 1st, 2nd, 5th, and 8th Pennsylvania Volunteer Regiments. (The Second and Third Brigades were commanded by Brigadier General George G. Meade and Edward C. Ord, a friend from Reynolds' Rogue River days.)

Arriving on September 16, just in time to see the division mustered into Federal service, Reynolds wrote home a description of his new command:

> *Since I have been here I have been assigned a Brigade in McCall's Division, and rode out today to see them and the ground they are occupying, in Camp near Tenallytown, not very far from the Chain Bridge, though not on the sacred soil of Virginia, being on this side of the Potomac. I am to have the 1st Brigade.*

General McClellan was determined to whip the volunteer army into shape before sending it again into action, thereby avoiding the hasty mistakes of Bull Run. Reynolds shared this philosophy and his skepticism of volunteers was reinforced in early October, when the division crossed into Virginia and his men plundered several houses left vacant by fleeing secessionists. Their commander had witnessed similar depredations in Mexico and was appalled by the volunteers. "I almost despair from what I have seen of them since I have been here."

On October 18, 1861, Reynolds made a reconnaissance in the direction of Dranesville, Virginia, which resulted in a small skirmish between one of his regiments and some Louisiana Cavalry, which cost the latter one casualty. Once again Reynolds was thoroughly disgusted, writing to his sister that his men "plundered and marauded most disgracefully .. I have however an officer and 3 men in arrest under charges for their plundering at Dranesville and hope to have them hung, if I can ... "

He was unable to arrange a hanging, but the severity of his response made a distinct impression on his volunteers. "He used few words but with a look he could crush an offender." Another young volunteer recalled that Reynolds' "dark, piercing eyes ... could burn right through a man." For himself, Reynolds decided that when he had concluded that volunteers were hopeless, he would try to return to the Fourteenth Infantry, for he was sure that he could succeed with "regulars."

Nor did the disgusted brigadier have much use for journalists: " ... you need not look for .. letter writing in the papers from our division for I am happy to say we are not favored with newspaper correspondents." Strange words, some would say, from the son of a former newspaper publisher and editor, but in this attitude he was at one with other "regular" officers such as William T. Sherman and John Buford. One of Reynolds staff officers recalled watching the general receive a pair of journalists coldly, and then, after directing them to apply to headquarters for information, turn his back and abruptly walk away.

Meanwhile, there was one more brief flurry of action for the Reserve Division near Dranesville. On December 20, Ord's Third Brigade engaged a mixed force of 1,200 Rebel infantry and cavalry commanded by General J.E.B. Stuart. Although Reynolds and Meade were within supporting distance, they were unable to arrive in time to participate. The whole affair lasted about an hour, with Ord winning the field, though he remained only long enough to collect his wounded before heading back to camp.

Afterwards, Reynolds wrote home critically of his brigade, stating that while he had confidence in his first and fifth regiments, they suffered like the others from the want of knowledgeable officers. It is significant that Reynolds cautioned his sister to keep this information to herself and not allow his letters to be shown outside the family. Clearly, there was a wariness and even secretiveness to Reynolds' personal makeup that had been reinforced by the political nature of the war and the highly politicized atmosphere. Perhaps, as a former Buchanan Democrat, he wished to avoid the suspicion of disloyalty that would taint the careers of George McClellan and Fitz John Porter, fellow West Point Democrats who were publicly critical of the Lincoln administration and the war effort, and who would later pay a price.

The Army Before Richmond

In the winter of 1862, the administration grew increasingly impatient with McClellan and the inactivity of the Army of the Potomac. Finally, in early February, "Little Mac" submitted a plan that called for shipping almost the entire army down the Potomac River to the Chesapeake Bay, to disembark at Fort Monroe, Virginia, on the peninsula between the York and James Rivers.

As the debate raged over the finer points of McClellan's scheme, President Lincoln took matters into his own hands and ordered the plan put into effect by March 18, 1862, but with a sufficient reserve force left before Washington, D.C., to protect it from attack. As a consequence, when the Army of the Potomac embarked to begin the Peninsula campaign, the Pennsylvania Reserves and Reynolds' Brigade were at the last moment detached and kept back to cover Washington.

Writing home on March 22, Reynolds speculated as to what the future might hold: " ... we are awaiting transportation, by water, where to is not known precisely, tho somewhere from Aquia Creek to Old Point [Virginia] ... " But, as events unfolded, the First Corps remained ashore and was marched instead to Fredericksburg, Virginia. Meanwhile, there came news of a great battle being fought in the West. While John Reynolds regarded Shiloh as a complete victory, he apparently had little confidence in the Federal commander: " ... the surprise of an Army under Grant, is not surprising to me." Grant's pre-war reputation as a heavy drinker was not forgotten by those who had known him in the regular army.

In early May the First Corps marched into Falmouth, on the Rappahannock River, opposite Fredericksburg. Here it was directed to remain on the northern side to protect Washington not only from the Rebels to the south, but also from General Stonewall Jackson who had begun wreaking havoc among Federal forces in the Shenandoah Valley. On May 24, corps commander McDowell was ordered into the valley with two divisions, thereby leaving McCall's Division in front of Fredericksburg. Two days later, John Reynolds took his brigade across the river, occupied the town, and for two weeks became its military governor. His rule there was both firm and courteous, and the inhabitants seemed well-behaved, though Reynolds believed them to be "secesh of the first water."

While sitting in Fredericksburg, Reynolds' letters began to exhibit a certain exasperation at being left out of the war. (Finally, on June 8, 1862, the Pennsylvania Reserves were ordered to embark aboard the steamer "Cannonius" to journey to the peninsula and the seat of war.) "We have just dropped our anchor in the York River below West Point...tomorrow we will be up at the White House, where we march to join the Army before Richmond."

Reynolds' Brigade was thrown into action almost immediately upon their arrival at White House, Virginia. Two days earlier, Jeb Stuart had undertaken the reconnaissance mission that would result in his celebrated ride around McClellan's army. On the evening of June 13, he attacked Turnstall's Station, a key supply depot on the Richmond and York Railroad, and Reynolds was ordered to march to its relief. His brigade arrived around midnight, just in time to catch a wisp of Stuart's dust and to assist in extinguishing fires set by the Gray Cavalier.

Six days later, McCall's Reserves were ordered to cross the Chickahominy River and report to General Fitz John Porter, whose newly created Fifth Corps held McClellan's right flank near the town of Mechanicsville. The Pennsylvanians were positioned furthest to the right behind Beaver Dam Creek, a small stream less than a mile from town. Reynolds was given the task of constructing the divisional defense line, and Porter was highly pleased by his performance, remarking that "he had the best reasons not only to be contented but thoroughly gratified with admirable arrangements of this accomplished officer." Unquestionably, Reynolds, the seasoned artillerist, had an eye for good ground.

Following his ride around McClellan, Stuart had reported to General Robert E. Lee that the Federal right flank was up "in the air." Lee, who had earlier replaced General Joseph Johnston as Confederate commander, realized that he could save Richmond only by launching a bold offensive strike. He regarded Porter's exposed flank as a golden opportunity and devised a plan wherein he would march the bulk of his infantry to the north, while leaving a small reserve to demonstrate in front of McClellan's main force opposite the Richmond trenches. Once in position, this larger force would be joined by Jackson's 18,000-man army coming down from the Shenandoah. In combination the two would hit and roll up Porter's flank, thereby throwing the Army of the Potomac into pandemonium - assuming, of course, perfect timing all around.

The Rebel assault was scheduled to commence at dawn on June 26, with Jackson hitting from the north while three divisions struck from the south. Unfortunately, Jackson was six hours late, and upon arriving, unaccountably failed to attack. By late afternoon, division commander A.P. Hill could wait no longer for Jackson. On his own authority, the impetuous Hill launched a head-on attack against Reynolds' defenses, with such results as Reynolds recorded in his official report of August 13 (unfinished):

The enemy appeared in force about 3:00 PM and opened with his batteries from the high ground around Mechanicsville. Impetuously, assailing with superior force and at the same time the right and left of our position by the roads leading from that place. He was repulsed in every effort to turn our position as well as in an attempt to the right by the ford and old dam where he was handsomely checked by the 2nd Regiment.

Further in the report, for the first time, the hard-bitten "regular" waxed eloquent in praise of his Union volunteers: "The conduct of the troops, most of them for the first time under fire was all that could be desired and was creditable to their state and country ... " Reynolds himself seemed to be all over the field that day, and was mentioned favorably in the dispatches of both Porter and McCall. Third Brigade commander Truman Seymour stated that "much of the credit of the day" belonged to Reynolds. Captain Evan Woodward remembered seeing him riding the lines and crying out, "Look at them, boys, in the swamp there, they are thick as flies on gingerbread; fire low, fire low."

While McClellan was pleased with the Fifth Corps' performance, he realized that his right flank was still vulnerable. Furthermore, if Jackson shook off his lethargy the following day, this corps would be in serious trouble. Therefore, that night he ordered Porter to fall back four miles to Gaines Mill, a small village overlooking Boatswain's Creek. Porter, in turn, decided to put the Pennsylvania division in reserve as a reward for their fine performance of the previous day.

Lee resumed his attack at 2:00 PM on the following afternoon. By 4:00 PM the weight of Confederate numbers began to tell, and the Reserve Division was called in. Reynolds now dashed to and fro, juggling his regiments to plug whatever holes occurred in the line. Later, in his official report, Porter praised the Pennsylvania Reserves and noted that John Reynolds had acted "under a true maxim and the generous spirit of a soldier," moving to the sound of the guns, and leading his men "wherever our hard-pressed forces required most assistance." The Fifth Corps was able to hold its own against vastly superior forces until about 7:00 PM, when a Confederate brigade broke through at the center, thereby forcing a Union retreat. McClellan, now on his heels, would shift his base to Harrison's Landing on the James River. There would be hard fighting to come, but for John Reynolds, the Peninsula campaign abruptly ended with his capture on the morning of June 28. He described the episode as follows:

After the second day's fight, I had withdrawn my brigade from the action around Gaines Mill. I went with my Adj. Gen. to the right of the line to post the artillery, or to get it changed to different position where I remained 'til nearly dark, when endeavoring to return to my brigade, I found the left of our line had given way and the Confederate pickets occupying the ground I had passed over, and taking what I thought a direct course through the woods to our rear, became entangled in the swamp with my horse wounded, and unable to extricate him, I remained there through the night, and when day broke made another effort to regain the position of our lines, but was unfortunately unsuccessful and taken prisoner.

Confederate Guest

In all, Reynolds would spend six weeks in captivity, and in the beginning, his accommodations were quite respectable, if not luxurious. He was confined to a room at the Spotswood, one of the finer hotels in Richmond, where he even ran up a bill of $44, although it is uncertain what he received or whether he ever paid for it. Later, when more prisoners arrived, including General McCall, who was captured at the Battle of New Market Crossroads (June 30, 1862), Reynolds was transferred to a tobacco warehouse. After an escape attempt by several officers, McCall, Reynolds, and the others were marched through the streets to Libby Prison. Following his release, Reynolds had very little to say concerning his experiences as a Confederate guest. General Abner Doubleday later wrote that Reynolds "must have suffered much during his captivity, for he disliked to refer to the subject, and I remember he said that he was confined in a cell with a negro and fed on refuse food." At the time, Reynolds notified his family that he was again back under the "old flag" and that he hoped never again to be "subjected to Rebel tyranny."

Strangely enough, during this period of distasteful captivity, Reynolds received a Rebel testimonial that may have played a role in his release. Upon hearing of his imprisonment, the citizens of Fredericksburg ("secesh of the first water") had drafted a formal petition informing the Confederate government of the fair and just treatment they had received at Reynolds hands, and included a request that he be "placed on parole," if it could be done without compromising military security. Whether this petition played a role in securing Reynolds release, it certainly indicates that he was widely perceived as an officer and gentleman of the old school, a man ever respectful of the rights of private citizens.

When Reynolds and McCall arrived at army headquarters at Harrison's Landing on August 13, the Pennsylvania Reserves lined up to greet them, cheering wildly. Unquestionably, a bond of affection and respect had been forged between Reynolds and his men at Mechanicsville and Gainesville. Despite his aloof exterior, the men had witnessed his valor and competence under fire and had responded in kind. Reynolds' pride in his brigade was revealed in his official report, and one of his aides, Charles Lamborn, wrote the Reynolds sisters that: "His whole brigade is most decidedly attached to him, and I do not think the love of any commander was ever felt more deeply or sincerely than his."

North to Manassas

Soon after, General McCall returned home in ill health and John Reynolds assumed command of the Pennsylvania Reserves, mustering now only 7,000 effectives.

Meanwhile, during Reynolds' absence the strategic picture had changed radically. At the conclusion of the Seven Days Battles, on July 1, Lee had accomplished his mission of driving McClellan from the gates of Richmond. From his base at Harrison's Landing, McClellan blamed the Lincoln administration for withholding troops and called for reinforcement. There followed an impasse of several days before the administration, in exasperation, ordered "Little Mac" to re-embark his army and steam north to reinforce General John Pope, who had been brought from the west to command the newly designated Army of Virginia, some 56,000 strong, in the Shenandoah.

In retaliation, McClellan went into a sulk and took his sweet time in reembarking the Army of the Potomac. Observing the Federal disarray from Richmond, Robert E. Lee saw an opportunity to bag Pope's army before the tardy McClellan could reassemble his. Lee sent Jackson's Corps north in mid-August and then, once he was certain that Richmond was safe, followed with Longstreet's Corps. The Peninsula campaign was over; the Second Manassas campaign had just begun.

Ordered north in support, Reynolds' Pennsylvania Division arrived at Rappahannock Station near Pope's headquarters on August 22. Not that Reynolds particularly cared for the movement or the political motives behind it: "I do not approve of the operation of leaving the line of the James River, to be sure I do not take political projects into consideration." He would sound this theme again and again, though circumspectly, and only in letters home. In Reynolds' mind, politics and war were separate entities and he believed that politicians should never influence or dictate the movements of armies. Still, he seemed resigned to the fact-" ... I suppose they [political considerations] will have, as they have heretofore, overruled all military ones."

By August 28, Pope had concentrated his army around Warrenton, Virginia. Two days earlier "Stonewall" Jackson had marched through Thoroughfare Gap, and the next day seized Pope's supply depot at Manassas Junction. In response, Pope chose to move toward Manassas, but by then, Jackson had abandoned the depot and moved down the Warrenton Turnpike to await him near the village of Groveton. As Reynolds marched up the turnpike on the morning of the 28th, his division brushed up against Jackson's men, and he prepared to go after them. A private in the ranks remembered seeing the general riding among the troops: " ... and with soldierly coolness and courage, he proceeded to arrange a line of battle." But, the Pennsylvania Reserves were now attached to McDowell's Third Corps of the Army of Virginia, and McDowell's intelligence placed Jackson at Manassas, not Groveton. Therefore, Reynolds was instructed to disengage and continue his march.

Very quickly, Pope's army began to unravel in confusion. Jackson was next reported to be at Centreville in force, though this force was only a single division commanded by A.P. Hill. As Reynolds' Reserves moved out, heavy firing could be heard in the direction of Groveton, where General John Gibbon's "Black Hat Brigade" had engaged Jackson's men in a savage fight that would result in over a thousand combined casualties. Reynolds spun about and spurred his mount toward Groveton, arriving there just as the fighting subsided. Realizing that the force he had earlier bumped against was indeed Jackson's, Reynolds urged Gibbon's division commander, General Rufus King, to hold his ground, on the promise that Reynolds would bring his reserve division up in support the following morning. Unfortunately, later that evening, King had a change of heart and decided to withdraw.

Reynolds would find the next day, August 29, equally as frustrating. That morning, believing that he had Jackson on the run, Pope attempted to pull his army together for a concerted attack near the old Bull Run Battlefield. Unfortunately, unbeknownst to Pope, that afternoon Lee had arrived with Longstreet's Corps on his extreme left flank. Giving little thought to his left, Pope continued to assault Jackson's Corps, though without much success. In his mind, the left flank would be handled by Fitz John Porter's Fifth Corps, which was supposedly marching up in support via the Manassas-Gainesville Road.

The following day, Pope ordered his troops north of the pike to advance, while to the south he expected the Fifth Corps to move up with Reynolds' Reserves in support on Porter's extreme left. Incredibly, Pope then misinterpreted Longstreet's re-shuffling of his corps as the beginning of a general Confederate retreat. Porter got his corps moving by mid-afternoon, but met with stiff resistance, and John Reynolds found the going especially rough. When his skirmishers began falling back on his own extreme left, Reynolds rode over and testily inquired as to the reason. Informed of a heavy concentration of Rebels, he rode on to see for himself, and was stunned by the sight of a line of skirmishers with cavalry behind it, " ... evidently masking a column of the enemy formed for an attack on my left." As Reynolds spun round, he was the target of a Rebel volley which killed one of his orderlies. Riding on, he reported this news at McDowell's headquarters and was ordered to pull his division back to Chinn Ridge covering the Warrenton Turnpike. One unsubstantiated story has it that Reynolds also went directly to Pope, only to have the latter discount his report of Longstreet's presence with the remark saying: "Oh I guess not." In any case, Reynolds' Division now had the task of covering the Union left against Longstreet's entire corps.

Porter was able to put up stiff resistance, but eventually the weight of Longstreet's attack caused the Fifth Corps to collapse. Reynolds' Division watched as Porter's men broke for the rear, and prepared for the coming onslaught. Just then, Reynolds received orders to march to the rear of the fleeing Fifth Corps in an attempt to rally them, which proved impossible. He was next ordered to Henry House Hill, where Pope was assembling a force to protect his line of retreat. This eminence became a key position as Longstreet pushed to the Warrenton-Sudley Road junction, in hopes of cutting Pope in half. Only the obstinate stand by

Reynolds' Division and other Union troops near Henry House Hill enabled Pope to save his army that day.

At one point, as a Confederate brigade presented an open flank to the Pennsylvanians, Reynolds grasped the flag of the Second Reserves, waved it aloft, shouted "Forward Reserves!", and led a downhill charge which stopped the Rebels in their tracks. Later, when his division showed signs of breaking, Reynolds seized the flag of the 6th Reserves, and rode up and down the line to steady it. In these moments he made himself such an easy mark for sharpshooters that one of his men thought that the general led a "charmed life." Such performances were becoming common with John Reynolds, and his heroism on Henry House Hill helped prevent Lee from converting a stunning victory into a staggering defeat for the Union cause.

Return of McLellan

Pope's army held until nearly dusk, and Reynolds' Reserves were some of the last regiments to leave the field. Fortunately, the Confederates were near exhaustion themselves and unable to mount a determined pursuit. Their victory, however, meant the end of General John Pope, who was transferred to the Minnesota Indian frontier, all the while protesting that he had been the victim of a conspiracy. He did, however, have words of high praise for a few, which included John Reynolds and the officers of the Reserves, " ... who performed their duties with ability and gallantry and in all fidelity to the government and to the army." In light of their later association at Gettysburg, it is significant that cavalryman John Buford received praise similar to Reynolds.

On September 2, President Lincoln ordered McClellan to assume command of all federal forces in the East and to prepare to defend the capital. By then, however, Lee had opted for another plan. Having suffered heavy casualties himself, the Gray Fox realized that his army lacked the strength to overcome the Washington fortifications. Unwilling to sacrifice the offensive momentum he had gained, he decided instead to invade Maryland. By September 6, 1862, his intentions were becoming clear to a number of Union officers, including John Reynolds, who wrote ... "I do not know what the [Rebel] movement portends except the enemy are evidently bent on an invasion of the North."

In McClellan's reorganization of the army, the Reserves were assigned to the First Army Corps under Major General Joe Hooker. The division had earned a reputation as a hard fighting unit, and its assignment to Hooker's Corps meant further opportunity to excel. Unfortunately, John Reynolds would not be available to share the opportunity, for at the same time that Lee led his army into Maryland, Reynolds was relieved of command and ordered to Pennsylvania, at the request of Governor Andrew Curtin.

When it became apparent that his state was in danger, Curtin had requested the return of the Pennsylvania Reserve Division to Harrisburg. The War Department refused to comply, assuring the governor that the Reserves could better serve Pennsylvania by remaining with the Army of the Potomac. In lieu of the Reserves, Curtin requested "an active energetic officer to command the forces in the field and one that could rally Pennsylvania. It is believed that General

Reynolds would be most as useful." After much wrangling between Harrisburg and Washington, the governor got his general and Reynolds, much to his disgust, was ordered to Harrisburg.

He arrived on September 13, set up headquarters at the state capital, and got down to the task of whipping the assembled mob into some semblance of a force that might fight. The situation was grim, and his letter to family was scarcely reassuring:

I think the threatening aspect of an invasion down the Cumberland Valley very serious, there is nothing to prevent their doing great injury, and in fact their marching to this place a well organized column of 20 or 30,000 men, cavalry and infantry, etc.; there is nothing in the valley to stop them.

Characteristically, he added a footnote to the letter, instructing his sister to "Burn this up and do not let anyone see it..." As events unfolded, there was very little that Reynolds could do about anything, for his state militia would refuse to cross into Maryland. In the next two weeks, while the Battles of South Mountain and Antietam were being fought, the commander of the Pennsylvania Militia would go no further south than Chambersburg. As for Antietam, in Reynolds' view, "we rather had the advantage ... though not much to boast of." Following Lee's retreat back into Virginia, he was permitted to disband the militia and return to the army, much to his relief. The militia wanted to defend their homes, he later wrote, but "they preferred to wait until the enemy actually reached their own door steps before they encountered him."

Upon return, Reynolds found himself in temporary charge of the First Corps, assuming command from General George Meade, who had led the corps since General Hooker's wounding at Antietam. As highly ambitious as Reynolds, and just as circumspect, Meade wrote to his wife that he wished Reynolds "would have stayed away." But, as an old army "regular" himself, Meade accepted the seniority system and would "subside gracefully into a division commander." Though the rivalry between these two would intensify as their stars began to rise, they were also developing a mutual respect that was rare among backbiting Federal corps commanders.

Following his narrow victory at Antietam, McClellan decided to refit and rebuild his army, much to the dismay of President Lincoln, who hoped that he would vigorously pursue Lee and bring him to battle before winter set in. Tensions escalated and by early November the President had enough of "Little Mac." On November 7, he was sacked for good and replaced as commander of the Army of the Potomac by Major General Ambrose Burnside, a meager talent at best.

In the meanwhile, Reynolds was becoming acquainted with his new corps. At a review held on October 2, he believed that the men demonstrated little enthusiasm, but one of them noted that Reynolds was "alertness personified." His artillery chief, Colonel Charles Wainwright, observed that the general "shows to advantage" on horseback, in one instance riding down a steep hill at such a rate that only a few of the staff could keep up. John Reynolds would command this corps to the end of his life, and take as much pride in his men as they did in him.

As one volunteer put it: "To the First Corps General Reynolds was the 'beau ideal' of a soldier."

I Have Hard Work Ahead of Me

The removal of McClellan was a great shock to the army, and in Reynolds' view the dismissal had been "unwise, injudicious, as it was uncalled for." Nonetheless, he was happy to write that McClellan's departure caused less ill will than he had feared, and that all must pull together in support of Burnside, who was "as noble a spirit as ever existed." Not everyone shared Reynolds' estimate of Burnside, but it is worth noting that Reynolds could always look past his own ambition and wholeheartedly support whomever commanded the army.

Burnside was now under extreme pressure from the administration to engage Lee before winter set in, and at least initially, he seemed up to the task. He submitted a plan for a rapid march around Lee's right flank at Culpeper, with the aim of occupying Fredericksburg so as to threaten Richmond from the north. Lincoln was reluctant to agree, feeling that Lee's army should be the target, not Richmond. Burnside set the Army of the Potomac quickly in motion on November 15, and had his leading elements in position on the Rappahannock River opposite Fredericksburg by the 18th. Pontoons were required to transport the army across, but unfortunately the orders for them had gone astray. By the time the pontoons did arrive on November 25, Lee had occupied the town and begun to fortify the heights commanding it.

Previously, the army had been reorganized into three "Grand Divisions" consisting of two corps apiece. Reynolds' First Corps, along with General William F. Smith's Sixth Corps, made up the "Left Grand Division," while the Third and Fifth Corps made up the "Center Grand Division," and the Second and Ninth Corps the "Right Grand Division." By the end of November, Franklin's Grand Division had been positioned along the river to the east of town, with Reynolds' First Corps posted on the extreme left flank. While awaiting further orders, on December 2, Reynolds received his commission as major general, backdated to November 29.

Finally, on the evening of December 10, the First Corps was ordered to march to the river and prepare to cross, while early on the 11th, engineers began the construction of pontoon bridges. Rebel snipers, however, slowed the operation considerably and the crossing was held up until the following afternoon. Further up river, the remainder of the army was having even greater difficulty; their pontoons would not be in place until late afternoon on December 11.

Grand Division Commander Franklin established his headquarters in a house owned by a man whom Reynolds had known during his own previous occupation of Fredericksburg. This gentleman, one Mr. Bernard, presented himself as a Union man, but the First Corps commander knew better, and had him arrested and unceremoniously escorted across the river. General Franklin later observed that "Reynolds on such occasions was a man of few words."

Franklin, Reynolds, and Smith concurred that an all-out assault with their entire force (two corps, three divisions each) was the only way to carry the heights to their front. They presented this plan to Burnside later in the day and he seemed to agree. The three generals waited that night at headquarters, but no orders came, and by 3:00 AM Reynolds could wait no longer. "I know I have hard work ahead of me and I must get some sleep."

Almost Gaining the Objective

Orders reached Franklin at 7:30 AM, December 13, but they were not what he had expected. Instead of a concentrated, all-out assault, Franklin was directed to attack with a division "at least" and seize the heights near Hamilton's Crossing. Reynolds' Corps was chosen to make the assault, and Reynolds selected his most trusted division-Meade's 4,000-man Pennsylvania Reserves-as the spearhead to lead it. A dense fog covered the Reserves as they moved across the Old Richmond Road to form a line of battle. The Confederates on the heights opposite Meade's troops, men of Jackson's Corps, could hear the sounds of their approach, but it was not until 10:00 AM that the fog lifted and presented the spectacle of the entire Left Grand Division. George Meade, the point commander, was supported by Doubleday's Division to the left, and Gibbon's to his right.

It was nearly noon by the time that Meade had everyone in position, but unfortunately, one of Reynolds' former West Point cadets managed to mischievously prolong the business. Just as Meade was preparing to step off, Major John Pelham of Stuart's Confederate Horse Artillery posted two guns on the Old Richmond Road and opened up, thereby scattering troops and prompting further delay.

Meade finally attacked at 1 :00 PM, though without the support of Doubleday, who now had to guard against Confederates on the left. The Reserves charged through the woods at the base of the hills and on up the heights, finding a gap in Jackson's line, and causing two Rebel brigades to fall back. The division next slammed into a brigade of South Carolinians, scattering them while killing their commander, General Maxcy Gregg. By now, however, Meade's troops were winded and desperately in need of support. Observing this, Reynolds ordered Gibbon to get his division moving, but despite his support the Reserves were forced to retreat.

Unfortunately, the business of getting out proved much more difficult than getting in. Meade was unable to form an effective rearguard on the downhill slopes and the division began to break apart. Reynolds and Meade worked feverishly to rally them behind the artillery near the Old Richmond Road, and Franklin was able to bring up enough supports to make the Confederates think twice about pressing their advantage. Furious at having received so little support during his attack, Meade rode up to his commander and exclaimed, "My God, General Reynolds, did they think my division could whip Lee's whole army?!" Although the Pennsylvania Reserves did not do all the fighting on the left, they certainly carried the heaviest load, suffering forty percent casualties. Their brief success proved to be the only bright spot in a very dark day for the Federals, as brigades of the other grand divisions battered themselves in futile assaults against "Marye's Heights."

Reynolds took a few moments that evening to write and give the home front some idea of the " ... events of the past few days." He criticized the tactics of the entire campaign, and believed that Franklin had interpreted his orders too narrowly. He was also surprisingly critical of his own First Corps:

> *My Corps, or two Divisions of it made the attack on the left and after almost gaining the object let it slip. They did not do as well as I expected tho' they advanced under Artillery fire very well. When it came to the attack of the wooded heights they faltered and failed-we are fortunate that it is not worse.*

The total Federal casualties were appalling; some 12,000 Union soldiers fell on a single day. Talked out of continuing the slaughter the next day, Burnside ordered a withdrawal to commence on the evening of the 15th. Straw was placed on the bridges to deaden the sound, and Reynolds himself rode the picket lines to make sure the evacuation was carried out quietly.

Burnside now began the process of identifying those officers responsible for his defeat, and in mid-January, after another failed offensive which became known as Burnside's "Mud March," he demanded the dismissal of his enemies, which by now included most of the Union high command. Looking on in dismay, Reynolds wrote home to say that "if we do not get someone who can command an Army without consulting 'Stanton and Halleck' at Washington, I do not know what will become of this army." In the end, the Lincoln administration allowed Sumner to resign, dismissed Franklin and Burnside, and appointed "Fighting Joe" Hooker as commander of the Army of the Potomac. Once again, Reynolds had survived a bloodletting of the top command with his reputation intact. Indeed, he had not only survived, but his own claim to the top command had grown stronger. In the midst of dismal failure, his star was on the rise.

In the winter of 1863, Hooker began the monumental task of rebuilding the army, now at its lowest ebb since Pope's debacle the previous August. He junked the "Grand Divisions," instituted some crucial reforms affecting health and sanitation, set up a furlough system, and began enforcing strict discipline in camp. Lincoln came to review the army in early April and Reynolds believed that the President was "much gratified with all he saw." He went on to quote Lincoln as saying that "if the troops only fight as well as they looked no expectations, however great, need be disappointed." Reynolds himself was optimistic and felt the army "with proper management. .. will achieve a success undoubtedly."

They Got More of the Spoils

In the spring campaign to come, Hooker planned to hold Lee below Fredericksburg with three Federal corps, while sneaking up river to cross and come down on the Confederate left flank with the remainder of his army.

Reynolds' First Corps was assigned to the Fredericksburg wing, which included the Third and Sixth Corps, under the overall command of General John Sedgwick. On the morning of April 28, as Hooker moved north, Sedgwick ordered Reynolds to move his corps down near the Rappahannock crossing, taking special care to keep his men concealed. As night fell, Chief Engineer Henry Benham began laying the bridges, but quickly fell behind schedule. Reynolds' nerves became exceptionally taut, and a staff member observed that he "swore pretty hard when things did not go to suit him." His composure received an extra jolt when a noticeably drunk Benham rode up, face bleeding from an accident, and loudly cried out, "Hurrah Josh, Hurrah for here and Buena Vista!" By now, the Confederates realized that something was up and began firing from the opposite bank, but Reynolds decided to wait until day before making any sudden moves.

A low fog hung close to the ground that morning of the 29th as Reynolds and his First Division commander, General James Wadsworth, sat on horseback, smoking cigars, gazing across the Rappahannock. When the fog lifted Wadsworth was ordered to send two regiments across the river to clear out enemy snipers; by late afternoon Reynolds had put two divisions across on the Fredericksburg side. Despite the delay, all was going tolerably well along Sedgwick's front.

Unfortunately, the same could not be said for Joe Hooker. After a promising start, in which his men had marched quickly, crossed the river, and come down on Lee's flank, "Fighting Joe" began to lose his nerve. Just when his plan was working well, Hooker ordered a halt, and then a withdrawal to the little crossroads known as Chancellorsville. That night John Reynolds wrote home praising the recent developments, but was still a bit uneasy: "The only thing I do not like about our operations has been that the bridges were thrown to soon here by a day." His fears were well grounded. By the evening of the 30th, Lee realized that Sedgwick's movements were merely a feint, and that Hooker's 70,000-man force around Chancellorsville was the main thrust.

Leaving but a single division in Sedgwick's front, Lee moved the remainder of his army, some 40,000 strong, to the west to confront Hooker, who by now had gone entirely on the defensive. On the evening of May 1, 1863, Lee and Jackson formulated a plan of attack that would seal the doom of "Fighting Joe." They would divide their inferior force and Jackson would march his 25,000-man corps around Hooker's right flank, while Lee held his front with the remaining 14,000. ? The plan worked almost to perfection. The following morning, Jackson marched out to circle round and at 5:00 PM delivered an attack that shattered the Federal Eleventh Corps and all but cut off the Union army from the river.

Somewhat earlier the nervous Hooker had ordered the Third and First Corps to come from Fredericksburg to his assistance. Reynolds' First Corps arrived at around 6:30 PM, just in time to reinforce the collapsing Federal right, and to provide stability as Jackson's attack sputtered in the darkness. (Jackson himself was mistakenly fired upon by his own men, and was to die of wound complications eight days later.)

On May 3, Jackson's Confederates resumed their attack under the command of Jeb Stuart. Anchoring the Federal right, Reynolds and Fifth Corps commander George Meade watched in amazement as Hooker allowed Stuart to assault his center without calling on the First and Fifth Corps for assistance. Indeed, Hooker refused their requests to join in. The following day brought more of the same as Hooker, feeling the effects of a near miss by a cannonball, ordered Sedgwick's lone corps to carry the heights beyond Fredericksburg and then come to his rescue. Sedgwick made a valiant effort but was fortunate merely to escape back across the Rappahannock with his corps intact, and never mind Joe Hooker.

John Reynolds was by now furious at the inactivity issuing from Hooker's headquarters. In the hope of getting his First Corps into the fight any kind of fight-he selected a brigade under Colonel Roy Stone and sent it out on "reconnaissance," fully expecting the fiery Stone to get into the kind of trouble that would require Reynolds to swoop in with the First Corps to rescue him. Stone pushed forward, brushed back Stuart's pickets, but upon encountering a heavier force, pulled back in the belief that he had accomplished what his general intended. When later told that the colonel could have gotten into a fight, Reynolds exclaimed, "I wish to God he had!"

On May 4, in the late evening, General Hooker called a conference of corps commanders to discuss the advisability of retreat. After reviewing the situation, Hooker excused himself to let his commanders come to a vote. Generals Meade and O. O. Howard voted to stand and fight; Generals Sickles and Couch voted for withdrawal; General Slocum was not present. John Reynolds agreed with Meade, but, since his corps had seen little action, felt reluctant to press his opinion. Having had his say, Reynolds lay down in a comer of the room to catch some sleep. Upon his return, despite the 3 to 2 vote to remain, Hooker announced the retreat, much to the irritation of Reynolds, who was heard to remark, loud enough for Hooker to hear: "What was the use of calling us together at this time of night when he intended to retreat anyhow?" This remark was as close to personal insubordination as John Reynolds would come in the whole of his military life.

By May 6, the army had re-crossed the Rappahannock and John Reynolds was in a foul mood. Visiting his headquarters during this period, General John Gibbon recalled that Reynolds "was the picture of woe and disgust and said plainly that we had been badly out-generaled and whipped by half our number." Completely discouraged, Reynolds wrote home expressing his bewilderment at a campaign that had begun so gloriously and ended so badly: "We did not effect much more by our crossing than to be slaughtered and to slaughter the Rebels. I think it will turn out that they got more of the spoils than we did."

Through the remainder of May the Army of the Potomac nursed its wounds, pulled itself together, and listened to gossip concerning the removal of Joe Hooker. Rumor had it that John Reynolds was being considered for the top job, and the rumors were on target. During its first few years, the eastern army had experienced incredible turmoil as Lincoln groped frantically for an army commander that could get the job done. In a ruthless winnowing process, army, corps, and division commanders had come and gone, some in disgrace, others shipped out to backwaters where they could do no harm. In the Union West a similar winnowing had taken place, and out there the makings of a winning command combination-Grant and Sherman, with George Thomas and Phil Sheridan in the wings-was becoming discernible. In the eastern theater where Union forces had almost always lost, the situation was more fluid. Even so, a number of younger men were coming to the fore—Winfield Scott Hancock, George Gordon Meade, John Buford-men who would make their mark in the coming campaign. As army commander, by late May, John Reynolds had emerged as the Lincoln administration's candidate in reserve.

On May 31, Reynolds took leave and traveled to Washington, where, on June 2, he had a lengthy discussion with the President concerning the leadership of the Army of the Potomac. The man whom Hooker had called "the ablest officer under me" was now very candid in discussing his superior's strengths and weaknesses. When sounded out himself on assuming command of the army, Reynolds replied that unless he was given free rein, he would prefer to decline it.

In retrospect, it is somewhat amazing that Reynolds was offered this command. For one thing, he was junior to corps commanders Sedgwick and Slocum. For another, he was a lifelong Democrat whose military career and advancement had been due, in part, to the patronage of one of the most vilified of Democrats, James Buchanan. Then too, although Reynolds had been extremely circumspect, he was widely perceived as a McClellan man (as indeed he was) and that alone was enough to bring a lesser man down. On the other hand, Reynolds' performance at brigade, divisional, and corps level had always been solid, if not sterling. That he possessed energy, intelligence, courage, and presence was obvious to all who met him. Moreover, he was a team player who had always served loyally under whomever he was placed. Lincoln undoubtedly sensed that Reynolds' primary loyalties were to the army and the Union, however much he might disagree with the policies of a Republican administration. In rejecting command of the Army of the Potomac, Reynolds was declining the chance of a lifetime, the capstone of a career. That he chose to do so on principle is yet another measure of his character.

Leaving that night to return to the army, Reynolds stopped in Baltimore to visit his sisters, to whom he divulged the substance of his Presidential interview. It is significant that he would also inform George Meade, but no one else. One can only guess at his state of mind. Perhaps in the wake of the interview he felt even more frustrated. Then again, perhaps he experienced a curious sense of release.

On June 12, General Hooker issued orders to set the Army of the Potomac in pursuit of Lee, who had earlier put his own army in motion to invade Pennsylvania. Ewell's was the first Confederate Corps to move via the Shenandoah Valley; A.P. Hill and Longstreet's Corps were still in the vicinity of Fredericksburg and Union intelligence had yet to figure the direction of Ewell's movements. On that day, Reynolds received notice that he was to temporarily command the "right wing" of the army, consisting of his own First Corps, Meade's Fifth Corps, and Howard's Eleventh Corps. This wing was to shadow the Confederates heading north, and Reynolds was instructed to keep his force between them and Washington. On June 15, 1863, Ewell attacked and seized Winchester, Virginia, capturing the Federal garrison. In the meantime, Lee put the remainder of his army on the march, ordering Hill and Longstreet into the Shenandoah in Ewell's wake. As it became obvious that Lee's objective was something other than Washington, Hooker now had to play catch up. For the men in ranks, this meant two weeks of forced marches in choking dust and stifling heat.

Reynolds' command of the Union "right wing" lasted until June 16, when Hooker moved his headquarters north to Fairfax Station. The army commander was now reduced to issuing orders calculated to keep the Army of the Potomac between the Rebels and Washington, as he searched for some clue to Lee's design.

During this period he fought constantly with the administration, and the relation had become so strained as to make a change of command almost inevitable. Unfortunately for Hooker, Lee too was feeling his way, as is indicated by his June 22 orders to Richard Ewell-as Ewell crossed into Pennsylvania he was to let his "progress and direction" be shaped by the "developments and circumstances." By June 22, John Reynolds was as befuddled as Joe Hooker, writing home that "it is almost impossible to say where the enemy is with any certainty."

On June 25, Reynolds was ordered to assume command of the "left" Union wing, consisting of the First, Third, and Eleventh Corps. General Doubleday met Reynolds that day at a Potomac River crossing, and later described him as feeling "that it was necessary to attack the enemy at once, to prevent his plundering the whole state ... He seemed to think if he could meet them with the First Corps there would be no doubt of the result."

On the same day that Reynolds assumed command of the "left wing," Ewell marched his corps out of Chambersburg, and accompanied two of his divisions to Harrisburg, while a third under General Jubal Early moved east toward York. Early brushed aside a regiment of militia west of Gettysburg and occupied the town on the 26th, but stayed only long enough to demand provisions, and when these were not forthcoming, moved through York to the banks of the Susquehanna the following day. He would have crossed the river and occupied Lancaster had the local militia not set fire to the bridge. As fate would have it, one of the militia soldiers was James Reynolds, John's youngest brother, who would remain with his company until July 2, when word reached him of his brother's fate.

On June 28, Abraham Lincoln relieved Joe Hooker and ordered General George Gordon Meade to assume command of the Army of the Potomac. Meade protested to the War Department courier that the army was expecting Reynolds, but finally accepted with the remark: "Well, I've been tried and condemned without a hearing, and I suppose I shall have to go to execution." Upon hearing of Meade's promotion, Reynolds dressed in his best uniform and went to his headquarters to pay his respects.

In this meeting, he found Meade anxious to talk to the man he considered "a lieutenant important to me in his services-a friend and a brother." The new commander went on to say how unwelcome the orders were, how he wished the position had been given to Reynolds, and how important it was to him to receive Reynolds' support at this critical time. In his turn, Reynolds assured Meade that the command had gone to the right man and that Meade could rely on him to support to the best of his ability, and with that the two generals mapped out plans to bring Lee to battle. On June 30, wing commander Reynolds, traveling with the First Corps, moved from Emmitsburg, Maryland into Pennsylvania and in mid-afternoon went into camp near Marsh Creek while setting up headquarters at the Moritz Tavern, some six miles south of Gettysburg. By now he was receiving a steady stream of information from John Buford, his cavalry commander, which he forwarded on to Meade and other pertinent commanders. "Buford sends reliable information that the enemy occupies Chambersburg in force and that they are moving down from Cashtown." Somewhat later: "Buford is in Gettysburg, and

Burning of the Wrightsville - Columbia Bridge. James Reynolds, brother of John, was present.

found a regiment of Rebel infantry advancing on the town, which retired as he advanced ... "- this from a dispatch sent to Howard in Emmitsburg, whom Reynolds instructed to be prepared to move "to his [Reynolds'] left, in case they move on him from Fairfield [Pennsylvania] and the mountain roads."

He spent the remainder of the day studying a variety of reports as he attempted to piece together Lee's intentions. Testimony from two different sources indicate that Reynolds experienced something of a mood swing between late afternoon and midnight. One of Meade's staff officers visiting in the afternoon recalled "his calm dignity, and true soldierly appearance as he courteously rose to receive me." General Howard, the Eleventh Corps commander, arrived late in the evening, and, after a light supper, joined Reynolds in pouring over the maps and messages. As they did so, Howard noticed that his commander seemed depressed. Before going to sleep, Reynolds sent Meade a message summarizing all the information he had received that day, along with his opinion that in the event of a defensive battle, a position north of Emmitsburg was the place to make a stand, but that Meade should consider this opinion as mere "surmise." If Reynolds was reeling somewhat from the immense responsibility of his position, John Buford's 10:30 PM dispatch certainly must have increased his anxiety:

I am satisfied that A.P. Hill's corps is massed just back of Cashtown, about nine miles from this place. Pender's division of this [Hill's] corps came up today, of which I advised you, 'saying the enemy in my front was increased'. The enemy's pickets, infantry and artillery, are within four miles of this place, at the Cashtown Road ... Ewell's corps is crossing the mountains from Carlisle ... Longstreet, from all I can learn, is still behind Hill.

Buford concluded his dispatch with a request for instructions: "Should I have to fall back, advise me by what route." Lying on the floor of the tavern, his mind teeming with possibilities, John Reynolds undoubtedly recalled one key passage from an earlier Meade dispatch: " ... If they advance against me, I must concentrate at that point where they show the strongest force."

What's the Matter John?

At approximately 4:00 AM, July 1, 1863, the General awakened Staff Officer Stephen Weld, "as he frequently had to do," and then turned to the First Corps, instructing Wadsworth at Marsh Creek to put his division on the road to Gettysburg. Observing Reynolds that morning, Colonel Wainwright noted that though "Doubleday is supposed to be in command of our troops [First Corps], all our orders came from Reynolds direct." Obviously, where Reynolds and the First Corps were concerned, old command habits died hard. He then ordered Doubleday to follow Wadsworth with his remaining divisions while sending a message confirming Howard's order to march in support of the First Corps, and instructing him where to place his own Eleventh Corps outside of town. Word was also sent to Third Corps commander Dan Sickles to verify his movement north of Emmitsburg. To most observers, this flurry of orders and messages conveyed a crackling sense of urgency, and yet, when asked of the prospects of a fight, Reynolds replied to staff officer: " ... that we were only moving to within supporting distance of Buford."

After signing all messages and paperwork, and after superintending all movements, Reynolds decided to accompany Wadsworth and rode to the head of the column, pausing only to confer before riding on. As he approached Gettysburg, Reynolds began to hear the faint sound of guns and soon met a courier from Buford with word that the Rebels were advancing on the Cashtown Road. He immediately sent Wadsworth an order to close up and hurry his column forward, and then put the spurs to "Fancy", his black stallion, and galloped toward town. Artillerist Reynolds had an eye for good ground, and as he rode up the Emmitsburg Pike he must have noticed the ridge anchored by two large hills to the east of the road. Still in the dark as to Buford's situation and the size of the force confronting him, Reynolds would have been looking for an appropriate place to position the First Corps in the event of withdrawal, and this ground from East Cemetery Hill to the Round Tops undoubtedly caught his eye.

About a half mile from town Reynolds encountered a civilian looking quite distressed, and when he inquired as to the reason, was told of the cavalry fight to the west of town. Riding on, he stopped at a house to inquire the way to Buford's headquarters at the Eagle Hotel. From there he rode into the town square and west on Chambersburg Street. Standing near the hotel that morning, Gettysburg resident Robert McClean recalled seeing Reynolds and his staff ride up to inquire about Buford. Further down, on the Chambersburg Pike, a young boy, one Daniel

Skelly, saw a general mount the ridge and then ride down a lane toward the Lutheran Seminary. Reynolds galloped up to the Seminary at approximately 9:30 AM and shouted up to Buford in the cupola of one of the buildings, "What's the matter, John?!" The cavalry commander yelled down, "The devil's to pay!"

As the two rode out to examine Buford's position, the latter apprised Reynolds of the situation, reporting that he had been fighting nearly since dawn against Henry Heth's Division of Hill's Corps, and that his scouts reported the advance of Ewell's Corps from the north.

Reynolds was now to make a momentous decision, the most important of his life. Should he commit his 8,000-man First Corps against heavy, soon-to-be overwhelming odds? If so, where should he position them? Should he assume Buford's place to the west and try to save the town, or should he abandon it to occupy and fortify the heights that he had seen to the south on the Emmitsburg Road? Very quickly he decided that he would join Buford in an attempt to save the town, reasoning that at the very least he could hold long enough to allow Meade to seize the heights to the south.

Reynolds and Buford "talked for two or three minutes" by the side of the road, and then Buford was given orders to stand and continue to hold his position. Reynolds then turned to his staff. To Captain Weld he said, "Weld, I am going to pick you out to go to General Meade with a message." He was to tell the army commander that the enemy were coming in strong force, that Reynolds was afraid that the enemy would reach the heights on the other side of town before he could, and that he would fight them all through town, and hold out as long as possible! With a sense of urgency, he ordered the captain to ride fast and hard and even kill his horse if necessary to reach Meade. Reynolds also sent messages to Howard and Sickles to come to Gettysburg with all dispatch, and then sent an aide into town to advise the civilians to stay in their homes.

The wing commander now knew that he was in a race and that time was of the essence. Riding back to hurry Wadsworth's Division along, he became momentarily lost on a Gettysburg side street, but resident Catherine Foster, standing in her balcony, pointed the way to the Emmitsburg Road. In departing, Reynolds requested she go to her cellar. Soon after, he arrived on the road near the Codori Farm and directed his escort to begin tearing down the fences lining the road.

While there, he was met by Major Henry Tremain of Dan Sickles' staff, who had come looking for orders. After receiving them, the major stood listening as Reynolds gazed at Cemetery Ridge and said, "That would be a good place ... but I would like to save the town. If I form there it might destroy the town. But I doubt if I shall have time to form the other side of the town ... " Uncertain as to whether Reynolds was addressing him, Tremain saluted and rode with orders for the Third corps to "come up."

When Wadsworth's Division reached the Codori Farm, Reynolds pointed him through the fence and sent the column at the double quick across fields on a direct line to the Lutheran Seminary. This column was led by Lysander Cutler's Brigade, followed by Captain James Hall's Second Maine Battery; bringing up the rear was General Solomon Meredith's black-hatted "Iron Brigade," regarded by many as the best brigade in the army. When Cutler's Brigade marched by, one soldier glanced up at the general, and later gave the following description: "General Reynolds sat on his horse on the west side of the highway facing us, and as we marched near the head of the column we had a fair look at his features ... the general looked careworn, and we thought, very sad." Very sad indeed. Judging from his earlier remark to Major Tremain, Reynolds was well aware of the desperate, double-sided gamble he had taken. He had committed Buford's cavalry to hold McPherson's Ridge until he could arrive and was wondering whether he could deliver the First Corps and his end of the bargain.

John Reynolds and the First Corps did just barely make it, arriving just as Buford's right flank was verging on collapse. Reynolds ordered Cutler up in relief, and the latter sent three regiments dashing across the Chambersburg Pike and the unfinished railroad cut to form a battle line facing west. Cutler's remaining two regiments went into position south of the Pike with their left resting against a wooded lot known as Herbst Woods (mistakenly referred to as McPherson's Woods).

Having placed Cutler's Brigade, Reynolds now summoned Hall's Maine Battery at a trot, and requested to see its commander. Sitting on horseback in the road near McPherson's Barn, the general gave Hall his instructions. "I desire you to damage the artillery to the greatest possible, and keep their fire from our infantry until they are deployed ... " At the same time, out of fear that the battery might be vulnerable, Reynolds ordered Wadsworth to provide infantry support on the right. Soon after, a messenger arrived from General Doubleday seeking orders. Reynolds replied that he (and Wadsworth) would handle the Cashtown Road and that Doubleday should deploy the two remaining divisions in defense of the Fairfield Road. Then, at approximately 10:30 AM, Reynolds glanced into the Herbst Woods beyond the unprotected left flank of the Fourteenth Brooklyn and was stunned by the sight of advancing Confederates.

For God's Sake Forward!

Somewhat earlier, Confederate commander Heth had ordered one of his brigades to cross the stream known as Willoughby Run and push into the woods beyond. As he advanced into them, Brigade Commander James Archer was unaware that his occupation of these woods (Herbst Woods) would severely compromise the entire Federal line. Reynolds knew, however, and having spotted the Rebels, moved quickly to improvise a solution.

Turning about, he spotted elements of Meredith's "Iron Brigade" moving down from the Seminary, and sent two aides to hurry them forward. He then galloped down toward the swale between the two ridges, saw the distinctive black hats of the Second Wisconsin and cried out, "Forward into line at the double quick!. .. " The Wisconsin men instantly swung into line, trying desperately to load their muskets on the run. As they reached the crest of the ridge they were staggered by a volley from the Rebel line, which inflicted heavy losses while grinding the regiment to a halt. Looking on, Reynolds rode down in among the men to rally them, shouting: "Forward, forward men! Drive those fellows out of that [the woods]. Forward! For God's sake forward!" With Reynolds leading the charge, the Second Wisconsin surged ahead, pushed to the north by tremendous Confederate pressure on their left. Reynolds' orderly, Sergeant Charles Veil, later wrote that "wherever the fight raged the fiercest, there the general was sure to be found, his undaunted courage always inspired the men with more energy and courage."

As the regiment crashed into the woods, riding to the left, Reynolds could see that the Rebels still overlapped his line by a considerable margin. Faced with the danger of being flanked and losing his entire line, he turned in the saddle, looking about for other "Iron Brigade" regiments. Suddenly, his horse bolted forward and the general tumbled to the ground. Three staff members—Captain Edward Baird, Captain Robert Mitchell, and Sergeant Veil—immediately jumped from their horses and went to his aide.

Reynolds was lying on his left side when Veil first reached him. The sergeant rolled him on his back, quickly checked for a wound, but found nothing except a bruise near the left eye. Their immediate concern, however, was not so much his wound as the Rebel firing line, which lay no more than "sixty paces" away. With Veil grabbing him under the arms, and the two captains each taking a leg, they managed to carry him out of the woods. Meanwhile, a number of orderlies rode up, relieving Baird and Mitchell so that they might inform the chain of command.

Sketch of the Death of Reynolds on the Gettysburg Battlefield

Veil and two orderlies carried the general back toward the seminary in hopes of finding medical assistance. Crossing the field between the two ridges, they heard Reynolds exhale, which led them to believe that he may only have been stunned by a spent mini ball. Veil immediately halted, laid him on the ground and tried to revive him with a drink of water. But, he could not drink, and upon further examination Veil found the wound beneath the general's uniform collar, a small bloodless hole behind the right ear. The men continued on, but at some point during their trek, Dr. J.T. Stillman, a surgeon of the 147th New York, examined the body and announced that the general had died within fifteen minutes of being hit. Quite possibly, the sigh heard by Sergeant Veil was the death gasp of John Reynolds.

At about 11:20 AM, just at the time that Reynolds was being carried from the field, Captain Weld arrived at army headquarters. Meade had received countless messages that morning, but was waiting most anxiously to hear from Reynolds. As Weld concluded his oral message, Meade exclaimed, "Good! That is just like Reynolds, he will hold on to the bitter end." Then, at approximately 1:00 PM, Major Riddle rode up with very bad news. Delivering the sad details of Reynolds death, Riddle noted the shock and sorrow on the face of the army commander, now without the services of his chief lieutenant when they were needed most.

If he died early in a desperate hour, John Reynolds did not die in vain. The example he set as a loyal subordinate had been crucial during the dark days between the Peninsula and Chancellorsville. The current of trust and confidence between Reynolds and George Meade provided badly needed stability to the army during the late spring of '63. At Gettysburg, he and John Buford ran and won perhaps the most dramatic and consequential race in U.S. military history. After his death, his men fought valiantly on where he had placed them, thereby enabling Hancock and Meade to seize and fortify the heights to the south. From this ground, two days later, the battle was won. Truly, when John Reynolds fell, the victorious "architect of the battle had fallen."

Epilogue

Reynolds' body was carried to the George House (where he had earlier asked for directions to John Buford) and laid there while staff members searched for a coffin. Two local women later claimed to have assisted the staff in their chores. While watching the body being carried to the rear, Mrs. John Sheads placed her white shawl under his head to comfort him, and upon recovering it found the shawl stained with his blood. Her sister-in-law, Mary Jane Sheads, later stated that the two walked to the George House, and washed the blood from his face while wrapping the body in sheets.

Veil and Captain Joe Rosengarten were unsuccessful in finding a coffin, but did locate a box at a marble cutters. Unfortunately, the length of the box was such that they were forced to knock out one end so that the body could fit. The box was placed in an ambulance at 1:00 PM and the sad escort proceeded to Union Bridge, Maryland, arriving in late evening. There they procured a coffin in which the corpse was packed with ice. The general was then sent to Baltimore where his brother-in-law made arrangements for embalming and a more suitable coffin. At midnight, July 2, 1863, the body arrived by train in Philadelphia and was taken to 1829 Spruce Street, the home of Mrs. Landis, his sister.

C

Catherine Mary (Kate) Hewitt

Dear Kate

While the body lay in the front parlor of the Landis home, a young lady came to the door, and John and Kate Hewitt's secret engagement was finally revealed to his family. During preparation of the body, a chain was discovered around his neck with a heart engraved medallion, and on his finger, where he normally would have worn his West Point class ring, a small ring was found with the inscription "Dear Kate." Inasmuch as John had never mentioned a "Kate" in any of his letters, the family was quite stunned at this discovery and by the arrival of Miss Hewitt at their door.

As she related the tale of her courtship to the Reynolds sisters, they came to regard her as a "superior person." She and John had met, she said, in California in 1860 and fallen in love, and when John had been ordered to West Point, she also had traveled east to attend the Academy of Sacred Heart in Torresdale, Pennsylvania. She was, yes, a Catholic, and she explained that she and John had decided to postpone marriage until after the war. Their agreement had also included Reynolds' permission for her to enter a convent should anything happen to him. This she now intended to do, as the world no longer held her interest.

The initial shock to the Presbyterian Reynolds family was considerable, but after hearing Kate's story, they embraced her as one of their own. Kate Hewitt would become "Sister Hildegardi" after entering the Sisters of Charity Convent in Emmitsburg, Maryland. She remained in touch with the family until 1868, when she disappeared, never to be seen or heard from again.

It is worth noting as well that the Reynolds family never again visited John's patron, former President James Buchanan, at his Wheatland estate in Lancaster. Upon John's death, the relation abruptly ceased. Obviously, the loss of their brother in a war with Buchanan's former associates, "secesh of the first water", was too much to bear.

John F. Reynolds arrived home in Lancaster, at 11:30 AM on July 4, 1863, accompanied by his family and the dedicated members of his staff Riddle, Mitchell, Rosengarten, Weld, Wilcox, and Veil. The family desired no martial display for they believed John would not have wanted it, but the streets were filled with people, with flags at half mast and draped with crepe, as the funeral cortège moved slowly to the cemetery. While members of the "Old Reserves" acted as pallbearers, the general was placed beside his mother and father. Captain Weld noted that "a chapter of the Bible was read, and prayer delivered, and then poor General Reynolds disappeared from us for some time to come." At the moment of interment, Major Riddle fell to the ground and wept.

A month after the battle the Reynolds family received a request from the "Old First Brigade" of the Reserve Division asking that one of their members be allowed to travel to Philadelphia to make a presentation. These men had decided after the Battle of Mechanicsville (June 1862) to present the general with a sword, belt, and sash "in a testimony of their love and admiration." The sword was made of the finest Damascus steel, and the scabbard was of pure gold. The grip was adorned with black onyx with his initials J.F.R. set in diamonds; on the reverse was a scroll with the Latin inscription "Vincer Amor Patriae" (Love of Country Conquers). The men had carried the sword in a company wagon during the Gettysburg campaign, in hopes of making the presentation themselves, but to their great sorrow, never had a chance.

In September 1863, the Reynolds family received another request, this one from the entire First Corps, asking permission to raise money for a monument to be erected "as a small tribute to his memory ... which would please the officers and men of the old Corps." Of the many tributes Reynolds received, those of the Pennsylvania Reserves and the First Corps would have undoubtedly meant the most.

The man whom Abraham Lincoln would call "our gallant and brave friend" had placed the good of the army and the cause of Union above personal ambition and made the ultimate sacrifice at Gettysburg. That he did so came as no surprise to those who loved him, and even Kate Hewitt accepted his priorities. In her heart she had given him first "to God, then to his country, and then to herself." About her own sacrifice there lingers a haunting sadness.

Afterword: Reynolds of Gettysburg

Great events are typically made up of a series of small incidents. This was certainly true of the titanic three days at Gettysburg in 1863. Some of these smaller incidents are significant in and of themselves in that they had critical impact on the course and outcome of the great event. The actions of Maj. Gen. John F. Reynolds on the first day of the battle were such significant and decisive incidents. It is appropriate to emphasize Reynolds' involvement, his last and finest hour. One may first identify him, to see him as a general officer.

In several ways, Reynolds was typical of the ranking generals of the Army of the Potomac. Thus he was politically conservative, a pre-war Democrat antagonistic to abolition. On the other hand, he was intensely committed to the Union, a patriot in a very real sense and angry about secession. His military philosophy was similarly conservative. Like McClellan, he believed that the war should have been in the hands of the military, free and clear of the political objectives and necessities of the government and uninhibited by civilian control. He perceived a nonexistent line between politics and war, and between the government and its military forces. Under this extra-constitutional view, the Washington administration should not have had the jurisdiction or the power to decide and direct the military establishment. Reynolds' inability to structure army command in this way caused him to reject the offer of command of the Army of the Potomac.

His concept of warfare was also traditional. He was initially skeptical of volunteer soldiers, was a strict disciplinarian, and believed in the protection of the private property of the enemy. Despite these characteristics, Reynolds was highly popular with his Washington superiors and his military peers and those he commanded, both officers and enlisted men. Unlike other major military figures of the eastern theater, he was discreet with his politics and was not an intriguer. The commands of Burnside and Hooker had been marked by political intrigue and jockeying. Reynolds and Meade, who was junior to Reynolds, had long been friendly rivals. They cooperated on Meade's appointment to command and brought on a needed period of stability to the army.

Douglas Southall Freeman has written that Lee's "army ... had been wrecked at Gettysburg." Without belaboring the classic issue of the decisiveness of that battle in terms of the war, it is surely fair to say that the Confederate defeat was highly damaging. It forever limited Lee's capacity to maneuver and thus predicted the ultimate siege which led to his surrender. There has been much careless writing about Gettysburg's first day. Confederate apologists sometimes speak of a Confederate victory on the first day, as if July 1 represented a battle in and of itself without reference to the succeeding two days and as if unmindful of what the stakes were on July 1. Other writers, referring to the Federals, use such words as "swept from the field," "collapsed," and "fled" to describe the action of the Eleventh and First Corps. The Federals were indeed defeated on the first day but their dogged and desperate fighting had permitted Federal possession of the key ground and had purchased the time for the Army of the Potomac to gather on that ground. Lee reported that the four Confederate divisions engaged on the first day were "weakened and exhausted by a long and bloody struggle," which surely contradicts the image of Federals that were "swept away."

The truth is that at stake on the first day of Gettysburg were two factors critical to the battle's outcome, field position and time. The key ground was the high ground south of the town: Cemetery Hill, Culp's Hill, Cemetery Ridge and the Round Tops. Possession of these heights-Porter Alexander called them "a position unique among all the battlefields of the war"-provided a significant Federal advantage. And time was essential so that the several missing corps of the Army of the Potomac could gather to defend this ground. These factors were what the first day of the battle was all about. The Federals held the ground and acquired the time. John F. Reynolds was the principle agent of these accomplishments.

Crediting Reynolds on the first day does not mitigate the contribution of Brig. Gen. John Buford. Screening the advance of the army's left wing, Buford initially established a cavalry line on July 1, west and north of Gettysburg as the divisions of Heth, Pender, Rodes and Early moved toward town. The horseman's skillful and tenacious defense afforded Reynolds his opportunity. Ordered by Meade to advance his First Corps to Gettysburg early on July 1, with the Eleventh Corps in support, it was Reynolds' decision to fight at McPherson's Ridge, and his bringing up the Eleventh Corps, that created the defense in depth of the high ground south of the town. This defense set up the ultimate battle site on that high ground.

It is only fair to note that Reynolds' decision was especially timely in the light of Meade's obvious uncertainty. Meade's order that sent the first corps to Gettysburg said that he would "assume position for offensive or defensive, as occasion requires, or rest to the troops." Uncertainty marked another of Meade's communications to Reynolds on July 1: "The commanding general cannot decide whether it is his best policy to move to attack until he learns something more definite of the point at which the enemy is concentrating ... Meanwhile, he would like to have your views upon the subject." This communication proceeded to discuss whether or not Gettysburg was the appropriate place for a Federal concentration and again solicited Reynolds' "suggestions." It is generally believed that Reynolds did not receive this latter communication, or the more or less simultaneous Pipe Creek Circular, but his actions plainly established his views of the proper role and place for the Army of the Potomac.

Significantly, after Reynolds' death a series of commanders on the field ratified Reynolds' decision. Doubleday, Howard, and finally Hancock clung to McPherson's and Seminary Ridges until the Federals were withdrawn, and the Federal Corps then assembled on the "position unique" from which Lee was heavily defeated. Lost Cause writers and Lee apologists have tried to diminish the Federal accomplishments on the first day by reiterating the "Ewell card": only Ewell's wrong-headed failure to attack Cemetery Hill permitted the Federals to hold the advantageous field position. These commentators forget that Lee was on the field and did not order such an attack. He also justified Ewell in his official report.

John F. Reynolds' death at Gettysburg has guaranteed his status as a romantic hero of the war. It is well to remember that this supreme contribution was matched by his tactical judgment.

Alan T. Nolan
Indianapolis, IN

EDITORS NOTE: Alan T. Nolan's writings include *The Iron Brigade* and *Lee Considered: General Robert E. Lee and Civil War History*. He has also published in the major Civil War and historical journals and resides in Indianapolis. He is a Fellow of the Company of Military Historians and a member of the Indianapolis Civil War Round Table.

READERS NOTE: The endnotes of this work have been placed on file for viewing purposes at the Gettysburg National Military Park Library. Readers may obtain a set of endnotes by sending $2.00 to the Farnsworth House Inn Book Store, 401 Baltimore St., Gettysburg, PA, 17325.

Select Bibliography

Aimone, Alan & Barbara. "Much to Sadden and Little to Cheer: The Civil War Years at West Point." *Blue and Gray Magazine*. Issue No.2 1991.

Bachelder, John. *Gettysburg in Their Own Words*. Volume 1. January 5, 1863 to July 27, 1880. Dayton, Ohio: Morningside House, Inc. 1994.

Cleaves, Freeman. *Meade of Gettysburg*. Oklahoma: Norman and London. University of Oklahoma Press, 1960.

Coddington, Edwin B. *The Gettysburg Campaign*. New York: Charles Scribner's Sons, 1968.

Doubleday, Abner. *Chancellorsville and Gettysburg*. New York: DaCapo Press, 1994.

Hassler Jr., Warren W. *Crisis at the Crossroads*. Tuscaloosa, Alabama: University of Alabama Press, 1970.

Hennessy, John J. *Return to Bull Run*. New York: Simon and Schuster Co., 1993.

Henry, Robert Selph. *The Story of the Mexican War*. New York: Da Capo Press, 1950.

Lewis, Lloyd. *Captain Sam Grant* 1822-1861. Volume 1. Boston: Little, Brown and Co., 1950.

Maloney, Mary. "General Reynolds and Dear Kate." *American Heritage Magazine*. Volume XV, No. 1.

Martin, David G. *Gettysburg July* 1. Conshohocken, Pennsylvania: Combined Books, 1995.

Morrison Jr., James L. *The Best School in the World, West Point, the Pre-Civil War Years* 1833-1866. Kent, Ohio: Kent State University Press, 1962.

Pfanz, Harry W. *Gettysburg: Culp's Hill and Cemetery Hill*. Chapel Hill and London: University of North Carolina Press, 1993.

Reynolds Family Papers (MS6), Archives and Special Collections Department, Franklin and Marshall College, Lancaster, PA.

Sears, Stephen W. *George B. McClellan, The Young Napoleon*. New York: Ticknor and Fields, 1968.

Scott, Colonel John Fulton Reynolds. "John Fulton Reynolds," Lancaster County Historical Society Papers. Volume LII. No.2, 1948.

Shue, Richard S. *Morning at Willoughby Run, July* 1, 1863. Gettysburg, Pennsylvania: Thomas Publications, 1995.

Smith, Major General William Farrar. "Franklin's Left Grand Division" *Battles and Leaders of the Civil War*. Retreat from Gettysburg. New York: Castle Books, 1956.

Steiner, Paul E. M.D., PH.D. *Medical-Military Portraits of Union and Confederate Generals,* Philadelphia: Whitemore Publishing Co., 1968.

Sypher, J.R. Esq. *History of the Pennsylvania Reserve Corps,* Pennsylvania: Elias Barr and Co., 1865.

United States War Department. *The War of the Rebellion: A Compilation of the Official Records of the Union and Confederate Armies*. Washington, D.C.: Government Printing Office, 1880-1901. Volume 27, Parts 1,2, and 3.

Viola, Herman J. *The Memoirs of Charles Henry Veil, The History of the American West*. New York: Orion Books, 1993.

Weld, Stephen Minot. *War Diary and Letters,* Boston: Massachusetts Historical Society, 1979.

Woodward, Evan Morrison. *Our Campaigns, The Second Regiment Pennsylvania Volunteers* 1861-1864. Edited by Stanley W. Zamonski. Pennsylvania: Burd Street Press, 1995.

Part II:

Reynolds:
The Last Six Miles

by

Diane E Watson

"...as we approached the house saw lights in the parlor, found your Uncle John reading there. He told us he had been with the President that day, and that Mr. Lincoln had offered him the command of the Army of the Potomac, which he told the President he would accept, if he was not interfered with from Washington. This the President would not promise him, therefore your Uncle declined the offer."

Eleanor Reynolds (1835-1923)

Statue of John Reynolds along the Chambersburg Pike

Introduction

This book is written to show the activities of the final hours of General John F. Reynolds who was killed around 10:30 AM on Wednesday, July 1, 1863, during the battle of Gettysburg. It is viewed from his perspective only. The reader will not follow anyone who leaves the General's presence. The reader will be privy to the Confederate activities only as they relate to Gen. Reynolds.

Gen. Reynolds was out of the battle so quickly that July morning that his influence is overlooked in some instances. Everything that happened the next few days depended on Gen. Reynolds' decisions, orders and actions during his short time on the field July 1, 1863.

I believe his part is important enough to devote this chapter to his hour-by-hour activities from 4:00 PM Tuesday, June 30, 1863 to 10:30 AM Wednesday, July 1, 1863. May the reader feel for this great man a fraction of what compels me to write this book.

The Man

Brilliant, decisive, honest and fair. A man of his word, a man of few words, a man you can trust. He is the consummate soldier. Tall, straight and elegant in the saddle, at one with the horse. His men adore him, would do anything for him.

Major General John Fulton Reynolds, Commander of the 1st Corps, United States Volunteers, Commander of the Left Wing, Army of the Potomac. Six feet tall, dark eyes, full, black, neatly trimmed whiskers, dark complexion and a natural charisma. He wears his kepi straight and tight, no tilt to it. His face is handsome with a combination of strength and sensitivity. His eyes, direct and sure, with a touch of sadness. An undeniable military genius.

An aggressive leader, he never goes into battle blind. He relies on his scouts and generals to keep him informed. He checks and double-checks maps, messages and charts. He listens carefully to the ideas and opinions of his generals.

He believes troops should be led and not directed. He can always be found leading his army - directing from the front lines. Finding the best ground for bivouac, as well as the best ground for battle. He cares about the needs of his men. They know it because he takes action to see to their needs. He is a good provider.

They also know he is almost fanatic about discipline. He can destroy an offender with a look. No crime goes unpunished in his command. In spite of, and maybe in some cases because of the discipline, his men love him. They agree he is generous, cares about them and makes certain they have everything in his power to get Major General John Reynolds for them.

He impresses everyone who meets him. He is strong, sure, fair, energetic, consistent, principled and unforgettable. When meeting with President

Lincoln, the general confided to his President that he would prefer not to have command of the Army of the Potomac unless he had free rein on all decisions in the field. He knew he could not take orders from Washington Bureaucrats. The general's loyalties are unmistakable - Army and the Union, but, he has his standards.

Later, upon hearing of George Meade's appointment, Gen. Reynolds dons his best dress uniform and rides to Meade to pay his respects and pledge his support and loyalty.

He is a soldier of the highest standard - loyal to his commanders, obeying orders. Now, with Meade in command, Gen. Reynolds feels a certain freedom. Meade knows he can trust Gen. Reynolds and gives him free rein to make decisions he thinks best. Reynolds feels the security of Meade's trust. Gen. Reynolds trusts Meade's instincts and military prowess more than the previous commanders. They have been soldiers together for a long time and know each other well. Gen. Reynolds knows Meade will approve his battle plans.

John Reynolds is a native of Lancaster, Pennsylvania, about 60 miles from his position on June 30, 1863, at the Moritz Tavern near Emmitsburg. He will not tolerate Confederates in his state. Robert E. Lee is near Gettysburg - six miles up the road - just six miles, the last six miles for Gen. John F. Reynolds.

The Moritz Inn

Already an Inn for at least sixty years by 1863, the Moritz (pronounced Mertz) Tavern is the perfect location to serve as headquarters for Gen. John F. Reynolds. It is a two-story, tin-roofed, brick building located where Bullfrog Road meets the Emmitsburg Road, just six miles from Gettysburg.

The Tavern's owner, Samuel Moritz, is married to Emily and they have two children, Catherine, three years old and David, five years old. Living with her family is Ann, Samuel's Mother, still grieving for her husband, Nicholas, who died in March. There is also a domestic and a farm hand in the employ of Mr. Moritz.

Downstairs is the dining room, the family area, a storeroom and a kitchen. Upstairs is a ballroom and five guest rooms. The barn is just south of the house and there is a well in the front yard. Beneath the house with the entrance out back under the kitchen is room enough to hide the family horses when the Rebels come around.

Tuesday, June 30, 1863

Gen. Reynolds and his staff are headquartered at the Moritz Tavern ... six miles from Gettysburg. He has established his office in the kitchen on the first floor just off the dining room in the rear of the house. There is ample space in the Tavern for his entire staff: Maj. William Riddle, Sr. Aide; Capt. William G. Mitchell, Aide; Lt. Joseph G. Rosengarten, Aide; Capt. Stephen

Weld, Aide (youngest of the General's Aides); Wm. H. Willcox, Aide; Sgt. Charles H. Veil, Orderly (18 years old).

The troops are camped in the fields between Emmitsburg and Marsh Creek, a mile to the north. It has been raining and the ground is wet and muddy. There are thousands of soldiers, tents and campfires. The men are wet, tired, hot, hungry, dirty - and ready for the Rebs.

On this day, the General is given command of the entire Left Wing of the Army of the Potomac. He spends the morning and early afternoon notifying and updating his Generals: Maj. Gen. Abner Doubleday, 1st Corps; Maj. Gen. Daniel Sickles, 3rd Corps; Maj. Gen. Oliver D. Howard, 11th Corps; Brig. Gen. John Buford, 2 Brigades of Cavalry.

He alerts Gen. Howard to be ready with his Eleventh Corps to move in support if and when necessary. The General orders Sickles' Third Corps to bivouac along Cat Tail Branch near Bridgeport, Maryland, and cover the roads leading toward Gettysburg. Wadsworth is north of the Moritz Tavern near Greenmount. Gen. Reynolds is responsible for almost half of Meade's 100,000 men since being assigned the Left Wing.

Brig. Gen. John Buford's Cavalry is already in Gettysburg and has been updating Gen. Reynolds throughout the day concerning Confederate activity. Gen. Reynolds can rely on Buford for detailed, timely messages.

4:00 PM Tuesday, June 30, 1863

Around 4:00 PM, an officer arrives from Taneytown. He says he has been sent by Gen. Meade to meet with Gen. Reynolds. He is ushered into the kitchen where Gen. Reynolds is lost in thought over a stack of papers and maps. The officer removes his hat and respectfully waits for the General to finish his thought. Realizing someone is standing there, the General looks up, stands, greets him warmly after returning his salute, and asks him to have a seat. The visitor notices a cup of tea and some crackers have been placed on the table where the papers are pushed aside. The General remarks "such a light repast with so much ahead of us tomorrow".

With the pleasantries over, the general and Meade's officer discuss what is known of the Confederate situation. Gen. Reynolds tells him of his plans for each of the three corps in his Left Wing (1st, 3rd and 11 th Corps). Doubleday's 1st Corps (his new command since Gen. Reynolds was given the Left Wing) is encamped around the Tavern. The 3rd Corps, commanded by Sickles is to bivouac along Cat Tail Branch, face Gettysburg, and cover the inroads. Howard's 11th Corps is situated about a mile north of the Tavern on Marsh Creek.

The meeting lasts about 20 minutes or so and the officer continues on his way to Buford in Gettysburg … just six miles away. He says he will return.

Shortly after this meeting, Gen. Reynolds sends word to Gen. Howard to join him at his headquarters.

Reynolds is not one to go into battle blind, even in his own state. He will be in constant touch with his generals. He continues to study his maps, reports and other documents. He will know every bit of information available about the Confederates, the land, and his options.

5:30 PM Tuesday, June 30, 1863

A message arrives from Buford at 5:30 PM. It states that the Confederate forces have increased considerably. The strongest Rebel position is behind Cashtown - about eight miles west of Gettysburg.

Buford's scouts have also sighted Southern troops north of Gettysburg near Mummasburg. There are Rebel pickets posted as close as three miles west of Gettysburg!

Sunset, Tuesday, June 30, 1863

Responding to the message from his commanding officer, Gen. Howard arrives at the Moritz Tavern. He and his staff join Gen. Reynolds and his staff for a late supper. Reynolds' demeanor is spirited and animated.

After supper, the two generals withdraw privately to his office in the kitchen. Together they discuss maps, battle plans and messages. Gen. Howard notices a dramatic change in his commander's mood. He becomes quiet, serious, almost depressed. Howard remembers how impressed he had been with John Reynolds at West Point when they were young instructors during the 1840's. He continues to hold him in the highest regard.

They discuss the reports from local citizens, as well as army scouts. He briefs Howard on Buford's latest communication. Gen. Reynolds listens intently to Howard's opinions, as he does all of his generals. Howard has the distinct feeling that his leader expects a battle soon; but, is not comfortable with the situation. He knows Meade's army is spread out and he knows little about Lee's location.

10:00 PM Tuesday, June 30, 1863

The Left Wing Commander sends for his Senior Aide, Major William Riddle. Gen. Meade is headquartered at Taneytown, and Maj. Riddle is to deliver several messages. Gen. Reynolds expects return orders from his commanding officer.

In the message, General Reynolds offers his best guess for what the enemy may have in mind. If they continue in their present venue, they may be thinking of coming in force through Gettysburg and attacking them just north of Emmitsburg, or possibly near St. Mary's College. However, he reminds Gen. Meade, it is only a guess. In conclusion, he suggests the necessity of an engineer officer to reconnoiter his present position, due to the Confederate main force being in the vicinity of Cashtown.

11:00 PM Tuesday, June 30, 1863

Major Riddle has not yet returned from Taneytown, so Gen. Howard takes his leave of Gen. Reynolds and heads back for his camp in Emmitsburg.

Shortly after Howard leaves, a courier arrives with a message from Gen. Buford in Gettysburg. The message is marked 10:30 PM, and contains detailed updates of the situation in Gettysburg:

> *I am satisfied that A. P. Hill's Corps is massed just back of Cashtown, about nine miles from this place. Pender's division of this Corps came up today ... The enemy's pickets are within four miles of this place on the Cashtown Road ... Longstreet is still behind Hill. I can get no forage nor rations; am out of both. Should I have to fall back advise me by what route.*

Reynolds regrets Buford's plight, but continued reconnaissance is essential. The enemy's next move is questionable, but whatever move they make, Reynolds is determined to be ready.

12:00 Midnight Tuesday, June 30, 1863

General Reynolds' downstairs room contains a table and chairs. An upstairs bedroom is made available if he wants it, but he chooses to stay where he is. He wraps himself in a blanket and sleeps on the floor.

4:00 AM Wednesday, July 1, 1863

General Reynolds' Senior Aide, Major Riddle, returns from Gen. Meade in Taneytown. He enters and finds his General sleeping soundly on the floor. Knowing the General has not slept well lately, he hesitates to awaken him from such a sound sleep. Actually, the General had been restless all night, perhaps even trying at first to sleep on five straight-back chairs. Maj. Riddle decides to read the orders and see if they merit waking his commanding officer ... they do.

General Reynolds lies on his back while Maj. Riddle reads the orders. He has the major read them three times:

> *The 1st Corp is to march to Gettysburg*
> *The 11th Corps to Gettysburg "or support distance"*
> *The 3rd Corp to Emmitsburg*

The message includes orders to lighten the load of the column. All unnecessary wagons, baggage, animals, etc., were to be sent to the rear. The orders continue with confirmation that Harrisburg and Philadelphia are relieved. The message concludes with the usual confidentiality cautions.

After brief contemplation, the General is on his feet - alert and ready to act upon the orders to head to Gettysburg ... just six miles away. Following his usual routine, he personally wakens his staff.

5:30 to 6:00 AM Wednesday, July 1, 1863

Christian Shriver and Alice, his wife, arrive with breakfast. Gen. Reynolds had sent a note and a pass to them the day before asking if they could provide food for breakfast. They were kind enough to bring the implements with which to prepare the food also. They start a cooking fire in an area known as "The Commons". The general and his staff have meat, eggs, potatoes and fresh bread. He offers the Shrivers five dollars. They decline, but he insists, knowing the war is as hard on the citizens as it is the troops. He thanks them for such kindness.

The General wants to be in Gettysburg as soon as possible. He changes the order of the march. Normally, the leading division would march last the next day, but he wants Wadsworth's Division to move first because they are closest to Gettysburg. He notifies Wadsworth, who, in turn, sends word to his regimental commanders.

Reynolds then writes a message to Gen. Meade in Taneytown reporting the increased Confederate activity. Reynolds ends the message with: from the scope of instructions he had so far received from him (Gen. Meade), " ... I feel at liberty to advance to Gettysburg and develop the strength of the enemy at that point."

6:00 AM Wednesday, July 1, 1863

General Howard sends word to two of his 11th Corps Division commanders to take an alternate route to avoid congestion on the Emmitsburg Road. His command will reform two miles outside of Gettysburg. General Reynolds agrees.

Another message is sent to Gen. Sickles near Bridgeport for his 3rd Corps to march to Emmitsburg.

The Left Wing Commander also sends a courier to Meade confirming action on his orders received earlier. The consummate soldier --- no detail is left undone.

7:00 to 7:30 AM Wednesday, July 1, 1863

Having been summoned by Gen. Reynolds, Doubleday arrives around 7:30 AM. They review the latest messages. Reynolds informs Doubleday that he will be moving out presently. He then orders Doubleday to call in the pickets and bring the 2nd and 3rd Divisions along with the artillery. In conclusion, he tells Doubleday to join him when the orders have been fulfilled.

8:00 AM Wednesday, July 1, 1863

General Reynolds mounts his huge, beautiful black horse, Fancy, and he and his staff begin the six mile journey to Gettysburg - the general's last six miles. The skies are cloudy now after an early morning shower. It is a comfortable morning with the temperature about 70. The marching troops look like a rolling blue wave moving up the Emmitsburg Road.

At one point Gen. Reynolds and Wadsworth dismount. They spread out a map and confer briefly by the side of the road near Greenmount.

Gen. Reynolds and his staff lead the march when it continues. Captain Baird thinks his General a bit quiet during the ride, but other staff members notice just a more relaxed demeanor. He knows Meade trusts him and he feels the freedom of this trust and knows he can make his own decisions.

A mile from the Moritz Tavern they cross Marsh Creek, a fairly wide creek with lovely trees on its banks. A mist just rising gives it a haunting look of peace in the midst of war. On the left as they cross the bridge, the creek splits around either side of a small "island".

9:00 AM Wednesday, July 1, 1863

The march proceeds - they are about a mile or so from Gettysburg now. The general and his attending officers are a good distance ahead of the troops. He becomes quiet and more pensive. They can hear the guns now, too. A rider comes in sight. He approaches the group, out of breath and very excited. He brings compliments to Gen. Reynolds from Buford, and proceeds to report Confederates coming down the road from Cashtown since daybreak. The commander knows this means he must move quickly and decisively. He will go to Buford and assess the situation for himself. Reynolds dismounts to prepare messages: one to Meade, one to urge Howard forward and another to Wadsworth to advance quickly to Gettysburg.

Biddles' Brigade and Cooper's Battery (1st Corps) are approaching Gettysburg from Pumping Station Road, across a covered bridge at Sock's Mill. They had camped the night before on Bullfrog Road west of the Moritz Tavern.

About this time Captain Hall, Battery B., Maine, joins the general and his officers. General Reynolds orders him to ride forward with his battery and get between the enemy and the town and "throw a few shells into them to keep them from plundering the town". After making all necessary contacts, Reynolds, his orderly, Veil, and one staff officer leave to meet Buford.

They hear cannon fire by now. The general races toward Gettysburg. Nothing escapes him, the two higher elevations sweeping down to a low ridge to his right. These may prove critical later.

Just outside of Gettysburg, a civilian comes running up, waving his arms, out of breath, shouting: "The cavalry has been driven back!" He is so distressed, they can get no further details from him. They hurry on, pausing at the edge of town, they elicit directions to the Seminary and Buford.

Civilians are in the streets, obviously scared and confused. However, one man, Peter Culp, is just sitting on his horse outside of the Eagle Hotel at the corner of Chambersburg and Washington Streets. Not wanting to waste valuable time with wrong turns, the general asks him to guide them to the Seminary. He gladly agrees and they head off toward the west of town.

About this time, General Reynolds sends a message to Wadsworth on the Emmitsburg Road to turn his leading brigade (Cutler's) into the field on the left and, at the double march, head toward the woods (Seminary Ridge). The general will meet the column and place the troops himself. He also orders Wadsworth to hurry the advance of the other brigades.

Matthew Brady picture of the Lutheran Theological Seminary soon after the battle in 1863.

9:15 AM Wednesday, July 1, 1863

General Reynolds sends his Aide, Captain Joseph Rosengarten, to warn the citizens of Gettysburg to stay in their homes. The consummate soldier, he thinks of everything. Citizens should not be caught in the middle of battle.

Knowing Buford is barely holding on, the general and his party hurry to the Lutheran Theological Seminary west of town. They approach the building with the cupola on top. The Confederates are in plain sight heading east on the Chambersburg Pike. As Reynolds enters, Buford is coming down the steps:

"What's the matter, John?", his general asks.

"The Devil's to pay", replies Buford.

"Can you hold?"

"1 reckon I can" says Buford, and then updates his commander on the situation as they walk outside.

9:30 AM Wednesday, July 1, 1863

Major E. P. Halstead of Doubleday's staff rides up to report on their progress. Gen. Reynolds' reply is to tell Doubleday to advance with all speed.

Also, at this time, General Reynolds sends Capt. Stephen Weld, the youngest of his aides, with a message to Gen. Meade still in Taneytown.

> *"Tell him the enemy is advancing in strong force and I fear he will get to the heights beyond the town before I can. I will fight him inch by inch and, if driven into the town, I will barricade the streets, and hold him back as long as possible."*

To Weld, he admonishes: "Don't spare your horse!"

Buford and Reynolds head for the front. They are showered by fire from the Confederate line. After slowing his horse only slightly, the general presses on. Buford, worried, cautions, "General, do not expose yourself so much."

Reynolds acknowledges with a nod, but is much more concerned with matters ahead. It was already obvious to the Left Wing Commander that the odds were overwhelming. He has 8,000 men in the First Corp alone. Where does he place them should he commit the entire corps, should he hold Buford's position, or move back to occupy the heights south of town? The decision is made quickly, but not without purpose and thought.

Just south of the Chambersburg Pike, Reynolds is ordering Buford to prevent the enemy from getting through town and seizing the high ground, remembering Cemetery Ridge and the higher slopes. His parting charge: "hold them in check from this position as long as you can. The 1st Corps will soon come to your relief."

At this time General Reynolds sends his aide Maj. Riddle to Gen. Howard with the message - "Bring up the 1st Corps with all possible speed, encamp along the Emmitsburg Road just outside Gettysburg and await further orders."

9:45 AM Wednesday, July 1, 1863

General Reynolds is anxious to get to General Wadsworth waiting near the Codori Farm on the Emmitsburg Road. On the way, they are briefly lost on a Gettysburg side street, but local, Catherine Foster, standing on her balcony, points the way toward the Emmitsburg Road. The general advises her to retreat to her cellar. He races across the fields. An excellent horseman, he and his beautiful black mount, Fancy, seem to float across the fences in his path. However, realizing foot soldiers would be slowed by these same obstacles, he has his and Wadsworth's staff, together with some engineers, take down as much of the fencing and posts as possible.

Major Henry Tremain of Sickles' Staff arrives looking for orders. Upon receiving them, the Major waits briefly listening as Reynolds gazes at Cemetery Ridge. The general says "That would be a good place ... but I would like to save the town. If I form there it might destroy the town. But, I doubt if I shall have time to form the other side of the town ... " Tremain salutes and returns to the Third Corps with orders to "come up".

As quickly as the infantry reach the fields they are turning left and marching double quick to Seminary Ridge. Gen. Reynolds pauses for awhile on the west side of the Emmitsburg Road and watches the advancement of the troops. He knows his men are eager to follow him and trust his judgment. This is a heavy burden for a man who cares so deeply about his men. These thoughts give the appearance of sorrow to some of the soldiers. However, he jokes a few minutes later with his aide, Rosengarten, about his dirty eyeglasses - asking if the townspeople threw mud at him after he told them to stay in their houses.

The 1st Corps band plays several songs to help the march as they pass, one of which is "The Girl I Left Behind Me".

10:00 to 10:20 AM Wednesday, July 1, 1863

Seeing all is being done to hurry the column, General Reynolds hurries toward Seminary Ridge. He meets up with Wadsworth who had ridden ahead with his men. They encounter Buford near McPherson's Ridge, along the Chambersburg Pike. His situation has deteriorated. Confederate General Heth's troops have crossed Willoughby Run, west on the Chambersburg Pike, and are pressing hard. Buford's men are fighting the impending necessity to fall back.

General Reynolds summons battery commander, Capt. Hall, and orders him to "put your battery on this ridge (Chambersburg Pike near McPherson's Barn) to engage those guns of the enemy." "I desire you to damage the artillery to the greatest possible, and keep their fire from our infantry until they are deployed ... " Knowing his leader's expectations, Hall moves quickly to follow his orders.

Reynolds has the ability to make critical decisions in the horrific throws of battle. Moreover, his military genius also allows him at the same time, to imagine all possible scenarios and what will be done should it become necessary to change tactics hurriedly.

North of the Cashtown Road, left to right, General Reynolds places the 147th New York, the 56th Pennsylvania, and the 76th New York. To the south of the Cashtown Road he sends the 14th Brooklyn left, and the 95th New York right.

62

Even with these placements his line is long and narrow. Reynolds is determined to hold – every move is deliberate and purposeful. He is now located at the edge of Herbst's Woods, about 200 yards from McPherson's Barn. From this vantage point he spots advancing Confederate soldiers. He looks toward Seminary Ridge and spots the Black-hatted Iron Brigade (1st Brigade, under Meredith). He sends two aides to hurry them forward. Sgt. Veil remains with his commander.

10:30 AM Wednesday, July 1, 1863

The urgency of the situation is on the general's mind. Confederates are pressing ever stronger from the west and north. Buford's exhausted men need relief. Caleb's depleted battery needs reinforced ...

The general dashes back and forth on Fancy, placing troops, encouraging them, directing them. Oblivious to the flying bullets, the thick smoke from the cannon, and the noise, he hastily but brilliantly performs his duty. " ... drive those fellows out..." Trying to follow the general's orders the regiment meets with heavy fire. They veer off to the right leaving Reynolds and Sgt. Yeil alone in front of the advancing Confederates. His thoughts going in different directions, yet completely focused. His eyes checking quickly but constantly for the support he knows is coming.

In the second it takes him to glance toward the Seminary, he's down. A bullet has found its mark. The general falls on his face, his arms outstretched. Sgt. Veil reacts instantly - springing from his horse, running to his leader's side. Reaching him Veil sees no blood or wound and briefly wonders why he fell. Veil turns the general over onto his back. Thinking Reynolds is perhaps only momentarily stunned by a minnie ball, the Sgt.'s main concern is to move him away from possibly falling into enemy hands.

As Sgt. Veil pulls the general back toward "safety", the Confederates are yelling "drop him". It is at this time Veil discovers the wound - a small bullet hole in the back of Reynolds' head. There is no external bleeding and his collar had covered the wound.

General John F. Reynolds' participation in the battle of Gettysburg is over.

Epilogue

General Reynolds' body is removed from the field to the George house and remains there until 1:00 PM when he is sent by rail to Baltimore. There his sister, Jennie, and her husband meet the train and accompany the body to Philadelphia.

On Saturday, July 4, 1863, General Reynolds is buried in Lancaster, Pennsylvania, in the family plot. At the moment of interment, Major Riddle collapses in a pool of tears.

Death of Reynolds (Painting at the Pennsylvania State Museum)

Biographical Sketch

21 Sep 1820 - Born in Lancaster, Pennsylvania

1833 - attending the John Beck School in Lititz, Pennsylvania, 12 miles from Lancaster

Jul 1835 - began attending the Long Green Academy, located in Baltimore, Maryland

1836 - attending the Academy in Lancaster, Pennsylvania

30 Jun 1837 - entered West Point Military Academy

1 Jul 1841 - graduated from West Point Military Academy

1842 - assigned to St. Augustine, Florida

Apr 1843 - assigned to Fort Moultrie on Sullivan's Island, Charleston, South Carolina

1846 - assigned to Corpus Christi

1847 - sent to Mexico

1849 - sent to Fort Preble Portland Harbor, Maine

1852 - sent to Fort Adams Newport, Rhode Island

Sep 1853 - sent to New Orleans, LA

Jan 1854 - sent to Fort Lafayette, given 3rd Artillery

1854 - New York Harbor, sent to Fort Leavenworth, Kansas

May 1855 - received rank of Captain

1856 - Fort Oxford, Oregon Fort Monroe, Virginia

1858 - Camp Floyd, Utah

1859 - Major Reynolds, Commandant of Cadets West Point Military Academy, NY

14 May 1861 - received rank of Lt. Colonel, New London, Conn.,

Sep 1861 - Brig. Gen. of Volunteers, Ft. Monroe, VA, given 1st Brigade PA Reserves (includes Bucktails)

9 Oct 1861 - Reserves to Tenleytown and into Fairfax, Co., VA

18 Oct 1861 - Dranesville, VA

24 Apr 1862 - Catlett's Station, VA

26 May 1862 - Military Governor of Fredericksburg for 16 days

15 Jun 1862 - Tunstall Station, VA

26 Jun 1862 - Mechanicsville, VA - led Brigade - proved himself in the way he placed artillery and covered the field

27 Jun 1862 - Gaines Mill - proved himself by the way he shuffled his Regiments to plug holes

28 Jun 1862 - captured - held prisoner six weeks in Richmond. Citizens of Fredericksburg appealed for his release

13 Aug 1862 - released (traded for Gen. Barksdale of Mississippi)

26 Aug 1862 - Manassas Junction - 2nd Battle of Bull Run

30 Aug 1862 - led division in 2nd Battle of Bull Run

Sep 1862 - commands PA Militia

26 Sep 1862 - his Militia discharged, he leaves for Hagerstown to rejoin the army of the Potomac

29 Sep 1862 - assumes temporary command of 1st Corp (which became permanent in October)

29 Nov 1862 - promoted to Major General

9 Dec 1862 - 1st Corp left Aquia Creek

19 Dec 1862 - Fredericksburg -led 1st Corp

25 Dec 1862 - Spent holidays on leave

Spring 1863 - Chancellorsville -led 1st Corps

15 Jun 1863 - Centreville, VA

27 Jun 1863 - Frederick, MD

29 Jun 1863 - Emmitsburg, MD

30 Jun 1863 - given left wing of Army of the Potomac

1 Jul 1863 - Gettysburg - killed on the battlefield around 10:30 AM

4 Jul 1863 - buried in Lancaster Cemetery, Lancaster, PA

Bibliography

Nichols, Edward J. *Toward Gettysburg, a Biography of General John F. Reynolds.* Penn State University Press, 1958.

Riley, Michael A. *For God's Sake Forward!.* Farnsworth House Military Impressions, 1995.

Shue, Richard S. *Morning at Willoughby Run, July 1, 1863.* Thomas Publication, 1995.

Veil, Charles Henry. *The Memoirs of Charles Henry Veil.* Orion Books, 1993.

Thanks

My unending gratitude to Brenda Wood, who so graciously allowed me to tour the Moritz Inn.

Thanks also to the Adams County Historical Society.

Part III:

Reynolds: His Own Words Before Gettysburg

by

Diane E Watson

"I will serve in any position the Government may call me to with all the energy and power I possess."

John Fulton Reynolds (1820-1863)

Preface

General Reynolds is, unfortunately, most remembered as the highest ranking officer killed at Gettysburg. He was down so early in the battle that his genius was barely felt. -- but it was there:

"...by his promptitude and gallantry he had determined the decisive field of the war, and had opened brilliantly a battle which required three days of hard fighting to close with a victory."

> Henry J. Hunt, Brevet Maj. Gen., USA
> Chief of Artillery, Army of the Potomac

This booklet covers Reynolds' battles up to, but not including, Gettysburg. In the pages to follow, you will read from letters, hearsay and battle reports. The eloquence and intelligence of the man shine through -- though he was not the kind of man to present himself in the light others see him. He is more apt to praise another -- which is why I have included quotes from others who were there. His letters home during the war were to his sisters, both of John's parents had died before the war. John was 39 years old in 1859. Remember to place yourself in the 19ᵗʰ Century while reading his words -- it was a different way of thinking and writing. Courtesy, decorum, phraseology, long sentences, all are a part of the written word in the 1860's. I have included only minimal narration -- nothing can improve on...his own words.

My heartfelt gratitude to Ann Upton and staff at the Franklin and Marshall College archives in Lancaster, PA., for allowing me to review the John F. Reynolds collection.

Introduction

John Fulton Reynolds is the ultimate soldier. He sits his horse like a Centaur -- tall and straight -- a master horseman. His dark eyes reveal nothing of his sense of humor, but can cut down an offending soldier without a word. He is about six feet all with black hair and a neatly trimmed beard. His military bearing impress all who see him and inspire his men to follow him anywhere in battle.

More important than Reynolds' physical appearance is his brilliance balanced with common sense. He speaks with weighed authority -- not as though the world revolves around him -- but as though he understands how the world revolves. He has little tolerance for indecision, incompetence, unprofessionalism and ... congressional interference. This last one is the reason he makes a decision which affects not only his military career, but his life.

Abraham Lincoln knows John Reynolds is supremely qualified to command the Army of the Potomac, and is about to make such an offer in June of 1863. When Reynolds is alerted to this fact, he hurries to Washington to meet with the President. He regrets to inform the President that unless he has complete freedom to run the army without congressional interference, he will have to say no. Lincoln respects Reynolds' decision. Meade is then ordered to take command.

Reynolds' men and peers (including Meade) are very disappointed. Most of them think he should have had the command long ago. They believe the war would have taken a different, perhaps shorter, direction with Reynolds in command.

After reading his words and those of others, I am certain the reader will clearly see his qualifications and come to the same conclusions.

The Words of Others

Captain Joseph G. Rosengarten, Reynolds' Adjutant described him:

Impetuous without rashness; rapid without haste, ready without heedlessness; he liked better to be at the head of a compact corps than to command a scattered army.

Col. Thomas F. McCoy thought:
Reynolds said little but, he (McCoy) liked his "gentlemanly manner" and considered Reynolds one of the few "old army" officers who held the respect and confidence of the volunteers.

Col. Frederick L. Hitchcock, one of Reynolds' regimental leaders, made an error in where his regiment should be in the line of march. Reynolds saw him hesitate, and came over and said to him:

"Part of your corps has gone in yonder. If I were you I would go in here and occupy this field to the right in columns...and you may say General Reynolds advised this of you, please."

Hitchcock says, "had he (Reynolds) chosen to do so, he could have given me orders as the senior officer present, but with gentle courtesy he accomplished his purpose without that, and to reassure me, gave his name and rank in this delicate way. I shall never forget his pleasant smile as he returned my salute." Hitchcock was clearly accepting Reynolds as "one of the few great commanders developed by the war."

He also describes the General's appearance: "He was a superb-looking man, dark-complexioned, wearing full black whiskers, and sat on his horse like a Centaur -- tall, straight, and graceful, the ideal soldier."

June 25th, 1862 -- Porter on Reynolds at Gaines Mill:

"Quite early in the day I visited General Reynolds and had the best reasons not only to be contented, but thoroughly gratified, with the admirable arrangements of this accomplished officer, and to be encouraged by the cheerful confidence of himself and his able and gallant assistants...."

Brigade Commander Truman Seymour on Reynolds at Gaines Mill:

"...much of the credit of the day belonged to Reynolds."

Gen. Fitz John Porter on Reynolds at Gaines Mill:

"...having repulsed the enemy on his front, and hearing the tremendous contest on his left, had, acting under a true maxim and with the generous spirit of the soldier, moved to the sound of the cannon, and led his men, regiment after regiment, where our hard-pressed forces required most assistance."

Charles Lamborn -- Aide to Gen. Reynolds, on Reynolds' absence during captivity:

"...and if he could return to-day to the command of the division he would be received with an earnest enthusiasm that no other man in the world could awaken."

Letter written by citizens of Fredericksburg appealing Reynolds' release:

"...We feel called upon to testify that Gen. Reynolds exhibited in a marked and efficient manner a desire and a determination to so conduct his military command here as to conserve and protect so far as practicable the personal rights and domestic comforts of the citizens and thus to mitigate, so far as his actions could avail, the evils and annoyances which are incident to such an occupation. Your own military experience will suggest to you how materially such conduct as this on the part of a commanding officer could avail in saving our citizens from the countless ills which an unbridled and licentious soldiery might inflict upon a helpless population; and while, sir, neither his kindness and consideration or any other act or line of conduct pursued by military authority now occupying our houses can avail in the slightest degree in modifying our sentiments touching the heinousness of our invasion or our devotion to our beloved cause and Government. Yet we do feel that inasmuch as when we were prisoners in the hands of General Reynolds we received from him a treatment distinguished by a marked and considerate respect for our feeble influence in invoking for him now a prisoner of our Government, a treatment as kind and considerate as was extended by him to us. We would, therefore, hope that he might be placed upon parole...."

Whether or not this letter had any influence on the decision is uncertain, but Reynolds was released on august 13, 1862, in a prisoner exchange.

Near Groveton during the 2nd Battle of Bull Run, August 28, 1862:

Alonzo F. Hill, a soldier, wrote:

"...The report of a cannon was heard a mile in our front, and a shell flew over our heads, striking in a field on our right. Half a dozen additional shell and shot now came crashing and smashing around us. General Reynolds -- brave fellow -- was among us; and, with soldierly coolness and courage he proceeded to arrange a line of battle."

Pope on Reynolds at 2nd Bull Run:

"Brig. Genl John F. Reynolds, commanding the Pennsylvania Reserves, merit's the highest commendations at my hands. Prompt, active, and energetic, he commanded his division with distinguished ability throughout all the operations and performed his duties in all situation with zeal and fidelity."

General Meade on hearing of Reynolds' promotion to Major General:

"I am very glad Reynolds is promoted, for I have always thought he deserved it for his services at Mechanicsville."

September 26, 1862, from Governor Curtin of Pennsylvania after Reynolds' stint as Commander of the Militia:

"...I deem it proper to express my strong sense of the gratitude which Pennsylvania owes for the zeal, spirit, and ability which you brot (sic) to her services when her homes and safety were threatened....."

Reynolds took a personal hand in placing Wainwrights' guns at Fredericksburg. Stonewall Jackson's opinion of the placement of those guns:

"The artillery of the enemy was so judiciously posted as to make an advance of our troops across the plain very hazardous....The first gun had hardly moved forward, a hundred yards when the enemy's artillery reopened, and so completely swept our front as to satisfy me that the proposed movement should be abandoned."

Winfield S. Hancock wrote:

"No officer in the Army of the Potomac had developed a character of usefulness and ability, in the highest grades of command, superior to that of General Reynolds."

.....from a letter dated March 8, 1880

Gen'l Darius N. Couch wired his regrets concerning General Reynolds' funeral July 4, 1863:

"...that the present emergency of the service prevent my sending such an escort to the funeral of Maj. Gen. Reynolds as his high rank and brilliant services so eminently deserve."

Reynolds' Orderly, 18-year-old Sgt. Charles Henry Veil, present at the general's fatal wounding in Gettysburg, July 1, 1863, wrote:

"The death of General Reynolds was a great loss to the Union cause deeply felt by all, but by no one person as much as myself...."

September 17, 1863, Captain R. W. Mitchell to the Reynolds sisters after his death:

"He was our favorite and every day by our camp fires we talk of him and the days his memory has taught us to love...."

Maj. William Riddle, Sr. Aide, to Reynolds' sister, Ellie, August 1863:

"...I was melancholy indeed to come back to the army and see no more the face of him we so loved and respected; I will never see the man who can fill his place in the hearts of those who knew him."

At the moment of interment, Maj. Riddle fell to the ground and wept.

Excerpts from Eulogy delivered by Rev. Walter Powell at the interment of John Fulton Reynolds July 4, 1863

It is with a sincere diffidence that I rise to speak on an occasion like this, made interesting by a thousand considerations. I feel that I may be able to speak some honest words if not elegant ones. The feelings with which we are inspired, or rather oppressed, are not such as require any elaborate language. We mourn with a profound sorrow, and must be indulged in the spontaneous words of the heart.

The fortune of War has brought us together in solemn state to mingle our tears over a soldier's grave. Our grief is not without some mixture of pride, for we remember that he stood high in the Nation's confidence and fell in leading brave men to the charge. The fatal instruments of death know no exempts in the favor of such honored ones, but the officer and the private alike fall before their destructive way. It gives no assurance of life to be elevated to the glory of command. Nay, the honor, it would seem, is only purchased by the greater hazard....

It is with propriety, my friends, that we mourn with those who mourn here to-day. He who died in the defense of our homes deserves more than a friendly funeral respect, the common decency of such occasions. The sacrifice he made of himself commands us to forget that we are not brothers and sisters by the affinities of blood. Our mourning should be, and is, of the sincerity which swells up the kindred hearts. We shall not allow him to be called theirs alone who base their claim on family ties. He was a nation's son, and all the people shall mourn him as their loss...

But we must restrain our words. It were fondness to linger longer at his open grave. The work is not yet wholly done in which he so gloriously died. Take up his fallen sword and go forth. Leave him to his quiet resting place. May the dust lie lightly upon his coffin and when the grass shall again start above him, may the tears of affection and love keep it ever green.

Prelude to War

September 20, 1859, on his assignment as Commandant of Cadets and instructor of Tactics at West Point Military Academy, New York, to sister Ellie in Lancaster, Pennsylvania:

"I have been on duty here for a week trying to persuade myself that I shall like it, but notwithstanding the kind of reception I have met with on all sides from my friends here I have not made up my mind fully on the subject. ...I shall try for a week or so longer the duties, which I find very disagreeable to me, so different from anything I have ever had before, and so confining, annoying and various, that I have hardly yet had time to test them fully -- then I can make up my mind as to whether I will remain or not. Of one thing I am certain, that the position to be filled is no sinecure for anyone. It is a most exacting one to the patience, industry and temper of any person, and of course very different from commanding men."

Fort Sumter bombarded April 13, 1861 - on the 25th he wrote to his Sister:

"What History will say of us, our Government, and Mr. B's (Buchanan) Administration makes one wish to disown him. ...I have said but little, except among ourselves here, on the present difficulties that surround the Government but a more disgraceful plot on the part of our friend B's Cabinet and the leading politicians of the South, to break up our Government, without cause, has never blackened the pages of history in any nation's record.
....Who would have believed when I came here last September and found Mr. Jeff Davis laboring with a Committee of Congress and civilians to re-organize the Academy; our national School! Whose sons, never until the seeds sown by his parricidal hand had filled it with the poisonous weed of secession, had known any other allegiance than that one to the whole country, or worshiped any other flag, than that which has moved our own youthful hopes and aspirations and under which we marched, so proudly in our boyish days - who! I say, would have believed, that he was brooding over his systematic plans for dis-organizing the whole country. The depth of his treachery has not been plumbed yet; but it will be."

July, 1861 - on his orders to report to New London, Connecticut, to recruit a regiment, he wrote to Ellie:

"I would, of course, have preferred the Artillery arm of the service, but could not refuse the promotion offered me under any circumstances, much less at this time, when the Government has a right to my services in any capacity."

On leaving West Point:

"I have had every expression of regret from both officers and Professors here at my leaving them, and what is more flattering, great rejoicing among the cadets at their being relieved of me."

September 6, 1861, in a letter home, on reporting to D.C. to headquarters and his assignment:

"Since I have been here I have been assigned a Brigade in McCall's Division, and rode out today to see them and the ground they are occupying, in camp near Tenallytown, not very far from the Chain Bridge, though not on the sacred soil of Virginia, being on this side of the Potomac. I am to have the 1st Brigade."

October 9, 1861 - at Camp Pierpont, VA, west of the Old Chain Bridge near Langley. In this position the division anchored the extreme right of the Army of the Potomac. It was a good position with an open field facing the enemy.

"...Should they advance upon us here, posted as we are in front of our line of works and we cannot stop them, we may as well give it up as a bad job. I begin to agree with somebody who, writing in one of the papers said, 'You cannot make soldiers of volunteers.' I thought in Mexico that I would never have anything to do with them under any circumstances, and nothing but this state of things in the country would have induced me to take command of any body of them. In coming over here they proceeded at once to plunder and destroy everything in the houses left by the people... I almost despair, from what I have seen of them since I have been here, of our ever making an attack upon any of the positions the enemy may take up."

Reynolds was not alone in his initial doubts about volunteers. In time, he would relent a little. After his volunteers' reconnaissance toward Dranesville:

"They plundered and marauded most outrageously and disgracefully....Of course it was stopped but not until great damage had been done. ...I have an officer and 3 men in arrest for their plundering at Dranesville and hope to have them hung if I can."

February 18, 1862, on other battles (Mill Springs, Kentucky, and Forts Henry and Donelson in Tennessee):

"What glorious news! The last three days have brought for the cause of the Union, from the South and West."

On naval successes:

"One good effect the gallant work of our navy has accomplished will be to show England that the spirit and pluck that lowered her proud banner as often in 1812 has not diminished in the last 50 years and will dissipate any idea of interference with the blockade if they even seriously contemplated any."

March 22, 1862:

"...we are awaiting transportation, by water, where to is not known precisely, tho' somewhere from Aquia Creek to Old Point (VA)..."
(they were, however, sent to Fredericksburg)

As Military Governor of Fredericksburg, Virginia

His term as Military Governor began May 26, 1862, and lasted 16 days. His headquarters were in the Virginia State Bank Building.

To his sister, Ellie:

"The people of Fredericksburg are secesh of the first water - the first almost we have seen of the real F.F.V.'s (First Families of Virginia) and tho' they were distant, the ladies especially, they behaved with much more dignity and propriety, than it appears they did in New Orleans. A family of Washington's on whose place I made my Hd. Qrs. Before we moved over to Fredericksburg, were very sensible and sociable, and as there were two young ladies (not bad looking either) your friend Mr. Lamborn became quite intimate with them. They had a brother in the army with Gen'l Pettigrew's command and as he was a prisoner were very anxious about him after the late battles."

From the Steamer "Cannonius" to his sister:

"We have just dropped our anchor in the York River below West Point (VA) having embarked in the Rappahannock yesterday morning. Tomorrow we will be up at the White House, where we march to join the Army before Richmond. ...Stanton's operations I do not like at all. They had no business to interfere with McClellan in the first instance when he left for the Peninsula... It makes me sick to think of the absurd ideas people have of military operations. I cannot write about them."

Fredericksburg (1863)

Mechanicsville and Gaines Mill, Virginia

To Headquarters
Dispatch Station
June 15, 1862

Sir: I have the honor to report that, in obedience to orders from headquarters, I proceeded with my brigade on the night of the 13th instant up the railroad to Tunstall's Station, which place I reached just about midnight. I approached as quietly as possible, sending one regiment out to occupy the hill, which commanded the whole place, another through the woods to the left, the remainder moving down after the advance. On reaching the depot I found a car loaded with corn on a side track on fire and partially consumed, the telegraph poles on the cross-road thrown down and the wires severed; the bridge beyond the depot on fire. Both fires were at once extinguished, the platform of the car and part of the corn alone being destroyed. One dead body on the track near the depot run over by the train...Another body afterward found in the woods with a gun-shot wound in the head...

"Though I did not assume any command over Gen. Emory or Gen. Cook...I coincided with measures taken by Gen. Emory and gave him such assistance as was in my power......

"The enemy appeared in force about 3 pm and opened with his batteries from the high ground around Mechanicsville, impetuously assailing with greatly superior force and at the same time the right and left of our position by the roads leading from that place. He was repulsed in every effort to storm our position, as well as in an attempt to turn our right by the ford and old dam where he was handsomely checked by the 2nd Regt., Lt. Col. McCandless."

Reynolds then shifted his lines:

"The action continued with undiminished vigor and the repeated efforts of the enemy to carry our position by assault was in every instance signally repulsed. Genl. Seymour was equally successful on the left in maintaining his position and night closed action with the enemy defeated and discomfited.

"The conduct of the troops, most of them for the first time under fire, was all that could be desired and was creditable to their State and County. I would particularly mention the conduct of Capts. DeHart, Smead, and Cooper for the coolness and judgment in which they directed the fire of their batteries. Lt. Piper of Smead's Battery was severely wounded.

"Cols. Simmons, Roberts, Lt. Col. McCandless and Major Stone, commanding Regts. Behaved with great coolness and executed my orders with a soldierly spirit and promptitude very gratifying to me."

June 19, 1862, Generals Reynolds and Seymour's brigades held the rifle pits skirting the east bank of Beaver Dam Creek and the field-works covering the only crossings near Mechanicsville and Elerson's Mill. This account was part of a rough draft he never finished.

"I received the order to fall back with my command to Cold Harbor, taking the upper road, Genls. Seymour and Meade to take the lower. Hastily arranging with Genl. Seymour the manner of withdrawing our troops, we put our commands in motion at once and by daylight the Batteries had already cleared the roads. I held the road on the right with the sharp shooters and the Rifle Regt., (Bucktails) now reduced to 5 Comps. And Cooper's 4 pieces. Genl. Seymour held the left road in a similar manner. The enemy's skirmishers advanced as soon as it was light enough to see and occupied the edge of the woods in our front and kept up a spirited fire upon the position while they endeavored to fill the woods in rear with their troops preparatory to an assault upon our position. Our fire kept them in check while our artillery shelled the woods until the Brigade had cleared the Bridge and the stream by Nunnally's Mill. I then ordered the withdrawal of the rear guard from its position, in effecting this unfortunately 2 Comps. Of the Rifle Regt., Capt. Niles, failed to get the order and were left behind in the rifle pits and after

making their way some two miles to the rear were overtaken and made prisoners.

"The services of Maj. Stone and Capt. Cooper in covering the withdrawal of the troops in the morning cannot be too highly extolled. They maintained their advanced positions alone for more than an hour in the face of greatly superior numbers and with a firmness and boldness that would have done credit to experienced veteran troops."

Captured!

Taken prisoner at Gaines Mill, VA, June 28, 1862. In a letter dated July 3, 1862, describing his capture:

"I went with my Adj. Gen. to the right of the line to post the artillery, or to get it changed to a different position, where I remained till nearly dark. When in endeavoring to return to my brigade, I found the left of our line had given way and the Confederate pickets occupying the ground I had passed over, and taking what I thought a direct course through the woods to our rear, became entangled in the swamp. With my horse wounded and unable to extricate him, I remained there through the night, and when day broke made another effort to regain the position of our lines, but was unfortunately unsuccessful and taken prisoner. We have since been in Richmond where we have been most kindly treated and cared for. My brigade in the first wo days behaved well and our loss was not great. The Capt. (Charles Kingsbury, his Adj.) is with me and is well."

Reynolds apparently told Hill (CSA) that he had fallen asleep that night (27th) - excusable if he had - he was on top of the only fighting the army did on the 26th, spent that night directing the move back, then added his harried day at Gaines Mill.

He was first held at the Spotswood Hotel in a comfortable room where he was allowed to have food sent in from a restaurant of his choice. When more prisoners arrived, they were transferred to a tobacco warehouse. After an attempted escape by several younger officers, they were all marched through the town to Libby Prison. He said he was confined in a cell and fed on refuse food, which was shameful treatment for any captured officer.

After being held for six weeks, Reynolds was released from Libby Prison August 13 in an exchange of prisoners.

2nd Bull Run, Virginia

August 15, 1862:

"We are on our way back to the Potomac to try to advance to Richmond by way of Fredericksburg and Pope's line...."

"I am very fearful of the operations in the valley. Pope's Army has not seen or met anything like the force we know left Richmond before we did."

Report of Brig. Gen. John F. Reynolds, U.S. Army, Commanding Third Division, of Operations August 21 - September 5, including Engagement near Gainesville and Battles of Groveton and Bull Run:

Headquarters Reynolds' Division
Camp near Munson's Hill, VA, September 5, 1862

Colonel Schriver,
Chief of Staff, Third Army Corps

Colonel: I have the honor to report the operations of this division since leaving Fredericksburg, on the 21st of August last, under orders from Major General Burnside to Proceed to Kelly's Ford, on the Rappahannock River.

The division having been united at Fredericksburg, with the exception of the Second Regiment, Colonel McCandless, not yet debarked at Aquia Creek, accompanied by an ammunition train supplied by General Burnside, proceeded to Kelly's Ford, where it arrived, after a severe and arduous march, on the evening of the 22nd ultimo, and relieved a brigade of Reno's division, under Colonel Farnsworth, of the Seventy-ninth New York.

On the morning of the 23rd the division joined the Army of Virginia under General Pope, then on its march to Warrenton from Rappahannock Station, and on arriving at Warrenton was attached temporarily to McDowell's army corps. On the 24th the division encamped on the Sulphur Springs road, 1 mile south of Warrenton, with Meade's brigade advanced 2 miles on that road. On the 26th we moved to the Waterloo road. On the 27th it marched with the army on the Alexandria and Warrenton turnpike, and encamped at Broad Run. On the 27th marched to Manassas by way of Gainesville. On the supposition that the enemy was at the former place, I was directed to follow General Sigel's corps until our arrival at Gainesville, where I was to form in columns of echelon on this left, King's division to form in like manner on my left, in which order we were to move on Manassas. On arriving at Gainesville the head of my column was fired upon by two pieces of the enemy in Ransom's battery, and Meade's brigade rapidly thrown into line of battle by that general. The range being too great for Ransom's guns his battery was replaced by the rifled guns of Captain Cooper, when the enemy withdrew, not, however before some loss had been sustained by Meade. Some force was displayed and skirmishers sent forward along the pike and through the woods on the right of the road. On the opening of fire upon the enemy from our rifled guns he retired from our front. This was supposed to be merely a demonstration by the enemy to save a wagon train which was seen moving off on the Sudley Springs Road, and the column continued its march toward Manassas.

About 5 o'clock I received orders to march upon Centreville, and the column turned off at Bethlehem Church and took the Sudley Springs road toward the Warrenton pike. About this time heavy cannonading was heard both to our front and left, the former supposed to be from Sigel's corps, and the latter from King's division, which had taken the Warrenton pike from Gainesville. I send word to the column to hasten its march, and proceeded to the left at once myself in the direction of the firing, arriving on the field just before dark, and found that Gibbon's brigade, of King's division, was engaged with the enemy, with Doubleday's and Patrick's brigades in the vicinity. After the firing ceased I saw General King, who, determining to maintain his position, I left about 9 o'clock PM to return to my division, promising to bring it up early in the morning to his support.

Before leaving, however, I heard the division moving off, and I learned from General Hatch that it was moving by Gainesville toward Manassas. I then returned to my own division, which I reached at daylight on the morning of the 28th (29th); closed up with General Sigel's command on the old battle-field of Bull Run. General Sigel reported the enemy in his immediate front, and requested my co-operation with him in an attack upon his position. I accordingly formed my division on the left of General Sigel's corps, next to the division of General Schenck. General McDowell joined the command at daylight, and directed my co-operation with General Sigel.

The right of the enemy's position could be discerned upon the heights above Groveton, on the right of the pike. The division advanced over the ground to the heights above Groveton, crossed the pike, and Cooper's battery came gallantly into action on the same ridge on which the enemy's right was, supported by Meade's brigade. While pressing forward our extreme left across the pike re-enforcements were sent for by General Sigel for the right of his line, under General Milroy, now hardly pressed by the enemy, and a brigade was taken from Schenck's command on my right. The whole fire of the enemy was now concentrated on the extreme right of my division, and, unsupported there, the battery was obligated to retire, with considerable loss in both men and horses, and the division fell back to connect with Schenck.

Later in the day General Pope, arriving on the right from Centreville, renewed the attack on the enemy and drove him some distance. My division was directed to threaten the enemy's right and rear, which it proceeded to do under a heavy fire of artillery from the ridge to the left of the pike. Generals Seymour and Jackson led their brigades in advance, but notwithstanding all the steadiness and courage shown by the men they were compelled to fall back before the heavy fire of artillery and musketry which met them both on the front and left flank, and the division resumed its original position. King's division engaged the enemy along the pike on our right, and the action was continued with it until dark by Meade's brigade.

On the morning of the 30th I was directed to take post with my division on the left of the pike near the Henry house, and ordered by Major General Pope to form my division in column by company at full distance, with the whole of my artillery on the left, that I would be the pivot in the attack which Porter's corps was to make on the enemy's right, then supposed to be on the pike and in retreat. Having formed my division in the position indicated, and opened with my rifled batteries to drive the enemy from the first ridge, the skirmishers advanced and the attack by Porter's corps commenced. When the skirmishers arrived in the thick woods opposite Groveton, I found the resistance so great that another regiment was deployed to support them, and finally a second, in all, three regiments.

The advanced skirmishers were the First Rifles, Colonel McNeil, and the First Infantry, Colonel Roberts, supported by the Seventh Infantry, Lieutenant Colonel Henderson. The Sixth Regiment, Colonel Sinclair, was thrown through the woods on our left flank. Becoming convinced that the enemy were not in retreat, but were posted in force on our left flank, I pushed through the skirmishers to the edge of the woods on the left, gaining sight of the open ground beyond, and advancing myself into the open ground, I found a line of skirmishers of the enemy nearly parallel to the line of skirmishers covering my left flank, with cavalry formed behind them, perfectly stationary, evidently masking a column of the enemy formed for attack on my left flank when our line should be sufficiently advanced. The skirmishers opened fire upon me, and I was obliged to run the gauntlet of a heavy fire to gain the rear of my division, losing one of my orderlies, who had followed me through the woods. I immediately communicated this to the commanding general of the corps, who came upon the ground and directed me to form my division to resist this attack, the dispositions for which were rapidly completed. Other troops were to be sent to my support, when the commanding general, observing the attack of Porter to have been repulsed, ordered me with my division across the field to the rear of Porter, to form, a line behind which the troops might be rallied. I immediately started my division in the direction indicated, but before the rear of my column had left the position the threatened attack by the enemy's right began to be felt, and the rear brigade, under Colonel Anderson, with three batteries of artillery, were obliged to form on the ground on which they found themselves to oppose it. Passing across the field to the right, with Meade's and Seymour's brigades and Ransom's battery, my course was diverted by the difficult nature of the ground, and the retreating masses of the broken columns among troops of Heintzelman's corps, already formed, by which much time was lost and confusion created, which allowed the enemy to sweep up with his right so far as almost to cut us off from the pike, leaving nothing but the rear brigade and the three batteries of artillery of my division and scattered troops of other commands to resist the advance of the enemy upon our left. It was here that the most severe loss of the division was sustained both in men and material, Kerns losing his four guns, but not until wounded and left on the field, Cooper his caissons.

Colonel Hardin, commanding Twelfth Regiment, was here severely wounded. The brigade under command of Colonel Anderson sustained itself most gallantly, and though severely pushed on both front and flank maintained its position until overwhelmed by numbers, when it fell back, taking up new position wherever the advantages of ground permitted. The two brigades and battery of artillery under my immediate command, finding

2nd Battle of Bull Run from Harper's Weekly

ourselves perfectly out of place, moved, by the direction of an officer of General Pope's staff, to a position to the right of the Henry house, which position was most gallantly maintained by the commands of Meade and Seymour and Ransom's battery for nearly two hours, when they were relieved by the division of regular troops under colonel Buchanan. My division was then united and marched during the early part of the night toward Centreville, and bivouacked with Sykes' division upon the east bank of cub Run. On the following morning it proceeded to Centreville.

On the afternoon of the 31st my division was directed to relieve the command of General Reno (Stevens' brigade), occupying the position of Cub run, where it remained during the night. On the 1st instant the division marched with the army from Centreville, and encamped near Fairfax Court-House. On the 2nd it proceeded by the Alexandria and Columbia turnpike to the vicinity of Hunter's Chapel and Arlington. On the afternoon of the 4th the division arrived at this place, and encamped in position to the rear of Munson's Hill.

The conduct of the officers and men during the several actions and the arduous marches they were subjected to since leaving Fredericksburg was generally good and commendable. Many straggled from the ranks, unable to keep up, and some few left the ranks on the field, but, rejoining their commands at Centreville, it is impossible to ascertain who were censurable. General Meade mentions the First Rifles, under Colonel McNeil, to whose lot the advance skirmishing principally fell, as deserving particular notice. The

First Infantry, under colonel Roberts, the Second, Colonel McCandless, the Sixth, Colonel Sinclair, the Seventh, Lieutenant-Colonel Henderson, and the Twelfth, Colonel Hardin, are also particularly mentioned.

Generals Meade and Seymour, as heretofore, led and conducted their brigades in the most skillful manner throughout the entire marches and actions, also General Jackson, commanding Third Brigade, up to the time that he was taken sick on the field and obliged to retire on the 30th. His command devolved upon Colonel Anderson, who conducted the brigade through that day. To the officers of my small staff, consisting of Captain Kingsbury, assistant adjutant-general Lieutenant Lamborn, aide-de-camp, and Lieutenant Snyder, of the Seventh Regiment, acting aide-de-camp, I am greatly indebted for their indefatigable efforts to execute my orders, rendered more arduous by the incompleteness of the division as well as brigade staffs, having neither quartermaster nor commissary with the division.

Division Surgeon King remained upon the field with Surgeon Read, of the First Infantry, to attend to our wounded. Not having a single ambulance with the division, it was impossible to bear our wounded any distance from the field.

I enclose a return of the killed, wounded, and missing in the several actions, also a list by name. I neglected to mention that the Second Regiment, under Colonel McCandless, joined the division at Warrenton, and that colonel McCandless was severely wounded in the action of the 30th.

Respectfully submitted,
Jno. F. Reynolds
Brigadier-General of Volunteers, Commanding Division

Rappahannock Station

August 25, 1862, to his sisters:

"...Our situation is very critical. I think the whole movement from the Peninsular wrong and if the army is to be managed from Washington, I am afraid there will be nothing but failures as there have been formerly. No one can conduct a campaign at a distance from the field or without being in the actual presence of the operating armies...."

Harrisburg, Pennsylvania

September, 1862, Pennsylvania Governor Curtin was terrified of the threatened Confederate invasion. He wrote to the President requesting John F. Reynolds to come to Harrisburg and form the militia - he would consider no one else. General Hooker worked hard to keep Reynolds, but Curtin won out. Reynolds reported to Harrisburg September 13, 1862. There were 50,000 men in the militia. Reynolds was not happy to be taken from the field, but he obeyed orders.

To his family:

"I think the threatening aspect of an invasion down the Cumberland Valley very serious, there is nothing to prevent their doing great injury, and in fact their marching to this place a well organized column of 20 or 30,000 men, cavalry and infantry, etc.; there is nothing in the valley to stop them."

September 14 to Curtin's Adjutant Col. John A. Wright:

"You will send 500 men to Greencastle at once to report to Captain Palmer for scouting and ranger duty. Select someone if possible familiar with the county."

Reynolds to Wright:

"Take immediate steps to obtain and transmit to these headquarters all the copies of the map of Franklin and Cumberland Counties to be found in those counties. Let the names and locations of each owner be affixed. Report any that may have been seized by the enemy."

Reynolds to Wright:

"Be particular to give orders to all commanders to arrest and send to the provost marshall of Harrisburg all persons suspected of gathering information for the enemy."

Reynolds to Gen. Henry W. Halleck, General-in-Chief of the Armies:

"Our pickets are across into Maryland 3 miles from Hagerstown. Rebel pickets falling back. Longstreet retired, moving east on Boonsboro Road today."

Reynolds to Edwin M. Stanton, Secretary of War:

"Can you direct the Ordnance Bureau to furnish us, at the earliest moment, with equipments and carbines for 3,000 cavalry? Please answer."

To his sisters:

"There is nothing in the Valley to stop them and our army is too far behind them to retard or overtake them if they push on boldly. ...Burn this up and do not let anyone see it."

Reynolds in Hagerstown to Militia officer Morton McMichael in Chambersburg:

"Send the troops already in the cars first to this place. Don't let there be any delay at Chambersburg afterwards. Send those men now at camp to this post. Order them to be prepared to move immediately..."

To his Adjutant, Kingsbury, at Chambersburg:

"I am going to join McClellan and to get the troops here and to Boonsboro if such a thing is possible. Send Rogers and McPherson on with horses at once. Veil can bring my horse and you can pay my bill at the hotel."

September 18, 1862, to his Sister Ellie:

"I think if the Pennsylvania Militia did not turn out to fight they had better have remained at home."

To Col. Vogdes at Hagerstown from McClellan's headquarters at the Pry House in Sharpsburg:

"Start all the troops out and urge them forward. Tell Governor Curtin to send Wright on to Chambersburg - that I am afraid I cannot get these troops forward. They only move when I am there in person to direct them. Some one ought to be sent to Hagerstown to command."

September 21 - a skirmish between the Militia and confederate Cavalry on the Williamsport Pike, one mile south of Hagerstown:

Reynolds to Gov. Curtin:

"The enemy cavalry drove in our picket and by great good luck I happened to be on the spot. Under my directions the picket opened fire on them and drove them back. But if I had not just happened to be on the spot the picket would have retired without firing a shot and might have stampeded the whole command. I really do not know what will be the result if they (the enemy) should undertake to charge down the road tonight. I am afraid to leave the command for a moment after what I saw in front this evening."

Some of his men agreed with Reynolds' thoughts on the lack of initiative of the militia. Gen Reynolds slept in the field with the militia.

The Militia was discharged by the governor on September 25.

Reynolds to his Sister Ellie on the 26th from Chambersburg:

"I leave for Hagerstown today at 11 o'clock to join Genl. McClellan, having finally dispersed all the militia to their homes - which they were so exceedingly anxious to defend, only they preferred to wait until the enemy

actually reached their own doorsteps before they encountered them. Harry (brother) can tell you something about the campaign. He left here yesterday morning for Philadelphia."

NOTE: September 29, 1862 promoted to Major General John F. Reynolds, USV

October, 1862 - On JEB Stuart's raid into Pennsylvania on October 10th:

"*I think it just as well for the south of the state that there were no militia in Chambersburg as I do not think from what I saw of them they would have been any use in preventing the raid of Rebel cavalry - unless a (more) 'courteous commander' would have instilled a proportionate amount more of courage in them than I was able to elicit. I must say that their escape has given me quite shock - I did not expect they could perform such a feat in our own country. On the chick hominy it was different.*"

October 26, 1862 the 1st Corps moved to Berlin - (now Brunswick) - on the Potomac.
On newspaper reporters:

"*They do more harm than good and are not at all reliable....*"
"*Your papers give the enemy too much information.*"

His pickets could expect him at any hour:

"*Who ordered that line? How far out is it? Push it out, push it out farther! ... Push it out until you feel something.*"

November 8, 1862, McClellan is relieved of command:

Reynolds and other officers paid their respects. At the end of the month Reynolds wrote to his sisters:

"*....It of course was a surprise to a greater part of the Army here, but take it altogether, it created less feeling than I feared such a step would have done. I saw more of him on this march than I have since he has been in command of the Army, had been with him most of the time in the advance and think the step taken by the authorities in Washington was as unwise, injudicious, as it was uncalled for, yet the prevailing spirit, with few exceptions, is obedience to the powers that be - and determine to do all they are capable of under the new chief....*"

November 30, 1862, to his sisters describing a group photograph by Brady:

"*I was taken in one with Burnside sitting on the stump of a tree, and it was very good. If you can ever get a copy of it do so - I saw only the plates.*"

In the photo Reynolds has just ridden up to the Burnside's Headquarters at Warrenton, almost too late to appear in one. Others have already posed and are beginning to leave.

General Ambrose E Burnside (seated, center) and officers, 1862. General Reynolds stands at Burnside's left shoulder.

Fredericksburg, Virginia

On December 9, 1862, the First Corps left Aquia Creek heading for Fredericksburg.

December 11, 1862, there was a consensus around 5:00 p.m. among the generals that the Sixth Corps (to which Reynolds was temporarily attached) must be relieved from its position in line, where it was covering the bridge - this would allow the 40,000 men of the Grand Left Division to divide into columns of assault on the right and left of the Richmond Road, carry the ridge and turn Lee's right flank. They await Burnside's official order for the plan - and wait. About 3:00 AM Reynolds says:

"I know I have hard work ahead of me and I must get some sleep. Send for me if I am wanted."

Orders came at 7:45 AM - Burnside still wanted to effect a "surprise"...and Fredericksburg was lost.

December 13, 1862 - to his sisters in Philadelphia, Pa.

"You are no doubt anxious to hear from me since the events of the past few days. The papers give you all the details of the crossing of the Rappahannock as well as the re-crossing, and are not very particular as to the truth of the facts, only so they have a telling effect and read well. My corps, or two division of it, made the attack on the left, and after almost graining the object let it slip. They did not do so well as I expected. Tho' they advanced under artillery fire very well, when it came to the attack of the wooded heights they faltered and failed. We are fortunate it is not worse. The crossing at this point was a failure from the fact that to have been successful it ought to have been a surprise, and we should have advanced at once and carried the heights as was intended. As it was we lost one day by the failure to throw over the bridges at the town without serious opposition - and to have risked more than we did would probably have cost the loss of the whole Army in case of another repulse. You must not show this to anyone."

In his official report he said of Gibbons' Division:

"They did not advance as vigorously as they should have, I think."

To the Congressional Committee:

"...The commanding officer of the whole force there must judge for himself as to the manner in which he will carry out the order he has received. We were fighting with the river to our backs, and in case of a serious reverse there, the army would have been destroyed. I suppose it would be necessary under such circumstances, for a general to hold a pretty large force in reserve. ...If a larger force had been up there in time, I would have put it into the attack at once. I was going to put General Doubleday's division in behind Meade, and carry the whole thing through as far as my corps was concerned. But the demonstration by the Enemy on our left was so strong that I had to turn Doubleday square off to the left to meet it, and he did not succeed in driving the enemy off until it was too late to move up again to support Meade."

December, 1862, battle report of Hamilton's Crossing, south of Fredericksburg:

"About 8:30 AM Meade's division advanced across the Smithfield ravine, formed in column of two brigades, with the artillery between them, the Third Brigade marching by the flank on the left and rear. It moved down the river some 500 or 600 yards, when it turned sharp to the right and crossed the Bowling Green road. The enemy's artillery opened fire from the crest and the angle of the Bowling Green road. I directed General Meade to put his column directly for the nearest point of wood, and, having gained the crest, to extend his attack along it to the extreme point of the heights, where most of the enemy's artillery was posted. As the column crossed the Bowling Green road the artillery of his division was ordered into position on the rise of the ground

between this road and the railroad, Cooper's and Ransom's batteries, to the front, soon joined by Amsden's, to oppose those of the enemy on the crest, while Simpson's had to be thrown to the left to oppose that on the Bowling Green road, which was taking the column in flank. Hall's battery was at the same time thrown to the front, on the left of Gibbon's division, which was advancing in line on Meade's right. The artillery combat here raged furiously for some time, until that of the enemy was silenced, when all of our batteries were directed to shell the woods, where his infantry was supposed to be posted. This was continued some half-hour, when the column of Meade, advancing in fine order and with gallant determination, was directed into the point of wood which extended this side of the railroad, with instructions, when they carried the crest the road which ran along it in their front, to move the First Brigade along the road, the Second Brigade to advance and hold the road, while the Third moved across the open fields, to support the First in carrying the extreme point of the ridge. At this time I sent orders to General Gibbon to advance, in connection with General Meade, and carry the wood in his front. The advance was made under the fire of the enemy's batteries on his right and front, to which Gibbon's batteries replied while those of Smith joined in on the right.

Meade's division successfully carried the wood in front, crossed the railroad, charged up the slope of the hill, and gained the road and edge of the wood, driving the enemy from his positions in the ditches and railroad cut, capturing the flags of 2 regiments and sending about 200 prisoners to the rear. At the same time Gibbon's division had crossed the railroad and entered the wood, driving back the first line of the enemy and capturing a number of prisoners, but, from the dense character of the wood, the connection between his division and Meade's column was vigorously assailed by the enemy's masked force, and, after a severe contest, forced back. Two regiments of Berry's brigade, Birney's division, arrived about this time, and were immediately thrown into the wood on Gibbon's left, to the support of the line, but they, too, were soon overpowered, and the whole line retired from the wood, Meade's in some confusion, and, after an ineffectual effort by General Meade and myself to rally them under the enemy's fire, that of the artillery having resumed almost its original intensity, I directed General Meade to re-form his division across the Bowling Green road, and ordered the remainder of Berry's brigade, which had come up, to the support of the batteries.

The enemy, showing himself in strong force in the wood, seemed disposed to follow our retiring troops, but the arrival of other brigades of Birney's division on the ground at this critical moment, to occupy our line of battle, materially aided in saving Hall's Battery, which was now seriously threatened by the enemy,. And, together with our artillery fire, soon drove him to his sheltered positions and cover, from which his infantry did not again appear. General Gibbon's division was assailed in turn in the same manner, and compelled to retire from the wood soon after Meade's."

January 30, 1863, to his sisters:

"We have been on the verge of moving ever since the first of the year and to-day finds us (the whole army) on the banks of the Rapp'k, with the idea of crossing above Fredericksburg. A violent stork interposed, however, and we are now 'stuck in the mud', unable to get up our artillery or supplies and Burnside goes to Washington to know what to do! If we do not get some one soon who can command an army without consulting 'Stanton and Halleck' at Washington, I do not know what will become of this army. No gen'l officer that I can find approved of the move and yet it was made. I have been all along afraid the weather would fall upon us in this way. No one who had not seen the roads in this country we have to move over could conceive of their wretched condition. We are of course anxious to know what is to be done, and it is about as difficult a problem to solve as ever fell to the lot of one man. I do not know how it is that the gen'l in command here is obliged to consult Washington every day, and yet there is no one there responsible for failure of operations here."

February 5, 1863, special order:

"...In separating from the Pennsylvania Reserve Corps, with which the commanding general has been so closely allied for the past eighteen months, he cannot but express his deep regrets. They are, however, lessened by the hope that soon their thin ranks will be filled, and they, once more restored and organized, will be returned to the field prepared to add new luster to a name already endeared to our patriotic state."

February 12, to a foraging expedition:

"You will enforce the strictest discipline...and summarily punish any unauthorized plundering, it being understood that anything taken is for the Government. Anything more than this is nothing more than robbery."

April, 1863, after a review by Lincoln of the First Corps, the president returned to the capital gratified with everything he saw:

"...as he ought to have been, and if the troops only fight as well as they looked, no expectation however great, need be disappointed..."
"Our troops here...with proper management, which bids fair to be the case, will achieve success undoubtedly."

April 14, 1863, to his sisters:

"Our operations may be said to have commenced, and all passes for the Army of the Potomac stopped for the present, tho' I do not know that this has been made public."

92

April 30, 1863, to his sisters (during Fredericksburg Campaign):

"We have got our bridges over the river - and three Corps have crossed and are moving down the right bank on the heights and in rear of Fredericksburg. We will cross at our bridges and attack when the heights of Fredericksburg are carried or pursue the enemy if he retreats. The weather has been unfavorable again and has retarded our movements very much or the attack would have been made to-day. The troops are in good spirits and I think will fight well if we meet with any success here. The only thing I do not like about our operations has been that the bridges were thrown too soon by a day and my bridges are not in a good position. I cannot write any more tonight as I am very busy."

Chancellorsville, Virginia

Maj. Gen. of the First Corps attached to Sedgwick.

May 1, 1863, 9:15 to Sedgwick:

"I think the proper view to take of affairs is this. If they have not detached more than A.P. Hill's division from our front, they have been keeping up appearances with a view of delaying Hooker, in tempting us to make an attack on their fortified position, and hoping to destroy us and strike for our depot over our bridges. We ought, therefore, in my judgment, to know something of what has transpired on the right. Do you not think this the correct view? Let me know, if you please, what you think of it."

May 5, 1863, upon hearing Hooker had been asleep and when wakened said the order to retreat stood. Reynolds remarked:

"Tell Gen. Meade that someone should be waked up to take command of this army."

Report of Maj. Gen. John F. Reynolds, U.S. Army, commanding Army Corps, with itinerary of the Corps, April 19 - May 26, 1863.

HDQRS. First Army Corps Army of the Potomac,
Camp near Pollock's Mill, Va. May, 1863

General, I have the honor to submit the following report of the operations of the First Corps from the 28th ultimo to the 7th instant:
The troops left their camp about noon on April 28, and were assembled by nightfall in the position designated for them, in rear of the point of crossing, the north of Pollock's Mill Creek.
At 10 o'clock the details called for to assist the engineer officer, Colonel Pettes, in carrying the boats by hand to the river, were furnished, viz., 75

men to each of the forty-four boats, and a brigade of 3,000 men were in readiness to be thrown across in them when they reached the river to cover the construction of the bridges. These details were under the direction of General Wadsworth, from whose division they were made.

Owing to the distance which the boats had to be carried, and the conditions of the road, they did not all reach the river until daylight of the 29th, twenty boats only being in the water when the enemy's pickets, in their rifle pits, opened with musketry and drove the working parties away. Our sharpshooters, disposed under cover along the bank of the river, were insufficient to dislodge the enemy who were soon re-enforced in their pits by another regiment. As soon as the fog cleared, and the force of the enemy could be discerned to be only that occupying the pits, General Wadsworth was directed to get the boats below them, and throw over two regiments, so as to flank the pits and clear them. The twenty-fourth Michigan and Sixth Wisconsin Regiments (Colonels Morrow and Braff), selected for this purpose, moved down to the river bank at double quick, were rapidly thrown across in the boats, ascended the bank, and drove off the enemy capturing some 90 men of the Sixth Louisiana and Twenty-third Georgia, including several officers. General Wadsworth crossed with the regiments and directed their movements in person. The remaining regiments of this brigade were then crossed in the boats, after which the bridges were constructed, under the direction of General Benham, who arrived from the upper crossing shortly after daylight.

By 10:30 o'clock the bridges were reported completed, and the other brigades of General Wadsworth's division were crossed and put in position to cover the bridge head. It was necessary, in order to do this completely, to extend the left wall toward the mouth of the Massaponax, to occupy the high bluff on the right bank of the river. Our loss reported in this operation was about 60 dead and wounded. The other two divisions of the corps were then brought down to the vicinity of the crossing and sheltered in the ravines of the creek. The enemy commenced moving into position in great strength from below about the time the bridges were completed, occupying the Bowling Green road with his skirmishers, and in the railroad cut and rifle pits just behind the crest (which was our line of battle on that part of the field December 13, 1862) he was apparently formed in two lines, with reserves in the woods.

The One hundred and thirty-fifth Regiment Pennsylvania volunteers was detailed in the morning to support the batteries (Taft's) on the extreme left, near Mrs. Gray's where it remained until the corps recrossed the river on the 2nd instant, when it rejoined its brigade.

On April 30 the troops remained in position, the division across the river throwing up some light defenses, rifle pits, etc., and during the day two batteries (Ransom's and Stewart's) were crossed, and placed so as to cover the bridges.

About 5 PM, the enemy opened fire from their battery on the hill, near Captain Hamilton's on our working parties and the bridges, which was replied to by our batteries on the north side of the river. The fire was kept up until nearly dark, during which time it became necessary to move the Second Division (massed in the ravines, where it sustained some loss) to the shelter of the river road. One boat of the bridge was struck and disabled. It was however, promptly replaced. The engineers received orders to take up one of the bridges at dark and move it to Banks' Ford. The One hundred and thirty-sixth Regiment Pennsylvania Volunteers was placed at the disposal of the engineer officer for this purpose, and accompanied the train to the ford, returning about noon the next day. At dark, Ransom's battery was replaced by Reynolds.

May 1 was passed with the troops occupying the same position. The enemy's force opposite us was very much diminished, though still strong on their extreme right, where their battery was posted. Their pickets along the Bowling Green road showed the same. The order for the demonstration at 1 o'clock did not reach me until 6 PM. The troops were at once put under arms, and a division of the Sixth Corps moved down in the direction of the lower bridge, the skirmishers on the left being advanced to the Massaponax, in which position they remained until dark.

At 7 AM on May 2, I received orders to withdraw the forces from the right bank of the river, take up the bridge, and proceed, with my command, to report to the commanding general, near Chancellorsville. The divisions of Doubleday and Robinson were at once put in motion up the river, while General Wadsworth was ordered to withdraw his to the left bank and follow the route of the other divisions. During the withdrawal of this division, the enemy opened fire from the battery doing effective service on the south side. The enemy soon ceased firing. I left General Wadsworth at this juncture and proceeded to the head of the column, by way of Bank's Ford, on intimation that probably I might find that the shortest line by which to communicate with the commanding general. On arriving at the ford, and finding there was no bridge thrown across, I continued to march the column to the United States Ford, where it arrived at sunset. I preceded the command, and reported in person to the commanding general at Chancellorsville at 6 PM, receiving his instructions for placing my corps.

On returning to the ford, I was joined by Captains Candler and Paine, of his staff, and conducted the troops under their guidance to the position designated, in which two divisions of the corps were established before daylight of the 3d though much delayed by the crowded condition of the road from the ford to Chancellorsville, which required the exertions of every officer of my staff to clear for the advance of the column. The First Division under General Wadsworth, which arrived shortly after daylight on the 3rd was soon gotten into position, and the line established by sunrise. Before the artillery of the corps reached the field, some of the Eleventh Corps was assigned to me, and I regret to report that two batteries, or parts of two, left the position assigned them without orders, and disgracefully retreated in the direction of the United States Ford, Colonel Schirmer was the officer who reported to me, in command of all the batteries of that corps. Two others were placed in different parts of the line, and retained their position until properly relieved by batteries of my own corps, Captain Dietrich's (First New York) artillery remaining until the position was evacuated. Three Batteries - Leppien's, Cooper's and Amsden's - went into action with the troops of other corps. The Fifth Maine Captain Leppien's suffered severe loss in men, horses, and materials.

The report of the chief of artillery of the corps (Col. C.S. Wainwright, First New York) is referred to for the services of the batteries actively engaged with enemy, as he also was detached at this time, under orders of the commanding general, for duty to the left and center of the position.

During the action of the morning, our pickets and scouts thrown out were constantly bringing in prisoners from the woods in front. The troops were actively engaged in strengthening their position and in clearing the ground for placing the artillery.

On Monday, the 4th, the corps remained in position, the skirmishers on the left of the line occupied by the corps joining General Meade being engaged more or less during the day. Later in the day those on the right, in front of the division of General Robinson, became engaged for a short time, when an attack was threatened.

During the afternoon two regiments of infantry with a section of artillery, General Robinson in command, were sent out, under orders from the commanding general, to reconnoiter the road to Ely's Fork, who reported the position occupied by the enemy in force.

Towards 5 o'clock, a brigade of the Third Division under Colonel Stone was sent out to follow up Hunting Creek, in the direction of the Plank Road nearly due south, which after having driven in the enemy's skirmishers, found itself in the presence of what appeared to be a brigade of infantry, with the road which it had followed barricaded by fallen trees. It being nearly dark at this time the brigade returned to its position. It having been decided on the night of the 4th to recross the river, the troops during the 5th were occupied in opening roads and building bridges over the small streams in the direction of the ford. The ambulances, wagons, artillery, etc., not required were sent across the river.

On the morning of the 6th, between 1 and 2 o'clock, the troops of the different divisions were withdrawn by separate routes and arrived in the vicinity of the ford about daylight, when, finding the bridges occupied by the troops of other corps in their passage, I drew up such portions of my corps as had not crossed the entire First division, the pickets, which had been withdrawn, under the direction of a staff officer from each division, and two batteries of artillery, Ransom's and Stewart's, detained when the bridges were reported as interrupted the night previous and remained with them until all the troops had crossed save the Fifth Corps, under Major General Meade, to whom had been assigned the duty of covering the passage of the army. As soon as the bridges were clear, the passage of the troops continued. The division of Generals Doubleday and Robinson were ordered to encamp for the night near the Wallace house, on the Falmouth and Belle Plain Road, the *division of General Wadsworth at Hamet's on the Warrenton Road. The next day the corps was assembled in rear of the place where we had thrown our bridge, near Pollock's Mill.*

Itinerary of the First Army Corps
April 19 - May 26, 1863

On April 19, the Third Division, General Doubleday, marched to Port Royal, returning the PM of the 22nd.

On the 22nd, the Twenty-fourth Michigan and Fourteenth New York State Militia regiments left camp near Belle Plain at 2 PM under command of Colonel Morrow, Twenty-fourth Michigan Volunteers, and marched to Port Royal on the Rappahannock River.

At daybreak on the 23rd, crossed the river, and entered Port Conway, capturing and destroying rebel property and mail. Recrossed river and marched back to camp same day. April 28, broke camp and moved to mouth of White Oak Creek, near Pollock's Mill, where bridges were thrown across the Rappahannock River during that night.

On the morning of the 29th, First Division crossed bridge, Second and Third Divisions remaining in position on north side of river.

April 30 position the same.

May 1, the First Division remained on the south side of the Rappahannock river, below Fredericksburg. The Second and Third Divisions lay on the road, on north side of the river, near the lower pontoon bridges, at Pollock's Mill Crossing.

May 2, the First Division recrossed and marched to United States Ford, a distance of 26 miles, leaving about 9 AM, the enemy shelling as it was leaving. Crossed the river at that point on the pontoons, and about 11 PM, the remaining divisions (Second and Third) reached the scene of action. May 3, about 1 AM, took position in line of battle on the extreme right of the army and on road leading to Ely's Ford. The First Division, having come up at daylight, during the day constructed breastworks.

May 4 and 5, remaining in same position. A part of the Third Division made a reconnaissance.

May 6, marched back to United States Ford, and recrossed the river at the same place; thence to near Berea Church, and bivouacked for the night.

May 7, marched to the present camp.

May 21, at daylight, the Second and Sixth Wisconsin Volunteers, Nineteenth Indiana, and Twenty-fourth Michigan Volunteers marched down the Northern Neck as a support to the Eighth Regiment Illinois Cavalry then scouting in the lower part of that section of the country. Bivouacked for the night at Millville.

May 22, marched to Mattox Creek and rebuilt the bridge over that stream; thence to Leesville and bivouacked for the night.

May 23, marched back to Oak Grove and in the direction of Westmoreland Court House.

May 24, marched to Westmoreland court house, where the command joined the Eighth Illinois Cavalry on their return.

May 25 and 26, marched back to camp, arriving there at 12m of the latter day.

On the Chancellorsville Campaign:

"We did not effect much more by our crossing then to be slaughtered and to slaughter the Rebels. My Corps was very little in action and has of course suffered very little tho' I do not consider its morale improved by the operations."

June 19th from Guilford Station near Alexandria, he wrote to his sisters:

"Ellie's letter of the 15th came yesterday. The Army has moved up so as to cover Washington but we have not yet been able to discern whereabouts the enemy is exactly. Our cavalry has been fighting on our flanks, but no large infantry force of the enemy has been discovered this side of the Blue Ridge. It is possible that Lee is yet in the Shenandoah Valley. Our cavalry drove them back yesterday to Upperville in the direction of Ashlay's Gap. We may have to move up after them by the gaps or through Harpers Ferry - tho' it is impossible to say where the enemy is with any certainty.

I am well. With much love to all at home and greetings to the newcomer, William R. Landis. Sam I have not seen or heard of since he was in Washington."

June, 1863, offered command of the Army of the Potomac:

General Halleck confidentially inquired of Reynolds if he was prepared to accept the command. Reynolds replied that he expected to obey all lawful orders coming to his hands, but as the communication seemed to imply the possession of an option in himself, he deemed it his duty to say frankly that he could not accept the command in a voluntary sense, unless a liberty of action should be guaranteed to him considerably beyond any which he had reason to expect. He was thereupon dropped, and the choice further and finally restricted to Hooker and Meade...Meade ultimately given the order.

When Reynolds heard the news, he dressed himself with scrupulous care and, handsomely attended, rode to headquarters to pay his respects to the new commander.

Meade, in the marching clothes he had hurriedly slipped on when awakened in his tent, understood the motive of the act, and after the exchange of salutations all around he took Reynolds by the arm, and, leading him aside, told him how surprising, imperative and unwelcome were the orders he had received, how much he would have preferred the choice to have fallen on Reynolds; how anxious he had been to see Reynolds and tell him these things and how helpless he should hold himself to be did he not feel that Reynolds would give him the earnest support he would have given to Reynolds in a like situation. Reynolds answered that, in his opinion, the command had fallen where it belonged, that he was glad such a weight of responsibility had not come upon him, and that Meade might count upon the best support he could give him.

June 30, 1863, given command of the Left Wing of the Army of the Potomac by General George Meade. Includes 1st, 3rd and 11th Corps and John Buford's Cavalry Brigades, along with reserves.

July 1, 1863 - on to Gettysburg.

Early photo of spot where General Reynolds fell.

His Assignments

Captain, 3rd Artillery (since March 3, 1855)

Lieutenant Colonel, 14th Infantry (May 14, 1861)

Brigadier General, USV (August 20, 1861)

Commanding 1 st Brigade, McCall's Division, Army of the Potomac (October 3, 1861 - March 13, 1862)

Commanding 1 st Brigade, 2nd Division, 1 st Corps, Army of the Potomac (March 13 - April 4, 1862)

Commanding 1 st Brigade, 2nd Division, Dept of the Rappahannock (April 4 - June 12, 1862)

Commanding 1 st Brigade, 3rd Division, 5th Corps, Army of the Potomac (June 18 - 27, 1862)

Commanding 3rd Division, 3rd Corps, Army of Virginia (August 26 - September 12, 1862)

Commanding Pennsylvania Militia (September 13 - ca. 29, 1862)

Commanding 1 st Corps, Army of the Potomac (Sept 29, 1862 January 2, 1863; January 4 - March 1, and March 9 July 1, 1863)

Commanding Left Wing (1 st, 3rd and 11 th Corps), Army of the Potomac (June 30 - July 1, 1863)

Chains of Command

Seven Days'
McClellan
Porter
McCall
Reynolds - Brigade: 1st PA Res - Roberts; 2nd PA Res - McCandless; 5th PA Res - Simmons; 8th PA Res – Harp; 13th PA Res - Stone

Second Bull Run
Pope until Porter came on the field
Reynolds - Division: 1st Brigade - Meade; 2nd Brigade - Seymour: 3rd Brigade - Jackson; Artillery - Ransom

Fredericksburg
Burnside
Franklin (Left Grand Division)
Reynolds - Corps: 1st Div - Doubleday; 2nd Div - Gibbon; 3rd Div - Meade;
    Artillery - Wainwright

Chancellorsville
Hooker
Reynolds - Corps: 1 st Div - Wadsworth; 2nd Div - Robinson; 3rd Div - Doubleday

Gettysburg
Meade
Reynolds - Left Wing: 1st Corps - Doubleday; 3rd Corps Sickles; 11th Corps -
    Howard

Battles

Battle	Date	Reynolds
Seven Days	June 25 - July 1, 1862	Brigade - fought at Mechanicsville and Gaines Mill - captured on June 28, held prisoner for six weeks
2nd Bull Run	August 28 – 30, 1862	Division - fought brilliantly on Henry House Hill - saved Porter's Army
Antietam	September 17, 1862	Assigned to lead militia in Harrisburg
Fredericksburg	December 1862	Corps - again, brilliantly fought at Hamilton's Crossing
Chancellorsville	May 1 – 4, 1863	Corps (mostly held in reserve) reinforced the collapsing Federal right and provided stability

Part IV:

The Relations of John Fulton Reynolds

by

Lawrence Knorr

Ancestors of John Fulton Reynolds

Generation No. 1

1. John Fulton Reynolds, born 20 Sep 1820 in Lancaster, PA; died 01 Jul 1863 in Battle of Gettysburg. He was the son of **2. John Reynolds** and **3. Lydia Moore**.

Generation No. 2

2. John Reynolds, born 30 Mar 1787 in Leacock, PA; died 11 May 1853. He was the son of **4. William Reynolds** and **5. Catherine Ferree LeFevre**. He married **3. Lydia Moore** 17 Jun 1813 in Lancaster, PA.
   3. Lydia Moore, born 24 Jan 1794 in Lebanon, PA; died 05 Aug 1843 in Lancaster, PA. She was the daughter of **6. Samuel Moore** and **7. Jane Fulton**.

More About John Reynolds and Lydia Moore:
Marriage: 17 Jun 1813, Lancaster, PA

Children of John Reynolds and Lydia Moore are:
   i. Samuel Moore Reynolds, born 14 Apr 1814 in Lancaster, PA; died 29 May 1888 in Philadelphia, PA; married Elizabeth Van Horn Murray 1858 in Castle Fin, PA; born 1827; died 1890.

   More About Samuel Reynolds and Elizabeth Murray:
   Marriage: 1858, Castle Fin, PA

   ii. William Reynolds, born 10 Dec 1815 in Lancaster, PA; died 05 Nov 1879 in Washington, DC; married Rebecca Krug 16 Aug 1842 in Holy Trinity Lutheran Church, Lancaster, PA; born 22 Aug 1816; died 12 Apr 1885.

   More About William Reynolds and Rebecca Krug:
   Marriage: 16 Aug 1842, Holy Trinity Lutheran Church, Lancaster, PA

   iii. Jane Moore Reynolds, born 07 Apr 1817 in Lancaster, PA; died 21 Apr 1817 in Lancaster, PA.
   iv. Lydia Moore Reynolds, born 27 Jul 1818 in Lancaster, PA; died 28 Dec 1896 in Fort Wayne, IN; married Nathaniel Evans 14 Apr 1846 in Cornwall Furnace, PA; born 23 Dec 1813; died 16 Oct 1893.

   More About Nathaniel Evans and Lydia Reynolds:

Marriage: 14 Apr 1846, Cornwall Furnace, PA

1   v.   John Fulton Reynolds, born 20 Sep 1820 in Lancaster, PA;
                  died 01 Jul 1863 in Battle of Gettysburg.
            vi.   James Lefevre Reynolds, born 08 Mar 1822 in Lancaster,
                  PA; died 05 Apr 1880 in Philadelphia, PA.
            vii. Mary Jane Reynolds, born 13 Feb 1824 in Lancaster, PA;
                  died 10 Dec 1901; married George Gildersleeve 04 Dec 1849
                  in St. James Episcopal Church, Lancaster, PA; born 24 May
                  1822; died 31 Dec 1900.

                  More About George Gildersleeve and Mary Reynolds:
                  Marriage: 04 Dec 1849, St. James Episcopal Church,
                  Lancaster, PA

            viii. Catherine Ferree Reynolds, born 11 Dec 1825 in Lancaster,
                  PA; died 10 Feb 1905 in Springfield, Montgomery County,
                  PA; married Henry D Landis 08 Aug 1854 in Lancaster, PA;
                  born 18 Oct 1824 in Philadelphia, PA; died 18 Feb 1895 in
                  Springfield, Montgomery County, PA.

                  More About Henry Landis and Catherine Reynolds:
                  Marriage: 08 Aug 1854, Lancaster, PA

            ix.   Anne Elizabeth Reynolds, born 26 Dec 1827 in Lancaster,
                  PA; died 07 Jun 1832.
            x.   Edward Coleman Reynolds, born 26 Dec 1827 in Lancaster,
                  PA; died 25 Sep 1828 in Lancaster, PA.
            xi.   Edward B Reynolds, born 26 May 1829 in Lancaster, PA;
                  died 06 Jul 1829 in Lancaster, PA.
            xii. Harriet Sumner Reynolds, born 29 Jul 1832 in Lancaster,
                  PA; died 14 Sep 1898.
            xiii. Eleanor Reynolds, born 13 Mar 1835 in Lancaster, PA; died
                  20 Feb 1923 in Washington, DC.

Generation No. 3

   4. William Reynolds, born 28 Jan 1743/44 in Kilraghts County, Ireland;
died 28 Aug 1801 in Paradise Township, Lancaster County, Pennsylvania. He
was the son of **8. William Reynolds.** He married **5. Catherine Ferree
LeFevre** 1778 in Lancaster, PA.
   5. Catherine Ferree LeFevre, born 09 Dec 1753 in Leacock/Strasburg
Township, PA; died 14 Dec 1822 in Paradise Township, Lancaster
County, Pennsylvania. She was the daughter of **10. Samuel LeFevre** and **11.
Lydia Ferree.**

More About William Reynolds and Catherine LeFevre:
Marriage: 1778, Lancaster, PA

Children of William Reynolds and Catherine LeFevre are:
  i.   Samuel Lefevre Reynolds, born 22 Aug 1779 in Leacock
        Township, Lancaster County,Pennsylvania; died 04 Feb
        1814 in Frederick,Maryland; married Eleanor ? Bef. 1805;
        born 1781; died 1855.

        More About Samuel Reynolds and Eleanor ?:
        Marriage: Bef. 1805

  ii.   William Reynolds, born 06 Aug 1784 in Leacock, PA; died
        05 Nov 1828 in St. Augustine, FL.
2 iii. John Reynolds, born 30 Mar 1787 in Leacock, PA; died 11
        May 1853; married Lydia Moore 17 Jun 1813 in Lancaster,
        PA.
  iv.   Lydia Reynolds, born 05 Jan 1792 in Lehman Place, PA;
        died 27 Apr 1857 in Lancaster, PA.

6. Samuel Moore, born 1749; died 1795. He married **7. Jane Fulton**
1791.
   7. Jane Fulton, born 1768; died 1847. She was the daughter of **14.
John Fulton** and **15. Elizabeth Harris.**

More About Samuel Moore and Jane Fulton:
Marriage: 1791

Child of Samuel Moore and Jane Fulton is:
3 i.   Lydia Moore, born 24 Jan 1794 in Lebanon, PA; died 05 Aug
        1843 in Lancaster, PA; married John Reynolds 17 Jun 1813
        in Lancaster, PA.

Generation No. 4

8. William Reynolds, died 1768.

Child of William Reynolds is:
4 i.   William Reynolds, born 28 Jan 1743/44 in Kilraghts
        County, Ireland; died 28 Aug 1801 in Paradise
        Township,Lancaster County,Pennsylvania; married
        Catherine Ferree LeFevre 1778 in Lancaster, PA.

10. Samuel LeFevre, born 28 Jun 1719 in
Strasburg,Lancaster,Pennsylvania; died 04 May 1789 in
Lancaster,Pennsylvania. He was the son of **20. Isaac LeFevre** and **21.
Catherine Ferree.** He married **11. Lydia Ferree** 1751.
   11. Lydia Ferree, born 1731 in Pequea Valley,Lancaster,Pennsylvania;

died 08 Feb 1778 in Lancaster,Pennsylvania. She was the daughter of **22. Daniel Ferree** and **23. Maria Leninger**.

More About Samuel LeFevre and Lydia Ferree:
Marriage: 1751

Children of Samuel LeFevre and Lydia Ferree are:

5   i.   Catherine Ferree LeFevre, born 09 Dec 1753 in Leacock/Strasburg Township, PA; died 14 Dec 1822 in Paradise Township,Lancaster County,Pennsylvania; married William Reynolds 1778 in Lancaster, PA.

        ii.   Elizabeth LeFevre, born 29 Nov 1755; died 23 Apr 1782.

        iii. Samuel LeFevre, born 27 Nov 1757; died 02 Jan 1813; married (1) Susanna Leaman 07 Sep 1780; born Abt. 1757; died Bef. 1783; married (2) Elizabeth Schofstall 23 Jan 1783.

More About Samuel LeFevre and Susanna Leaman:
Marriage: 07 Sep 1780

        iv. Joseph LeFevre, born 03 Apr 1760; died 17 Oct 1826; married (1) Catherine Messenkop; born 15 Feb 1767; died 13 Jan 1835; married (2) Salome Carpenter 14 Apr 1785; born 25 May 1766; died 09 May 1795; married (3) Lydia Ferree 20 Sep 1796; born 11 Oct 1766; died 11 Jul 1802; married (4) Catherine Messenkop Eckman 03 Mar 1803; born 15 Feb 1767; died 13 Jan 1835.

More About Joseph LeFevre and Salome Carpenter:
Marriage: 14 Apr 1785

        v.   Sarah LeFevre, born 02 Jan 1763; died 31 Aug 1830; married Hugh McCalley.

        vi. Andrew LeFevre, born 15 Apr 1767; died Bef. 1805.

        vii. Lydia LeFevre, born 10 Jul 1770; died Feb 1829; married Thomas Algeo.

        viii. Mary LeFevre, born 10 Jan 1773; died 24 Mar 1817.

14. John Fulton, born 1724; died 1803. He married **15. Elizabeth Harris**.
  15. Elizabeth Harris, born 1732; died 1831.

Child of John Fulton and Elizabeth Harris is:

7   i.   Jane Fulton, born 1768; died 1847; married Samuel Moore 1791.

Generation No. 5

20. Isaac LeFevre, born 26 Mar 1669 in Chateau-Chinon, France; died 01 Oct 1751. He was the son of **40. Abraham Lefevre.** He married **21. Catherine Ferree** 1704 in Bavaria, Germany.

21. Catherine Ferree, born 1679 in Lindau, BAVARIA; died 1749 in Strasburg Twp., Lancaster Co., PA. She was the daughter of **42. Daniel Ferree** and **43. Marie de la Warembur.**

More About Isaac LeFevre and Catherine Ferree:
Marriage: 1704, Bavaria, Germany

Children of Isaac LeFevre and Catherine Ferree are:

i. Abraham LeFevre, born 09 Apr 1706 in Germany; died 20 Nov 1735; married Elizabeth Ferree Abt. 1728; born 1710.

More About Abraham LeFevre and Elizabeth Ferree:
Marriage: Abt. 1728

ii. Philip G LeFevre, born 16 Mar 1709/10 in New Pfaltz, New York; died Sep 1761; married Maria Catherine Herr 1730; born 13 Oct 1714 in West Lampeter Twp, Lancaster Co, PA; died Abt. 1766.

More About Philip LeFevre and Maria Herr:
Marriage: 1730

iii. Daniel LeFevre, born 29 Mar 1713 in Pequea Valley, Lancaster Co, PA; died Apr 1781; married Mary Catherine Kerr 1736.

More About Daniel LeFevre and Mary Kerr:
Marriage: 1736

iv. Mary LeFevre, born 24 Aug 1715; died 25 Feb 1774; married (1) David Ferree WFT Est. 1729-1748; born WFT Est. 1698-1718; died WFT Est. 1732-1804; married (2) David Deshler 20 Mar 1737/38; born 1711 in England; died 1792 in America.

More About David Deshler and Mary LeFevre:
Marriage: 20 Mar 1737/38

v. Esther LeFevre, born 03 May 1717; died Bef. 1751; married Daniel Harmon WFT Est. 1731-1748; born WFT Est. 1700-1720; died WFT Est. 1735-1806.

More About Daniel Harmon and Esther LeFevre:
Marriage: WFT Est. 1731-1748

10   vi.   Samuel LeFevre, born 28 Jun 1719 in
              Strasburg,Lancaster,Pennsylvania; died 04 May 1789 in
              Lancaster,Pennsylvania; married Lydia Ferree 1751.

22. Daniel Ferree, born 1676; died 10 Aug 1750 in Strasburg Twp,
Lancaster Co, PA. He was the son of **42. Daniel Ferree** and **43. Marie de la
Warembur.** He married **23. Maria Leninger** Bef. 1710.
      23. Maria Leninger, born 1678; died Aft. 1731.

More About Daniel Ferree and Maria Leninger:
Marriage: Bef. 1710

Children of Daniel Ferree and Maria Leninger are:
        i.   Elizabeth Ferree, born 1710; married Abraham LeFevre Abt.
             1728; born 09 Apr 1706 in Germany; died 20 Nov 1735.

             More About Abraham LeFevre and Elizabeth Ferree:
             Marriage: Abt. 1728

11   ii. Lydia Ferree, born 1731 in Pequea
             Valley,Lancaster,Pennsylvania; died 08 Feb 1778 in
             Lancaster,Pennsylvania; married Samuel LeFevre 1751.

Generation No. 6

40. Abraham Lefevre, born 1632 in Strasbourg, France; died Oct 1685
in Martyred by Roman Catholics. He was the son of **80. Andrew Lefevre.**

Children of Abraham Lefevre are:
        i.   Judith Lefevre, born 20 Oct 1660; died Oct 1685 in
             Martyred by Roman Catholics.
        ii. Philip Lefevre, born 01 May 1664; died Oct 1685 in
             Martyred by Roman Catholics.
        iii. Jacob Lefevre, born 20 Dec 1666; died Oct 1685 in Martyred
             by Roman Catholics.
20   iv. Isaac LeFevre, born 26 Mar 1669 in Chateau-Chinon,
             France; died 01 Oct 1751; married Catherine Ferree 1704 in
             Bavaria, Germany.
        v.   Mary LeFevre, born 15 Jan 1670/71.
        vi. Mary Lefevre, born 15 Jan 1671/72; died Oct 1685 in
             Martyred by Roman Catholics.
        vii. Susanna Lefevre, born 12 Sep 1672; died Oct 1685 in
             Martyred by Roman Catholics.
        viii. Charles Lefevre, born 24 Oct 1680; died Oct 1685 in
             Martyred by Roman Catholics.

42. Daniel Ferree, born 10 Mar 1646/47 in Picardie, France; died 1708 in Lindau, Bavaria, Germany. He was the son of **84. Jean La Verree.** He married **43. Marie de la Warembur** 1675 in Picardie, France.

43. Marie de la Warembur, born 1653 in Bavaria; died 1716 in Pequea Valley, Lancaster Co, PA.

More About Daniel Ferree and Marie la Warembur:
Marriage: 1675, Picardie, France

Children of Daniel Ferree and Marie la Warembur are:

	i.	Mary Ferree, born 1683 in France; married Thomas Faulkner.
	ii.	Philip Ferree, born 1687 in France; died 10 Mar 1773 in Lancaster Co, PA; married Mary Unknown.
22	iii.	Daniel Ferree, born 1676; died 10 Aug 1750 in Strasburg Twp, Lancaster Co, PA; married Maria Leninger Bef. 1710.
21	iv.	Catherine Ferree, born 1679 in Lindau, BAVARIA; died 1749 in Strasburg Twp., Lancaster Co., PA; married Isaac LeFevre 1704 in Bavaria, Germany.
	v.	John Ferree, born 1685; died 1754; married (1) Mary Musgrave; married (2) Ruth Buffington WFT Est. 1702-1734; born WFT Est. 1681-1700; died WFT Est. 1702-1785.
	vi.	Jane Ferree, born 1685 in France; died 1754; married Richard Davis WFT Est. 1701-1732; born WFT Est. 1670-1690; died WFT Est. 1704-1776.

More About Richard Davis and Jane Ferree:
Marriage: WFT Est. 1701-1732

Generation No. 7

80. Andrew Lefevre, born 1604 in Chateau-Chinon, France. He was the son of **160. Philip Lefevre.**

Children of Andrew Lefevre are:

40	i.	Abraham Lefevre, born 1632 in Strasbourg, France; died Oct 1685 in Martyred by Roman Catholics; married Abt. 1658.
	ii.	Andrew Lefevre, born 1636 in Strasburg, France; died 1696 in NY State.
	iii.	Simon Lefevre, born 1640 in Strasburg, France; died 1690 in New Pfaltz, NY; married Elizabeth Deyo 1678.

More About Simon Lefevre and Elizabeth Deyo:
Marriage: 1678

	iv.	Judith Lefevre, born 1644 in Strasburg, France; died 1690 in Strasburg, France.

v. Isaac Lefevre, born 1648 in Chateau-Chinon, France; died 13 Jun 1702 in Martyred by Roman Catholics.

vi. Issac LeFevre, born 1648 in Chateau-Chinon, Province of Nivernois, France; died 13 Jun 1702 in Martyred by Roman Catholics.

84. Jean La Verree, born Abt. 1624.

Child of Jean La Verree is:
42 i. Daniel Ferree, born 10 Mar 1646/47 in Picardie, France; died 1708 in Lindau, Bavaria, Germany; married Marie de la Warembur 1675 in Picardie, France.

Generation No. 8

160. Philip Lefevre, born 1574 in Valley of the Yonne, France; died Aft. 1604. He was the son of **320. John Lefevre.**

Child of Philip Lefevre is:
80 i. Andrew Lefevre, born 1604 in Chateau-Chinon, France.

Generation No. 9

320. John Lefevre, born 1540 in Lorraine, France; died Aft. 1574. He was the son of **640. Mengen Lefevre.**

Child of John Lefevre is:
160 i. Philip Lefevre, born 1574 in Valley of the Yonne, France; died Aft. 1604.

Generation No. 10

640. Mengen Lefevre, born Abt. 1510 in Lorraine, France; died Aft. 1540.

Child of Mengen Lefevre is:
320 i. John Lefevre, born 1540 in Lorraine, France; died Aft. 1574.

John Reynolds Sr. (1787 - 1853)

Lydia Moore Reynolds (1794 - 1843)

Gen. John Fulton Reynolds

Descendants of Mengen Lefevre

Generation No. 1

1. MENGEN[1] LEFEVRE was born Abt. 1510 in Lorraine, France, and died Aft. 1540.

Notes for MENGEN LEFEVRE:
This Record begins with Mengen LeFevre, of 1510, who, it is believed, is the Ancestor of, not only the Pennsylvania LeFevres, but also of the New York LeFevres, the New Jersey and the Virginia LeFevres.

1-001 Mengen LeFevre, Born 1510 in Lorraine, France. He was ennobled by Royal Duke Antoine, the "Good Duke of Lorraine," and granted a Coat-of-Arms, which was registered in 1543.

The coat of arms displayed above is that used by George Newton LeFevre in his book The Pennsylvania LeFevres. It was granted, he writes, to a man named Mengen LeFevre in 1510 and he further states that Simon and Andre LeFevre (of New York) and Isaac LeFevre (of Pennsylvania) were his descendants. This same statement has been found in other sources as well. The HHS uses a different coat of arms which may be seen on their website under the section headed "Museum Shop Menu."

"The old people, in noting the family characteristics of the LeFevres, said that they lacked the energy of the Hasbroucks and DuBoises; they would not work hard themselves, nor make their slaves work hard; they were not so noted for book learning as the Beviers; they could not talk well; but on the other hand they knew when to keep the mouth shut. This is a most important quality, meaning prudence and oftentimes good sense and judgement. The LeFevres certainly held their own very well among the other settlers; when the church sought release from Holland rule and when the country sought release from British rule they were on the right side; in building each of the old stone churches they contributed a full share, and in the war of the Revolution they did not waver; no feuds or family quarrels are reported among the LeFevres in the olden days."
-Ralph LeFevre in A History of New Paltz, New York, and its Old Families..."

Although I am linked to by the Huguenot Historical Society in New Paltz- the authority on many of the old families of that town and the group responsible for preserving the old homes there- I am not affiliated with them. If you have questions for them, or just want to get some wonderful information on the New Paltz Huguenots, I highly recomend that you visit their website at www.hhs-newpaltz.org.

In the northeastern part of France was situated the beautiful Province of Alsace, with its magnificent city of Strasburg, founded by the Romans near the beginning of the Christian Era. The neighboring Province of Lorraine was formally ceded to France by the Treaty of Bonn in 921, and became a part of Alsace. It was the home of Mengen LeFevre, of 1510. It was subsequently held by many kings and dukes until 1477 when Charles of Burgundy, who then held it, lost his life at the battle of Nancy, Jan. 4, 1477. After this, Lorraine merged more and more into the stream of French history. At the death of Rene II (1508), his eldest son Anthony, who had been educated in the court of France, inherited Lorraine with its dependencies. He became known as the "Good Duke of Lorraine," and was the one who granted the Coat-of-Arms to Mengen LeFevre, of 1510. In 1525 the country was invaded by German insurgents, and Lutheranism began to spread in the towns. At this time the LeFevres may have become Protestants.

The Coat-of-Arms of Mengen LeFevre of 1510, granted by the Royal Duke Antoine, the "Good Duke of Lorraine," was registered in 1543. The following is the official description, as translated from the French: Blue field, Three Crosses, re-crossed, of Gold, so constructed as to permit being driven, -- Stag head of Silver. (It was traced by R. G. LeFevre, of Cleveland, Ohio.)

In 1552, just after the LeFevre Coat-of-Arms was registered, war broke out by the Elector of Saxony and some German princes against the German Emperor Charles V, and Lorraine was overrun by the Emperor's troops. Then the LeFevres may have fled to the French province of Nivernois, southwest of Strasburg, and over one hundred miles from Lorraine. Here in the shelter of the Vosges mountains where they meet the ridge running southeast from Paris, in the valley of the river Yonne, near Chateau-Chinon, the LeFevres made their home until 1685. By Geo. N. LeFevre.

About the middle of the sixteenth century the French Protestants were nicknamed Huguenots by the Roman Catholics. In 1562 a struggle began between the Huguenots and the government, for religious freedom. This was the beginning of the eight religious wars which covered more than thirty years.

On Sunday, August 24, 1572, when a large number of Huguenots had gathered in Paris for the wedding of one of their chiefs, the Roman Catholics made an attack and killed several thousand. This was known as the Massacre of St. Bartholomew. Massacres were ordered in other parts of France, and all together seventy thousand perished. The Pope sent congratulations to Catherine de Medici, the queen regent, and both felt that they were finished with the Huguenots. But the Huguenots rallied and fought on. (From "The Growth of the Christian Church" by Nichols.)

Catherine de Medici ruled her son, Charles IX, with an iron hand. He became very discouraged and despondent, and died in 1574, being only twenty-four years of age. His brother Henry III then ascended the throne, but disaster befell him in 1589 when he was stabbed by a monk. Being childless, he called for Henry, King of Navarre, and declared him as his successor to the throne of France.

This man was crowned as Henry IV. Being a friend of the Huguenots he did much to aid them and to lessen their persecution. In April of 1598 he issued the famous Edict of Nantes, which put an end to the religious wars for a short time.

Henry IV met his death at the hand of an assassin on May 14, 1610. His son Prince Louis being only a child, Henry's wife Maria de Medici, was regent queen. She became interested in Cardinal Richelieu and they governed young Louis until he took the throne as Louis XIII in 1617.

Persecutions gradually began again, and many Huguenots endeavoring to flee were pursued and killed. Cardinal Richelieu was made prime minister of France and became very powerful. He expressed his desire to break the Huguenot party that was opposing the Pope, and to completely wipe out the new Reformed religion.

Louis XIII died in 1643, and the throne passed to his son Louis XIV, who turned out to be one of the most cruel rulers of recent times.

(From Judge Edgar O. LeFevre's Family History.)

In 1666 a new set of Regulations, comprising Fifty-nine Articles, was issued, the provisions of which so invaded all the rights of humanity that they evoked a remonstrance from several Protestant Sovereigns in whose continued friendship Louis XIV was interested. This had some effect, and in 1669 several of the most inhuman Articles were revoked and others were modified. (Stapleton, p.15.)

The Regulations of 1666 was the occasion of the first emigration of the Huguenots, and in a short time thousands of the better class had sought refuge in foreign lands. Louis XIV, whose immoralities had greatly scandalized his court, professed in 1676 to have reformed, and in order to signalize his devotion to the Roman Catholic church undertook anew the complete destruction of Protestant Christianity. This was the beginning of the end.

On October 18, 1685, Louis XIV signed the Revocation of the Edict of Nantes. The Huguenots were not allowed to hold public offices any longer. Protestant marriages were declared illegal. Pastors were ordered to leave the country in fifteen days. Parents could no longer instruct their children in the Reformed faith, but were compelled, under heavy penalty, to have them baptized and instructed by the priests. They were forbidden to emigrate, and those who had done so must return in four months or suffer the confiscation of their property. Churches and records were destroyed. Notwithstanding the most strenuous efforts to prevent it, there was a stampede of the Protestants to leave the kingdom, and we are told that about 400,000 of them left France.

Many of the refugees settled in England, and their descendants have been an honor to the land of their adoption. Among them was a LeFevre, speaker of the House of Commons, who was elevated to the peerage as Lord Eversly.

In October, 1685, after the Revocation of the Edict of Nantes, the parents of our ancestor, Isaac of 1669, and his three brothers and three sisters were murdered by the Roman Catholics, he alone escaping. But Isaac, then a boy of sixteen, took with him his father's Bible, which his mother had concealed by baking it in a loaf of bread. This Bible he clung to and cherished during all his journeyings and hardships for sixty-six years.

Our French ancestors, beginning with Mengen LeFevre of 1510, are then: His son John of 1540; Philip of 1574, son of John; Andrew of 1604, son of Philip; Abraham of 1632, son of Andrew; and Isaac of 1669, son of Abraham, who is our American ancestor.

The record of our French ancestry is based in part on circumstantial evidence. We must remember that the Roman Catholics besides killing the Protestants, also wrecked their churches and destroyed all Huguenot records they could lay their hands on, as I found out when I was in Strasburg, France, in 1929. I tried to get records of Protestants in the Strasburg Cathedral, and in the Strasburg City Archives.

Geo. N. LeFevre

Child of MENGEN LEFEVRE is:
2.   i.   JOHN^2 LEFEVRE, b. 1540, Lorraine, France; d. Aft. 1574.

Generation No. 2

2. JOHN^2 LEFEVRE *(MENGEN^1)* was born 1540 in Lorraine, France, and died Aft. 1574.

Child of JOHN LEFEVRE is:
3.   i.   PHILIP^3 LEFEVRE, b. 1574, Valley of the Yonne, France; d. Aft. 1604.

Generation No. 3

3. PHILIP^3 LEFEVRE *(JOHN^2, MENGEN^1)* was born 1574 in Valley of the Yonne, France, and died Aft. 1604.

Child of PHILIP LEFEVRE is:
4.   i.   ANDREW^4 LEFEVRE, b. 1604, Chateau-Chinon, France.

Generation No. 4

4. ANDREW^4 LEFEVRE *(PHILIP^3, JOHN^2, MENGEN^1)* was born 1604 in Chateau-Chinon, France.

Notes for ANDREW LEFEVRE:
Andrew Unknown LeFevre, b 1604 Unknown near Chateau-Chinon, France.

His Huguenot paster, in speaking of Andrew and his wife, said: "They were the best people amongst us." It was also said of them by another: "Having walked before God in Christian simplicity, and performed their duty, they died at a good old age." Andrew had five children as follows:

Children of ANDREW LEFEVRE are:

5. i. ABRAHAM[5] LEFEVRE, b. 1632, Strasbourg, France; d. Oct 1685, Martyred by Roman Catholics.

    ii. ANDREW LEFEVRE, b. 1636, Strasburg, France; d. 1696, NY State.

    Notes for ANDREW LEFEVRE:
    Andrew, b Unknown 1636 in France; d 1696 at Kingston, N.Y. He and his younger brother Simon (5-003) being Huguenots, left France about 1655. They fled to the Bavarian Palatinate, and lived a while at a place called Paltz, on the river Rhine, near Manheim. From there they went down the Rhine to Holland. In April, 1660, they left Holland, and between 1662 and 1665 they came to the Indian village of Wiltwyck, or what was called by the Dutch, Esopus, and later by the English, Kingston, in Ulster county, New York. On April 23, 1665, they were in Wiltwyck and united with the Kingston church. Andrew and Simon were two of the twelve Huguenot Patentees who on May 26, 1677, made a treaty with the Indians and bought 36,000 acres, called the New Paltz tract. Andrew was never married.

6. iii. SIMON LEFEVRE, b. 1640, Strasburg, France; d. 1690, New Pfaltz, NY.

    iv. JUDITH LEFEVRE, b. 1644, Strasburg, France; d. 1690, Strasburg, France.

    Notes for JUDITH LEFEVRE:
    Judith, b about 1644 in France; d there about 1690. She was an earnest and faithful Huguenot, and encouraged and helped her brother Isaac while he was persecuted, although she was often threatened. Finally she was imprisoned in a convent till her death.

    v. ISAAC LEFEVRE, b. 1648, Chateau-Chinon, France; d. 13 Jun 1702, Martyred by Roman Catholics.

    Notes for ISAAC LEFEVRE:
    Isaac, b 1648 near Chateau-Chinon, in the valley of the river Yonne, in the Province of Nivernois, France. He died a martyr June 13, 1702, after seventeen years of suffering from the murderous cruelty of the Roman Catholic church authorities. In 1663, when fifteen years old he was sent to school in Geneva, Switzerland. Later he studied law at Orleans. His testimonials of character and learning were so high that he was admitted as

one of the Advocates of the Court of Parliament. But he was a sincere and Christian Huguenot, and encouraged and helped other Huguenots to be faithful. On account of his ability and eminence, the Roman Catholic church authorities made every effort to get Isaac to recant and leave the Huguenot faith. Failing in such efforts, they determined to put him out of the way. He was seized on Sunday, Feb. 4, 1686. They took everything he had, and put him in irons. After three weeks in prison he was tried and convicted of heresy, i.e. of following Christ instead of the Pope of Rome. While before the Court, a Counsellor of the Court said to Isaac: "When a person is convinced that he is in the true belief, he must suffer even unto death." Isaac answered , what he said was very true, and that he was on the way to it. He was then condemned to the galleys. From ill treatment and bad food in the prison, he became sick. In August 1686 he arrived in Marseilles, and was put in a hospital of the galley slaves. When he was a little better, although he could not stand, he was carried to a galley for rowing, and fastened with chains. He had to sleep on a board without clothing, and the galley slaves in pity for him gave of their own scanty clothes to shelter him. He was able to remain on the galleys only until April 1687, when he was put in a dungeon in Fort St. John in Marseilles harbor. The dungeon had been a stable, but being too damp and ill ventilated to keep a horse in, they put him in it till his death. And there the body of Isaac LeFevre, the Martyr, was buried.

vi.   ISSAC LeFevre, b. 1648, Chateau-Chinon, Province of Nivernois, France; d. 13 Jun 1702, Martyred by Roman Catholics.

Notes for ISSAC LeFevre:
Isaac, b 1648 near Chateau-Chinon, in the valley of the river Yonne, in the Province of Nivernois, France. He died a martyr June 13, 1702, after seventeen years of suffering from the murderous cruelty of the Roman Catholic church authorities. In 1663, when fifteen years old he was sent to school in Geneva, Switzerland. Later he studied law at Orleans. His testimonials of character and learning were so high that he was admitted as one of the Advocates of the Court of Parliament. But he was a sincere and Christian Huguenot, and encouraged and helped other Huguenots to be faithful. On account of his ability and eminence, the Roman Catholic church authorities made every effort to get Isaac to recant and leave the Huguenot faith. Failing in such efforts, they determined to put him out of the way. He was seized on Sunday, Feb. 4, 1686. They took everything he had, and put him in irons. After three weeks in prison he was tried and convicted of heresy, i.e. of following Christ instead of the Pope of Rome. While before the Court, a Counsellor of the Court said to Isaac: "When a person is

convinced that he is in the true belief, he must suffer even unto death." Isaac answered , what he said was very true, and that he was on the way to it. He was then condemned to the galleys. From ill treatment and bad food in the prison, he became sick. In August 1686 he arrived in Marseilles, and was put in a hospital of the galley slaves. When he was a little better, although he could not stand, he was carried to a galley for rowing, and fastened with chains. He had to sleep on a board without clothing, and the galley slaves in pity for him gave of their own scanty clothes to shelter him. He was able to remain on the galleys only until April 1687, when he was put in a dungeon in Fort St. John in Marseilles harbor. The dungeon had been a stable, but being too damp and ill ventilated to keep a horse in, they put him in it till his death. And there the body of Isaac LeFevre, the Martyr, was buried.

Generation No. 5

5. ABRAHAM[5] LEFEVRE *(ANDREW[4], PHILIP[3], JOHN[2], MENGEN[1])* was born 1632 in Strasbourg, France, and died Oct 1685 in Martyred by Roman Catholics.

Notes for ABRAHAM LEFEVRE:
Abraham, b Unknown 1632 (In Vol. 5 of some book, the name not now recalled, it is recorded--"Abraham LeFevre b near Strasburg, France, in 1632.") m about 1658; d 1685. He and his family being Huguenots, French Protestants, were killed by the Roman Catholics after the Revocation of the Edict of Nantes, Oct. 18, 1685, except Isaac, his third son, then a boy of 16, who escaped to Bavaria, and later came to America.

More About ABRAHAM LEFEVRE:
Fact 1: 1685, Huguenot martyr after revocation of the Edict of Nantes

Children of ABRAHAM LEFEVRE are:
      i.   JUDITH[6] LEFEVRE, b. 20 Oct 1660; d. Oct 1685, Martyred by Roman Catholics.

           Notes for JUDITH LEFEVRE:
           Judith, b Oct. 20, 1660, martyred 1685 by the Roman Catholics after the Revocation of the Edict of Nantes.

           More About JUDITH LEFEVRE:
           Fact 1: 1685, martyred

     ii.   PHILIP LEFEVRE, b. 01 May 1664; d. Oct 1685, Martyred by Roman Catholics.

           More About PHILIP LEFEVRE:
           Fact 1: 1685, martyred

iii. JACOB LEFEVRE, b. 20 Dec 1666; d. Oct 1685, Martyred by Roman Catholics.

More About JACOB LEFEVRE:
Fact 1: 1685, Martyred

7. iv. ISAAC LEFEVRE, b. 26 Mar 1669, Chateau-Chinon, France; d. 01 Oct 1751.
   v. MARY LEFEVRE, b. 15 Jan 1670/71.

More About MARY LEFEVRE:
Fact 1: 1685, martyred

vi. MARY LEFEVRE, b. 15 Jan 1671/72; d. Oct 1685, Martyred by Roman Catholics.
vii. SUSANNA LEFEVRE, b. 12 Sep 1672; d. Oct 1685, Martyred by Roman Catholics.

More About SUSANNA LEFEVRE:
Fact 1: 1685, martyred

viii. CHARLES LEFEVRE, b. 24 Oct 1680; d. Oct 1685, Martyred by Roman Catholics.

More About CHARLES LEFEVRE:
Fact 1: 1685, martyred

6. SIMON[5] LEFEVRE *(ANDREW[4], PHILIP[3], JOHN[2], MENGEN[1])* was born 1640 in Strasburg, France, and died 1690 in New Pfaltz, NY. He married ELIZABETH DEYO 1678.

Notes for SIMON LEFEVRE:
Simon, b 1640 in France; d 1690 at New Paltz, N.Y. m in 1678 Elizabeth Deyo. Simon and Andrew (5-002) worked together, and were noble examples of Huguenot brothers. In 1713 Simon's four children--Andrew, Isaac, John and Mary--owned 6,000 acres of the New Paltz tract. For the record of Simon's descendants, the New York LeFevres, get a copy of Ralph LeFevre's History of New Paltz (Price $20.)

More About SIMON LEFEVRE and ELIZABETH DEYO:
Marriage: 1678

Children of SIMON LEFEVRE and ELIZABETH DEYO are:
   i. ANDREW[6] LEFEVRE.
   ii. ISAAC LEFEVRE.
   iii. JOHN LEFEVRE.
   iv. MARY LEFEVRE.

7. ISAAC[6] LeFEVRE *(ABRAHAM[5], ANDREW[4], PHILIP[3], JOHN[2], MENGEN[1])* was born 26 Mar 1669 in Chateau-Chinon, France, and died 01 Oct 1751. He married CATHERINE FERREE 1704 in Bavaria, Germany, daughter of DANIEL FERREE and MARIE LA WAREMBUR. She was born 1679 in Lindau, BAVARIA, and died 1749 in Strasburg Twp., Lancaster Co., PA.

Notes for ISAAC LeFEVRE:
Isaac LeFevre, founder of the Pennsylvania family of LeFevres, was born March 26, 1669, near Chateau-Chinon, in the valley of the River Yonne in France. Died Oct. 1, 1751.

Married in Bavaria, Germany, about 1704 to Catherine Fuehre, who was born at Landau, France, about 1679 and died in 1749.

From a statement made by John LeFevre, his grandson, who knew him for twenty years, Isaac LeFevre was "lively, active, and took a great deal of exercise, even in his old age, and was very temperate." He prospered in his new home and at the time of his death owned about 1500 acres of land.

The place of his burial cannot be definitely stated. At the side of Madame Ferree's grave however, in a space wide enough for two other graves, there is a small dark colored natural stone with the initials I.L. carved on the side of it. It is reasonable to believe that Isaac and Catherine would have been buried beside her mother but it is not certain.

[Brøderbund WFT Vol. 3, Ed. 1, Tree #2268, Date of Import: Nov 9, 1996]

Isaac and family first arrived in Boston in 1710, then moved to New York, Lancaster and finally Cumberland County, Pa. Isaac's son Daniel was the first white child born in Pequea Valley.

EARLY LEFEVRE CHURCH CONNECTIONS
Early History of LeFevre and Ferree Families
As one becomes more deeply involved in his family's genealogy, the cold records can become living guideposts to be assembled into a contemporary concept of who those earlier people really were. Inasmuch as the LeFevre family in France were killed because of their Protestant Christian beliefs, that faith of our early LeFevres must have been very real, bringing forth many new facets to their lives.

One should stop to realize what 16 year old Isaac LeFevre experienced in the blood bath he saw with has own eyes when his parents and brothers and sisters were slaughtered in 1685 in their home by the soldiers from the Roman Catholic state. His religious convictions must have registered heavily enough upon him so that he gathered up his family Bible. He took it with him as a momento or symbol of his beloved family as he hastily fled his native and familiar country to be traded for a foreign land. That was the Bible printed in 1608 in the French language in Calvin's Geneva. Just possessing such a Bible could bring instant death in France at that time.

That he was finally taken in as an orphan by the Daniel Ferree family, also Huguenots and also fleeing their native land leaving behind all their own prized possessions, is a matter of historical record. We don't know exactly where they met, but it is believed to have been near Strasbourg. Isaac's family were most likely very modest, probably workers in agriculture and vine growers and dressers. That's what the English noted on Isaac's listing for instruments to be provided by England's Queen Anne for her first boat load of new settlers for her new country. He was listed as a vine dresser.

The Daniel Ferree family (Fiere, Fire, etc.) were more likely from a much wealthier background, for Daniel was described as a wealthy silk manufacturer. He and his family had come under the heel of the French government because he was a professing Huguenot, a despised Protestant in that Roman Catholic comitted country. Instead of merely killing them as the soldiers had done to the LeFevres, it is believed they dragooned the Ferrees, sending a large band of perhaps 20 soldiers to live in their home. Usually under such circumstances the homes were upset, furniture broken, women desecrated, food taken or destroyed -- all in an effort to force the Huguenots to give up their Protestant religion and return to the Roman Catholic church. The Ferrees chose not to obey the soldiers. Instead they departed under cover of night, leaving all their possessions behind, and fleeing for their lives to depart their native country. That near part of Germany at that time was under the control of Lutheran Protestants, having
been sold to them by Mad Ludwig to try to pay for the exorbitant castles he built for himself.

So together, the Ferrees and Isaac LeFevre fled to the small town of Steinweiler in the mayoralty of Bittingham very likely about 1686, or within a year or so of fleeing their homes in France. This town was on the west side of the Rhine River, southwest of Mannheim and Heidelberg yet northeast of Karlsruhe. To help set the dates, Daniel Ferree was born in France circa 1650, and died in Germany circa 1708 before his family left for America. Circa 1669 he married Maria Warembauer born in France 1653, and died in Pennsylvania 1716.

Among the Ferree family keepsakes is a church letter giving permission for them to leave for America. It was written on behalf of the pastor and elders of the Reformed Walloon Church of Pelican in the Palatinate of Germany. It was dated 5/10/1708 and granted permission for Daniel Ferree (son) and wife Anne Marie Leininger and their family to leave with their church's blessings. Records for the childrens' baptisms were included. Andrew Ferree was baptised in the Steinweiler Church 9/28/1701, sponsors being Andrew Leininger and wife Margaret. John Ferree was baptised 2/8/1703 in the
church at Rhorbac with sponsors Abraham Ptillian and Judith Miller, both of Steinweiller. Though no such record for Isaac LeFevre, wife Catherine Ferree

and son Abraham is known to exist, it would seem logical to believe they, too, had a similar church letter. They were so closely related, and were surely together members of the same Protestant Reformed Church there.

The term Walloon in the Reformed Church in Germany referred largely to French people who had been heavily influenced by the Germans, especially in the so called low countries of Flanders, Luxembourg and Belgium. The language and custom might have been Germanic. It is known that the New York LeFevres were Walloons. They had helped settle New Paltz, New York with Louis DuBois, known as Louis the Walloon who established the Huguenot related Walloon Reformed Church in New Paltz. And the Daniel Ferree and Isaac LeFevre families came under that influence both in Germany and again in New York. However, it is this writer's conviction Isaac LeFevre wasn't thoroughly a Walloon. He preferred the French language, as evidenced by the fact his notes in the LeFevre Bible were in French, as well the notations of the birth of each of his children in French, even long after he had arrived in
America. The French Huguenot influence seemed to have been dominant.

In summary, the LeFevres were French Huguenots, encouraged in the Reformation by the Calvin group in Switzerland, and when persecuted they fled to Germany where they became members of the local Protestant Walloon Reformed Church so akin to their Huguenot Church.

Old Dutch Church
When the Ferrees and the LeFevres arrived in New York in 1709 there was an already existing Dutch Reformed Church awaiting them both in New Amsterdam (New York City) and in Kingston, not far from New Paltz. When Philip LeFevre was born the New Paltz Walloon Reformed church was without a minister, so they journeyed to Kingston for his baptism. Domine Petrus Vas was the minister for that baptism April 1,1710. Witnesses were Isaak and Rachel Duboy (DuBois). When the group arrived in Pennsylvania the fall of 1712 there were very few people in the area, and of course, no churches. It is believed they conducted worship services within their homes, including the reading of the Scriptures from the French language Bible, prayers, a brief devotional talk by one of the elders, and the singing of hymns and psalms such as were printed in the LeFevre Bible. This constituted the Reformed tradition.

Also having arrived in Pennsylvania in 1710, two years earlier, were a group of Mennonites frorn Switzerland. Principally the group consisted of Christian and Hans Herr who conducted worship services in their manner in their homes. Eventually the minister Christian Herr built a stately stone house after German architecture in 1717, and put his initials on the lintel over the doorway. And this is where the group met for their Sunday worship every Sunday. It is of interest to note the Herrs had settled only a short distance, a couple miles, from where the Ferrees and LeFevres took up their warrant or deed for 2000 acres from the same Martin Kindig who sold the

Herrs their land. There were also some German Lutherans who had arrived in the area, and they were forced to worship in their homes because they had no church building.

The Old Dutch Church in the Beaver Creek valley, also called Beaver Creek Congregation is one of the county's oldest shared union churches by the Reformed and Lutheran congregations. It was built of logs about 20 feet square with the door facing west and the small cemetery at the bottom of the hill. Today that is on Rt. 896 at Iva Road. The oldest notation for the Reformed Church is in German language an infant baptism of Catherine born 9/1/1740 and baptised 5/31/1741, daughter of Henry and Esther Eckman. The next is infant baptism 2/25/1744 for Johannes, son of Johannes and Maria
Eckman.

The earliest record for the Lutherans is in Lancaster County Historical Society Volume 9, p 179, "On 5/1/1730 the Lutheran Pastor Johann Casper Stoever baptised children at Millcreek, Pequea and Beber Creek." Historian Clyde L. Groff also discovered in archives of Trinity Lutheran Church of New Holland: "On 3/23/1746 William Phillipse had six children baptised at the Dedication of the Beber Krick Church". While the baptism is not so important, it suggests the date of the new church building but not of the beginning of the congregation. There are records of two civil weddings by justices of the peace in 1739, probably because there were no ministers available out in the country area. "This much is certain: that before a house of worship could be erected a congregation must have been in existence, and further, that before that congregation assumed a definite organization the Reformed people held religious meetings in their homes", thus said Pastor Shepherdson at a church anniversary of Zion Reformed church in 1921. After the structure was completed, it is said the Reformed group used it only for special occasions and for Communion, whereas the Lutherans used it regularly each Sunday until about 1795 when the Lutherans built the new St. Michael's Lutheran Church edifice in nearby Strasburg. The Reformed group built a new stone church near New Providence, and called it the Zion German Reformed Church. Both groups had had their early roots shared in the old log Dutch Church.

Some have thought that this Old Dutch Church may be the one referred to by Rev. Conrad Templeman who wrote in a letter to Holland deputies February 1733 in reference to a Reformed congregation near Lancaster. He said, "This church took its origin at Conestoga with a small gathering here and there in houses with the reading of a sermon and singing and praying according to the German Reformed Church order upon all Sundays and holidays."

October 11, 1921 the Reverend Harry E. Shepherdson, pastor of Zion Reformed Church at New Providence gave the historical sermon as part of an Anniversary of their church. It is preserved by having been published by the

Quarryville Sun, a copy available at the Lancaster County Historical Society.

"The Old Dutch Church was erected by the German Lutherans and Reformed residing between Pequea and the Mine hill, that for a number of years the German Reformed were known as the Pequea Congregation. The German Reformed did not worship regularly in the church as we are told the German Lutherans did. They only repaired to the Old Dutch Church for special occasions and for the celebration of the Lord's Supper. Worship was conducted in the homes and barns of the members. There are no extant records telling us when the Old Dutch Church was erected, nor of the agreement between the
Lutheran and Reformed in regard to the use of their sanctuary. Rev. Christian Brubaker of Strasburg brought greetings from the New Providence Mennonite Church. He said he learned that the Old Dutch Church near Strasburg, on land which his father bought and in 1876 removed the debris of the church, was the original church of New Providence Reformed Church."

But the custom of sharing a common "Union" church building by the Reformed and the Lutherans is described more as a rule than the exception in Lancaster and Berks Counties, typically settled by those of German extraction, commonly called Pennsylvania Dutch. This extensive quote is taken from a book titled "The Pennsylvania Dutch" by Frederic Kleer, 1952, taken from pages 72-74:

There is a gnawing question as to the exact identity of the wife of Philip LeFevre, blacksmith and gunsmith, the second son of Isaac and Catherine LeFevre. The standard Herr family genealogy says Christian Herr's daughter Maria was married to someone else other than a LeFevre. But in the rear of the volume under title of Errata, errors, it is noted that "current researchers believe she was married to Philip LeFevre." THE PENNSYLVANIA LEFEVRES book indicates her as Philip's wife. The Herrs were all Mennonites, and very devout in their faith. They did not believe in infant baptism. Philip's background was Reformed. He had been baptised as an infant in 1710 in Kingston Old Dutch Reformed Church.

The geographical proximity is very close. The Christian Herr House is on Hans Herr Drive, just west of Rt. 222, a short distance South of Willow Street. The 350 acre tract Isaac LeFevre had purchased for use by his son Philip is also on Rt. 222, at Gypsy hill Road. The two properties, Herr and LeFevre, had a common boundry between the two tracts. They lived less than a mile apart. Did Philip join the Mennonites, or did Mary join the Reformed group? Unfortunately for us, the librarian at the Lancaster Mennonite Historical Society informs us the Mennonites did not keep written records of their adult baptism or church memberships until circa 1905. Also unfortunately, the early Reformed Church records do not reveal Philip or Mary's names. But indeed those records do reveal the names of several of

126

Philip's grandchildren being presented for infant baptism by his children. This tends to indicate the continuation of the Reformed tradition among those families, rather than a Mennonite tradition of only adult baptisms. Philip died unexpectedly at age 56, so he died intestate. But the Orphan's Court record of his estate settlement definitely named his widow as "the widow Mary". The brutal fact is that we may never know positively which church Philip and Mary attended. And of course, we do not have positive proof Philip's wife was Mary Herr, only that her name was Mary, believed to be Herr.

For Baptism Records see APPENDIX A

Isaac and Catherine Ferree LeFevre

It is known that Catherine Ferree LeFevre's brother Daniel Ferree and wife Anna Maria Leininger were members of the Walloon Reformed Church in Pelican, Palatinate of Germany in 5/10/1708, when they were granted a church letter to move to Pennsylvania. Probably they had been members for perhaps as long as 20 years before that. Though no document is known today for Isaac LeFevre and his family, it would certainly seem that Daniel Ferree's sister and her husband would have been eligible, for they were there during the same period of time. They were certainly of the same church connection.

They arrived in New York City January 1, 1709. Sometime the following Spring they moved from the Newburgh colony site offered them by England's Queen Anne as part of her deal with them to settle her new country. Because of dissension that broke out within that colony, the Ferrees and LeFevres went farther north up the Hudson River to New Paltz, New York, just a very few miles south of Kingston, New York. While living there on 3/16/1710 the second child was born to Catherine and Isaac LeFevre, and the New Paltz Church was without a minister at that time. So they journeyed to Kingston where in the Old Dutch Reformed Church Domine Petrus Vas baptised young infant Philip 4/1/1711. Witnesses were French friends Isaak and Rachel Duboy (DuBois). This baptism would seem to indicate their preferred church connection was still to the Reformed Church.

Very likely they were part of the organizing group who started the Pequea Congregation of the Reformed Church in the small log "union church," built just to the southern boundry of their tracts, the Old Dutch Church, or went to Lancaster churches. Such were the very likely church experiences that were open to them in these early years in Pennsylvania. The oldest records of these churches have been searched for any records of their children, grandchildren and great-grandchildren so we can to try to glean what their church preferences were.

Special gratitude must be expressed to George Newton LeFevre and Franklin

D. Lefever for their book entitled THE PENNSYLVANIA LEFEVRES, and for the unique manner their numbering system employed, making it easy to identify so many of the family by name and birth date, thereby giving access to their
genealogy.

Isaac LeFevre died October 1, 1751 in Lancaster, Pa., and is believed to be buried with his wife, Catherine Ferree LeFevre, in graves beside her mother, Madam Marie Warambauer Ferree, in Carpenter's Cemetery on Black Horse Road at the Strasburg Railroad in Paradise, Pa. Isaac's will was
recorded in Will Book J, volume 1, at page 135, located in the Lancaster County Court Archives in Lancaster, Pa.

"A boy of sixteen who prized his father's Bible above everything else to save from his wrecked home, LeFevres are not ashamed of."
George Newton LeFevre

History of the LeFevre Bible
This Bible, the only item that Isaac LeFevre rescued from his home following the martyrdom of his entire family, was printed in Geneva in 1608, one of thousands spread undercover throughout France by the Calvinists. How it came into his family's possession is Unknown, though it was likely acquired at great risk. To be caught in possession of a Bible could bring instant death in France at that time. Isaac joined the Ferree family in their escape from France following the Revocation of the Edict of Nantes, and smuggled the Bible to safety in Bavaria. According to tradition it was concealed in a loaf of bread.
Isaac LeFevre was indeed a Frenchman, using the French language to list the birth of each of his children, even after they had come to America. After the name of each child is in French "est ne" meaning "is born."

Abraham LeFevre est ne April 9, 1706.
Philip LeFevre est ne March 16, 1710.
Daniel LeFevre est ne March 29, 1713.
Mary LeFevre est ne August 24, 1715.
Ester LeFevre est ne May 3, 1717.
Samuel LeFevre est ne June 28, 1719.

Isaac remained loyal to his Huguenot Christian faith and carried this Bible with him throughout his travels until his homegoing at the age of 83. Afterwards, it was passed down through several generations before finally reaching its permanent home at the Lancaster County Historical Society. This Bible remains the greatest treasure of the Pennsylvania LeFevres.

The Recent Preservation Effort
Another old Lancaster County Family Bible had recently been conserved, and that sparked the idea in Paul S. Lefever's mind concerning our almost 400 year old LeFevre Bible. At the Lancaster County Historical Society auditorium

there was a meeting with the conservator, Mr. Rolf Kat, who was highly trained in this work in his native Holland. He explained that temperature changes cause some condensation of moisture even in a large volume such as a Bible. Those pages were made with the use of acids, some of which yet remained on the page. The reaction of the introduction of the water condensation is what causes the pages to crumble and fall. Therefore the conservator takes the Bible completely apart, washes out the acid from every page, then reassembles the Bible and replaces the old binding, now kept in a clam-shell box cover for added protection.

Hopefully this will preserve our old family Bible for at least another 400 years! Since the Bible now officially belongs to the Lancaster County Historical Society, they made all the arrangements, but the LeFevre Cemetery and Historical Association paid that cost of $3,000 through the good office of Franklin D. Lefever, at that time their Secretary/Treasurer. This work was done in 1998 by the Conservation Center, 264 South 23rd Street, Philadelphia, PA 19103, telephone 215-545-1013. Mr. Rolf Kat is the conservator of Bibles. View the LeFevre Bible at the Lancaster County Historical Society

The LeFevre Family Bible may be viewed by appointment. The Society requests that at least one week's advance notice be given. Appointments can be made with Archivist Heather Tennies. For contact information, hours of operation, and directions, visit the Society's web site.

On Sept. 10, 1712, William Penn's Commissioners granted and confirmed to Daniel Ferree and Isaac LeFevre 2000 acres of land for 140 pounds, in what was then Chester County, Pa. (Lancaster County was not organized until the year of 1729.)--Rupp's History.

According to the above record the land was deeded to Daniel and Isaac, and not to Madame Ferree.

They arrived at their destination late in the fall of 1712. After all their trials and travels, it looked so good to them that they called the place "Paradise," and so the town and the township remains to this day.

From an Unknown early writer we have the following:

"It was on the evening of an autumn day when the Huguenots reached the verge of a hill commanding the view of the valley of the Pequea. It was a woodland scene, a forest inhabited by wild beasts, for no indication of civilized life was very near. Scattered along the Pequea among the dark green hazel inhabited by wild beast could be discerned the Indian wigwams, and the smoke coming therefrom.

"Suddenly a number of Indians darted from the woods. The females shrieked when an Indian advanced and in broken English said to Madame Ferree, 'Indian no harm white; white good to Indian; go to our Chief; come to Beaver.' Few were the words of the Indian. They went with him to Beaver Cabin, and Beaver, with the humanity which distinguishes the Indian of that period, gave to the emigrants his wigwam.

"The next day Beaver introduced them to Tawana, who lived on the great flats of Pequea and was a chief of a band of Conestoga Indians who at that time occupied this region."--Stapleton.

The above mentioned Tawana was one of the Chiefs who signed the famous treaty made by William Penn at Shackamaxon on Nov. 4, 1682. His remains rest in the burying ground used by the Episcopal Church in Paradise, Pa.

Four years after their arrival, in 1716, after she had through much hardship and trouble established a home for each of her children in the New World, Madame Ferree passed from the scenes of this life. Her body was laid to rest in what is now known as Carpenter's Cemetery, a plot one mile south of Paradise, which she herself had selected before her death.

The 2000 acre tract was later found to contain 2300 acres. Its western boundary was near to where U.S. 30 crosses the Pequea Creek and included the area now known as Gordonville, Paradise and Leaman Place, and extended southward to the Strasburg-Gap Road. It was about 1 1/3 miles wide, its northern and southern boundaries running east and west; and almost 3 miles long, its eastern and western boundaries running slightly north-west and south-east. The tract was divided among the Ferree Children. Isaac LeFevre's share was 383 1/3 acres near the center and extended the entire width of the tract.

Isaac later purchased three additional tracts thus having one for each of his four boys. Abraham's 300 acres lay north of Strasburg and east of Hartman Bridge Road. (See deed on opposite page -- also house and cemetery on page 14) Philip got 350 acres northeast of Willow Street, Pa. It extended north from the intersection of Route 222 and Gypsy Hill Road. Daniel's 300 acres lay north of Abraham's tract and Samuel inherited his father's Paradise ground.

More About ISAAC LeFEVRE and CATHERINE FERREE:
Marriage: 1704, Bavaria, Germany

Children of ISAAC LeFEVRE and CATHERINE FERREE are:

8.   i.   ABRAHAM[7] LeFEVRE, b. 09 Apr 1706, Germany; d. 20 Nov 1735.
9.   ii. PHILIP G LeFEVRE, b. 16 Mar 1709/10, New Pfaltz, New York; d. Sep 1761.
10.   iii. DANIEL LeFEVRE, b. 29 Mar 1713, Pequea Valley, Lancaster Co, PA; d. Apr 1781.
         iv. MARY LeFEVRE, b. 24 Aug 1715; d. 25 Feb 1774; m. (1) DAVID FERREE, WFT Est. 1729-1748; b. WFT Est. 1698-1718; d. WFT Est. 1732-1804; m. (2) DR. DAVID DESHLER, 20 Mar 1737/38; b. 1711, England; d. 1792, America.

         Notes for MARY LeFEVRE:
         Mary, b Aug. 24, 1715, d Feb. 25, 1774.
         m Mar. 20, 1738, to Dr. David Deshler, of Philadelphia, Pa. b in England 1711, came to America 1730, d 1792.

More About DAVID FERREE and MARY LeFEVRE:
Marriage: WFT Est. 1729-1748

More About DAVID DESHLER and MARY LeFEVRE:
Marriage: 20 Mar 1737/38

11.   v.   ESTHER LeFEVRE, b. 03 May 1717; d. Bef. 1751.
12.   vi. SAMUEL LeFEVRE, b. 28 Jun 1719,
          Strasburg,Lancaster,Pennsylvania; d. 04 May 1789,
          Lancaster,Pennsylvania.

Generation No. 7

8. ABRAHAM[7] LeFEVRE *(ISAAC[6], ABRAHAM[5], ANDREW[4], PHILIP[3], JOHN[2], MENGEN[1])* was born 09 Apr 1706 in Germany, and died 20 Nov 1735. He married ELIZABETH FERREE Abt. 1728, daughter of DANIEL FERREE and MARIA LENINGER. She was born 1710.

Notes for ABRAHAM LeFEVRE:
Abraham, b in Germany April 9, 1706, d Nov. 20, 1735. m about 1728 Elizabeth Firre, b 1710, daughter of Daniel Firre.

Abraham, with the assistance of his father Isaac, built a two-story log house one mile north of Strasburg, Pa., on the tract which was to be in his inheritance at the time of his father's death. But dying in 1735 before its completion, his father finished the building, and thus its remains are the only tangible work left of our French ancestor Isaac LeFevre of 1669. The house stood a little west of the present brick dwelling erected in 1836, and the foundation, even with the surface of the ground, is shown to visitors. A dozen or more of the great logs from the building, some measuring twenty-one inches wide, are still in the large bank barn built in 1837, the year following the erection of the brick house by George, the great-grandson of Isaac and the the grandfather of the Compiler, George N. LeFevre, who remodeled the house in 1891.

We believe Abraham's body was the first to be buried in the LeFevre Cemetery but there is no marker to that effect. The cemetery is located a quarter mile west of the big house and contains the remains of six generations of LeFevres.

Abraham 7-001

Abraham LeFevre, the oldest son, had been born in Germany and came with the family from New Paltz to Pennsylvania as a young child. His father Isaac had purchased a 300 acre tract for him. Today that is on North Star Road, just north of Strasburg. Abraham had two sons, John and Peter. When Abraham died 11/20/1735 at the young age of 29, father Isaac on the back of the sheepskin warrant (deed from Penn) signed over that 300 acre tract to his grandsons John and Peter. It must have been a sad occasion. For this only son who had made the voyage with them from Europe Isaac was

required to
put up 200£ surety to settle his son's estate. Circa 1728 in Pennsylvania Abraham married Elizabeth Fiere, his first cousin, the daughter of brother-in-law and wife, Daniel Fiere and Anne Marie Leininger Ferree.

Of John LeFevre's children Elizabeth (9-002), Catherine (9-003), Abraham (9-004), and John (9-005) were baptised as infants according to Zion Reformed Church records. Of Peter LeFevre's children Catherine (9-009), and Elizabeth (9-012) were baptised as infants according to Zion Reformed Church records, but Mary (9-010) wife of Peter Eckman was baptised as an adult in 1789 at the First Reformed Church of Lancaster. Marie Eckman, daughter of the above Marie LeFevre Eckman was baptised as an infant at First Reformed Church at Lancaster, too. Additionally, a granddaughter of Peter, Margaret LeFevre (10-009) daughter of Jacob (9-006) and wife Rebecca, son of John (8-001) and Margaret LeFevre was baptised as an infant 8/3/1800 in First Reformed Church in Lancaster.

There are other later LeFevres listed in records of Zion Reformed Church as active participants: Richard G. (14-075), Marion B. (14-077), Margaret N. (14-078), and Mary Catherine (14-081) known today as Kitty LeFevre Yohn. Their brother Roy Park LeFevre (14-083) at age 12 was presented for baptism there In 1931. They were children of Roy R. LeFevre (13-064) who with his parents Martin B. LeFevre (12-032) were members of the Mennonite Church. Their line continues back through David N.(11-016), John (10-002), John (9-005 who had married Elizabeth Howry), John (8-001) to Abraham (7-001). It seems possible the whole line could have been Mennonites, but Kitty knows her grandparents and father were Mennonites until her father and mother were married. Because of their marriage he was ejected from his church because his wife was not of the Mennonite faith. Mrs. Yohn and her husband Henry M. maintain membership in the Lancaster Church of God.

Franklin Dabler Lefever (13-126) is the author of THE PENNSYLVANIA LEFEVRES, a person unusually well versed in things concerning the LeFevre family. He spent his life as an accountant, many years for Ezra Martin swine abbatoire of Lancaster, and has membership in Calvary Independent Church of Lancaster. He is the son of Harry Kreider LeFevre (12-069), Isaac Denlinger LeFevre (11-032), George LeFevre (10-004), John LeFevre (9-005 who had married Elizabeth Howry), John LeFevre (8-001) and Abraham LeFevre (7-001). Franklin is convinced that the Howrys were staunch Mennonites, and his
family all the way from John (9-005) and wife Elizabeth Howry were Mennonites, he being the first one of his family to break away from his early Mennonite youth training.

More About ABRAHAM LeFEVRE and ELIZABETH FERREE:

Marriage: Abt. 1728

Children of ABRAHAM LeFEVRE and ELIZABETH FERREE are:
13.   i.   JOHN[8] LeFEVRE, b. 21 Jun 1730; d. 18 Oct 1810, LeFevre Cemetery, Strasburg, PA.
14.   ii.   PETER LeFEVRE, b. 05 Jan 1732/33; d. 12 Jan 1799, LeFevre Cemetery, Strasburg, PA.

9.   PHILIP G[7] LeFEVRE (ISAAC[6], ABRAHAM[5], ANDREW[4], PHILIP[3], JOHN[2], MENGEN[1]) was born 16 Mar 1709/10 in New Pfaltz, New York, and died Sep 1761. He married MARIA CATHERINE HERR 1730, daughter of CHRISTIAN HERR and SALOME HAAS. She was born 13 Oct 1714 in West Lampeter Twp, Lancaster Co, PA, and died Abt. 1766.

Notes for PHILIP G LeFEVRE:
Philip, b March 16, 1710, New Paltz, N. Y., d Sept. 1766.
m about 1730 Mary Herr, a daughter of Christian Herr who was a son of Hans Herr.

     Philip's tract lay about five miles west of Abraham's home and about four miles south of Lancaster, in what is now West Lampeter Township. In the "Biographical Annals of Lancaster County," published in 1903, published in 1903, it is said (p.337) that Philip LeFevre, the son of Isaac, received by deed his large property in West Lampeter Township, The consideration being "natural love and affection."

     He was a gunsmith and blacksmith. Besides various tools and farming implements, he made smoothbore guns that were used in the Revolutionary War.

The Philip Lefever Burying Ground

ABOUT THIS CEMETERY

     The Reverend Mr. William F. Worner went about Lancaster County copying all the old grave markers he could find, which he recorded as librarian of the Lancaster County Historical Society. He wrote, "The Lefever graveyard, approximately 50 by 100 feet, was originally on the farm of Christian Lefever 10-098] now owned by Furry H. Frey in West Lampeter Township. The graveyard, if an almost impenetrable blackberry thicket may be referred to as a graveyard, is about two hundred feet from Gypsy Hill Road that leads from Lancaster to Route No. 222. The graveyard is about three hundred yards north-east of the "Big Spring," which has long been a landmark in Lancaster County. On July 13, 1935 we paid our first visit to the blackberry patch and copied as many of the inscriptions as we could under the most scratching conditions. Doubtless we missed some of the tombstones; if we did, it could not be avoided for it was almost impossible thoroughly to penetrate the jungle. We counted 20 headstones, 10 foot stone s, and a number of field stones." We wonder how many graves could be there.

Circa 1985 a Lefever descendant wrote to Franklin D. Lefever, publisher of THE PENNSYLVANIA LEFEVRES, about this old cemetery. Franklin investigated, had a difficult time finding it, and when he finally located it in the thicket, most of the markers had been tramped down into the soft earth by cattle who used that cool shady area as a standing place. Painstakingly he cleared it, set up the markers he could find, and wired together many of the broken remaining markers. It took him more than a week! Then the farmer fenced the cemetery to keep the cattle away. In 1995 Franklin succeeded in finding a Lefever descendant who was willing to keep the cemetery grass mowed.

Of these remaining records the earliest burial here recorded was for Peter Eckman who died 9/1/1799. However, this was always known as the Philip Lefever (7-002) Cemetery, and it would be natural to believe he (who died September 1766) and his wife Maria Herr Lefever who died 6/6/1786 were buried here, but markers no longer exist. So Philip may have been the first to have been buried here in 1766, and his wife some twenty years later.

The latest burial according to these records was for Elizabeth Smeltz, likely the mother of Elizabeth Smeltz Gall Lefever, the second wife of Henry Lefever 9-029. She died 12/6/1841.

Paul S. Lefever 1996

Philip 7-002

Philip was born near New Paltz, New York 1710, and came with his family to Pennsylvania in 1712 as an infant. Somewhere he learned the trade of blacksmith and gunsmith, as well as continuing as a tanner. But he died unexpectedly in 1766, only 56 years of age. Though his guns were surely used
in the Revolutionary War, he can not be used as a Patriot for DAR or SOR, because he wasn't alive to make a decision on which side to sympathize and fight at the outbreak of the war. He had married a wife named Mary, and many believe she was daughter of nearby Christian Herr of the Hans Herr Mennonite tradition.

In the early records of Lancaster First Reformed Church there are many references to Mecks and Manderbaughs. It would seem likely they were cousins or relatives of sons-in-law who married daughters of Philip and Mary LeFevre, but further research will have to be made for those proofs.

More About PHILIP LEFEVRE and MARIA HERR:
Marriage: 1730

Children of PHILIP LEFEVRE and MARIA HERR are:

15.   i.   ISAAC[8] LeFevre, b. 1732; d. Jul 1783.
            ii. CATHERINE LeFevre, b. 02 Mar 1733/34; d. 02 Oct 1804; m. NICHOLAS MECK; b. 12 Dec 1731; d. 16 Apr 1803.
16.   iii. GEORGE LeFevre, b. 18 Feb 1738/39; d. 20 Aug 1820.
           iv. ELIZABETH LeFevre, b. 1742; d. 1791; m. HENRY CHRISTY.
17.   v. ADAM LeFevre, b. 27 Feb 1744/45; d. 15 Feb 1814.
           vi. ESTHER LeFevre, b. 1747; m. HENRY ECKMAN, 09 Feb 1769; b. 09 Feb 1769; d. 1795.

More About HENRY ECKMAN and ESTHER LeFevre:
Marriage: 09 Feb 1769

      vii. EVE LeFevre, b. 1748; m. RUDOLPH HAUP, 06 Aug 1764.

More About RUDOLPH HAUP and EVE LeFevre:
Marriage: 06 Aug 1764

     viii. ANNA LeFevre, b. Aft. 1754; m. JONATHAN WEBER, WFT Est. 1747-1793; b. WFT Est. 1721-1758; d. WFT Est. 1747-1836.

More About JONATHAN WEBER and ANNA LeFevre:
Marriage: WFT Est. 1747-1793

      ix. LUDWIG LeFevre, b. Aft. 1754; d. WFT Est. 1751-1839; m. JARUNCIA MARTIN, WFT Est. 1751-1797; b. WFT Est. 1730-1766; d. WFT Est. 1751-1846.

More About LUDWIG LeFevre and JARUNCIA MARTIN:
Marriage: WFT Est. 1751-1797

18.   x. JACOB LeFevre, b. 24 Feb 1753, West Lampeter Twp, Lancaster Co, PA; d. 08 Jan 1827, Spring Garden Twp, York Co, PA.

10. DANIEL[7] LeFevre *(ISAAC[6], ABRAHAM[5], ANDREW[4], PHILIP[3], JOHN[2], MENGEN[1])* was born 29 Mar 1713 in Pequea Valley, Lancaster Co, PA, and died Apr 1781. He married MARY CATHERINE KERR 1736.

Notes for DANIEL LeFevre:
Daniel, b March 29, 1713, d April, 1781.
m about 1736 Mary Catherine Kerr. He was the first white child born in Pequea Valley, his birthplace being within sight of the Pennsylvania Railroad bridge at Leaman Place, Pa. He lived on a 300 acre tract just north of and adjoining Abraham's tract.

More About DANIEL LeFevre and MARY KERR:
Marriage: 1736

Children of DANIEL LeFevre and MARY KERR are:

19.	i.	CHRISTIAN[8] LeFevre, b. 26 Aug 1737; d. 15 Jan 1801.
20.	ii.	MARY LeFevre, b. Nov 1738.
21.	iii.	CATHERINE LeFevre, b. 18 Feb 1739/40; d. 27 Jul 1802.
22.	iv.	ELIAS LeFevre, b. May 1743.
23.	v.	DAVID LeFevre, b. Apr 1745; d. Oct 1821.
	vi.	ESTHER LeFevre, b. Sep 1748; m. JACOB LUTTMAN.
	vii.	SOLOMON LeFevre, b. Jan 1749/50.
24.	viii.	DANIEL LeFevre, b. 15 Apr 1752; d. 09 Nov 1814.

11. ESTHER[7] LeFevre (*ISAAC[6], ABRAHAM[5], ANDREW[4], PHILIP[3], JOHN[2], MENGEN[1]*) was born 03 May 1717, and died Bef. 1751. She married DANIEL HARMON WFT Est. 1731-1748. He was born WFT Est. 1700-1720, and died WFT Est. 1735-1806.

More About DANIEL HARMON and ESTHER LeFevre:
Marriage: WFT Est. 1731-1748

Child of ESTHER LeFevre and DANIEL HARMON is:
    i. JOHN[8] HARMON, b. WFT Est. 1735-1751; d. WFT Est. 1740-1835.

12. SAMUEL[7] LeFevre (*ISAAC[6], ABRAHAM[5], ANDREW[4], PHILIP[3], JOHN[2], MENGEN[1]*) was born 28 Jun 1719 in Strasburg,Lancaster,Pennsylvania, and died 04 May 1789 in Lancaster,Pennsylvania. He married LYDIA FERREE 1751, daughter of DANIEL FERREE and MARIA LENINGER. She was born 1731 in Pequea Valley,Lancaster,Pennsylvania, and died 08 Feb 1778 in Lancaster,Pennsylvania.

Notes for SAMUEL LeFevre:
Samuel, b June 28, 1719, d May 4, 1789.
m about 1751 Lydia Firre, b about 1731, d Feb. 8, 1778.
Samuel inherited his father's 383 acre tract in Paradise. He was a miller, living north of Leaman Place, Pa. After his death the mill was sold to Jacob Eshleman. Samuel and Lydia are both buried in the Carpenter Cemetery at Paradise, Pa.

More About SAMUEL LeFevre:
Burial: Carpenter's Cemetery one mile south of Paradise,Lancaster County,Pennsylvania

More About LYDIA FERREE:
Burial: Carpenter's Cemetery one mile south of Paradise,Lancaster County,Pennsylvania

More About SAMUEL LeFevre and LYDIA FERREE:
Marriage: 1751

Children of SAMUEL LEFEVRE and LYDIA FERREE are:

25.   i.   CATHERINE FERREE[8] LEFEVRE, b. 09 Dec 1753, Leacock/Strasburg Township, PA; d. 14 Dec 1822, Paradise Township, Lancaster County, Pennsylvania.

        ii.   ELIZABETH LEFEVRE, b. 29 Nov 1755; d. 23 Apr 1782.

26.   iii.   SAMUEL LEFEVRE, b. 27 Nov 1757; d. 02 Jan 1813.

27.   iv.   CONGRESSMAN JOSEPH LEFEVRE, b. 03 Apr 1760; d. 17 Oct 1826.

        v.   SARAH LEFEVRE, b. 02 Jan 1763; d. 31 Aug 1830; m. HUGH MCCALLEY.

Notes for SARAH LEFEVRE:
Sarah, b Jan. 20, 1763, d Aug. 31, 1830.
Sarah died in Indiana, was m to Hugh McCalley

      vi.   ANDREW LEFEVRE, b. 15 Apr 1767; d. Bef. 1805.

     vii.   LYDIA LEFEVRE, b. 10 Jul 1770; d. Feb 1829; m. THOMAS ALGEO.

    viii.   MARY LEFEVRE, b. 10 Jan 1773; d. 24 Mar 1817.

Generation No. 8

13. JOHN[8] LEFEVRE *(ABRAHAM[7], ISAAC[6], ABRAHAM[5], ANDREW[4], PHILIP[3], JOHN[2], MENGEN[1])* was born 21 Jun 1730, and died 18 Oct 1810 in LeFevre Cemetery, Strasburg, PA. He married MARGARET HENNING. She was born 07 Jan 1728/29, and died 16 Feb 1786.

Children of JOHN LEFEVRE and MARGARET HENNING are:

        i.   MARY[9] LEFEVRE, b. 1754; m. JOHN SHULTZ, Baden, Germany.

Notes for JOHN SHULTZ:
Mary, b 1754 Unknown m to John Shultz b in Baden, Germany. John came to America at the age of seventeen.

More About JOHN SHULTZ:
Fact 1: Born In Germany
Fact 2: Came to America at age 17

More About JOHN SHULTZ and MARY LEFEVRE:
Marriage: Baden, Germany

       ii.   ELIZABETH LEFEVRE, b. 13 Jul 1756; d. 15 Mar 1812; m. JOSEPH LEAMAN, 13 Dec 1781; b. May 1757; d. 11 Jul 1833.

More About JOSEPH LEAMAN and ELIZABETH LEFEVRE:
Marriage: 13 Dec 1781

28.   iii.   CATHERINE LEFEVRE, b. 21 Oct 1758; d. Bef. 1813.

      iv.   ABRAHAM LEFEVRE, b. 1761; d. Aft. 1791.

29.   v.   JOHN LEFEVRE, b. 1763; d. 20 Oct 1795.
30.   vi.   JACOB LEFEVRE, b. 24 Mar 1766; d. 08 Nov 1844, Ohio.
31.   vii. GEORGE LEFEVRE, b. 22 Apr 1771; d. 16 Dec 1847, LeFevre Cemetery.

14. PETER[8] LEFEVRE (ABRAHAM[7], ISAAC[6], ABRAHAM[5], ANDREW[4], PHILIP[3], JOHN[2], MENGEN[1]) was born 05 Jan 1732/33, and died 12 Jan 1799 in LeFevre Cemetery, Strasburg, PA. He married CATHERINE LEFEVRE, daughter of DANIEL LEFEVRE and MARY KERR. She was born 18 Feb 1739/40, and died 27 Jul 1802.

Notes for PETER LEFEVRE:
Peter, b Jan. 5, 1733, d Jan. 12, 1799. M.D. LeFevre Cemetery.
m Catherine LeFevre (8-013) b Feb. 18, 1740, d July 27, 1802.
John and Peter received the 300 acre tract gotten by Isaac for their father, Abraham. They divided the tract equally between them, John having the southern half adjoining Strasburg borough, and Peter having the northern half. George Newton LeFevre, the compiler of this Record, a great-grandson of John, was in 1918 the owner of 150 acres, the southern half of this tract, on which he lived from 1880 till his death. He had the Patent for this tract from William Penn with his great seal in wax, four inches in diameter and 3/8 of an inch thick. On this Patent Isaac LeFevre wrote and signed a transfer of it to his two grandsons, John and Peter. In the body of the transfer and in his signature the LeFevre name is written correctly as here given, but in the Old French form. In the Old French a capital letter was made by doubling the small letter, thus a capital A was written "aa"; a capital E was "ee," and a capital F was written "ff." As time went on some began to drop the one "f" and write it LeFevre. Then pronouncing it wrong, they began to write it Lefever. Many LeFevres thus got to writing the name wrong and it has been written in six different ways, but in the early legal documents the name is found written in its correct form. It was the original compiler's request that all names in this record be spelled correctly, LeFevre.

Children of PETER LEFEVRE and CATHERINE LEFEVRE are:
32.   i.   JOSEPH[9] LEFEVRE, b. 16 Sep 1765; d. 20 Dec 1835.
      ii.   CATHERINE LEFEVRE, b. 23 Sep 1769; d. 27 Jan 1771.
      iii. MARY LEFEVRE, b. Abt. 1771; m. PETER ECKMAN.
33.   iv. DR. PETER LEFEVRE, b. 06 May 1774; d. Jul 1844.
      v.   ELIZABETH LEFEVRE, b. 1777; m. JOHN VALENTINE VONDERSMITH.

Notes for JOHN VALENTINE VONDERSMITH:
He was a gunsmith in Donegal Township

More About JOHN VALENTINE VONDERSMITH:
Fact 1: Gunsmith in Donegal, Pennsylvania

15. ISAAC[8] LEFEVRE (PHILIP G[7], ISAAC[6], ABRAHAM[5], ANDREW[4], PHILIP[3], JOHN[2],

MENGEN[1]) was born 1732, and died Jul 1783. He married (1) EVE UNKNOWN 1766. She died Bef. 1773. He married (2) MARY CUNKLE 13 Jan 1773. She died 16 May 1786.

Notes for ISAAC LEFEVRE:
Isaac, b 1732, d July 1783. m 1766 to Eve (last name Unknown).
Then m Jan. 13, 1773 Mary Cunkle, who d May 16, 1786.

More About ISAAC LEFEVRE and EVE UNKNOWN:
Marriage: 1766

More About ISAAC LEFEVRE and MARY CUNKLE:
Marriage: 13 Jan 1773

Child of ISAAC LEFEVRE and EVE UNKNOWN is:
34.   i.   JOHN[9] LEFEVRE, b. 03 Apr 1768; d. 01 Nov 1791.

16. GEORGE[8] LEFEVRE (*PHILIP G[7], ISAAC[6], ABRAHAM[5], ANDREW[4], PHILIP[3], JOHN[2], MENGEN[1]*) was born 18 Feb 1738/39, and died 20 Aug 1820. He married ANNA BARBARA SLAYMAKER Feb 1761. She was born 1745, and died 1790 in buried Big Spring Cem. Newville, PA.

Notes for GEORGE LEFEVRE:
George LeFevre born 1739, a grandson of Isaac, was an Ensign (or First Lieutenant) in the Revolutionary War.

George, b Feb. 18, 1739, d Aug. 20, 1820. Newville, Pa.
m Feb. 1761 Anne B. Slaymaker. Then m Mrs. Quigley.
George LeFevre of West Lampeter Township, Lancaster County, Pa., on June 1, 1762, bought 100 acres west of the Susquehanna River. On Jan. 14, 1767, he bought 10 acres 145 perches. On May 8, 1769, Christian Schlemmer of Windsor Township, York County, Pa., deeded to George LeFevre of Windsor Township, York Co., Pa., a tract of land called "Locust Hills," containing 68 acres 71 perches, also another tract of 91 acres 23 perches for pounds 325, equal to about $1600.
    When the Revolutionary War occurred, when he was thirty-six years old, George in 1775 joined as Ensign (corresponding to First Lieutenant now) the 3rd Battalion, under Col. David Jamison. After the War he returned to his home in York County, Pa. On May 1, 1780, he sold the last three tracts he had bought in 1767 and 1769, containing 170 acres 79 perches, to Jacob Dritt for pounds 6000, almost $30,000. Also on the same date to the same person he sold the 100 acres he bought in 1762 for pounds 7035.
    In 1785 George LeFevre with his family moved to Cumberland County, Pa., and bought a farm near Newville, and built a large stone house, that is still standing and good for another 150 years.

George LeFevers house at Newville is still standing. My husband and I went to see it a couple of years ago and the young man that was at home showed us on the inside. The cemetery where George is buried is nearby and they also have a LeFever Street.

Ruby Casto

More About GEORGE LEFEVRE and ANNA SLAYMAKER:
Marriage: Feb 1761

Children of GEORGE LEFEVRE and ANNA SLAYMAKER are:
35.   i.   ELIZABETH[9] LEFEVRE, b. 08 Dec 1761; d. 07 Feb 1835, buried Big Spring Cem, Newville, Pa..
36.   ii. LAWRENCE LEFEVRE, b. 15 Dec 1764; d. 24 Feb 1830, Newville, Pennsylvania.
37.   iii. ISAAC LEFEVRE, b. 11 Feb 1767; d. 1854.
       iv. MARY LEFEVRE, b. 06 Apr 1769; d. 05 Jul 1825.

         Notes for MARY LEFEVRE:
         Of unsound mind, and lived with Lawrence until her death.

38.   v. JACOB LEFEVRE, b. 14 Sep 1771; d. 20 May 1855.
      vi. GEORGE LEFEVRE, b. 1773; d. 1791, buried Seitz Graveyard.
39.   vii. ADAM LEFEVRE, b. 30 Dec 1775; d. 22 Aug 1861.
40. viii. PETER LEFEVRE, b. 24 Jul 1778.
41.   ix. ANNA BARBARA LEFEVRE, b. 18 Sep 1780; d. 22 Aug 1850.
42.   x. SAMUEL LEFEVRE, b. 22 Jan 1783; d. 01 Apr 1840.
43.   xi. JOHN L. LEFEVRE, b. 17 Jan 1786; d. 24 Mar 1849.
44.   xii. COLONEL DANIEL LEFEVRE, b. 23 Nov 1788; d. 13 Jan 1855.

17. ADAM[8] LEFEVRE (*PHILIP G[7], ISAAC[6], ABRAHAM[5], ANDREW[4], PHILIP[3], JOHN[2], MENGEN[1]*) was born 27 Feb 1744/45, and died 15 Feb 1814. He married ELIZABETH PAULES. She was born 04 Jul 1743, and died 30 Aug 1816.

Children of ADAM LEFEVRE and ELIZABETH PAULES are:
       i. CATHERINE[9] LEFEVRE, b. 15 Dec 1767; d. 18 Dec 1854; m. HENRY MANDERBAUGH; b. 29 Aug 1762; d. 20 Aug 1825.
45.   ii. MARY LEFEVRE, b. 16 Oct 1769; d. 20 Aug 1825.
     iii. ELIZABETH LEFEVRE, b. 28 Sep 1770; d. 14 Sep 1857; m. DANIEL ESBENSHADE; b. 11 Aug 1765; d. 24 Sep 1856.
46.   iv. HENRY B LEFEVRE, b. 11 Apr 1772; d. 26 Sep 1844.
47.   v. JACOB LEFEVRE, b. 24 Jul 1773; d. 06 Jul 1826.
     vi. GEORGE LEFEVRE, b. 25 Sep 1774; d. 15 Oct 1815.
48.   vii. JOHN LEFEVRE, b. 13 Dec 1776; d. 13 Oct 1851.
49. viii. PHILIP LEFEVRE, b. 06 Apr 1778; d. 1813.
50.   ix. ADAM LEFEVRE, b. 21 Feb 1779; d. 26 Mar 1847.
51.   x. PETER LEFEVRE, b. 08 May 1780, Lancaster Co, PA; d. 22 Jul 1830, York Co, PA.
52.   xi. DANIEL LEFEVRE, b. 03 Feb 1783; d. Feb 1852.

xii.   HESTER LEFEVRE, b. 06 Dec 1784; m. JACOB RATHFON; b. Philadelphia.

More About JACOB RATHFON:
Fact 1: Born in Philadelphia

xiii.   SAMUEL LEFEVRE, b. 26 Feb 1786; d. 18 Apr 1808.

18. JACOB[8] LEFEVRE (*PHILIP G*[7], *ISAAC*[6], *ABRAHAM*[5], *ANDREW*[4], *PHILIP*[3], *JOHN*[2], *MENGEN*[1]) was born 24 Feb 1753 in West Lampeter Twp, Lancaster Co, PA, and died 08 Jan 1827 in Spring Garden Twp, York Co, PA. He married (1) SUSANNA UNKNOWN 1774. She was born Abt. 1753, and died 1780. He married (2) CATHERINE PETERMAN 29 Aug 1775 in , York County, Pennsylvania, daughter of MICHAEL PETERMAN and ANNA UNKNOWN. She was born 22 May 1756 in Windsor Twp, York Co, PA, and died 22 Jul 1845 in Spring Garden Twp, York Co, PA.

Notes for JACOB LEFEVRE:
[peterman.FTW]

Jacob & Catherine had children: Ester, Susanna, Anna Maria, Johannes, Catherine, Elizabeth, Maria Barbara, Sarah, & Lydia.Jacob, b Feb. 24, 1753, d Jan. 8, 1827.
m 1774 to Susanna (last name Unknown) who d 1780.
m 1782, Catherine Peterman, b May 22, 1756, d July 22, 1845.

Jacob LeFevre of West Lampeter Township, Lancaster County, Pa., was the founder of the York County, Pa., family of LeFevres. His father Philip died in 1766. Being a minor under fourteen years of age then, the Orphans' Court of Lancaster County, Pa., on November 8, 1766, appointed his father's nephew John LeFevre (8-001) of Strasburg Township the guardian of his estate, as his father was quite wealthy. In 1773 he lived in West Lampeter Township, Lancaster County, but in the spring of 1774 it is believed he moved to York County, Pa. On Nov. 3, 1773 he bought from Christian Schibly, of York Township, York Co., Pa., 200 acres of land in York Township for pounds 1050 ($5100). His brother George (8-005) was one of the witnesses to the deed. The tract had been bought from the Penns on Oct. 30, 1736.
    After the death of his wife Susanna, he married on Aug. 28, 1782, Catherine Peterman of Windsor Township, York Co., Pa. On Mar. 11, 1783, John Peterman of Windsor Township sold to Jacob LeFevre of York Township 200 acres 46 perches for pounds 382, about $1860. On Dec. 15, 1783 he bought from Ulry Neff for pounds 22 all the grain in the ground of 22 acres, also 1 cow, 3 heifers, 2 feather beds, 1 chaff bed, 1 chest, and 1 large Bible. On May 21, 1787 he bought from Christian Rathfon, of Windsor Township, 100 1/4 acres, neat measure, including dower rights, for pounds 1050, about $5100. He was Justice of the Peace in 1804.

More About JACOB LEFEVRE and SUSANNA UNKNOWN:

Marriage: 1774

Notes for CATHERINE PETERMAN:
[peterman.FTW]

Her sponsors were Daniel Peterman & Catherine Loreyen.

More About CATHERINE PETERMAN:
Christening: 13 Jun 1756, , York County, Pennsylvania

Marriage Notes for JACOB LEFEVRE and CATHERINE PETERMAN:
[peterman.FTW]

They were married at the Trinity First Reformed Church.

More About JACOB LEFEVRE and CATHERINE PETERMAN:
Marriage: 29 Aug 1775, , York County, Pennsylvania

Children of JACOB LEFEVRE and SUSANNA UNKNOWN are:
  i. ESTHER[9] LEFEVRE, b. 20 May 1776, York County, PA; m. MICHAEL SCHAEFFER.
  ii. SUSANNA LEFEVRE, b. 01 Mar 1778, York County, PA; d. 10 Nov 1858, Somerset Co, PA; m. (1) DAVID ZUK; m. (2) HENRY HOLTZAPFEL, 14 Jan 1798, Christ German Reformed Church, York, PA.

    More About HENRY HOLTZAPFEL and SUSANNA LEFEVRE:
    Marriage: 14 Jan 1798, Christ German Reformed Church, York, PA

  iii. ANNA MARIA LEFEVRE, b. 21 Feb 1780, York County, PA; d. 26 Sep 1849, York County, PA; m. (1) DAVID MAISH; m. (2) JOHANN PHILIP KING, 23 Sep 1798, Trinity First Reformed Church, York, PA; d. Bef. 1826; m. (3) PHIIP KING, 23 Sep 1798.

    More About JOHANN KING and ANNA LEFEVRE:
    Marriage: 23 Sep 1798, Trinity First Reformed Church, York, PA

    More About PHIIP KING and ANNA LEFEVRE:
    Marriage: 23 Sep 1798

Children of JACOB LEFEVRE and CATHERINE PETERMAN are:
53.   iv. JOHN[9] LEFEVRE, b. 29 Nov 1783; d. 26 Jan 1866.
       v. CATHERINE LEFEVRE, b. 01 Dec 1784, York County, PA; d. Bef. 20 Jan 1827; m. JACOB NEFF, 05 Jun 1803, St John's Union Church (Blymir's), York Twp, York, PA.

    More About JACOB NEFF and CATHERINE LEFEVRE:

Marriage: 05 Jun 1803, St John's Union Church (Blymir's), York Twp, York, PA

54. vi. JACOB LEFEVRE, b. 14 Feb 1785, York County, PA; d. 21 Nov 1833.

vii. ELIZABETH LEFEVRE, b. 20 Apr 1787, York County, PA; m. GEORGE LANTZ.

55. viii. MARIA BARBARA LEFEVRE, b. 15 Oct 1789, Windsor Twp, York County, PA; d. 06 Jun 1878, Newberry Twp, York Co, PA.

ix. MAGDALENA LeFEVRE, b. 17 Feb 1792; d. 25 Feb 1842, York County, PA; m. GEORGE MUSSER, 10 Mar 1814.

More About GEORGE MUSSER and MAGDALENA LeFEVRE:
Marriage: 10 Mar 1814

x. SARAH LEFEVRE, b. 18 Aug 1794, York County, PA; d. 10 Aug 1863, Frederick Co, MD; m. SAMUEL S BOYER, 20 Aug 1820, First Reformed and Trinity First Reformed Church, York, PA.

More About SAMUEL BOYER and SARAH LEFEVRE:
Marriage: 20 Aug 1820, First Reformed and Trinity First Reformed Church, York, PA

xi. LYDIA LEFEVRE, b. 09 Dec 1796; m. (1) HENRICH SCHMID, 19 Feb 1818, First Reformed and Trinity First Reformed Church, York, PA; m. (2) HENRY SMITH, 19 Feb 1818; d. Bef. 1837.

More About HENRICH SCHMID and LYDIA LEFEVRE:
Marriage: 19 Feb 1818, First Reformed and Trinity First Reformed Church, York, PA

More About HENRY SMITH and LYDIA LEFEVRE:
Marriage: 19 Feb 1818

19. CHRISTIAN[8] LEFEVRE *(DANIEL[7], ISAAC[6], ABRAHAM[5], ANDREW[4], PHILIP[3], JOHN[2], MENGEN[1])* was born 26 Aug 1737, and died 15 Jan 1801. He married ANNE FERREE.

Notes for CHRISTIAN LeFEVRE:
Christian, b Aug. 26, 1737, d Jan. 15, 1801. m Anne Firre.
On July 27, 1771, he sold 124 acres and allowances to Peter LeFevre (8-002) of 1733. He moved to Frederick, Md.

Children of CHRISTIAN LeFEVRE and ANNE FERREE are:
i. CATHERINE[9] LeFEVRE, b. 22 Sep 1762; d. Bef. 1780.
ii. HENRY LeFEVRE, b. 03 Feb 1764; d. Bef. 1780.
iii. ANNE LeFEVRE, b. 21 Nov 1765; m. PETER REESE.
iv. MARY LeFEVRE, b. 10 Apr 1767; m. GEORGE DERR.

	v.	SARAH LEFEVRE, b. 15 May 1769.
56.	vi.	DANIEL LEFEVRE, b. 27 Apr 1771; d. 06 Aug 1856.
57.	vii.	GEORGE LEFEVRE, b. 14 Oct 1773; d. 24 Dec 1850.
	viii.	ELIZABETH LEFEVRE, b. 19 Dec 1775; m. GEORGE PRICE.
	ix.	ESTHER LEFEVRE, b. 28 Mar 1778.
	x.	SAMUEL LEFEVRE, b. 10 Mar 1780; d. Bef. 1790.
58.	xi.	CHRISTIAN LEFEVRE, b. 07 Jun 1786; d. Feb 1871.

20. MARY[8] LEFEVRE (DANIEL[7], ISAAC[6], ABRAHAM[5], ANDREW[4], PHILIP[3], JOHN[2], MENGEN[1]) was born Nov 1738. She married DAVID FERREE. He was born WFT Est. 1698-1718, and died WFT Est. 1732-1804.

Child of MARY LEFEVRE and DAVID FERREE is:
59.   i.   LYDIA[9] FERREE, b. 11 Oct 1766; d. 11 Jul 1802.

21. CATHERINE[8] LEFEVRE (DANIEL[7], ISAAC[6], ABRAHAM[5], ANDREW[4], PHILIP[3], JOHN[2], MENGEN[1]) was born 18 Feb 1739/40, and died 27 Jul 1802. She married PETER LEFEVRE, son of ABRAHAM LEFEVRE and ELIZABETH FERREE. He was born 05 Jan 1732/33, and died 12 Jan 1799 in LeFevre Cemetery, Strasburg, PA.

Notes for PETER LEFEVRE:
Peter, b Jan. 5, 1733, d Jan. 12, 1799. M.D. LeFevre Cemetery.
m Catherine LeFevre (8-013) b Feb. 18, 1740, d July 27, 1802.
John and Peter received the 300 acre tract gotten by Isaac for their father, Abraham. They divided the tract equally between them, John having the southern half adjoining Strasburg borough, and Peter having the northern half. George Newton LeFevre, the compiler of this Record, a great-grandson of John, was in 1918 the owner of 150 acres, the southern half of this tract, on which he lived from 1880 till his death. He had the Patent for this tract from William Penn with his great seal in wax, four inches in diameter and 3/8 of an inch thick. On this Patent Isaac LeFevre wrote and signed a transfer of it to his two grandsons, John and Peter. In the body of the transfer and in his signature the LeFevre name is written correctly as here given, but in the Old French form. In the Old French a capital letter was made by doubling the small letter, thus a capital A was written "aa"; a capital E was "ee," and a capital F was written "ff." As time went on some began to drop the one "f" and write it LeFevre. Then pronouncing it wrong, they began to write it Lefever. Many LeFevres thus got to writing the name wrong and it has been written in six different ways, but in the early legal documents the name is found written in its correct form. It was the original compiler's request that all names in this record be spelled correctly, LeFevre.

Children are listed above under (14) Peter LeFevre.

22. ELIAS[8] LEFEVRE (DANIEL[7], ISAAC[6], ABRAHAM[5], ANDREW[4], PHILIP[3], JOHN[2],

$MENGEN^1$) was born May 1743.

Notes for ELIAS LEFEVRE:
Elias, b May, 1743 Unknown m Moved to Maryland

More About ELIAS LEFEVRE:
Fact 1: Unknown, Married - moved to Maryland

Children of ELIAS LEFEVRE are:
60.   i.   ELIAS[9] LEFEVRE, b. 20 Jul 1770, Maryland.
        ii.   ELIZABETH LEFEVRE, b. 1778; m. MR. BIGGER.
61.   iii. GEORGE LEFEVRE, b. 15 Jun 1790; d. 11 Mar 1840.

23. DAVID[8] LEFEVRE (*DANIEL[7], ISAAC[6], ABRAHAM[5], ANDREW[4], PHILIP[3], JOHN[2], MENGEN[1]*) was born Apr 1745, and died Oct 1821. He married MARY ZELLER.

Notes for DAVID LEFEVRE:
David, b April, 1745, d Oct. 1821. m Mary Zeller.
Some time before the Revolutionary War he moved to Washington County, Md., and settled along the Potomac River on what is called "the neck."

Children of DAVID LEFEVRE and MARY ZELLER are:
62.   i.   JOHN[9] LEFEVRE, b. 1770; d. 1815.
        ii.   CATHERINE LEFEVRE, b. 1773; m. FREDERICK HOUSEHOLDER, Bef. 1816.

              More About FREDERICK HOUSEHOLDER and CATHERINE LEFEVRE:
              Marriage: Bef. 1816

63.   iii. HENRY LEFEVRE, b. 1776.
64.   iv.   GEORGE LEFEVRE, b. 23 Dec 1779; d. 20 Apr 1850, Williamsport, Maryland.
        v.   MARY LEFEVRE, b. 1781; m. HENRY FRENCH, Bef. 1816.

              More About HENRY FRENCH and MARY LEFEVRE:
              Marriage: Bef. 1816

24. DANIEL[8] LEFEVRE (*DANIEL[7], ISAAC[6], ABRAHAM[5], ANDREW[4], PHILIP[3], JOHN[2], MENGEN[1]*) was born 15 Apr 1752, and died 09 Nov 1814. He married ELIZABETH PECK Apr 1773. She was born 10 Jun 1752, and died 19 Nov 1809.

More About DANIEL LEFEVRE and ELIZABETH PECK:
Marriage: Apr 1773

Children of DANIEL LEFEVRE and ELIZABETH PECK are:

i. MARY[9] LeFEVRE, b. 13 Feb 1774; d. 21 Sep 1843; m. HENRY STROHM, 28 Sep 1793; b. 08 Jul 1764; d. 09 Jul 1835.

More About HENRY STROHM and MARY LeFEVRE:
Marriage: 28 Sep 1793

ii. SUSANNA LeFEVRE, b. 22 Jan 1776; d. 12 Apr 1838; m. JACOB HARTMAN; b. 24 Nov 1768; d. 08 Apr 1846.

iii. ELIZABETH LeFEVRE, b. 10 Sep 1777; m. JACOB FERREE; b. 19 Dec 1779.

Notes for JACOB FERREE:
Jacob Ferree was a resident of Adams Co., Pa., in 1816.

iv. LYDIA LeFEVRE, b. 24 Apr 1779; m. ABRAHAM FERREE, 14 Jun 1800; b. 05 Mar 1771.

Notes for LYDIA LeFEVRE:
They moved from Anne Arundel Co., Md. to Indiana

More About ABRAHAM FERREE and LYDIA LeFEVRE:
Marriage: 14 Jun 1800

v. CATHERINE LeFEVRE, b. 17 Feb 1781; m. JAMES FERREE, 16 Jan 1798; b. 16 Jun 1778.

Notes for CATHERINE LeFEVRE:
They moved from Anne Arundel Co., Md. to N. Carolina.

More About JAMES FERREE and CATHERINE LeFEVRE:
Marriage: 16 Jan 1798

vi. SARAH LeFEVRE, b. 09 Nov 1783; d. 01 Jan 1854; m. JOHN SEITZ; b. 25 Dec 1782.

vii. DANIEL LeFEVRE, b. 31 Jan 1786; d. 31 Dec 1851.

viii. LEAH LeFEVRE, b. 15 Nov 1788; d. Strasburg Township; m. ANDREW OATMAN.

ix. ISAAC LeFEVRE, b. 24 Sep 1790; m. NANCY ANNE HARRIS, 25 Apr 1815.

More About ISAAC LeFEVRE and NANCY HARRIS:
Marriage: 25 Apr 1815

x. RACHEL LeFEVRE, b. 22 Feb 1794; m. CHRISTIAN DENLINGER.

25. CATHERINE FERREE[8] LeFEVRE *(SAMUEL[7], ISAAC[6], ABRAHAM[5], ANDREW[4], PHILIP[3], JOHN[2], MENGEN[1])* was born 09 Dec 1753 in Leacock/Strasburg Township, PA, and died 14 Dec 1822 in Paradise Township, Lancaster

County,Pennsylvania. She married WILLIAM REYNOLDS 1778 in Lancaster, PA, son of WILLIAM REYNOLDS. He was born 28 Jan 1743/44 in Kilraghts County, Ireland, and died 28 Aug 1801 in Paradise Township,Lancaster County,Pennsylvania.

Notes for CATHERINE FERREE LeFEVRE:
Catherine F. b Dec. 9, 1753, d Dec. 14, 1822.
m to Wm. Reynolds, b Jan. 28, 1744, d Aug. 28, 1801.
Grandparents of Gen. John H. Reynolds, killed in the Civil War at the battle of Gettysburg, Pa., on July 1, 1863. Catherine and William are buried in the Carpenter's Cemetery in Paradise.

More About CATHERINE FERREE LeFEVRE:
Burial: Carpenter's Cemetery one mile south of Paradise,Lancaster County,Pennsylvania

Notes for WILLIAM REYNOLDS:
[BKGlenn.FTW]

Grandparent of General John Reynolds killed at Battle of Gettysburg

1821 Unknown - appointed Secretary to the Spanish Governor of Florida.
1822 - appointed to the Legislative Council of the territory of Florida by James Buchanan.
- appointed "Keeper of the Public Archives."
1825 - elected mayor of St. Augustine, Florida.

More About WILLIAM REYNOLDS:
Burial: Carpenter's Cemetery one mile south of Paradise,Lancaster County,Pennsylvania

More About WILLIAM REYNOLDS and CATHERINE LeFEVRE:
Marriage: 1778, Lancaster, PA

Children of CATHERINE LeFEVRE and WILLIAM REYNOLDS are:
    i.   SAMUEL LEFEVRE[9] REYNOLDS, b. 22 Aug 1779, Leacock Township, Lancaster County,Pennsylvania; d. 04 Feb 1814, Frederick,Maryland; m. ELEANOR ?, Bef. 1805; b. 1781; d. 1855.

       More About SAMUEL REYNOLDS and ELEANOR ?:
       Marriage: Bef. 1805

    ii. WILLIAM REYNOLDS, b. 06 Aug 1784, Leacock, PA; d. 05 Nov 1828, St. Augustine, FL.
65.   iii. JOHN REYNOLDS, b. 30 Mar 1787, Leacock, PA; d. 11 May 1853.
    iv. LYDIA REYNOLDS, b. 05 Jan 1792, Lehman Place, PA; d. 27 Apr

1857, Lancaster, PA.

Notes for LYDIA REYNOLDS:
The unmarried sister of John Reynolds (Sr.) who took charge of the East King Street house and of the permanent Duke Street house in which all of the family remaining in Lancaster lived from 1848 to 1857.

In a letter from nephew William, he stated '...I suppose she has deserted Mr. Buckwheat altogether.' "Mr. Buckwheat" was the nickname of the Reynolds children for then Senator James Buchanan. The reference to his relationship with Aunt Lydia is unclear.

26. SAMUEL[8] LEFEVRE *(SAMUEL[7], ISAAC[6], ABRAHAM[5], ANDREW[4], PHILIP[3], JOHN[2], MENGEN[1])* was born 27 Nov 1757, and died 02 Jan 1813. He married (1) SUSANNA LEAMAN 07 Sep 1780. She was born Abt. 1757, and died Bef. 1783. He married (2) ELIZABETH SCHOFSTALL 23 Jan 1783.

More About SAMUEL LEFEVRE and SUSANNA LEAMAN:
Marriage: 07 Sep 1780

More About SAMUEL LEFEVRE and ELIZABETH SCHOFSTALL:
Marriage: 23 Jan 1783

Children of SAMUEL LEFEVRE and SUSANNA LEAMAN are:
  i.   HANNAH[9] LEFEVRE, d. Aft. 1839; m. JACOB WITMER; d. Aft. 1839.

       Notes for JACOB WITMER:
       A grocer in Philadelphia

  ii. SARAH LEFEVRE, b. 1781; d. 28 Dec 1840.
  iii. LYDIA LEFEVRE, b. 1793.

27. CONGRESSMAN JOSEPH[8] LEFEVRE *(SAMUEL[7], ISAAC[6], ABRAHAM[5], ANDREW[4], PHILIP[3], JOHN[2], MENGEN[1])* was born 03 Apr 1760, and died 17 Oct 1826. He married (1) CATHERINE MESSENKOP. She was born 15 Feb 1767, and died 13 Jan 1835. He married (2) SALOME CARPENTER 14 Apr 1785. She was born 25 May 1766, and died 09 May 1795. He married (3) LYDIA FERREE 20 Sep 1796, daughter of DAVID FERREE and MARY LEFEVRE. She was born 11 Oct 1766, and died 11 Jul 1802. He married (4) CATHERINE MESSENKOP ECKMAN 03 Mar 1803. She was born 15 Feb 1767, and died 13 Jan 1835.

Notes for CONGRESSMAN JOSEPH LEFEVRE:
Hon. Joseph LeFevre born 1760, of near Paradise, Pa., was a member of Congress from 1811 to 1813.

Joseph, b Apr. 3, 1760, d Oct. 17, 1826.
m April 14, 1785, Salome Carpenter, daughter of Dr. John Carpenter, b May 25, 1766, d May 9, 1795. Then m Sept. 20, 1796, Lydia Ferree, daughter of David Ferree (8-012) b Oct. 11, 1766, d July 11, 1802. Then m Mar. 3, 1803, Mrs. Catherine Eckman (nee Messenkop), b Feb. 15, 1767, d Jan. 13, 1835.

In Harris' History of Lancaster County, Pa., it is recorded: Hon. Joseph LeFevre, a leading politician, and member of Congress from 1811 till 1813, was a citizen of Strasburg (now Paradise) Township.

More About CONGRESSMAN JOSEPH LeFEVRE:
Fact 1: Bet. 1811 - 1813, Member of Congress

More About JOSEPH LeFEVRE and SALOME CARPENTER:
Marriage: 14 Apr 1785

More About JOSEPH LeFEVRE and LYDIA FERREE:
Marriage: 20 Sep 1796

More About JOSEPH LeFEVRE and CATHERINE ECKMAN:
Marriage: 03 Mar 1803

Children of JOSEPH LeFEVRE and SALOME CARPENTER are:
  i. SUSANNA[9] LeFEVRE, b. 12 May 1786; d. 1860; m. JOEL LIGHTNER, Abt. 1822; b. 1779; d. 1850.

       More About JOEL LIGHTNER and SUSANNA LeFEVRE:
       Marriage: Abt. 1822

  ii. LYDIA LeFEVRE, b. 26 Apr 1789; d. 10 Jul 1789.
  iii. SALOME LeFEVRE, b. 12 Feb 1791; d. Aug 1795.
66. iv. JOHN CARPENTER LeFEVRE, b. 09 Apr 1793; d. 01 Dec 1863.
67. v. JOSEPH SMITH LeFEVRE, b. 08 May 1795; d. 10 Apr 1875.

Children of JOSEPH LeFEVRE and LYDIA FERREE are:
  vi. MARY ANN[9] LeFEVRE, b. 13 Oct 1797.
  vii. LYDIA FERREE LeFEVRE, b. 27 Jun 1800.

Generation No. 9

28. CATHERINE[9] LeFEVRE (*JOHN[8], ABRAHAM[7], ISAAC[6], ABRAHAM[5], ANDREW[4], PHILIP[3], JOHN[2], MENGEN[1]*) was born 21 Oct 1758, and died Bef. 1813. She married DANIEL KEEPORTS 17 Dec 1782.

More About DANIEL KEEPORTS and CATHERINE LeFEVRE:
Marriage: 17 Dec 1782

Child of CATHERINE LeFEVRE and DANIEL KEEPORTS is:

68.   i.   ELIZABETH[10] KEEPORTS, b. 03 Jan 1784; d. 25 Sep 1864.

29. JOHN[9] LEFEVRE *(JOHN[8], ABRAHAM[7], ISAAC[6], ABRAHAM[5], ANDREW[4], PHILIP[3], JOHN[2], MENGEN[1])* was born 1763, and died 20 Oct 1795. He married ELIZABETH HOWERY 1789. She was born 12 Sep 1764, and died 13 Aug 1834.

More About JOHN LEFEVRE and ELIZABETH HOWERY:
Marriage: 1789

Children of JOHN LEFEVRE and ELIZABETH HOWERY are:
    i.   DANIEL[10] LEFEVRE, b. 29 Sep 1790; d. 11 May 1863; m.
         BARBARA NEFF, 13 Apr 1813; b. 24 Sep 1790; d. 12 Aug 1856.

         More About DANIEL LEFEVRE and BARBARA NEFF:
         Marriage: 13 Apr 1813

    ii. JOHN LEFEVRE, b. 27 Feb 1792; d. 14 Aug 1856; m. MAGDALENE
         NEFF, 23 Sep 1817; b. 19 Nov 1797; d. 02 Oct 1831.

         More About JOHN LEFEVRE and MAGDALENE NEFF:
         Marriage: 23 Sep 1817

    iii. SAMUEL LEFEVRE, b. Dec 1793; d. Jan 1797.
    iv. GEORGE LEFEVRE, b. 17 Sep 1795; d. 21 May 1863; m. BARBARA
         DENLINGER, 11 Apr 1820; b. 24 Jan 1802; d. 14 Feb 1851.

         More About GEORGE LEFEVRE and BARBARA DENLINGER:
         Marriage: 11 Apr 1820

30. JACOB[9] LEFEVRE *(JOHN[8], ABRAHAM[7], ISAAC[6], ABRAHAM[5], ANDREW[4], PHILIP[3], JOHN[2], MENGEN[1])* was born 24 Mar 1766, and died 08 Nov 1844 in Ohio. He married REBECCA PACHTEL 1790. She was born 04 Dec 1770, and died 03 Feb 1829.

More About JACOB LEFEVRE and REBECCA PACHTEL:
Marriage: 1790

Children of JACOB LEFEVRE and REBECCA PACHTEL are:
    i.   DAVID[10] LEFEVRE, b. 21 Apr 1791; d. 28 Sep 1843.
    ii. SAMUEL LEFEVRE, b. 26 Jan 1793, Chester County,
         Pennsylvania; d. 22 Feb 1888; m. REBECCA KELSEY, Apr 1816; b.
         30 Jul 1795; d. 13 Mar 1891.

         Notes for SAMUEL LEFEVRE:
         Samuel was born in Chester county, where his father had

moved when he left Strasburg Township, Lancaster Co., Pa. In the War of 1812 he enlisted in the army, and served till its close. In 1818 they moved to Missouri, where they lived on a farm which they took up in 1820. They lived together nearly three-quarters of a century. On Jan. 26, 1888, he celebrated his 95th birthday, and their united age was 188 years.

More About SAMUEL LeFEVRE:
Fact 1: Served in War of 1812

More About SAMUEL LeFEVRE and REBECCA KELSEY:
Marriage: Apr 1816

   iii. ISAAC LeFEVRE, b. 20 Jun 1795; d. 07 Mar 1798.
   iv. JACOB LeFEVRE, b. 02 Apr 1797; d. 12 Jan 1867; m. (1) CATHERINE HITE KEMP, 23 Sep 1819; b. Nov 1800; d. 1843; m. (2) LUCY DAVIS, 13 Jan 1847; b. 26 Oct 1808.

Notes for JACOB LeFEVRE:
Jacob, b Apr. 2, 1797, d Jan. 12, 1867. Lived in Pa., Ohio, & Mo.
m Sept. 23, 1819, Catherine Hite Kemp, b Nov., 1800, d 1843
Then m Jan. 13, 1847, Lucy M. Davis, b Oct. 26, 1808.
Went to Calif. in the "gold rush" of 1849, and returned to Mo.

More About JACOB LeFEVRE and CATHERINE KEMP:
Marriage: 23 Sep 1819

More About JACOB LeFEVRE and LUCY DAVIS:
Marriage: 13 Jan 1847

   v. MARGARET LeFEVRE, b. 06 Jan 1799; d. 02 Jan 1879; m. WILLIAM KELSEY.
   vi. ISAAC LeFEVRE, b. 23 Jun 1801; d. 20 Mar 1821.
  vii. MARY LeFEVRE, b. 05 Oct 1803; d. 30 Apr 1811.
 viii. REBECCA LeFEVRE, b. 10 Oct 1805; d. 15 Aug 1887; m. THOMAS SWOPE, 31 Dec 1827.

More About THOMAS SWOPE and REBECCA LeFEVRE:
Marriage: 31 Dec 1827

   ix. JOHN LeFEVRE, b. 03 Dec 1807; d. 27 Dec 1890; m. (1) RACHEL SWOPE; b. 12 Feb 1808; m. (2) ELVIRA REED, 18 Sep 1849; b. 13 May 1814; d. 10 Feb 1902.

More About JOHN LeFEVRE and ELVIRA REED:
Marriage: 18 Sep 1849

   x. ELIZABETH LeFEVRE, b. 03 Sep 1809; d. 27 Sep 1886; m. WESLEY

LONG, 03 Apr 1845; d. 03 Dec 1867.

More About WESLEY LONG and ELIZABETH LeFEVRE:
Marriage: 03 Apr 1845

xi.   WILLIAM LeFEVRE, b. 11 Feb 1812; d. 08 Dec 1867; m. NAOMI
TWIGG, 09 Nov 1842; b. 11 Mar 1819; d. 14 Nov 1880.

More About WILLIAM LeFEVRE and NAOMI TWIGG:
Marriage: 09 Nov 1842

xii. SARAH ANN LeFEVRE, b. 03 Apr 1815; d. 11 Mar 1855.

31. GEORGE[9] LeFEVRE *(JOHN[8], ABRAHAM[7], ISAAC[6], ABRAHAM[5], ANDREW[4],
PHILIP[3], JOHN[2], MENGEN[1])* was born 22 Apr 1771, and died 16 Dec 1847 in
LeFevre Cemetery. He married SUSSANA HARTMAN Apr 1796. She was born
Mar 1774, and died 11 Feb 1872.

Notes for SUSSANA HARTMAN:
  "Grandmother LeFevre" (9-007) known to so many for so many years (she
was nearly 100 years old), was tall, straight as a soldier, and quick on her
feet. One winter morning in her 98th year, when a mist had put an icy
coating on the kitchen porch, she went out quickly to feed her chickens. Not
noticing the icy surface of the floor, she slipped, and falling, broke her hip.
The shock and injury was too much for her system, and in a couple of weeks
Grandmother departed from earthly scenes.

More About GEORGE LeFEVRE and SUSSANA HARTMAN:
Marriage: Apr 1796

Children of GEORGE LeFEVRE and SUSSANA HARTMAN are:
        i.   ANNE[10] LeFEVRE, b. 26 Apr 1797; d. 21 Apr 1870; m. MARTIN
              BUCKWALTER; b. 19 May 1795; d. 04 Apr 1842.
        ii.   SARAH LeFEVRE, b. 15 Feb 1799; d. 09 Sep 1890; m. JACOB
              WITMER, 11 Mar 1817; b. 07 Sep 1791; d. Jun 1864.

              More About JACOB WITMER and SARAH LeFEVRE:
              Marriage: 11 Mar 1817

        iii. ABRAHAM LeFEVRE, b. 06 Jul 1803; d. 27 Aug 1875; m. ANNE
              FRITZ, 24 Oct 1826; b. 10 Sep 1803; d. 14 Feb 1850.

              More About ABRAHAM LeFEVRE and ANNE FRITZ:
              Marriage: 24 Oct 1826

69.   iv.   GEORGE LeFEVRE, b. 15 Nov 1810; d. 22 Apr 1852, LeFevre
              Cemetery.
        v.   CHRISTIAN HERR LeFEVRE, b. 24 Jan 1813; d. 16 Jan 1890; m.

MARTHA ESHLEMAN, Apr 1840; b. 08 Jan 1815; d. Jun 1876.

More About CHRISTIAN LeFEVRE and MARTHA ESHLEMAN:
Marriage: Apr 1840

32. JOSEPH[9] LeFEVRE *(PETER[8], ABRAHAM[7], ISAAC[6], ABRAHAM[5], ANDREW[4], PHILIP[3], JOHN[2], MENGEN[1])* was born 16 Sep 1765, and died 20 Dec 1835. He married SUSANNA BOWMAN Jan 1786. She was born 17 Apr 1769, and died 23 Jan 1840.

Notes for JOSEPH LeFEVRE:
Joseph, b Sept. 16, 1765, d Dec. 20, 1835.
m Jan. 1786 Susanna Bowman, b Apr. 17, 1769, d Jan. 23, 1840.
They moved to Adams Co., Pa. On Apr. 25, 1819, he bought 315 acres and 20 perches at $120.00 per acre, at what is now LeFevre Railroad Station in Adams County. He paid the cost of $37,815 with silver dollars brought in kegs by wagon from Lancaster County. It took several days to count the money. Buried in Christ Church Cemetery at LeFevre Station, near Littlestown, Adams Co., Pa.

More About JOSEPH LeFEVRE and SUSANNA BOWMAN:
Marriage: Jan 1786

Children of JOSEPH LeFEVRE and SUSANNA BOWMAN are:
  i. BENJAMIN[10] LeFEVRE, b. Jul 1789; d. Sep 1849, Gettysburg Cemetery; m. BARBARA WEAVER, Mar 1813; b. 15 Sep 1793; d. Aug 1850.

     More About BENJAMIN LeFEVRE and BARBARA WEAVER:
     Marriage: Mar 1813

  ii. ELIZABETH LeFEVRE, b. 12 Aug 1791; d. 06 Oct 1827, Lancaster County; m. JOHN KEEPORTS, Abt. 1812.

     More About JOHN KEEPORTS and ELIZABETH LeFEVRE:
     Marriage: Abt. 1812

  iii. JOSEPH LeFEVRE, b. 12 Jun 1793; d. 15 Sep 1864; m. MARY HOSTETTER; b. 1791; d. 23 Feb 1836.
  iv. SUSANNA LeFEVRE, b. 12 Aug 1795; d. 05 Oct 1877; m. DAVID ZOOK, 30 Mar 1813; b. 17 Aug 1791; d. 23 Jul 1875.

     More About DAVID ZOOK and SUSANNA LeFEVRE:
     Marriage: 30 Mar 1813

  v. ISAAC LeFEVRE, b. 22 Jul 1797; m. CATHERINE SHRODER.

     Notes for ISAAC LeFEVRE:

Lived in Illinois

    vi.   CATHERINE LEFEVRE, b. 15 Aug 1800; d. 02 Oct 1835; m. EPHRAIM SWOPE, 02 May 1821; b. 04 Jul 1796; d. Mar 1862.

        More About EPHRAIM SWOPE and CATHERINE LEFEVRE:
        Marriage: 02 May 1821

    vii. LYDIA LEFEVRE, b. 01 Apr 1804; d. 29 Jul 1836; m. CHRISTIAN HELLER.
    viii. AMOS LEFEVRE, b. 25 Oct 1806; d. 11 Nov 1872; m. JULIA C WERTZ, 01 Sep 1831; b. 14 Mar 1813; d. 03 Jan 1884.

        More About AMOS LEFEVRE and JULIA WERTZ:
        Marriage: 01 Sep 1831

    ix.   ENOCH LEFEVRE, b. 19 Apr 1809; d. 06 Apr 1877; m. CATHERINE SHRIVER, 12 May 1831; b. 21 Dec 1808; d. 02 Feb 1890.

        More About ENOCH LEFEVRE and CATHERINE SHRIVER:
        Marriage: 12 May 1831

33. DR. PETER[9] LEFEVRE (*PETER*[8], *ABRAHAM*[7], *ISAAC*[6], *ABRAHAM*[5], *ANDREW*[4], *PHILIP*[3], *JOHN*[2], *MENGEN*[1]) was born 06 May 1774, and died Jul 1844. He married MARY LEFEVRE, daughter of ADAM LEFEVRE and ELIZABETH PAULES. She was born 16 Oct 1769, and died 20 Aug 1825.

More About DR. PETER LEFEVRE:
Fact 1: Buried in LeFevre cemetery

Children of PETER LEFEVRE and MARY LEFEVRE are:
    i.   JOHN WESLEY[10] LEFEVRE, b. 05 Jan 1797; d. 31 Dec 1872; m. MARY ESBENSHADE, 23 Mar 1818; b. Sep 1796; d. Oct 1859.

        Notes for JOHN WESLEY LEFEVRE:
        In 1847 he sold his farm in Strasburg Township, Lane. Co., Pa., and moved to Illinois. There he bought 200 acres of land where the city of Sterling now stands.

        More About JOHN LEFEVRE and MARY ESBENSHADE:
        Marriage: 23 Mar 1818

    ii.   ADAM LEFEVRE, b. 13 Mar 1798; d. 16 Apr 1816, LeFevre Cemetery.
    iii. LEVI LEFEVRE, b. 12 Feb 1804; d. 25 Jun 1879; m. (1) SUSAN FRITZ, 03 Jan 1828; b. 12 Jun 1807; d. 26 Apr 1842; m. (2) ELIZABETH HERR, 19 Apr 1852; b. 16 Jul 1816; d. Jul 1875.

More About LEVI LeFEVRE and SUSAN FRITZ:
Marriage: 03 Jan 1828

More About LEVI LeFEVRE and ELIZABETH HERR:
Marriage: 19 Apr 1852

    iv.   HESTER LeFEVRE, b. 05 Oct 1805; d. 28 May 1874; m. GEORGE LEAMAN, 14 Nov 1827; b. 26 Aug 1797; d. Apr 1890.

More About GEORGE LEAMAN and HESTER LeFEVRE:
Marriage: 14 Nov 1827

    v.   PETER LeFEVRE, b. 30 Mar 1808; d. 26 Apr 1893; m. CATHERINE MILLER, 09 May 1844; b. 09 Apr 1817; d. Apr 1886.

Notes for PETER LeFEVRE:
He was a dry goods merchant in Philadelphia for many years. At the beginning of the Civil War he bought up large quanities of mourning goods. As a result of the War, there was a great demand for these goods, and while other stores were short, he sold great quanities. When he retired he bought land and built a large residence at Chatham, Chester Co., Pa.

More About PETER LeFEVRE and CATHERINE MILLER:
Marriage: 09 May 1844

34. JOHN[9] LeFEVRE (*ISAAC[8], PHILIP G[7], ISAAC[6], ABRAHAM[5], ANDREW[4], PHILIP[3], JOHN[2], MENGEN[1]*) was born 03 Apr 1768, and died 01 Nov 1791. He married MAGDELENA SHAEFER 14 Oct 1788.

More About JOHN LeFEVRE and MAGDELENA SHAEFER:
Marriage: 14 Oct 1788

Child of JOHN LeFEVRE and MAGDELENA SHAEFER is:
    i.   ELIZABETH[10] LeFEVRE, b. 01 Feb 1791; d. 01 Jul 1808; m. JOHN KUNKLE.

35. ELIZABETH[9] LeFEVRE (*GEORGE[8], PHILIP G[7], ISAAC[6], ABRAHAM[5], ANDREW[4], PHILIP[3], JOHN[2], MENGEN[1]*) was born 08 Dec 1761, and died 07 Feb 1835 in buried Big Spring Cem, Newville, Pa.. She married PETER TRITT 1777. He was born 05 Mar 1755 in possibly born in Spain, and died 24 Feb 1839 in buried Big Spring Cem, Newville, Pa.

More About PETER TRITT:
Fact 3: Was A Revolutionary War Soldier.

More About PETER TRITT and ELIZABETH LeFEVRE:

Marriage: 1777

Children of ELIZABETH LEFEVRE and PETER TRITT are:

i. BARBARA[10] TRITT, b. 10 May 1778; d. WFT Est. 1779-1872, died young.

ii. JACOB TRITT, b. 18 Jan 1780; d. 14 Dec 1856.

iii. PETER TRITT, b. 28 Jan 1782; d. 24 Jan 1860, buried Centerville, Pa.; m. (1) SARAH LINE, WFT Est. 1799-1830; b. 1783; d. 1861; m. (2) SARAH LINE, WFT Est. 1800-1817; b. 18 Feb 1738/39; d. 20 Jul 1820, buried Centerville, Pa..

More About PETER TRITT and SARAH LINE:
Marriage: WFT Est. 1799-1830

More About PETER TRITT and SARAH LINE:
Marriage: WFT Est. 1800-1817

iv. ELIZABETH TRITT, b. 18 Jan 1784; d. 17 Oct 1831; m. DAVID PALM, WFT Est. 1799-1826; b. WFT Est. 1775-1801; d. 1884.

More About DAVID PALM and ELIZABETH TRITT:
Marriage: WFT Est. 1799-1826

v. JOSEPH TRITT, b. 16 Jan 1787; d. 30 May 1873.

vi. BARBARA TRITT, b. 01 Mar 1789; d. WFT Est. 1790-1883, died young.

vii. GEORGE TRITT, b. 03 Nov 1791; d. 04 Oct 1882.

viii. CATHERINE TRITT, b. 05 Jul 1794; d. 10 Jan 1871.

70. ix. CHRISTIAN TRITT, b. 25 Jul 1796; d. 10 Jan 1871, Lutheran Cem, Centerville, Pa..

x. ANNE TRITT, b. 21 Nov 1798; d. 01 Jan 1837.

xi. JOHN TRITT, b. 18 Jan 1801; d. Sep 1884; m. CATHERINA LINE, WFT Est. 1818-1849; b. 28 Dec 1802; d. 12 Dec 1879.

More About JOHN TRITT and CATHERINA LINE:
Marriage: WFT Est. 1818-1849

xii. SAMUEL TRITT, b. 14 Sep 1803; d. 22 Feb 1873.

xiii. WILLIAM K. TRITT, b. 26 May 1807; d. 07 Feb 1855, Buried Centerville, Pa.; m. CATHERINE BLOCK, WFT Est. 1826-1848; b. 1813; d. 1902, Buried Centerville, Pa..

More About WILLIAM TRITT and CATHERINE BLOCK:
Marriage: WFT Est. 1826-1848

36. LAWRENCE[9] LEFEVRE *(GEORGE[8], PHILIP G[7], ISAAC[6], ABRAHAM[5], ANDREW[4], PHILIP[3], JOHN[2], MENGEN[1])* was born 15 Dec 1764, and died 24 Feb 1830 in Newville, Pennsylvania. He married (1) VERONICA ALTER 01 May 1792. She was born 09 Oct 1769, and died 15 Nov 1817. He married (2) SALOME LINE 29 Oct 1822, daughter of JOHN LINE and ANNA LEFEVRE. She was born WFT Est. 1782-1820, and died WFT Est. 1792-1902.

Notes for VERONICA ALTER:
Miss Alter was a sister to the wife of Gov. Ritner.

More About VERONICA ALTER:
Fact 1: Sister to the wife of Governor Ritner

More About LAWRENCE LEFEVRE and VERONICA ALTER:
Marriage: 01 May 1792

More About LAWRENCE LEFEVRE and SALOME LINE:
Marriage: 29 Oct 1822

Children of LAWRENCE LEFEVRE and VERONICA ALTER are:

	i.	MARGARET[10] LEFEVRE, b. 26 Apr 1793; d. 28 Mar 1806.
	ii.	GEORGE LEFEVRE, b. 11 Jul 1794; d. 27 Jul 1794.
71.	iii.	JACOB LEFEVRE, b. 31 May 1795; d. 26 Apr 1875.
	iv.	ELIZABETH LEFEVRE, b. 08 May 1797; d. 22 Mar 1818.
72.	v.	JOHN B. LEFEVRE, b. 11 Mar 1799; d. 13 Sep 1864.
	vi.	ISAAC LEFEVRE, b. 16 Jan 1801; d. 19 Sep 1881; m. ELIZABETH RINE, Jan 1823; b. 22 Nov 1801; d. 27 Mar 1881.

More About ISAAC LEFEVRE and ELIZABETH RINE:
Marriage: Jan 1823

	vii.	FANNY LEFEVRE, b. 29 Nov 1802; d. 14 Feb 1880, Indiana; m. GEORGE WHITMYER, Mar 1820; b. 23 Aug 1797; d. Mar 1880.

More About GEORGE WHITMYER and FANNY LEFEVRE:
Marriage: Mar 1820

	viii.	ESTHER LEFEVRE, b. 22 Oct 1804; d. 12 Mar 1840; m. JOHN HAMM, 14 Mar 1822; b. 05 Aug 1800; d. 03 Apr 1872.

More About JOHN HAMM and ESTHER LEFEVRE:
Marriage: 14 Mar 1822

73.	ix.	DAVID ALTER LEFEVRE, b. 30 Dec 1806; d. 02 May 1885.
	x.	JOSEPH RITNER LEFEVRE, b. 16 Jul 1810; d. 16 Aug 1876; m. ELIZABETH SNYDER, Mar 1830; b. 16 Aug 1813; d. Mar 1874.

More About JOSEPH LEFEVRE and ELIZABETH SNYDER:
Marriage: Mar 1830

Child of LAWRENCE LEFEVRE and SALOME LINE is:

xi.   SALOME ANN[10] LEFEVRE, b. 12 Jun 1824; d. 13 Sep 1908; m. ANTHONY FISHBURN, WFT Est. 1838-1871; b. WFT Est. 1807-1827, Dauphin Co, Pa.; d. WFT Est. 1841-1913.

More About ANTHONY FISHBURN and SALOME LEFEVRE:
Marriage: WFT Est. 1838-1871

37. ISAAC[9] LEFEVRE (*GEORGE[8], PHILIP G[7], ISAAC[6], ABRAHAM[5], ANDREW[4], PHILIP[3], JOHN[2], MENGEN[1]*) was born 11 Feb 1767, and died 1854. He married NANCY MCGAHAN Jun 1807. She was born 17 Apr 1784, and died Aug 1829.

More About ISAAC LEFEVRE and NANCY MCGAHAN:
Marriage: Jun 1807

Children of ISAAC LEFEVRE and NANCY MCGAHAN are:
   i.   GEORGE[10] LEFEVRE, b. 24 Mar 1808.
   ii.   JOSEPH LEFEVRE, b. 02 Nov 1809; d. 25 Jul 1890.
   iii. ELIZABETH LEFEVRE, b. 01 Nov 1811; m. JOHN JOHNSON.
   iv.   ISAAC LEFEVRE, b. Abt. 1813; m. PERMELIA FRENCH; b. Abt. 1820.
   v.   NANCY LEFEVRE, b. 26 Feb 1814; d. 23 Dec 1892; m. ISSAC D. ROSS.
   vi.   DANIEL LEFEVRE, b. Abt. 1820.
   vii. SUSAN FOWKES LEFEVRE, b. 15 Oct 1822; d. 1903; m. GEORGE W MARTIN, 29 Oct 1848.

          More About GEORGE MARTIN and SUSAN LEFEVRE:
          Marriage: 29 Oct 1848

   viii. JESSE LEFEVRE, b. Abt. 1826.
   ix.   MARY PAGE LEFEVRE, b. Abt. 1827; m. (1) ELISHA SHINN; m. (2) DR. JACOB FORTNEY.

38. JACOB[9] LEFEVRE (*GEORGE[8], PHILIP G[7], ISAAC[6], ABRAHAM[5], ANDREW[4], PHILIP[3], JOHN[2], MENGEN[1]*) was born 14 Sep 1771, and died 20 May 1855. He married MARY A. FULWEILER.

Children of JACOB LEFEVRE and MARY FULWEILER are:
   i.   MARY A.[10] LEFEVRE, b. 05 Nov 1798; d. 30 May 1873; m. (1) HAWLEY DAUCHEY; m. (2) DR. ROBERT W. WOOD, 11 Dec 1818.

          More About ROBERT WOOD and MARY LEFEVRE:
          Marriage: 11 Dec 1818

74.   ii.   ELIZABETH LEFEVRE, b. 23 Apr 1801; d. Jun 1852, Oregon Trail.
      iii. SARAH LEFEVRE, b. 13 Feb 1804; d. 01 Apr 1847; m. WILLIAM

POWERS, 06 May 1826.

More About WILLIAM POWERS and SARAH LeFEVRE:
Marriage: 06 May 1826

39. ADAM[9] LeFEVRE *(GEORGE[8], PHILIP G[7], ISAAC[6], ABRAHAM[5], ANDREW[4], PHILIP[3], JOHN[2], MENGEN[1])* was born 30 Dec 1775, and died 22 Aug 1861. He married (1) MARY JANE PORTER 1804. She was born 17 Apr 1788, and died 1822. He married (2) MARY DENNY 25 Mar 1823. She was born 24 Aug 1796, and died Jun 1861.

More About ADAM LeFEVRE and MARY PORTER:
Marriage: 1804

More About ADAM LeFEVRE and MARY DENNY:
Marriage: 25 Mar 1823

Children of ADAM LeFEVRE and MARY PORTER are:
  i.   GEORGE[10] LeFEVRE, b. 06 Jun 1805; d. 02 Jan 1861; m. ANNE E. HERRICK.
  ii. WASHINGTON LeFEVRE, b. 24 Mar 1807; d. 20 Oct 1872.
  iii. ELIZABETH LeFEVRE, b. 07 Aug 1809; d. 28 Jul 1843; m. AMASA WHEELER, Sep 1831; b. 01 Nov 1810; d. 29 Apr 1839.

       Notes for ELIZABETH LeFEVRE:
       Went to Illinios

       More About AMASA WHEELER and ELIZABETH LeFEVRE:
       Marriage: Sep 1831

  iv. SAMUEL LeFEVRE, b. 18 Aug 1811; d. 29 Apr 1839; m. MIRIAM COLE, 18 May 1837; b. 31 Jul 1815.

       More About SAMUEL LeFEVRE and MIRIAM COLE:
       Marriage: 18 May 1837

  v.   JACOB LeFEVRE, b. 09 Nov 1816; d. 13 Mar 1891.
  vi. JOHN PORTER LeFEVRE, b. 21 Nov 1818; d. 03 Feb 1870; m. JUDITH WHITING.
  vii. EVALINE LeFEVRE, b. 18 May 1820; d. 06 Jun 1844; m. CHARLES FRAZIER ADAMS; b. 16 Apr 1816.

Children of ADAM LeFEVRE and MARY DENNY are:
  viii. LEANDER FLEMING[10] LeFEVRE, b. 10 Mar 1824; d. 23 Apr 1890; m. MARY LYDIA DAVID, 04 Jul 1848; b. 25 Aug 1830.

       More About LEANDER LeFEVRE and MARY DAVID:

Marriage: 04 Jul 1848

    ix.   WILLIAM DENNY LEFEVRE, b. 02 Jul 1826; d. 03 Sep 1888; m. DELILAH HARPER, Jun 1854; b. 22 Apr 1835; d. 25 Oct 1905.

More About WILLIAM LEFEVRE and DELILAH HARPER:
Marriage: Jun 1854

    x.   MARY MATILDA LEFEVRE, b. 28 Feb 1829; d. 27 Aug 1890; m. JAMES JOHNSTON, 11 Apr 1854; b. 31 Jan 1827.

More About JAMES JOHNSTON and MARY LEFEVRE:
Marriage: 11 Apr 1854

    xi.   WALTER D. LEFEVRE, b. 07 Apr 1833; d. Jul 1880, Hastings, Nebraska; m. LOUISA MOISER; b. 16 Apr 1836; d. 31 Oct 1865.
    xii.   JOSEPH RITNER LEFEVRE, b. 05 May 1835; d. 12 Jan 1896; m. ELIZABETH MALZENA REED; b. 09 May 1836.

40. PETER[9] LEFEVRE (*GEORGE[8], PHILIP G[7], ISAAC[6], ABRAHAM[5], ANDREW[4], PHILIP[3], JOHN[2], MENGEN[1]*) was born 24 Jul 1778. He married AGNES CURRY.

Children of PETER LEFEVRE and AGNES CURRY are:
    i.   JOHN CURRY[10] LEFEVRE, b. Abt. 1805; m. SIDNEY PARKS.
    ii.   ELIZABETH W. LEFEVRE, b. Abt. 1806; m. ROBERT SPEER.
    iii.   GEORGE W. LEFEVRE, b. 27 Jan 1807; m. MARY HICKEY.
    iv.   SAMUEL SLAYMAKER LEFEVRE, b. 24 Apr 1809; m. MRS. PHELPS.
    v.   DANIEL LINE LEFEVRE, b. 31 Mar 1811; m. MARGARET SPEERS.
    vi.   MARY ANN LEFEVRE, b. 19 Aug 1813; m. JACOB LANE.
    vii.   PETER PERRY LEFEVRE, b. Abt. 1815; m. SARAH LEONARD.
    viii.   WILLIAM ALTER LEFEVRE, b. Abt. 1817; m. MISS WILLS.
    ix.   JOSIAH W. LEFEVRE, b. Abt. 1819; m. ELIZABETH DRAM.
    x.   AGNES J. LEFEVRE, b. Abt. 1821; m. CHRISTOPHER LUTZ.
    xi.   SARAH M. LEFEVRE, b. Abt. 1822; m. ROBERT WILLS.

41. ANNA BARBARA[9] LEFEVRE (*GEORGE[8], PHILIP G[7], ISAAC[6], ABRAHAM[5], ANDREW[4], PHILIP[3], JOHN[2], MENGEN[1]*) was born 18 Sep 1780, and died 22 Aug 1850. She married JOHN A LINE WFT Est. 1777-1820. He was born 29 Jan 1763, and died 08 Jan 1827.

More About JOHN LINE and ANNA LEFEVRE:
Marriage: WFT Est. 1777-1820

Children of ANNA LEFEVRE and JOHN LINE are:
75.   i.   SALOME[10] LINE, b. WFT Est. 1782-1820; d. WFT Est. 1792-1902.
    ii.   MARY ANN COULTER LINE, b. WFT Est. 1782-1820; d. WFT Est.

1792-1902.
        iii. DAVID LINE, b. WFT Est. 1782-1820; d. WFT Est. 1793-1899,
             burned to death in childhood.
76.   iv. GEORGE L. LINE, b. WFT Est. 1786-1818; d. 05 Nov 1885.
         v. CATHERINA LINE, b. 28 Dec 1802; d. 12 Dec 1879; m. JOHN
             TRITT, WFT Est. 1818-1849; b. 18 Jan 1801; d. Sep 1884.

        More About JOHN TRITT and CATHERINA LINE:
        Marriage: WFT Est. 1818-1849

42. SAMUEL[9] LeFEVRE (GEORGE[8], PHILIP G[7], ISAAC[6], ABRAHAM[5], ANDREW[4], PHILIP[3], JOHN[2], MENGEN[1]) was born 22 Jan 1783, and died 01 Apr 1840. He married (1) HANNAH WIEGNER Bef. 1809. She died Bef. 1823. He married (2) MARY ANN CAMP May 1823. She was born Dec 1790, and died 14 Jun 1868.

More About SAMUEL LeFEVRE and HANNAH WIEGNER:
Marriage: Bef. 1809

More About SAMUEL LeFEVRE and MARY CAMP:
Marriage: May 1823

Children of SAMUEL LeFEVRE and HANNAH WIEGNER are:
         i. GEORGE[10] LeFEVRE, b. 15 Sep 1809; m. ELEANOR ADAMS; b. Abt.
             1815.
        ii. ELIZABETH LeFEVRE, b. 23 Sep 1811; m. PARDON KING, 28 Apr
             1830.

            More About PARDON KING and ELIZABETH LeFEVRE:
            Marriage: 28 Apr 1830

       iii. SARAH LeFEVRE, b. 19 Jan 1814; m. THOMAS B. BARNUM, 22 Nov
             1835.

            More About THOMAS BARNUM and SARAH LeFEVRE:
            Marriage: 22 Nov 1835

        iv. JOHN WIEGNER LeFEVRE, b. 15 Jul 1818; m. (1) POLLY CAMP; d.
             22 Jun 1868; m. (2) CHRISTIANA FOREMAN, 27 Feb 1850; b.
             1823.

            More About JOHN LeFEVRE and CHRISTIANA FOREMAN:
            Marriage: 27 Feb 1850

         v. MARY ANN LeFEVRE, b. 15 Aug 1820; d. 29 Nov 1893; m.
             ALEXANDER H. SMITH, 27 Jun 1850.

            More About ALEXANDER SMITH and MARY LeFEVRE:
            Marriage: 27 Jun 1850

Children of SAMUEL LEFEVRE and MARY CAMP are:

  vi. SAMUEL A[10] LEFEVRE, b. 09 Jul 1824; d. 17 Feb 1853; m. PHOEBE ROGERS, 23 Jan 1851.

       More About SAMUEL LEFEVRE and PHOEBE ROGERS:
       Marriage: 23 Jan 1851

 vii. JACOB CAMP LEFEVRE, b. 15 Aug 1826; d. 29 May 1874; m. PAMILA POND.

viii. HANNAH MATILDA LEFEVRE, b. 19 Sep 1828; d. 21 Aug 1865; m. DAVID W. HOPKINS, 14 Oct 1858.

       More About DAVID HOPKINS and HANNAH LEFEVRE:
       Marriage: 14 Oct 1858

  ix. BARBARA LINE LEFEVRE, b. 05 May 1830; m. GEORGE KEPLER, 10 Sep 1848.

       More About GEORGE KEPLER and BARBARA LEFEVRE:
       Marriage: 10 Sep 1848

   x. RHUHANA C. LEFEVRE, b. 03 Jan 1835; m. LORENZO SMITH, 24 Dec 1863.

       More About LORENZO SMITH and RHUHANA LEFEVRE:
       Marriage: 24 Dec 1863

43. JOHN L.[9] LEFEVRE (*GEORGE*[8], *PHILIP G*[7], *ISAAC*[6], *ABRAHAM*[5], *ANDREW*[4], *PHILIP*[3], *JOHN*[2], *MENGEN*[1]) was born 17 Jan 1786, and died 24 Mar 1849. He married ELIZABETH LINE 18 Mar 1807. She was born 14 Oct 1788, and died 15 Apr 1866.

More About JOHN LEFEVRE and ELIZABETH LINE:
Marriage: 18 Mar 1807

Children of JOHN LEFEVRE and ELIZABETH LINE are:

   i. ABRAHAM[10] LEFEVRE, b. 04 Jan 1808; d. 27 May 1858; m. (1) MARGARET CEASE, 1833; d. May 1834; m. (2) REBECCA HUBER, 1835; b. 1818; d. 1898.

       Notes for ABRAHAM LEFEVRE:
       Abraham died as result of being mangled by a neighbor's bull

       More About ABRAHAM LEFEVRE and MARGARET CEASE:
       Marriage: 1833

More About ABRAHAM LEFEVRE and REBECCA HUBER:
Marriage: 1835

    ii. ANNE BARBARA LEFEVRE, b. 11 Dec 1809; d. 25 Dec 1884; m. DAVID HARPER, 19 May 1831.

More About DAVID HARPER and ANNE LEFEVRE:
Marriage: 19 May 1831

    iii. GEORGE LINE LEFEVRE, b. 09 Nov 1820; d. 30 Jul 1879; m. PRISCILLA SMITH, 21 Jan 1847.

More About GEORGE LEFEVRE and PRISCILLA SMITH:
Marriage: 21 Jan 1847

44. COLONEL DANIEL[9] LEFEVRE (*GEORGE[8], PHILIP G[7], ISAAC[6], ABRAHAM[5], ANDREW[4], PHILIP[3], JOHN[2], MENGEN[1]*) was born 23 Nov 1788, and died 13 Jan 1855. He married HENRIETTA LOUISA VON COLSON Dec 1818 in Meadville, Pennsylvania. She was born 27 Jun 1802 in Hamburg, Germany, and died Jul 1892 in Jamestown, New York.

Notes for COLONEL DANIEL LEFEVRE:
Daniel LeFevre born 1788, youngest son of the above George, was a Colonel in the War of 1812

More About COLONEL DANIEL LEFEVRE:
Fact 1: 1812, Colonel in War of 1812

More About DANIEL LEFEVRE and HENRIETTA VON COLSON:
Marriage: Dec 1818, Meadville, Pennsylvania

Child of DANIEL LEFEVRE and HENRIETTA VON COLSON is:
    i. CAROLINE E[10] LEFEVRE, b. 24 Mar 1822; d. Nov 1900; m. NATHAN BROWN.

45. MARY[9] LEFEVRE (*ADAM[8], PHILIP G[7], ISAAC[6], ABRAHAM[5], ANDREW[4], PHILIP[3], JOHN[2], MENGEN[1]*) was born 16 Oct 1769, and died 20 Aug 1825. She married DR. PETER LEFEVRE, son of PETER LEFEVRE and CATHERINE LEFEVRE. He was born 06 May 1774, and died Jul 1844.

More About DR. PETER LEFEVRE:
Fact 1: Buried in LeFevre cemetery

Children are listed above under (33) Peter LeFevre.

46. HENRY B[9] LEFEVRE (*ADAM[8], PHILIP G[7], ISAAC[6], ABRAHAM[5], ANDREW[4],

PHILIP³, JOHN², MENGEN¹) was born 11 Apr 1772, and died 26 Sep 1844. He married (1) ELIZABETH HESS 04 Aug 1822. She was born 29 Aug 1792, and died 04 Sep 1826. He married (2) ELIZABETH SMELTZ GALL 1830. She was born 25 Sep 1787, and died 03 Sep 1875.

More About HENRY LeFEVRE and ELIZABETH HESS:
Marriage: 04 Aug 1822

More About HENRY LeFEVRE and ELIZABETH GALL:
Marriage: 1830

Children of HENRY LeFEVRE and ELIZABETH HESS are:

    i.   CHRISTIAN¹⁰ LeFEVRE, b. 24 Nov 1823; d. 29 Jul 1903; m. ANNE HOUSER; b. 11 May 1833; d. 05 Jul 1920.

        Notes for CHRISTIAN LeFEVRE:
        Christian served as director of both the Farmers' Bank and the Lancaster County National Bank, Lancaster, Pa.

   ii.   ADAM LeFEVRE, b. 11 May 1825; d. 02 Feb 1889; m. CATHERINE KENDIG, Nov 1850; b. 08 Oct 1830; d. 08 Sep 1902.

        Notes for ADAM LeFEVRE:
        Adam served on the board of directors of the Lan. Co. Natl. Bk.

        More About ADAM LeFEVRE and CATHERINE KENDIG:
        Marriage: Nov 1850

47. JACOB⁹ LeFEVRE (*ADAM⁸, PHILIP G⁷, ISAAC⁶, ABRAHAM⁵, ANDREW⁴, PHILIP³, JOHN², MENGEN¹)* was born 24 Jul 1773, and died 06 Jul 1826. He married CATHERINE MEEK 09 Mar 1802. She was born 22 Nov 1780, and died May 1857.

More About JACOB LeFEVRE and CATHERINE MEEK:
Marriage: 09 Mar 1802

Children of JACOB LeFEVRE and CATHERINE MEEK are:

    i.   GEORGE¹⁰ LeFEVRE, b. 17 Jan 1803; d. Dec 1887, Brick Church Cemetery; m. CHRISTIANA FORRER, Aug 1825; b. 21 Apr 1805; d. May 1886.

        More About GEORGE LeFEVRE and CHRISTIANA FORRER:
        Marriage: Aug 1825

   ii.   JACOB LeFEVRE, b. 29 Oct 1805; d. 09 May 1880, Oreville, OH; m. ANNE FORRER, 20 May 1830; b. 06 Nov 1810; d. 08 Oct 1888.

        Notes for JACOB LeFEVRE:

Moved west in 1833 by stage coach

More About JACOB LEFEVRE and ANNE FORRER:
Marriage: 20 May 1830

   iii. ELIZABETH LEFEVRE, b. 22 Sep 1807; d. 28 Oct 1853; m. DANIEL
         LEFEVRE, 1830; b. 13 Aug 1805; d. 15 Jul 1880, Drumore, PA.

More About DANIEL LEFEVRE and ELIZABETH LEFEVRE:
Marriage: 1830

   iv.   PHILIP LEFEVRE, b. 14 Aug 1810; d. 22 Jun 1882, Mylin's
         Cemetery; m. (1) CATHERINE LEFEVRE, 09 May 1833; b. 21 Oct
         1805; d. Dec 1841; m. (2) MARY LEFEVRE, 14 May 1843; b. 22
         Sep 1811; d. 26 Nov 1853.

More About PHILIP LEFEVRE and CATHERINE LEFEVRE:
Marriage: 09 May 1833

More About PHILIP LEFEVRE and MARY LEFEVRE:
Marriage: 14 May 1843

    v.   CATHERINE LEFEVRE, b. 19 Nov 1813; d. 15 Dec 1884.
   vi.   SAMUEL LEFEVRE, b. 18 Mar 1817; d. 02 Nov 1901.
  vii.   LYDIA LEFEVRE, b. 23 Dec 1819; d. 06 Feb 1897, Longeneckers
         Cemetery; m. JOHN HOUSER, 05 Oct 1843; b. 23 Oct 1808; d. 26
         May 1882.

More About JOHN HOUSER and LYDIA LEFEVRE:
Marriage: 05 Oct 1843

48. JOHN[9] LEFEVRE (ADAM[8], PHILIP G[7], ISAAC[6], ABRAHAM[5], ANDREW[4], PHILIP[3],
JOHN[2], MENGEN[1]) was born 13 Dec 1776, and died 13 Oct 1851. He married
ELIZABETH KEEPORTS 31 Mar 1804, daughter of DANIEL KEEPORTS and
CATHERINE LEFEVRE. She was born 03 Jan 1784, and died 25 Sep 1864.

More About JOHN LEFEVRE and ELIZABETH KEEPORTS:
Marriage: 31 Mar 1804

Children of JOHN LEFEVRE and ELIZABETH KEEPORTS are:
    i.   DANIEL[10] LEFEVRE, b. 13 Aug 1805; d. 15 Jul 1880, Drumore,
         PA; m. (1) ELIZABETH LEFEVRE, 1830; b. 22 Sep 1807; d. 28 Oct
         1853; m. (2) SUSAN E SWEINHART, 30 May 1854; b. 03 Oct 1831.

More About DANIEL LEFEVRE and ELIZABETH LEFEVRE:
Marriage: 1830

More About DANIEL LEFEVRE and SUSAN SWEINHART:

Marriage: 30 May 1854

- ii. CATHERINE LEFEVRE, b. 21 Dec 1807; d. 27 Dec 1807.
- iii. JOHN LEFEVRE, b. 17 Feb 1809; d. 12 Apr 1815.
- iv. CHRISTIAN LEFEVRE, b. 20 Aug 1811; d. 03 Jul 1894; m. SUSAN GROFF, 13 Feb 1834; b. 24 Feb 1809; d. 16 Mar 1891.

More About CHRISTIAN LEFEVRE and SUSAN GROFF:
Marriage: 13 Feb 1834

- v. BARABARA LEFEVRE, b. 30 Nov 1813; d. 05 Apr 1815.
- vi. MARY LEFEVRE, b. 31 Mar 1816; d. 27 Nov 1851.
- vii. ELIZABETH LEFEVRE, b. 25 May 1819; m. (1) BENJAMIN GROFF; m. (2) DR. R B MCALLISTER.

Notes for DR. R B MCALLISTER:
Indiana

- viii. CATHERINE LEFEVRE, b. 16 Jun 1822; d. 15 May 1861, Mt Hope Church; m. JOHN STANTON; b. 22 Jul 1818; d. 26 Mar 1888.
- ix. SAMUEL LEFEVRE, b. 15 Nov 1825; d. 15 Nov 1825.

Notes for SAMUEL LEFEVRE:
lived 11 hours

- x. BENJAMIN LEFEVRE, b. 03 Aug 1827; d. 06 May 1914; m. SUSAN BRUBAKER, 12 Jul 1855; b. 09 Jul 1835; d. Mar 1922.

More About BENJAMIN LEFEVRE and SUSAN BRUBAKER:
Marriage: 12 Jul 1855

49. PHILIP[9] LEFEVRE *(ADAM[8], PHILIP G[7], ISAAC[6], ABRAHAM[5], ANDREW[4], PHILIP[3], JOHN[2], MENGEN[1])* was born 06 Apr 1778, and died 1813. He married ELIZABETH CLACK.

Children of PHILIP LEFEVRE and ELIZABETH CLACK are:
- i. DANIEL[10] LEFEVRE, b. 25 Apr 1803; d. 08 Mar 1889; m. MARTHA SHANK; b. 27 Jun 1810; d. 03 Nov 1896.

Notes for DANIEL LEFEVRE:
He was in the tannery business at Chatham, Chester Co, PA. As there was another Daniel LeFevre (-9-036) who was in the tannery business at Paradise, PA this Daniel was known as "Chatam Tanner Dan."

- ii. HESTER LEFEVRE, b. Abt. 1805; m. DANIEL RANKIN.

Notes for HESTER LEFEVRE:

Went West

   iii.   GEORGE W LEFEVRE, b. 1807; d. 26 May 1872.

        Notes for GEORGE W LEFEVRE:
        Was an extensive Drover for many years and lived at Chatham,
        Chester Co, PA

   iv.   SAMUEL LEFEVRE, b. 1810; m. ADALINE BRADEN.

        Notes for SAMUEL LEFEVRE:
        Went to Iowa

   v.   PHILIP LEFEVRE, b. 1814.

50. ADAM[9] LEFEVRE (ADAM[8], PHILIP G[7], ISAAC[6], ABRAHAM[5], ANDREW[4], PHILIP[3], JOHN[2], MENGEN[1]) was born 21 Feb 1779, and died 26 Mar 1847. He married CATHERINE ERB. She was born 27 May 1781, and died 27 Aug 1853.

Notes for ADAM LEFEVRE:
Founder of the Manor Township (Lanc. Co., Pa.) LeFevres.

Children of ADAM LEFEVRE and CATHERINE ERB are:
   i.   MESHACH[10] LEFEVRE, b. 16 Apr 1804; d. 18 Sep 1874; m. CHRISTIANA RIPLEY, Mar 1829; b. 03 Oct 1800; d. Oct 1875.

        More About MESHACH LEFEVRE and CHRISTIANA RIPLEY:
        Marriage: Mar 1829

   ii.   CATHERINE LEFEVRE, b. 21 Oct 1805; d. Dec 1841; m. PHILIP LEFEVRE, 09 May 1833; b. 14 Aug 1810; d. 22 Jun 1882, Mylin's Cemetery.

        More About PHILIP LEFEVRE and CATHERINE LEFEVRE:
        Marriage: 09 May 1833

   iii.   ELIZABETH LEFEVRE, b. 09 Jan 1808; d. 09 Dec 1808.
   iv.   JOHN ERB LEFEVRE, b. 29 Sep 1809; d. 19 Sep 1887; m. ELIZABETH MARTIN; b. 03 Aug 1806; d. 02 Feb 1875.
   v.   MARY LEFEVRE, b. 22 Sep 1811; d. 26 Nov 1853; m. (1) JOHN RUCH, 1835; b. WFT Est. 1806-1834, Lancaster Co., Pennsylvania; d. WFT Est. 1859-1921, Warren Co., Ohio; m. (2) PHILIP LEFEVRE, 14 May 1843; b. 14 Aug 1810; d. 22 Jun 1882, Mylin's Cemetery.

        More About JOHN RUCH and MARY LEFEVRE:
        Marriage: 1835

More About PHILIP LEFEVRE and MARY LEFEVRE:
Marriage: 14 May 1843

vi.   HENRY LEFEVRE, b. 23 Jan 1814; d. 22 Feb 1864; m. RACHEL
      HESS, 20 Sep 1838; b. 05 Dec 1819; d. 1905.

More About HENRY LEFEVRE and RACHEL HESS:
Marriage: 20 Sep 1838

vii. ADAM LEFEVRE, b. 15 Jan 1816; d. 06 Jul 1888; m. ELIZABETH
      SCHENK; b. 31 Oct 1818; d. 21 Feb 1893.
viii. RUDOLPH LEFEVRE, b. 13 Dec 1818; d. 06 May 1885.
ix.   ESTHER LEFEVRE, b. 08 Mar 1820; d. 09 Dec 1897; m. JACOB
      GAUL, 10 Nov 1839; b. 21 Jun 1813; d. 07 May 1905.

More About JACOB GAUL and ESTHER LEFEVRE:
Marriage: 10 Nov 1839

x.   RACHEL LEFEVRE, b. 25 Dec 1822; d. 09 Jun 1860; m. (1)
      SAMUEL HARMON; m. (2) JOHN NAYLOR; b. 1810; d. 26 Feb 1885.
xi.   EDMUND LEFEVRE, b. 27 Feb 1825; d. 04 Jan 1900, Sterling, IL;
      m. MARY WATSON, 01 Mar 1853; b. 31 Oct 1833; d. 15 Dec
      1904.

More About EDMUND LEFEVRE and MARY WATSON:
Marriage: 01 Mar 1853

51. PETER[9] LEFEVRE *(ADAM[8], PHILIP G[7], ISAAC[6], ABRAHAM[5], ANDREW[4], PHILIP[3], JOHN[2], MENGEN[1])* was born 08 May 1780 in Lancaster Co, PA, and died 22 Jul 1830 in York Co, PA. He married MARIA BARBARA LEFEVRE Feb 1812, daughter of JACOB LEFEVRE and CATHERINE PETERMAN. She was born 15 Oct 1789 in Windsor Twp, York County, PA, and died 06 Jun 1878 in Newberry Twp, York Co, PA.

Notes for PETER LEFEVRE:
Mr. LeFevre went to York County, Pa., with his uncle, Jacob LeFevre (8-010) of 1753, and bought a farm near York, Pa. In 1820 he bought a farm in northern York county near Goldsboro, Pa., to which he moved. On July 22, 1830, while harvesting, there was a thunder-gust, and he took shelter under a large tree and was killed by lightning that struck the tree.

The 1830 census for Peter Lefeber lists 1 male under 20, 1 male under 30, 1 female under 15 and 1 female under 40. It appears this census was taken after his death.

Notes for MARIA BARBARA LEFEVRE:
Listed in the 1850 census aged 60 in Newberry Twp with son Daniel - 19.

Lafever, Barbara   View Image Online
  State: Pennsylvania Year: 1850
  County: York Roll: M432_840
  Township: Newberry Twp Page: 366
  Image: 506

More About PETER LeFEVRE and MARIA LEFEVRE:
Marriage: Feb 1812

Children of PETER LeFEVRE and MARIA LEFEVRE are:

77.   i.   SAMUEL[10] LEFEVRE, b. 26 Feb 1812, York County, PA; d. 07 Jul
              1899.
        ii.   ELIZABETH LEFEVRE, b. 1813, York County, PA; d. 02 Feb 1887,
              Parkville, York Co, PA; m. JOHN FELTY.
       iii.   JACOB LEFEVRE, b. 12 Nov 1815, York, PA; d. 07 Aug 1881,
              Gettysburg, PA; m. (1) NANCY ARNOLD, 23 Dec 1847; b. 01 Mar
              1823; d. 01 Jul 1853; m. (2) MARGARET WOLF, 01 Jan 1854; b.
              16 Mar 1832; d. Apr 1913.

              More About JACOB LEFEVRE and NANCY ARNOLD:
              Marriage: 23 Dec 1847

              More About JACOB LEFEVRE and MARGARET WOLF:
              Marriage: 01 Jan 1854

        iv.   MARY LEFEVRE, b. 09 Apr 1817; d. 14 Nov 1894, Dover, PA; m.
              ELIJAH GLATFELTER, Abt. 1839.

              More About ELIJAH GLATFELTER and MARY LEFEVRE:
              Marriage: Abt. 1839

78.   v.   LYDIA LeFEVRE, b. 09 Mar 1818, York County, Pennsylvania; d.
              02 Sep 1852, Highspire, PA.
        vi.   PETER LEFEVRE, b. 16 Feb 1819, York County, PA; d. 01 Jan
              1871, Newberry Twp, York Co, PA.
       vii.   JOHN LEFEVRE, b. 14 Feb 1822, Goldsboro, York, PA; d. 13 Jan
              1844, Newberry Twp, York Co, PA.
      viii.   GEORGE LEFEVRE, b. 09 Apr 1824, Goldsboro, York, PA; d. 04
              Aug 1898, York County, PA; m. ELIZA SULTZABERGER, Mar 1853;
              b. 02 Oct 1831; d. May 1914.

              More About GEORGE LEFEVRE and ELIZA SULTZABERGER:
              Marriage: Mar 1853

        ix.   LEAH LEFEVRE, b. 28 May 1828, York, PA; d. 17 Jun 1920, St
              Johns Lutheran, Lewisberry, York Co, PA; m. SAMUEL Z
              GRISSINGER.

x.   DANIEL LEFEVRE, b. 14 May 1830; d. 15 Nov 1860, Newberry Twp, York Co, PA.

52. DANIEL[9] LEFEVRE (*ADAM[8], PHILIP G[7], ISAAC[6], ABRAHAM[5], ANDREW[4], PHILIP[3], JOHN[2], MENGEN[1]*) was born 03 Feb 1783, and died Feb 1852. He married ESTHER WITMER, daughter of DAVID WITMER and ESTHER KENDIG. She was born 02 Sep 1785, and died 30 Aug 1854.

More About DANIEL LEFEVRE:
Note: Called "Paradise Tanner Dan" to distinquish him from another Daniel Lefevre that was a Tanner in Paradise, Pennsylvania

Children of DANIEL LEFEVRE and ESTHER WITMER are:

　　　i.   DAVID W[10] LEFEVRE, b. 09 Jan 1809; d. 25 Mar 1892; m. CATHERINE KOCH; b. 20 Oct 1821; d. 15 Jun 1901.
　　　ii.   ELIZABETH LEFEVRE, b. 21 Jan 1811; d. 13 Aug 1878; m. JOHN KREIDER, 06 Nov 1834; b. 23 May 1799; d. 17 Jan 1861.

　　　　　More About JOHN KREIDER and ELIZABETH LEFEVRE:
　　　　　Marriage: 06 Nov 1834

　　　iii.   ANNE LEFEVRE, b. 25 Dec 1813; d. 28 May 1888; m. JOHNATHAN WEAVER; b. 23 Feb 1803; d. 14 Oct 1849.
79.　iv.   HENRY W LEFEVRE, b. 12 May 1818; d. 02 Apr 1892.
　　　v.   DANIEL LEFEVRE, b. 16 Apr 1821; d. 17 May 1890; m. MARY GRYDER, 30 Apr 1861; b. 31 Mar 1832; d. Feb 1906.

　　　　　More About DANIEL LEFEVRE:
　　　　　Burial: Paradise Cemetery, Paradise Township, Lancaster County, Pennsylvania

　　　　　More About DANIEL LEFEVRE and MARY GRYDER:
　　　　　Marriage: 30 Apr 1861

　　　vi.   JACOB B LEFEVRE, b. 1823; d. 14 Feb 1860.
　　　vii.   HIRAM LEFEVRE, b. Dec 1825; d. 1853; m. SUSAN BRUA; b. Sep 1830; d. 1898.
　　　viii.   EMMA JANE LEFEVRE, b. 30 Sep 1833; d. 18 Mar 1904; m. MARIS KERNS, 10 Feb 1854; b. 17 Mar 1831; d. 18 Sep 1884.

　　　　　More About MARIS KERNS and EMMA LEFEVRE:
　　　　　Marriage: 10 Feb 1854

　　　ix.   EMMA JANE LEFEVRE, b. 20 Sep 1833, Lancaster County, Pennsylvania; d. 18 Mar 1904, Lancaster County, Pennsylvania.

53. JOHN[9] LEFEVRE (*JACOB[8], PHILIP G[7], ISAAC[6], ABRAHAM[5], ANDREW[4], PHILIP[3],*

JOHN², MENGEN¹) was born 29 Nov 1783, and died 26 Jan 1866. He married CATHERINE HAMMER 15 Feb 1807 in York County, PA. She was born 01 Dec 1784.

More About JOHN LEFEVRE and CATHERINE HAMMER:
Marriage: 15 Feb 1807, York County, PA

Children of JOHN LEFEVRE and CATHERINE HAMMER are:

    i.   JACOB L¹⁰ LEFEVRE, b. 13 Dec 1815; d. 08 May 1896; m. MARY ANN KUHN, 30 May 1839; b. Aug 1818; d. Dec 1903.

       More About JACOB LEFEVRE and MARY KUHN:
       Marriage: 30 May 1839

    ii. GEORGE LEFEVRE, b. 25 Nov 1817; d. 24 Feb 1893, Hagerstown, MD; m. MARY STRICKLER, Dec 1839; b. 02 Feb 1820; d. 06 Aug 1889.

       More About GEORGE LEFEVRE and MARY STRICKLER:
       Marriage: Dec 1839

    iii. JOHN LEFEVRE, b. 17 Nov 1819; d. 18 Apr 1891; m. CATHERINE REINHART, 1842; b. 28 Jun 1822; d. 22 Sep 1890.

       More About JOHN LEFEVRE and CATHERINE REINHART:
       Marriage: 1842

    iv. LYDIA LEFEVRE, b. Abt. 1820; m. JOHN WITMER.
    v. WILLIAM HENRY LEFEVRE, b. 20 Jul 1827; d. 24 Jan 1898, Mt Zion Cemetery York Co, PA; m. SUSANNA IRVIN; b. 30 Oct 1818; d. 02 Nov 1883, Mt Zion Cemetery York Co, PA.
    vi. RACHEL LEFEVRE, b. Mar 1829; d. 30 Nov 1903; m. JOHN STARK, 1846.

       More About JOHN STARK and RACHEL LEFEVRE:
       Marriage: 1846

    vii. JESSE LEFEVRE, b. 1832; d. 15 Jan 1900; m. JULIA WAMBAUGH.
    viii. DANIEL LEFEVRE, b. Abt. 1833.

54. JACOB⁹ LEFEVRE (*JACOB⁸, PHILIP G⁷, ISAAC⁶, ABRAHAM⁵, ANDREW⁴, PHILIP³, JOHN², MENGEN¹)* was born 14 Feb 1785 in York County, PA, and died 21 Nov 1833. He married MARY JACKSON 01 May 1804. She was born 24 Dec 1784, and died 06 Jun 1883.

Notes for JACOB LEFEVRE:
He was raised from childhood and lived with his uncle, Major Baltzell, in Western Maryland, until his marriage.

Notes for MARY JACKSON:
In 1839 (after her husband's death), Mary (& children) Elias, Henry J., Amasa H., Jacob and Nimrod D. moved from near Cincinnati up to Port Jefferson, Shelby County, Ohio, and are buried in Glen Cemetery near Sidney, Ohio.

More About JACOB LEFEVRE and MARY JACKSON:
Marriage: 01 May 1804

Children of JACOB LEFEVRE and MARY JACKSON are:
- i. AMELIA[10] LEFEVRE, b. Mar 1805; d. 1805.
- ii. MARY LEFEVRE, b. 26 Mar 1806; d. 07 Dec 1865; m. JAMES BAXTER, 06 Jul 1829; d. 06 Dec 1885.

  More About JAMES BAXTER and MARY LEFEVRE:
  Marriage: 06 Jul 1829

- iii. MATILDA LEFEVRE, b. 24 Feb 1808; d. 19 Sep 1871; m. JOSEPHUS DODDS, Oct 1825; b. 24 Jan 1804; d. 21 May 1887.

  More About JOSEPHUS DODDS and MATILDA LEFEVRE:
  Marriage: Oct 1825

- iv. ELIAS LEFEVRE, b. 10 Dec 1809; d. Aug 1882; m. HENRIETTA INGERSOL, Nov 1832; b. 04 Feb 1811; d. Jun 1892.

  More About ELIAS LEFEVRE and HENRIETTA INGERSOL:
  Marriage: Nov 1832

- v. CATHERINE LEFEVRE, b. 13 Apr 1811; m. GILBERT BARTON, 13 Nov 1832.

  More About GILBERT BARTON and CATHERINE LEFEVRE:
  Marriage: 13 Nov 1832

- vi. HENRY J LEFEVRE, b. 06 Mar 1813; d. 18 Sep 1846; m. ELEANOR MORGAN, Sep 1837; b. 25 Dec 1821; d. 20 Feb 1895.

  More About HENRY LEFEVRE and ELEANOR MORGAN:
  Marriage: Sep 1837

- 80. vii. REBECCA LEFEVRE, b. Feb 1815; d. Terre Haute, IN.
- viii. AMASA LEFEVRE, b. 22 Dec 1817; d. 02 Oct 1894; m. NIMROD DUVALL; b. 1815; d. 10 Oct 1876.
- ix. SARAH LEFEVRE, b. 30 Nov 1819; m. MILTON COULSON, 10 Oct 1844; b. 08 May 1806.

  Notes for MILTON COULSON:

Descendent of William Penn

More About MILTON COULSON and SARAH LEFEVRE:
Marriage: 10 Oct 1844

  x.   JACOB LEFEVRE, b. 25 Apr 1823; d. 30 Oct 1871; m. ELIZABETH
    BELCH; b. 04 Mar 1824; d. 08 Mar 1888.
  xi.   NIMROD D LEFEVRE, b. 11 Nov 1825; d. 21 May 1889; m.
    REBECCA TOBIAS, Mar 1855; b. 22 Sep 1838; d. 02 Oct 1914.

More About NIMROD LEFEVRE and REBECCA TOBIAS:
Marriage: Mar 1855

55. MARIA BARBARA[9] LEFEVRE (*JACOB*[8], *PHILIP G*[7], *ISAAC*[6], *ABRAHAM*[5], *ANDREW*[4], *PHILIP*[3], *JOHN*[2], *MENGEN*[1]) was born 15 Oct 1789 in Windsor Twp, York County, PA, and died 06 Jun 1878 in Newberry Twp, York Co, PA. She married PETER LEFEVRE Feb 1812, son of ADAM LEFEVRE and ELIZABETH PAULES. He was born 08 May 1780 in Lancaster Co, PA, and died 22 Jul 1830 in York Co, PA.

Notes for MARIA BARBARA LEFEVRE:
Listed in the 1850 census aged 60 in Newberry Twp with son Daniel - 19.

Lafever, Barbara View Image Online
  State: Pennsylvania Year: 1850
  County: York Roll: M432_840
  Township: Newberry Twp Page: 366
  Image: 506

Notes for PETER LEFEVRE:
Mr. LeFevre went to York County, Pa., with his uncle, Jacob LeFevre (8-010) of 1753, and bought a farm near York, Pa. In 1820 he bought a farm in northern York county near Goldsboro, Pa., to which he moved. On July 22, 1830, while harvesting, there was a thunder-gust, and he took shelter under a large tree and was killed by lightning that struck the tree.

The 1830 census for Peter Lefeber lists 1 male under 20, 1 male under 30, 1 female under 15 and 1 female under 40. It appears this census was taken after his death.

More About PETER LEFEVRE and MARIA LEFEVRE:
Marriage: Feb 1812

Children are listed above under (51) Peter LeFevre.

56. DANIEL[9] LEFEVRE (*CHRISTIAN*[8], *DANIEL*[7], *ISAAC*[6], *ABRAHAM*[5], *ANDREW*[4],

PHILIP[3], JOHN[2], MENGEN[1]) was born 27 Apr 1771, and died 06 Aug 1856. He married ANNE MARGARET SULSER. She was born 1773, and died 26 Dec 1859.

Children of DANIEL LEFEVRE and ANNE SULSER are:

     i.   ANNE[10] LEFEVRE, b. 01 Jan 1797; d. 16 Dec 1863, Hopewell, NY; m. JOSEPH THATCHER.
    ii.   CHRISTIAN LEFEVRE, b. 21 May 1798; d. 10 Jun 1889, Michigan; m. GRATA KNAPP, 31 Mar 1839; d. 10 Jun 1885.

> More About CHRISTIAN LEFEVRE and GRATA KNAPP:
> Marriage: 31 Mar 1839

    iii.   GEORGE LEFEVRE, b. 1800, Maryland.
    iv.   SARAH LEFEVRE, b. 1802, New York; d. 1838, Michigan; m. MICHAEL BOWERMAN.
    v.   CATHERINE LEFEVRE, b. 1803; m. SAMUEL COUGH.
    vi.   DAVID LEFEVRE, b. 31 Mar 1806; d. 13 Aug 1838, Ontario Co, NY; m. GRATA KNAPP, 22 Dec 1827; d. 10 Jun 1885.

> More About DAVID LEFEVRE and GRATA KNAPP:
> Marriage: 22 Dec 1827

    vii.   MARGARET LEFEVRE, b. 1807; m. HENRY STEPHENS.
    viii.   JOSEPH LEFEVRE, b. 1809; d. 10 Jun 1849.
    ix.   ELIZABETH LEFEVRE, b. 1814; d. 25 Dec 1860; m. AARON CORNELL.
    x.   DANIEL LEFEVRE, b. 29 Apr 1818; d. 24 Aug 1908, Jonesville, MI; m. CHRISTINA DERR, Jul 1848; b. 26 Jun 1830; d. 28 Feb 1905.

> More About DANIEL LEFEVRE and CHRISTINA DERR:
> Marriage: Jul 1848

57. GEORGE[9] LEFEVRE (CHRISTIAN[8], DANIEL[7], ISAAC[6], ABRAHAM[5], ANDREW[4], PHILIP[3], JOHN[2], MENGEN[1]) was born 14 Oct 1773, and died 24 Dec 1850.

Child of GEORGE LEFEVRE is:

     i.   DAVID[10] LEFEVRE, b. 25 Aug 1806; d. Bef. 1870; m. MARY ANN McKEE; b. 1815; d. 07 Apr 1907.

58. CHRISTIAN[9] LEFEVRE (CHRISTIAN[8], DANIEL[7], ISAAC[6], ABRAHAM[5], ANDREW[4], PHILIP[3], JOHN[2], MENGEN[1]) was born 07 Jun 1786, and died Feb 1871. He married JELY MELOY 17 Mar 1808. She was born 17 May 1789, and died Aug 1871.

Notes for CHRISTIAN LeFEVRE:
He was six feet tall and well muscled, had deep set gray eyes and thick, bristling hair. His bearing was very military, and he was a commissioned officer in the War of 1812. He lived this life as a part of the life to come. Eternity was only the morrow of today with him. His Bible was his dearest companion.

More About CHRISTIAN LeFEVRE:
Fact 1: Officer in War of 1812

More About CHRISTIAN LeFEVRE and JELY MELOY:
Marriage: 17 Mar 1808

Children of CHRISTIAN LeFEVRE and JELY MELOY are:
     i.   SARAH[10] LeFEVRE, b. 15 Mar 1809; d. 02 Oct 1866; m. FIELDING DYE, 13 Dec 1827.

        More About FIELDING DYE and SARAH LeFEVRE:
        Marriage: 13 Dec 1827

    ii.   JOHN LeFEVRE, b. 12 Oct 1810; d. 25 Apr 1900; m. ELIZABETH STATLER, 18 Oct 1832.

        More About JOHN LeFEVRE and ELIZABETH STATLER:
        Marriage: 18 Oct 1832

   iii.   ELIZABETH LeFEVRE, b. 20 Jan 1812; d. 28 Mar 1853; m. JACOB FRENCH, 14 Oct 1831.

        More About JACOB FRENCH and ELIZABETH LeFEVRE:
        Marriage: 14 Oct 1831

    iv.   WILLIAM C MINOR LeFEVRE, b. 11 Jan 1814; d. 27 Dec 1869; m. MARTHA JEWETT, 09 Jun 1840; d. 1863.

        More About WILLIAM LeFEVRE and MARTHA JEWETT:
        Marriage: 09 Jun 1840

     v.   NAOMI LeFEVRE, b. 29 Apr 1815; d. 13 May 1851; m. GEORGE B REED, 26 Oct 1843.

        More About GEORGE REED and NAOMI LeFEVRE:
        Marriage: 26 Oct 1843

    vi.   AMY H LeFEVRE, b. 01 Mar 1817; d. 01 Mar 1845; m. HENRY IDDINGS, 23 Mar 1843.

        More About HENRY IDDINGS and AMY LeFEVRE:
        Marriage: 23 Mar 1843

vii. REZON LeFEVRE, b. 06 Aug 1818; d. 09 Mar 1839.
viii. JAMES V LeFEVRE, b. 24 Apr 1820; d. 27 Jun 1875; m. MALISSA TULLIS, 18 Nov 1841.

More About JAMES LeFEVRE and MALISSA TULLIS:
Marriage: 18 Nov 1841

81. ix. DR. ALFRED LeFEVRE, b. 23 Apr 1822; d. 02 Jul 1897.
x. CYRUS H LeFEVRE, b. 23 Oct 1824; d. 28 Oct 1894; m. (1) CAROLINE BABB; b. 18 Nov 1828; d. Jan 1875; m. (2) MINERVA BABB, Feb 1886; b. 18 Sep 1840; d. 13 Jun 1904.

More About CYRUS LeFEVRE and MINERVA BABB:
Marriage: Feb 1886

xi. CHRISTIAN LeFEVRE, b. 12 Oct 1826; d. 31 Jul 1886; m. NANCY CECIL, 13 Oct 1853; b. 30 May 1833; d. 20 May 1924.

More About CHRISTIAN LeFEVRE and NANCY CECIL:
Marriage: 13 Oct 1853

xii. SOLOMON LeFEVRE, b. 23 Aug 1828; d. 29 Nov 1841.
xiii. MARY LeFEVRE, b. 12 Jul 1830; d. 06 Dec 1854; m. (1) HENRY TENEYCKE, Dec 1848; d. Bef. Nov 1854; m. (2) E CORY SAYLOR, Nov 1854.

More About HENRY TENEYCKE and MARY LeFEVRE:
Marriage: Dec 1848

More About E SAYLOR and MARY LeFEVRE:
Marriage: Nov 1854

59. LYDIA[9] FERREE *(MARY[8] LeFEVRE, DANIEL[7], ISAAC[6], ABRAHAM[5], ANDREW[4], PHILIP[3], JOHN[2], MENGEN[1])* was born 11 Oct 1766, and died 11 Jul 1802. She married CONGRESSMAN JOSEPH LeFEVRE 20 Sep 1796, son of SAMUEL LeFEVRE and LYDIA FERREE. He was born 03 Apr 1760, and died 17 Oct 1826.

Notes for CONGRESSMAN JOSEPH LeFEVRE:
Hon. Joseph LeFevre born 1760, of near Paradise, Pa., was a member of Congress from 1811 to 1813.

Joseph, b Apr. 3, 1760, d Oct. 17, 1826.
m April 14, 1785, Salome Carpenter, daughter of Dr. John Carpenter, b May 25, 1766, d May 9, 1795. Then m Sept. 20, 1796, Lydia Ferree, daughter of David Ferree (8-012) b Oct. 11, 1766, d July 11, 1802. Then m Mar. 3, 1803, Mrs. Catherine Eckman (nee Messenkop), b Feb. 15, 1767, d Jan. 13, 1835.

In Harris' History of Lancaster County, Pa., it is recorded: Hon. Joseph LeFevre, a leading politician, and member of Congress from 1811 till 1813, was a citizen of Strasburg (now Paradise) Township.

More About CONGRESSMAN JOSEPH LeFEVRE:
Fact 1: Bet. 1811 - 1813, Member of Congress

More About JOSEPH LeFEVRE and LYDIA FERREE:
Marriage: 20 Sep 1796

Children are listed above under (27) Joseph LeFevre.

60. ELIAS[9] LeFEVRE (*ELIAS[8], DANIEL[7], ISAAC[6], ABRAHAM[5], ANDREW[4], PHILIP[3], JOHN[2], MENGEN[1]*) was born 20 Jul 1770 in Maryland. He married CATHERINE MATHIOT. She was born Feb 1775.

Children of ELIAS LeFEVRE and CATHERINE MATHIOT are:
  i. GEORGE[10] LeFEVRE, b. 19 Jul 1795.
 ii. CATHERINE LeFEVRE, b. 29 Jun 1799.
iii. SARAH LeFEVRE, b. 29 Jun 1801; d. 28 Feb 1883; m. MR. ROCKHILL; d. 1865.
 iv. POLLY LeFEVRE, b. 28 Apr 1804; d. 01 Aug 1809.
  v. ELIZABETH LeFEVRE, b. 15 May 1806; m. PERSINGER.
 vi. JACOB LeFEVRE, b. 14 Oct 1808; d. 21 Aug 1810.
vii. DANIEL LeFEVRE, b. 28 Oct 1810.
viii. PETER LeFEVRE, b. 25 Oct 1812; d. 04 Mar 1868; m. MARTHA ROUTH IORNS, 1836; b. 01 Nov 1805; d. 04 Mar 1897.

      Notes for PETER LeFEVRE:
      A trustee of Antioch College, Yellow Springs Ohio

      More About PETER LeFEVRE and MARTHA IORNS:
      Marriage: 1836

 ix. MARY LeFEVRE, b. 15 Sep 1814.
  x. SUSAN LeFEVRE, b. 08 Aug 1816.

61. GEORGE[9] LeFEVRE (*ELIAS[8], DANIEL[7], ISAAC[6], ABRAHAM[5], ANDREW[4], PHILIP[3], JOHN[2], MENGEN[1]*) was born 15 Jun 1790, and died 11 Mar 1840. He married CATHERINE BROWN. She was born 27 Aug 1792, and died 17 Oct 1867.

Children of GEORGE LeFEVRE and CATHERINE BROWN are:
  i. ELIAS[10] LeFEVRE, b. 12 Apr 1812.
 ii. ELI LeFEVRE, b. 18 Mar 1814; d. 20 Oct 1842; m. MARY DAVIS, 29 Nov 1835; b. 12 Nov 1812; d. 09 Nov 1887.

      More About ELI LeFEVRE and MARY DAVIS:

Marriage: 29 Nov 1835

    iii.   MARIA LeFEVRE, b. 21 Apr 1817.
    iv.   LYDIA LeFEVRE, b. 22 Nov 1818.
    v.   ENOS LeFEVRE, b. 14 Jun 1820; m. REBECCA IORNS.
    vi.   PETER LeFEVRE, b. 24 Feb 1822; d. Edinburg, IN; m. SARAH COX.
    vii.   SARAH LeFEVRE, b. 16 Sep 1824.
    viii.   REBECCA LeFEVRE, b. 22 Jul 1828; m. MORRIS.
    ix.   JOHN LeFEVRE, b. 12 Feb 1832; d. 01 Jun 1909; m. ELIZABETH HATFIELD, Jul 1859; b. 19 Mar 1836; d. 05 Oct 1898.

       More About JOHN LeFEVRE and ELIZABETH HATFIELD:
       Marriage: Jul 1859

    x.   SUSANNA LeFEVRE, b. 12 Jan 1834; m. LEWIS DeLAWTER, 23 Sep 1856.

       More About LEWIS DeLAWTER and SUSANNA LeFEVRE:
       Marriage: 23 Sep 1856

    xi.   DAVID LeFEVRE, b. 08 Jun 1838; m. REBECCA T RICHMOND.

62. JOHN[9] LeFEVRE *(DAVID[8], DANIEL[7], ISAAC[6], ABRAHAM[5], ANDREW[4], PHILIP[3], JOHN[2], MENGEN[1])* was born 1770, and died 1815. He married CHRISTIANNA HOUSEHOLDER. She was born 1778, and died 15 May 1863 in Williamsport, PA.

Notes for JOHN LeFEVRE:
John was born on the farm that his father David took up and improved. It belonged to this family until 1865, almost 100 years. In 1823 John's widow moved with the children to Williamsport, Md., where she died, aged 85 years.

Children of JOHN LeFEVRE and CHRISTIANNA HOUSEHOLDER are:
    i.   MARY[10] LeFEVRE, b. 03 Jul 1801; d. 26 Nov 1822; m. ROBERT THORNBERG.
    ii.   CATHERINE LeFEVRE, b. 1804; m. BENJAMIN CROWE; b. 1791; d. 23 Jun 1878.
    iii.   ISAAC LeFEVRE, b. 20 Aug 1806; d. 04 Jan 1895, Dayton Ohio; m. ANNE MARTIN, 16 Dec 1830; b. 14 Aug 1813; d. 21 Jul 1888.

       Notes for ISAAC LeFEVRE:
       In the spring of 1835 Isaac with his little family moved from Williamsport, Md., to Dayton, Ohio. After a few months he bought a farm near Lebanon, Ohio, about seven miles south of Dayton. After farming several years, about 1844 he sold that farm and bought a larger farm three miles nearer to Dayton. Here the family lived for many years, and Mr. LeFevre and his wife died here. They are buried in the Martin Church Cemetery,

located three miles south of Dayton.

More About ISAAC LEFEVRE and ANNE MARTIN:
Marriage: 16 Dec 1830

    iv.   HENRY LEFEVRE, b. 01 Jul 1808; d. 17 Feb 1883, Cumberland, MD; m. REBECCA SYSTER, 27 Dec 1832; b. 11 Feb 1808; d. May 1891.

More About HENRY LEFEVRE and REBECCA SYSTER:
Marriage: 27 Dec 1832

    v.   ELIZABETH LEFEVRE, b. 1810.
    vi.   MARIA LEFEVRE, b. 12 Sep 1811; d. 24 Sep 1859; m. BENJAMIN CROWE; b. 1791; d. 23 Jun 1878.
    vii.   DR. JOHN LEFEVRE, b. 1812; d. 1887; m. ANNE E SOMERS; d. 1885.

Notes for DR. JOHN LEFEVRE:
MD in Cincinnati, OH

    viii.   SAMUEL LEFEVRE, b. 20 May 1815; d. 07 Feb 1904, Williamsport, MD; m. ANNE W HERR, Jun 1854; b. 30 Sep 1830; d. 13 Nov 1905.

Notes for SAMUEL LEFEVRE:
Samuel was born on the same farm on which his father was born in 1770. In 1842 he established a tannery in Williamsport, which he operated till 1852. He then became a dealer in lumber, coal and general merchandise; he also had a saw-mill and planing-mill. He was very active in securing the extension of the Western Maryland R.R. to Williamsport in 1873. He retired in 1876. During the Civil War Mr. LeFevre was a staunch Union man. He had three sons who were also prominent citizens of Williamsport and vicinity.

More About SAMUEL LEFEVRE and ANNE HERR:
Marriage: Jun 1854

63. HENRY[9] LEFEVRE *(DAVID[8], DANIEL[7], ISAAC[6], ABRAHAM[5], ANDREW[4], PHILIP[3], JOHN[2], MENGEN[1])* was born 1776. He married EVE MARGARET LINGENFELTER.

Children of HENRY LEFEVRE and EVE LINGENFELTER are:
    i.   JOHN T[10] LEFEVRE, b. 24 Sep 1798; d. 1828; m. NANCY C HILL, 1819; b. 12 Nov 1802; d. 05 Oct 1876.

More About JOHN LEFEVRE and NANCY HILL:
Marriage: 1819

ii. DAVID LEFEVRE, b. 1800.
iii. JACOB LEFEVRE, b. 06 Jan 1802; d. 16 Nov 1859, Bedington, WV; m. MARIA SPEROW, 30 Aug 1827; b. 08 Apr 1809; d. Nov 1883.

More About JACOB LEFEVRE and MARIA SPEROW:
Marriage: 30 Aug 1827

iv. DANIEL L LEFEVRE, b. 02 Aug 1813; d. 01 Oct 1877, Bunker Hill, WV; m. (1) ELIZABETH FALCK, Feb 1835; b. 31 May 1810; d. 27 Feb 1842; m. (2) MARGARET SPECK, Nov 1844; b. 24 Apr 1817; d. 09 Jun 1897.

More About DANIEL LEFEVRE and ELIZABETH FALCK:
Marriage: Feb 1835

More About DANIEL LEFEVRE and MARGARET SPECK:
Marriage: Nov 1844

v. ELIZABETH LEFEVRE, b. Abt. 1815.
vi. SARAH LEFEVRE, b. Abt. 1815.

64. GEORGE[9] LEFEVRE (DAVID[8], DANIEL[7], ISAAC[6], ABRAHAM[5], ANDREW[4], PHILIP[3], JOHN[2], MENGEN[1]) was born 23 Dec 1779, and died 20 Apr 1850 in Williamsport, Maryland. He married ELIZABETH LINGENFELTER. She was born 25 Sep 1779, and died 05 Mar 1826.

Children of GEORGE LEFEVRE and ELIZABETH LINGENFELTER are:
i. MARY[10] LEFEVRE, b. 11 Oct 1807; d. 15 Apr 1836; m. WILLIAM DELLINGER.
ii. DAVID LEFEVRE, b. 1809; d. 1830.
iii. HENRY LEFEVRE, b. 20 Aug 1810; d. 06 Jul 1852, Washington Co, MD; m. CATHERINE STERLING, 1834; b. 18 Sep 1811; d. 22 Oct 1859.

More About HENRY LEFEVRE and CATHERINE STERLING:
Marriage: 1834

iv. ELIZABETH LEFEVRE, b. 26 Apr 1812; d. 04 Dec 1856; m. JOSEPH BYERS, Bef. 1848; b. 27 Jul 1808; d. 06 Mar 1856.

More About JOSEPH BYERS and ELIZABETH LEFEVRE:
Marriage: Bef. 1848

v. SARAH LEFEVRE, b. Abt. 1815; m. JOHN F DELLINGER; b. 24 Dec 1808; d. 11 Jun 1856.
vi. DANIEL LEFEVRE, b. 14 Aug 1820; d. 25 Nov 1855, Bakersville,

MD; m. ELIZABETH C LOWMAN; b. 03 Jan 1822; d. 30 Aug 1862.

65. JOHN[9] REYNOLDS (*CATHERINE FERREE[8] LEFEVRE, SAMUEL[7], ISAAC[6], ABRAHAM[5], ANDREW[4], PHILIP[3], JOHN[2], MENGEN[1]*) was born 30 Mar 1787 in Leacock, PA, and died 11 May 1853. He married LYDIA MOORE 17 Jun 1813 in Lancaster, PA, daughter of SAMUEL MOORE and JANE FULTON. She was born 24 Jan 1794 in Lebanon, PA, and died 05 Aug 1843 in Lancaster, PA.

Notes for JOHN REYNOLDS:
John Reynolds was a solid citizen and participant in community affairs. He had begin as a printer's apprentice, been a clerk of a newly formed Lancaster bank, captain of a volunteer infantry company, and county treasurer before purchasing the weekly Lancaster Journal, which he published from 1820 to 1834 from the family home on West King St. During the years son William served with the Exploring Expedition, his family lived in the Coleman house at Cornwall Furnace, about twenty miles north of Lancaster, where his father was occupied full time as guardian of his friend Thomas Bird Coleman's six children and their iron furnaces and forges. (from "Voyage to the Southern Ocean' by Cleaver & Stann)

1802/10 Unknown - apprenticed under Archibald Bartram, Phila.printer; later became a partner.
1814 - 1817 - cashier at Farmer's State Bank of Lancaster.
1820 - purchased the "Lancaster Journal" and functioned as printer and publisher of the newspaper.
1822 - 1824 - member of the Pennsylvania State Legislature.
1834 - sold the "Lancaster Journal."
1836 - manager of Coleman Iron Works, Cornwall (Lebanon County, PA) and guardian of Coleman heirs.
1837. - moved to Cornwall.
1848 - moved back to Lancaster City

Reynolds, John
 State: Pennsylvania Year: 1850
 County: Lancaster Roll: M432_788
 Township: Lancaster City N E Ward Page: 329
 Image: 658

More About JOHN REYNOLDS and LYDIA MOORE:
Marriage: 17 Jun 1813, Lancaster, PA

Children of JOHN REYNOLDS and LYDIA MOORE are:
82.   i.   SAMUEL MOORE[10] REYNOLDS, b. 14 Apr 1814, Lancaster, PA; d. 29 May 1888, Philadelphia, PA.
83.   ii.   ADMIRAL WILLIAM REYNOLDS, b. 10 Dec 1815, Lancaster, PA; d. 05 Nov 1879, Washington, DC.

          iii.   JANE MOORE REYNOLDS, b. 07 Apr 1817, Lancaster, PA; d. 21 Apr 1817, Lancaster, PA.

84.   iv.   LYDIA MOORE REYNOLDS, b. 27 Jul 1818, Lancaster, PA; d. 28 Dec 1896, Fort Wayne, IN.

          v.   JOHN FULTON REYNOLDS, b. 20 Sep 1820, Lancaster, PA; d. 01 Jul 1863, Battle of Gettysburg.

Notes for JOHN FULTON REYNOLDS:
1841 - graduated from U.S. Military Academy, West Point, NY; commissioned Lieutenant, Third U.S. Artillery.
1846 - promoted to First Lieutenant; served under Gen. Zachary Taylor in the war withMexico; breveted Captain after Battle of Monterey.
1847 - breveted Major for special gallantry after Battle of Buena Vista.
1858 - served in the Utah Expedition under Albert Sidney Johnston.
1860 - assigned to U.S. Military Academy; served as Commandant of Cadets.
1861 - commissioned as Lieutenant Colonel of 14th Infantry; appointed Brigadier-General and assumed command of First Brigade, Pennsylvania Reserves.
1862 - appointed Military Governor of Fredericksburg, VA; captured by Confederate Army and held in Libby Prison; after prisoner exchange appointed Major General and given command of First Corps of the Army of the Potomac.
1863 Jul 1 - killed on first day of the Battle of Gettysburg, PA

More About JOHN FULTON REYNOLDS:
Fact 3: Was Killed First day in Battle of Gettysburg.

         vi.   JAMES LEFEVRE REYNOLDS, b. 08 Mar 1822, Lancaster, PA; d. 05 Apr 1880, Philadelphia, PA.

Notes for JAMES LEFEVRE REYNOLDS:
Graduated from Marshall College in Mercersburg, PA an 1841 with honors. Admitted to the bar in 1844 after studying with John R Montgomery of Lancaster and John Weidman of Lebanon, he was in active practice for only ten years. In 1854, he refused a position on the Pennsylvania Supreme Court, apparently devoting his time to study and politics. An ardent Democrat, he was Buchanan's lawyer and chief political aide until the civil war, when he became an ardent Republican and quartermaster general of the Pennsylvania militia on Governor Andrew Curtin's staff. He was a member of the Pennsylvania

Constitutional Convention of 1872, but, rather typically, refused to sign the resulting document because he objected to a portion. His 1880 obituaries stress his scholarship, vast library, powers as a conversationalist, and warm circle of friends. Like his father, he was 'tall, portly and commanding.'

1841 - graduated from Marshall College, Mercersburg, PA
1844 - admitted to the bar, Lancaster, PA
1862 - appointed Superintendent of the Union Army draft for Lancaster County, PA
1863 - appointed Quarter-Master General for the State of Pennsylvania.
1872 - elected member of the Constitutional Convention of Pennsylvania.

85.	vii.	MARY JANE REYNOLDS, b. 13 Feb 1824, Lancaster, PA; d. 10 Dec 1901.
86.	viii.	CATHERINE FERREE REYNOLDS, b. 11 Dec 1825, Lancaster, PA; d. 10 Feb 1905, Springfield, Montgomery County, PA.
	ix.	ANNE ELIZABETH REYNOLDS, b. 26 Dec 1827, Lancaster, PA; d. 07 Jun 1832.
	x.	EDWARD COLEMAN REYNOLDS, b. 26 Dec 1827, Lancaster, PA; d. 25 Sep 1828, Lancaster, PA.
	xi.	EDWARD B REYNOLDS, b. 26 May 1829, Lancaster, PA; d. 06 Jul 1829, Lancaster, PA.
	xii.	HARRIET SUMNER REYNOLDS, b. 29 Jul 1832, Lancaster, PA; d. 14 Sep 1898.
	xiii.	ELEANOR REYNOLDS, b. 13 Mar 1835, Lancaster, PA; d. 20 Feb 1923, Washington, DC.

66. JOHN CARPENTER[9] LeFEVRE (*JOSEPH[8], SAMUEL[7], ISAAC[6], ABRAHAM[5], ANDREW[4], PHILIP[3], JOHN[2], MENGEN[1]*) was born 09 Apr 1793, and died 01 Dec 1863. He married ELIZABETH MCCLUNG Jul 1823. She was born Jan 1792, and died 29 Jun 1855.

More About JOHN LeFEVRE and ELIZABETH MCCLUNG:
Marriage: Jul 1823

Children of JOHN LeFEVRE and ELIZABETH MCCLUNG are:
  i. DR. JOSEPH HENRY[10] LeFEVRE, b. 14 May 1824; d. 20 Oct 1875; m. CHRISTIANA FOSTER; b. 20 Sep 1824; d. 13 Nov 1902.
  ii. SALOME LeFEVRE, b. 08 Jul 1826; d. 02 Aug 1826.
  iii. SUSANNA ELIZABETH LeFEVRE, b. 09 Aug 1827; d. 03 Oct 1900; m. JOHN C FREELAND; b. 1828; d. 1899.
  iv. CHARLES MCCLUNG LeFEVRE, b. 16 Jun 1831; d. 18 Mar 1832.

67. JOSEPH SMITH[9] LEFEVRE *(JOSEPH[8], SAMUEL[7], ISAAC[6], ABRAHAM[5], ANDREW[4], PHILIP[3], JOHN[2], MENGEN[1])* was born 08 May 1795, and died 10 Apr 1875. He married RACHEL FOSTER. She was born 24 Dec 1799, and died 10 Feb 1874.

Children of JOSEPH LEFEVRE and RACHEL FOSTER are:
    i. JOHN F[10] LEFEVRE, b. 24 Mar 1821; d. 28 May 1888; m. (1) HANNAH TROUT, 26 Jul 1844; b. 12 Dec 1823; d. Oct 1854; m. (2) ELIZABETH BAIR, Jan 1855; b. 14 Feb 1838; d. 11 Jun 1913.

Notes for JOHN F LEFEVRE:
A Civil War vet

More About JOHN LEFEVRE and HANNAH TROUT:
Marriage: 26 Jul 1844

More About JOHN LEFEVRE and ELIZABETH BAIR:
Marriage: Jan 1855

    ii. ALBERT T LEFEVRE, b. 20 Nov 1822; d. 15 Feb 1824.
   iii. JOEL LIGHTNER LEFEVRE, b. 28 Nov 1824; d. 28 Nov 1855.
    iv. SAMUEL S LEFEVRE, b. 26 Aug 1827; d. 26 Jan 1831.
     v. NATHANIEL LEFEVRE, b. 27 Sep 1829; d. 22 Aug 1851.
    vi. SALOME LEFEVRE, b. 16 Jul 1831; d. 24 Jun 1857; m. ADAM TROUT, 21 Nov 1848; b. 06 Jul 1820; d. 06 Feb 1870.

More About ADAM TROUT and SALOME LEFEVRE:
Marriage: 21 Nov 1848

   vii. ELI MCCALLEY LEFEVRE, b. 31 Jan 1834; d. 08 Feb 1834.
  viii. SUSAN A LEFEVRE, b. 24 Jan 1835; d. 02 Apr 1867; m. WILLIAM H HITCHMAN, 03 Apr 1860.

More About WILLIAM HITCHMAN and SUSAN LEFEVRE:
Marriage: 03 Apr 1860

    ix. JOSEPHINE LEFEVRE, b. 20 Jul 1837; d. 04 Feb 1881.
     x. MARGARET LEFEVRE, b. 19 Mar 1840; d. 21 Jan 1907; m. (1) GEORGE ECKERT, 25 Dec 1865; b. 16 Sep 1839; d. 18 Oct 1883; m. (2) SAMUEL F MCBRIDE, 21 Feb 1905.

More About GEORGE ECKERT and MARGARET LEFEVRE:
Marriage: 25 Dec 1865

More About SAMUEL MCBRIDE and MARGARET LEFEVRE:
Marriage: 21 Feb 1905

68. ELIZABETH[10] KEEPORTS (*CATHERINE[9] LeFevre, John[8], Abraham[7], Isaac[6], Abraham[5], Andrew[4], Philip[3], John[2], Mengen[1]*) was born 03 Jan 1784, and died 25 Sep 1864. She married JOHN LeFevre 31 Mar 1804, son of ADAM LeFevre and ELIZABETH PAULES. He was born 13 Dec 1776, and died 13 Oct 1851.

More About JOHN LeFevre and ELIZABETH KEEPORTS:
Marriage: 31 Mar 1804

Children are listed above under (48) John LeFevre.

69. GEORGE[10] LeFevre (*George[9], John[8], Abraham[7], Isaac[6], Abraham[5], Andrew[4], Philip[3], John[2], Mengen[1]*) was born 15 Nov 1810, and died 22 Apr 1852 in LeFevre Cemetery. He married ANNE HERR 11 Feb 1837. She was born 31 Mar 1815, and died 05 Jul 1911.

More About GEORGE LeFevre and ANNE HERR:
Marriage: 11 Feb 1837

Children of GEORGE LeFevre and ANNE HERR are:

      i. SUSAN SALOME[11] LeFevre, b. 14 Nov 1837, Lancaster Co, PA; d. 03 Sep 1925, Lancaster Co, PA.

         Notes for SUSAN SALOME LeFevre:
         Served as missionary to Burma for one term

87.   ii. GEORGE NEWTON LeFevre, b. 31 Jul 1850, Strasburg, Lancaster Co, PA; d. 29 Nov 1943, Strasburg, Lancaster Co, PA.

70. CHRISTIAN[10] TRITT (*Elizabeth[9] LeFevre, George[8], Philip G[7], Isaac[6], Abraham[5], Andrew[4], Philip[3], John[2], Mengen[1]*) was born 25 Jul 1796, and died 10 Jan 1871 in Lutheran Cem, Centerville, Pa.. He married (1) LYDIA JANE STOUGH Nov 1820. She was born 05 Oct 1803, and died 09 Sep 1849 in Lutheran Cem, Centerville, Pa.. He married (2) FLORENCE CHARLOTTE MCCULLOUGH WFT Est. 1831-1859. She was born 16 Mar 1818, and died 28 Feb 1899.

More About CHRISTIAN TRITT and LYDIA STOUGH:
Marriage: Nov 1820

More About CHRISTIAN TRITT and FLORENCE MCCULLOUGH:
Marriage: WFT Est. 1831-1859

Children of CHRISTIAN TRITT and LYDIA STOUGH are:
88.   i. J. MILLER[11] TRITT, b. WFT Est. 1816-1838; d. WFT Est. 1855-

1921.

89.   ii.   PETER TRITT, b. 24 Jun 1821, Huntsdale, Pa.; d. 16 Mar 1887, Huntsdale, Pa. buried Pa. German Baptist Church, Huntsdale,Pa..

71. JACOB[10] LeFEVRE *(LAWRENCE[9], GEORGE[8], PHILIP G[7], ISAAC[6], ABRAHAM[5], ANDREW[4], PHILIP[3], JOHN[2], MENGEN[1])* was born 31 May 1795, and died 26 Apr 1875. He married ELIZABETH FERGUSON 24 Jun 1819. She was born 30 Mar 1798, and died 10 Dec 1871.

Notes for JACOB LeFEVRE:
In 1818 Jacob LeFevre began publication at Gettysburg, Pa., of The Gettysburg Compiler, which he continued until August, 1835. Then his son Isaac, of 1820, published it until February, 1845, when it was sold and the LeFevres moved to Cumberland Co., Pa. On Jan. 25, 1839, Governor Porter appointed Mr. LeFevre the Recorder for Adams Co., Pa., and he was also appointed Clerk of the Adams County Orphans Court.

More About JACOB LeFEVRE and ELIZABETH FERGUSON:
Marriage: 24 Jun 1819

Children of JACOB LeFEVRE and ELIZABETH FERGUSON are:

90.   i.   DR. ISSAC[11] LeFEVRE, b. 15 Jun 1820, Adams County, PA; d. 25 Oct 1893, 411 Cumberland St, Harrisburg, PA.

         ii.   ESTHER LeFEVRE, b. 09 Sep 1822; d. 15 May 1900; m. PETER CALVERT, Jun 1844; b. 29 Mar 1819; d. 19 Sep 1898.

               More About PETER CALVERT and ESTHER LeFEVRE:
               Marriage: Jun 1844

        iii.   REBECCA LeFEVRE, b. 16 Jan 1825; d. 11 Apr 1900; m. (1) SAMUEL SOUDER, 02 Dec 1847; b. 27 Oct 1823; d. 20 Sep 1860; m. (2) BENJAMIN BLOSSER, 19 Dec 1867; b. 01 Jul 1826; d. 09 Oct 1909.

               More About SAMUEL SOUDER and REBECCA LeFEVRE:
               Marriage: 02 Dec 1847

               More About BENJAMIN BLOSSER and REBECCA LeFEVRE:
               Marriage: 19 Dec 1867

        iv.   LAWRENCE LeFEVRE, b. 26 Apr 1827; d. 22 Apr 1902.
         v.   JACOB F. LeFEVRE, b. 26 Jan 1830; d. 04 Jul 1855.
        vi.   CAROLINE E. LeFEVRE, b. 28 Feb 1833; d. 04 Dec 1896.
       vii.   FANNY LeFEVRE, b. 13 Dec 1835; d. 30 Oct 1870; m. HENRY WHITE, 13 Aug 1857; b. 30 Dec 1826; d. 19 Jul 1902.

               More About HENRY WHITE and FANNY LeFEVRE:

Marriage: 13 Aug 1857

viii. DAVID PORTER LEFEVRE, b. 05 Jan 1839; d. 1917; m. ELIZABETH BOGGS, 25 Aug 1857; b. 27 Sep 1837; d. 1918.

More About DAVID PORTER LEFEVRE:
Fact 1: lost arm in Civil War at Chancellorsville

More About DAVID LEFEVRE and ELIZABETH BOGGS:
Marriage: 25 Aug 1857

ix. ANNE B. LEFEVRE, b. 19 Oct 1843; d. 25 Jan 1916; m. JOHN SHEARER, 08 Sep 1864; b. 01 Oct 1837; d. 18 May 1907.

More About JOHN SHEARER and ANNE LEFEVRE:
Marriage: 08 Sep 1864

72. JOHN B.[10] LEFEVRE (*LAWRENCE*[9], *GEORGE*[8], *PHILIP G*[7], *ISAAC*[6], *ABRAHAM*[5], *ANDREW*[4], *PHILIP*[3], *JOHN*[2], *MENGEN*[1]) was born 11 Mar 1799, and died 13 Sep 1864. He married REBECCA RINE 07 Jun 1821. She was born 16 Jan 1798, and died 17 Dec 1875.

Notes for JOHN B. LEFEVRE:
In 1835 Mr. LeFevre was appointed Associate judge of Cumberland Co., Pa., by Governor Ritner. He resigned from that office with honor. At the age of forty he was converted, and some time later he rode fifty-one miles on horseback to a church near Beaver Creek, in Washington Co., Md., to be baptized. He later became a minister in the Church of Christ near his home.

More About JOHN B. LEFEVRE:
Fact 1: 1835, Appointed Associate Judge of Cumberland County

More About JOHN LEFEVRE and REBECCA RINE:
Marriage: 07 Jun 1821

Children of JOHN LEFEVRE and REBECCA RINE are:
91.   i. DAVID[11] LEFEVRE, b. 05 Mar 1823; d. 1904.
      ii. MARGARET LEFEVRE, b. 10 Dec 1825; d. 08 Jul 1850; m. HENRY BAER, 01 Feb 1848; b. 17 Mar 1824.

More About HENRY BAER and MARGARET LEFEVRE:
Marriage: 01 Feb 1848

     iii. GEORGE LEFEVRE, b. 07 Apr 1828; d. 02 Aug 1830.
      iv. MARIA LEFEVRE, b. 14 Nov 1830; m. JOHN MYERS, 03 Dec 1855.

More About JOHN MYERS and MARIA LEFEVRE:
Marriage: 03 Dec 1855

92.   v.   HENRY LEFEVRE, b. 02 Jan 1833, Cumberland County; d. 15 Jul 1868.
      vi.   JOHN LEFEVRE, b. 11 Apr 1838; d. 20 Jun 1840.

73. DAVID ALTER[10] LEFEVRE *(LAWRENCE[9], GEORGE[8], PHILIP G[7], ISAAC[6], ABRAHAM[5], ANDREW[4], PHILIP[3], JOHN[2], MENGEN[1])* was born 30 Dec 1806, and died 02 May 1885. He married HARRIET WILT 10 Mar 1827. She was born 28 Nov 1807, and died 02 May 1883.

Notes for DAVID ALTER LEFEVRE:
Minister

More About DAVID LEFEVRE and HARRIET WILT:
Marriage: 10 Mar 1827

Children of DAVID LEFEVRE and HARRIET WILT are:
      i.   CATHERINE A.[11] LEFEVRE, b. 11 Mar 1828; d. 01 May 1856; m. SAMUEL BLACK; b. 28 Nov 1824; d. Mar 1905.
      ii.   MARY ELLEN LEFEVRE, b. 17 Apr 1830; d. 18 Apr 1853; m. AUGUSTUS CLARK, 20 Feb 1851; b. 26 Dec 1828; d. Apr 1898.

      More About AUGUSTUS CLARK and MARY LEFEVRE:
      Marriage: 20 Feb 1851

93.   iii.   ISSAC LAWRENCE LEFEVRE, b. 08 Sep 1832, Cumberland County, Pennsylvania; d. 07 Jan 1905.
      iv.   PETER WILT LEFEVRE, b. 06 Nov 1834; d. 20 Jan 1913.
94.   v.   JOHN ALTER LEFEVRE, b. 28 Mar 1837; d. 30 Nov 1915.
      vi.   HETTIE VERONICA LEFEVRE, b. 16 Sep 1839; d. 13 Feb 1934; m. WILLIAM SIMS, Sep 1862; b. 12 Apr 1840; d. 17 Nov 1872.

      More About WILLIAM SIMS and HETTIE LEFEVRE:
      Marriage: Sep 1862

95.   vii.   DAVID SLAYMAKER LEFEVRE, b. 05 Sep 1841; d. 02 May 1911, Lafayette, Indiana.
      viii.   JACOB SAILER LEFEVRE, b. 21 May 1844; d. 04 Jun 1922, Denver, Colorado; m. ELIZA ADAMS, 25 Feb 1868; b. 25 Mar 1852; d. 17 Feb 1934.

      More About JACOB LEFEVRE and ELIZA ADAMS:
      Marriage: 25 Feb 1868

      ix.   JOSEPH LINES LEFEVRE, b. 13 Aug 1846; d. 24 Oct 1910, Glendora, California; m. LEAH KUHNS, 22 Oct 1874; b. 15 Oct 1854; d. 17 Nov 1883.

More About JOSEPH LeFEVRE and LEAH KUHNS:
Marriage: 22 Oct 1874

    x.   HARRIET SUE LeFEVRE, b. 10 Mar 1850; d. 10 Mar 1910; m. JOHN MOORE, 14 Oct 1869; b. 10 Feb 1846; d. 30 Jun 1917.

More About JOHN MOORE and HARRIET LeFEVRE:
Marriage: 14 Oct 1869

    xi.   PHILLIP LeFEVRE, b. 09 Feb 1854; d. 22 Feb 1854.

74. ELIZABETH[10] LeFEVRE *(JACOB[9], GEORGE[8], PHILIP G[7], ISAAC[6], ABRAHAM[5], ANDREW[4], PHILIP[3], JOHN[2], MENGEN[1])* was born 23 Apr 1801, and died Jun 1852 in Oregon Trail. She married JOHN DOUGLAS 30 Nov 1819.

Notes for ELIZABETH LeFEVRE:
Elizabeth and two sons-in-law died on their way to Oregon.

More About JOHN DOUGLAS and ELIZABETH LeFEVRE:
Marriage: 30 Nov 1819

Children of ELIZABETH LeFEVRE and JOHN DOUGLAS are:
    i.   JOHN[11] DOUGLAS, d. 1852.
    ii.   ELIZABETH DOUGLAS.

75. SALOME[10] LINE *(ANNA BARBARA[9] LeFEVRE, GEORGE[8], PHILIP G[7], ISAAC[6], ABRAHAM[5], ANDREW[4], PHILIP[3], JOHN[2], MENGEN[1])* was born WFT Est. 1782-1820, and died WFT Est. 1792-1902. She married LAWRENCE LeFEVRE 29 Oct 1822, son of GEORGE LeFEVRE and ANNA SLAYMAKER. He was born 15 Dec 1764, and died 24 Feb 1830 in Newville, Pennsylvania.

More About LAWRENCE LeFEVRE and SALOME LINE:
Marriage: 29 Oct 1822

Child is listed above under (36) Lawrence LeFevre.

76. GEORGE L.[10] LINE *(ANNA BARBARA[9] LeFEVRE, GEORGE[8], PHILIP G[7], ISAAC[6], ABRAHAM[5], ANDREW[4], PHILIP[3], JOHN[2], MENGEN[1])* was born WFT Est. 1786-1818, and died 05 Nov 1885. He married MARIA LINE WFT Est. 1811-1854. She was born WFT Est. 1794-1820, and died 27 Nov 1869.

More About GEORGE LINE and MARIA LINE:
Marriage: WFT Est. 1811-1854

Children of GEORGE LINE and MARIA LINE are:
    i.   ELIZABETH M.[11] LINE, b. WFT Est. 1815-1857; d. WFT Est. 1834-

1938; m. HIMMINGER, WFT Est. 1834-1889; b. WFT Est. 1808-1855; d. WFT Est. 1834-1933.

More About HIMMINGER and ELIZABETH LINE:
Marriage: WFT Est. 1834-1889

     ii.   EMMANUEL C. LINE, b. WFT Est. 1815-1857; d. WFT Est. 1829-1935.
96.   iii.   JOHN A. LINE, b. 09 Apr 1834; d. WFT Est. 1870-1925.
97.   iv.   ABRAM L. LINE, b. 02 Mar 1841; d. WFT Est. 1869-1932.

77. SAMUEL[10] LEFEVRE *(PETER[9], ADAM[8], PHILIP G[7], ISAAC[6], ABRAHAM[5], ANDREW[4], PHILIP[3], JOHN[2], MENGEN[1])* was born 26 Feb 1812 in York County, PA, and died 07 Jul 1899. He married CATHERINE HOFFSTOTT 22 Oct 1837 in Newberry Twp, York, PA. She was born 16 Oct 1818, and died 26 Feb 1875.

Notes for SAMUEL LEFEVRE:
Moved to Jonesborough, IN and then to Dayton, OH.

Lafever, Samuel   View Image Online
  State: Pennsylvania Year: 1850
  County: York Roll: M432_840
  Township: Newberry Twp Page: 366
  Image: 506

More About SAMUEL LEFEVRE and CATHERINE HOFFSTOTT:
Marriage: 22 Oct 1837, Newberry Twp, York, PA

Children of SAMUEL LEFEVRE and CATHERINE HOFFSTOTT are:
    i.   HARRISON[11] LAFEVER, b. 1839.
    ii.   SUSAN LAFEVER, b. 1846.
    iii.   WILLIAM F LAFEVER, b. 1850.

78. LYDIA[10] LEFEVRE *(PETER[9], ADAM[8], PHILIP G[7], ISAAC[6], ABRAHAM[5], ANDREW[4], PHILIP[3], JOHN[2], MENGEN[1])* was born 09 Mar 1818 in York County, Pennsylvania, and died 02 Sep 1852 in Highspire, PA. She married GEORGE W WOLF Abt. 1836, son of JACOB WOLF and SUSAN FORREY. He was born 01 Mar 1809 in York County, Pennsylvania, and died 05 Mar 1869 in Highspire, PA.

Notes for GEORGE W WOLF:
[Broderbund Family Archive #305, Census Microfilm Records: PA, 1850, Disk 11, Date of Import: Jun 5, 1999, Internal Ref. #1.305.1.70155.16]

Individual: Wolf, George S.
Year: 1850

State: PA
County: York
Location: Fairview Township
National Archives Series Number: M432
National Archives Microfilm Number: 840
Census Page Number: 372

George S Wolf was an innkeeper in Fairview Twp, York Co. A son, Franklin (3) was found on the roster. This is the closest match to Franklin (who was supposedly born in 1849). Believed to be the father of our Franklin Lefever Wolf.

[Brøderbund Family Archive #316, Ed. 1, Census Index: U.S. Selected Counties, 1840, Date of Import: Jun 5, 1999, Internal Ref. #1.316.1.12779.188]

Individual: Wolf, George
County/State: York Co., PA
Location: Fairview Twp
Page #: 190
Year: 1840

This (1840) record lists a male aged 20-30, a female aged 20-30, a male under 5 and a female under 5. This profile fits the family = as both parents fit and only Barbara and David (children) were born at that time - both under 5.

Tombstone in Highspire reads George W Wolf (1809-1869) and wife Lydia L Wolf (1819-1858). They match very closely with the census - as do the names of other children buried with them - David, Daniel & Sarah.

From the "Commemorative Biographical Encyclopedia of Dauphin County, PA - 1896 (JM Runk & Co):

Pg 815 -816 (Portrait on 773)

Wolf, Franklin, farmer, Highspire PO, was born in York county, PA, December 29, 1849. He was the son of George W and Lydia (LeFevre) Wolf, natives of York county, PA. His father was a farmer and tobacco raiser. He was an active member of the Lutheran church. He was Republican in politics. He died in 1868, his wife in 1852. They had nine children, two of whom are now living; Annie, wife of Peter Shingle, or Goldsboro, York county, and Franklin.

The link to Jacob Wolf is based on circumstantial evidence. The Jacob Wolf 1830 census record includes Jacob aged 50-60, a son aged 15-20 (John), a son aged 20-30 (George), a daughter less than 5 (Susan), a daughter 15-20 (probably daughter in law Lydia) and wife 50-60 (Susan Forry.) The older siblings Barbara, Jacob & Peter were likely out of the home. This record fits the family tree attached from Ancestry.com - and is likely the same family. That tree had precise birthdates for all siblings but George - stating his only as '1808'. This is very class to March 1 1809. Also, our George Wolf appears in Fairview Twp in the 1840 & 1850 census - and not in the 1830. Thus, it is likely - if he lived in York County - he still lived in his father's home. Of course, he could have been from a different family, but none of these check out as closely. As of October 2002 - I am 80% certain this is the correct family for him.

More About GEORGE W WOLF:
Record Change: 07 Aug 2002

More About GEORGE WOLF and LYDIA LeFEVRE:
Marriage: Abt. 1836

Children of LYDIA LeFEVRE and GEORGE WOLF are:

      i.   BARBARA[11] WOLF, b. 1836, York County, PA.

     ii.   DAVID WOLF, b. 11 Jun 1839, Fairview Twp, York, PA; d. 09 Dec 1850, Highspire, PA.

98.   iii.   DANIEL LEFEVRE WOLF, b. 22 Oct 1842, York, PA; d. 30 Dec 1882, Highspire, PA.

     iv.   LYDIA ANN WOLF, b. 1845; d. Aft. 1920, Goldsboro, York County, PA; m. PETER SHINDLE; b. 1839; d. Aft. 1920, Goldsboro, York County, PA.

        Notes for PETER SHINDLE:

        Civil War Service Records
        Viewing records 1-2 of 2 Matches

        Surname Given Name Middle Initial Company Unit Rank - Induction Rank - Discharge Notes Allegiance
        Shindle Peter W. E 23 Pennsylvania Inf. Private Private Shindel Peter W. Union
        Shindle Peter W. 105 2 Batt'n Veteran Res. Corps. Private Private 23 Pa. Vols. Union

        Found in the 1920 Census in Goldsboro.

     v.   SARAH WOLF, b. 13 Jun 1846, Fairview Twp, York, PA; d. Abt. 1858, Highspire, PA.

99.   vi.   FRANKLIN LeFEVERE WOLF, b. 29 Dec 1849, York County, PA; d. 02 Mar 1933, Highspire, PA.

79. HENRY W[10] LeFEVRE *(DANIEL[9], ADAM[8], PHILIP G[7], ISAAC[6], ABRAHAM[5], ANDREW[4], PHILIP[3], JOHN[2], MENGEN[1])* was born 12 May 1818, and died 02 Apr

1892. He married HANNAH BAUGHMAN Jan 1847. She was born 02 Jun 1825, and died Nov 1916.

More About HENRY LeFEVRE and HANNAH BAUGHMAN:
Marriage: Jan 1847

Child of HENRY LeFEVRE and HANNAH BAUGHMAN is:
       i. SUSAN W[11] LeFEVRE, b. 1849.

80. REBECCA[10] LEFEVRE *(JACOB[9], JACOB[8], PHILIP G[7], ISAAC[6], ABRAHAM[5], ANDREW[4], PHILIP[3], JOHN[2], MENGEN[1])* was born Feb 1815, and died in Terre Haute, IN. She married THOMAS MOORE.

Child of REBECCA LEFEVRE and THOMAS MOORE is:
100.   i. ELIZABETH[11] MOORE, b. 19 Apr 1850.

81. DR. ALFRED[10] LeFEVRE *(CHRISTIAN[9], CHRISTIAN[8], DANIEL[7], ISAAC[6], ABRAHAM[5], ANDREW[4], PHILIP[3], JOHN[2], MENGEN[1])* was born 23 Apr 1822, and died 02 Jul 1897. He married LAVINA WILHELM 17 Mar 1847. She was born 29 Nov 1829.

Notes for DR. ALFRED LeFEVRE:
He was the father of Judge Owen E Lefevre of Denver Colorado

More About ALFRED LeFEVRE and LAVINA WILHELM:
Marriage: 17 Mar 1847

Child of ALFRED LeFEVRE and LAVINA WILHELM is:
      i. OWEN E[11] LeFEVRE.

            Notes for OWEN E LeFEVRE:
            Judge in Denver, CO

82. SAMUEL MOORE[10] REYNOLDS *(JOHN[9], CATHERINE FERREE[8] LeFEVRE, SAMUEL[7], ISAAC[6], ABRAHAM[5], ANDREW[4], PHILIP[3], JOHN[2], MENGEN[1])* was born 14 Apr 1814 in Lancaster, PA, and died 29 May 1888 in Philadelphia, PA. He married ELIZABETH VAN HORN MURRAY 1858 in Castle Fin, PA. She was born 1827, and died 1890.

Notes for SAMUEL MOORE REYNOLDS:
He took over management of Cornwall Furnace in 1840, but that same year journeyed Clarion County to inspect Lucinda Furnace, worked by a bankrupt Lancaster man; his father and James Buchanan subsequently bought Lucinda and 4351 acres of timberland and put Sam in charge. Thus, on WIlliam's return, Sam was once again managing an 'out of repair' property

with a 'poor house' and talking of future success.

Reynolds, Samuel   View Image Online
   State: Pennsylvania Year: 1850
   County: Lancaster Roll: M432_787
   Township: Drumore Twp Page: 75
   Image: 151

1860 United States Federal Census about Samuel M Reynolds
Name: Samuel M Reynolds
Age in 1860: 46
Birth Year: abt 1814
Birthplace: Pennsylvania
Home in 1860: Lower Chanceford, York, Pennsylvania
Gender: Male
Post Office: McCalls Ferry
Value of real estate: View image
Household Members:
NameAge
Samuel M Reynolds 46
Elizabeth Reynolds 33
Sarah H Coy Reynolds 19
Margret Hopkins 25

More About SAMUEL REYNOLDS and ELIZABETH MURRAY:
Marriage: 1858, Castle Fin, PA

Child of SAMUEL REYNOLDS and ELIZABETH MURRAY is:
        i.   SARAH McCOY[11] REYNOLDS, b. 1841.

83. ADMIRAL WILLIAM[10] REYNOLDS (JOHN[9], CATHERINE FERREE[8] LeFEVRE, SAMUEL[7], ISAAC[6], ABRAHAM[5], ANDREW[4], PHILIP[3], JOHN[2], MENGEN[1]) was born 10 Dec 1815 in Lancaster, PA, and died 05 Nov 1879 in Washington, DC. He married REBECCA KRUG 16 Aug 1842 in Holy Trinity Lutheran Church, Lancaster, PA, daughter of GEORGE HOPSON KRUG. She was born 22 Aug 1816, and died 12 Apr 1885.

Notes for ADMIRAL WILLIAM REYNOLDS:
Voyage to the Southern Ocean; The Letters of Lieutenant William Reynolds from the U.S. Exploring Expedition, 1838-42 by edited by Anne Hoffman Cleaver and E. Jeffrey Stann.

William Reynolds was the older brother of Maj. Gen. John Fulton Reynolds who, while commander of the left wing of the Army of the Potomac on July 1, 1863, became the first general officer killed at Gettysburg. Brother William was then a Navy commander and senior officer afloat at Port Royal, SC under Admiral Dahlgren. He was to go on to become an admiral and even acting

Secretary of the Navy--twice. This book contains his letters home during the 4-year U. S. Navy Exploring Expedition (the Wilkes Expedition). It also interweaves entries from both his official and personal journal and responses from home--mostly from sister Lydia. Anyone with an interest in the pre-Civil War Navy or even social life (in Lancaster, Pennsylvania, his home) will find this book extremely informative.

Lancaster Native Explored Islands Over a Century Ago, Pushed First Treaty With U.S.

When happy Hawaiians trooped to the polls this past week, they were paying unconscious tribute to a Lancaster sailing-man who was among the first Americans to explore the islands, and also among the first to fall in love with them. He was Rear Admiral William Reynolds. If the name sounds familiar, it should. For this was a brother to the Hero of Gettysburg, Maj. Gen. John Fulton Reynolds. Historically, the admiral has always been overshadowed by his more famous brother-almost as much as was another brother, Gen. James L. Reynolds. Two generals and an admiral in the same generation-it's a record that few other families could boast.

Lancaster may be proud of the fact that all three of these distinguished military men were born in this city. a reminder of this coincidence turned up fortuitously this past week in a collection of material presented to Frackenthal Library at Franklin & Marshall College by Thomas R. Brendle, of Egypt, Pa., a retired minister, who was a member of the class of 1908 at F&M. Together with a great quantity of Pennsylvania Dutch folk literature, there came the Brendle library of assorted books and pamphlets. Among them was "A Memoir" of the Reynolds triumvirate, delivered by J. G. Rosengarten before the Historical Society of Pennsylvania, later printed in "The United Service" and reprinted as a pamphlet by the Lippincott Co. of Philadelphia in 1880. {Rosengarten, incidentally, was treasurer of the Reynolds Memorial Association which in 1884 dedicated an equestrian statue of Gen. John F. Reynolds at Broad & Market Streets, Philadelphia . A souvenir booklet of this occasion is also included in the Brendle collection}

OLD LANCASTER STOCK
The Reynolds brothers were of old Lancaster stock. John, their father, was born near Lancaster, the son of William Reynolds who married the great granddaughter of Mary Ferree, pioneer of the Paradise area who came here in 1709. John published the Lancaster Journal 1820-1836. Their mother was Lydia Moore, a descendant of early Scotch-Irish settlers in this country. The three, in order of birth:
WILLIAM REYNOLDS, born Dec. 10, 1815, became an admiral. JOHN FULTON REYNOLDS, born Sept. 20, 1820, became a major general and died from a sniper's bullet at Gettysburg. JAMES LeFEVRE REYNOLDS, born March 8, 1822, became a lawyer and was Quartermaster General of Pennsylvania under Gov. Curtin throughout the Civil War.
It is William whose career is particularly topical today. In the Rosengarten memoir, which is also available in part in a Lancaster County Historical

195

Society paper of 1934, it is recalled that William was appointed a Navy midshipman in 1831-before his 15th birthday. Congressman James Buchanan, a friend of the family, obtained the appointment.

EXPLORED ISLANDS

Seven years later William sailed with the Wilkes Exploring Expedition, which probed odd cor as Lieutenant caught up with him while he was assigned to his duty. One of the areas he helped explore was the Sandwich Islands. Today we call them Hawaii, the 50th State. Nine years after the Wilkes Expedition returned to port, William Reynolds regretfully went on the retired list because of recurring ill health. But he remembered the romantic isles of the Pacific, and had himself assigned to Hawaii. Ten years in the islands so renewed his health that he applied for active duty in 1861, and was made commander of naval forces at Port Royal. He became a commodore in 1870; served as Chief of Bureau and acting Secretary of the Navy in 1873, and again in 1874, having been made Rear Admiral in the former year; was appointed to the command of the U.S. naval force in the Asiatic Station but was stricken down and obliged to return home. While in Japanese waters, he made his will, mentioning especially the famous sword which the enlisted men of the Pennsylvania Reserves had ordered for their beloved general before his death at Gettysburg. William left his brother's sword to their nephew, Lt. John Fulton Reynolds Landis, a West Pointer. A press clipping enclosed with the memoir-there is also a pencilled Reynolds genealogy, and obituaries of William and his father-reveals that the heir to the sword died suddenly in Georgia at the age of 31. When William died at 64, in 1879, tributes from old comrades revealed something of his service in Hawaii. Although on the inactive list, he was serving as naval storekeeper there, and this gave him opportunity to find out something about the economic importance of the islands. He became impressed with Hawaii's strategic position with relation to both navy and merchant marine. He pointed out that more intimate commercial relations between Hawaii and the United States would increase business and tend to strengthen this country's position of leadership in the world. William Reynolds pushed successfully the negotiation of a Hawaiian treaty of reciprocity. His opinion reportedly carried great weight with the many public men who consulted him on the subject. Hawaiians "have always borne in grateful memory his long residence in their midst, and his action in forwarding the treaty which has secured them a strong alliance with the United States, and saved them from the risks of an unwelcome protectorate from some distant power." according to one of the tributes from a Hawaiian representative in Washington.

From the evidence, Reynolds was a sort one man lobby for the Hawaiian treaty, an indispensable way-station on the road to statehood.

Admiral Reynolds's last voyage was his most glamorous. Sailing aboard his flagship, the "Tennessee." he passed through the Suez Canal, receiving "unusual honors" from the Khetive of Egypt and later from the British officers in India. Rosengarten said that, "In China and Japan, in Siam and Singapore, he discharged with great success the large discretion necessarily vested in our naval commanders in the East."

WIFE WALKED WITH EMPRESS

He sailed his ship close in by the Great Wall of China where it comes down to the sea, and his wife, the former Rebecca King of Lancaster, was the first American women permitted to walk on the wall with the Empress of China. The mention of Gen. John F. Reynolds' sword in Admiral Reynolds' will is a reminder that brother never forgot brother. The other "forgotten" Reynolds, the bachelor lawyer James, became a student of the life of John at Gettysburg. So it is that the other Reynolds brothers, long over-shadowed may shine again in some of the reflected glory of their hero brother. E.J. Nichols, Penn State professor who wrote the John F. Reynolds biography "Towards Gettysburg," has contributed to a remembering of William and James. And perhaps the Civil War centennial, now close upon us, will give them still more of the attention they have deserved.

The Sunday News, August 2,

1831 Nov 17 - appointed Midshipman/U.S. Navy
1836 - 37 - attended naval school, Norfolk, VA
1837 Jun 15 - passed Midshipman.
1838 - 1842 - served as an officer on the U.S.Exploring Expedition (aka the Wilkes Expedition.)
1841 Sep - received commission as Lieutenant.
1852 - 1861 - resided in Kauai and Honolulu, Hawaii during leave of absence from Navy; placed on Reserve list.
1855 Sep 24 - placed on reserved list due to ill health.
1857 Feb 23 - appointed Naval Store Keeper at Honolulu.
1862 Jun 9 - appointed Commander of U.S.S. Tennessee,South Atlantic Blockading Station, Port Royal, S. Carolina.
1866 Jul 25 - Promoted to Captain; U.S.S. Lackawanna toHawaii.
1867 - Took possession of Midway Island for the U.S.
1870 - appointed Commodore.
1870 - 1875 - appointed Chief of the Bureau of Equipment and Recruiting.
1873 - 1874 - Acting Secretary of the Navy.
1873 Dec 12 - appointed Rear Admiral.
1875 - appointed Commander of the naval forces bases at the "Asiatic Station" (Japan, China, Siam).
1877 Dec 10 - placed on Retired List.
1879 Nov 5 - died.

GENERAL JOHN REYNOLDS: Searching for names and birthdates of the children of two brothers of Civil War General John Fulton Reynolds. One brother, Admiral William Reynolds 1815-1879), married Rebecca Krug. The other, Samuel Moore Reynolds (1814-1888) married Elizabeth Van Horn. William had children and Samuel presumably did too, but the childrens' names are unkown. Samuel's place of death is even unkown. One missing child is believed to be attorney and poet J. Mason Reynolds (probably John or James), who moved to Belmont, Michigan around 1870, married Hannah,

and died young in 1891. Which brother was J. Mason's father is of enormous importance to the very few descendants of this Lancaster family.
Alan Reynolds <AReynolds@aol.com>
Reston, VA USA - Wednesday, February 04, 1998 at 11:46:05 (EST)

1850 United States Federal Census about William Reynolds
Name: William Reynolds
Age: 35
Estimated birth year: abt 1815
Birth Place: Pennsylvania
Gender: Male
Home in 1850 (City, County, State): Washington Ward 1, Washington, District of Columbia
Family Number: 942
Household Members:
Name Age
William Reynolds 35
Mrs.   Reynolds 28

1870 United States Federal Census about William Reynolds
Name: William Reynolds
Birth Year: abt 1815
Age in 1870: 55
Birthplace: Pennsylvania
Home in 1870: Washington Ward 1, Washington, District of Columbia
Race: White
Gender: Male
Value of real estate:
Post Office: Washington
Household Members:
Name Age
William Reynolds 55
Rebecca Reynolds 48
Rebecca King 9
Frederick King 6
Emma Herbert 30
Rachel Johnson 50

More About WILLIAM REYNOLDS and REBECCA KRUG:
Marriage: 16 Aug 1842, Holy Trinity Lutheran Church, Lancaster, PA

Child of WILLIAM REYNOLDS and REBECCA KRUG is:
101.   i.   JOHN MASON[11] REYNOLDS, b. Abt. 1845.

84. LYDIA MOORE[10] REYNOLDS (*JOHN*[9], *CATHERINE FERREE*[8] *LEFEVRE, SAMUEL*[7], *ISAAC*[6], *ABRAHAM*[5], *ANDREW*[4], *PHILIP*[3], *JOHN*[2], *MENGEN*[1]) was born 27 Jul 1818 in Lancaster, PA, and died 28 Dec 1896 in Fort Wayne, IN. She married NATHANIEL EVANS 14 Apr 1846 in Cornwall Furnace, PA. He was born 23 Dec 1813, and died 16 Oct 1893.

Notes for NATHANIEL EVANS:
Cornwall ironmaster.
1850 United States Federal Census about Nathan Evans
Name: Nathan Evans
Age: 36
Estimated birth year: abt 1814
Birth Place: Pennsylvania
Gender: Male
Home in 1850 (City, County, State): Washington, Clarion, Pennsylvania
Family Number: 742
Household Members:
Name Age
Nathan Evans 36
Lydia M Evans 31
Mary Evans 3
Catharine Evans 1
Robert Montgomery 26
Joseph Thompson 26
Lena Foglebacher 20
Caroline Emerline 17

1860 United States Federal Census about Nathan Evans
Name: Nathan Evans
Age in 1860: 46
Birth Year: abt 1814
Birthplace: Pennsylvania
Home in 1860: London Grove, Chester, Pennsylvania
Gender: Male
Post Office: Cochranville
Value of real estate:
Household Members:
Name Age
Nathan Evans 46
Lydia M Evans 41
Mary Evans 13
Hale Evans 10
John Evans 8
Frank Burel 33
Sarah J Burel 33

1870 United States Federal Census about Nathan Evans
Name: Nathan Evans
Birth Year: abt 1814

Age in 1870: 56
Birthplace: Pennsylvania
Home in 1870: Fort Wayne Ward 3, Allen, Indiana
Race: White
Gender: Male
Value of real estate: View image
Post Office: Fort Wayne
Household Members:
Name Age
Nathan Evans 56
Lydia Evans 52
Mary Evans 23
John Evans 19
Harry Evans 10
Julia Somers 24

1880 United States Federal Census about Nathan Evans
Name: Nathan Evans
Home in 1880: West Goshen, Chester, Pennsylvania
Age: 66
Estimated birth year: abt 1814
Birthplace: Pennsylvania
Relation to Head of Household: Self (Head)
Spouse's name: Lydia M
Father's birthplace: Pennsylvania
Mother's birthplace: Pennsylvania
Neighbors: View others on page
Occupation: Farmer
Marital Status: Married
Race: White
Gender: Male
Household Members:
Name Age
Nathan Evans 66
Lydia M Evans 51
Harry L. Evans 19
Mary Bullock 64

More About NATHANIEL EVANS and LYDIA REYNOLDS:
Marriage: 14 Apr 1846, Cornwall Furnace, PA

Children of LYDIA REYNOLDS and NATHANIEL EVANS are:
102.   i.   MARY[11] EVANS, b. 1847.
        ii.   CATHARINE EVANS, b. 1849; d. Bef. 1860.
        iii. HALE EVANS, b. 1850; d. Bef. 1870.
103.   iv.   JOHN FULTON REYNOLDS EVANS, b. 11 Aug 1851, Lancaster, PA;
              d. 27 Aug 1882, Lancaster, PA.

104.   v.   HARRY L EVANS, b. 1860.

85. MARY JANE[10] REYNOLDS *(JOHN[9], CATHERINE FERREE[8] LEFEVRE, SAMUEL[7], ISAAC[6], ABRAHAM[5], ANDREW[4], PHILIP[3], JOHN[2], MENGEN[1])* was born 13 Feb 1824 in Lancaster, PA, and died 10 Dec 1901. She married GEORGE GILDERSLEEVE 04 Dec 1849 in St. James Episcopal Church, Lancaster, PA. He was born 24 May 1822, and died 31 Dec 1900.

More About GEORGE GILDERSLEEVE and MARY REYNOLDS:
Marriage: 04 Dec 1849, St. James Episcopal Church, Lancaster, PA

Child of MARY REYNOLDS and GEORGE GILDERSLEEVE is:
     i.   WILLIAM REYNOLDS[11] GILDERSLEEVE, b. 1851; d. 1869.

86. CATHERINE FERREE[10] REYNOLDS *(JOHN[9], CATHERINE FERREE[8] LEFEVRE, SAMUEL[7], ISAAC[6], ABRAHAM[5], ANDREW[4], PHILIP[3], JOHN[2], MENGEN[1])* was born 11 Dec 1825 in Lancaster, PA, and died 10 Feb 1905 in Springfield, Montgomery County, PA. She married HENRY D LANDIS 08 Aug 1854 in Lancaster, PA. He was born 18 Oct 1824 in Philadelphia, PA, and died 18 Feb 1895 in Springfield, Montgomery County, PA.

Notes for CATHERINE FERREE REYNOLDS:
1900 United States Federal Census about Henry Landis Mrs
Name: Henry Landis Mrs
[Landis Mrs]
Home in 1900: Springfield, Montgomery, Pennsylvania
Age: 74
Birth Date: Dec 1825
Birthplace: Pennsylvania
Race: White
Gender: Female
Relationship to Head of House: Head
Father's Birthplace: Pennsylvania
Mother's Birthplace: Pennsylvania
Mother: number of living children: 5
Mother: How many children: 5
Marital Status: Widowed
Residence : Springfield Township, Montgomery, Pennsylvania
Occupation:
Neighbors:
Household Members:
Name Age
Henry Landis 74
Bertha L Landis 28
Eleanor Landis 63
Ella Jones 36
Rosetta Mc Intyre 20

Lizzie Mc Intyre 32
Emma Steel 41
Samuel Donald   25

More About HENRY LANDIS and CATHERINE REYNOLDS:
Marriage: 08 Aug 1854, Lancaster, PA

Children of CATHERINE REYNOLDS and HENRY LANDIS are:
  i.   HENRY G[11] LANDIS, b. 04 Jun 1848; d. 22 May 1888.
105. ii. MARY L LANDIS, b. Abt. 1850.
  iii. WILLIAM REYNOLDS LANDIS, b. Abt. 1850; m. (1) SARAH ANGENY, WFT Est. 1863-1906; b. WFT Est. 1843-1874; d. WFT Est. 1863-1956; m. (2) BERTHA LEFEVRE, WFT Est. 1863-1906; b. WFT Est. 1843-1874; d. WFT Est. 1863-1956.

      More About WILLIAM LANDIS and SARAH ANGENY:
      Marriage: WFT Est. 1863-1906

      More About WILLIAM LANDIS and BERTHA LEFEVRE:
      Marriage: WFT Est. 1863-1906

  iv. JOHN FULTON REYNOLDS LANDIS, b. 21 Oct 1856, Pennsylvania; d. Aft. 1934.

      Notes for JOHN FULTON REYNOLDS LANDIS:
      Former US Military Attache to Rome.

      New York Passenger Lists, 1820-1957 about John F R Landis
      Name: John F R Landis
      Arrival Date: 23 Oct 1934
      Estimated birth year: 1856
      Age: 78
      Gender: Male
      Port of Departure: Genoa, Italy
      Ship Name: President Adams
      Port of Arrival: New York, New York
      NATIVITY: Pennsylvania
      Line: 3
      Microfilm Serial: T715
      Microfilm Roll: T715_5566
      Birth Location: Pennsylvania
      Birth Location Other: Philadelphia
      Page Number: 13

106. v.   EDWARD KNEASS LANDIS, b. 06 Feb 1859; d. 15 Jan 1904.
  vi. KATE FERREE LANDIS, b. 1868; d. 1870.
  vii. BERTHA LEFEVRE LANDIS, b. Sep 1871; d. 1943.

87. GEORGE NEWTON[11] LeFEVRE (GEORGE[10], GEORGE[9], JOHN[8], ABRAHAM[7], ISAAC[6], ABRAHAM[5], ANDREW[4], PHILIP[3], JOHN[2], MENGEN[1]) was born 31 Jul 1850 in Strasburg, Lancaster Co, PA, and died 29 Nov 1943 in Strasburg, Lancaster Co, PA. He married LAURA LONG. She was born 02 May 1855 in Lancaster Co, PA, and died 08 Mar 1930 in Strasburg, Lancaster Co, PA.

More About GEORGE NEWTON LeFEVRE:
Burial: Lefevre Cemetery,Strasburg Township,Lancaster
County,Pennsylvania

Children of GEORGE LeFEVRE and LAURA LONG are:

    i.   LINCOLN L[12] LeFEVRE, b. 25 May 1875, Strasburg, Lancaster Co, PA; d. 31 Dec 1925, Strasburg, Lancaster Co, PA.

        More About LINCOLN L LeFEVRE:
        Burial: Lefevre Cemetery,Strasburg Township,Lancaster
        County,Pennsylvania

    ii. EDITH VIOLA LeFEVRE, b. 01 May 1897, Strasburg, Lancaster Co, PA; m. PAUL M MARVEL; b. 03 Mar 1898, Lancaster Co, PA.

88. J. MILLER[11] TRITT (CHRISTIAN[10], ELIZABETH[9] LeFEVRE, GEORGE[8], PHILIP G[7], ISAAC[6], ABRAHAM[5], ANDREW[4], PHILIP[3], JOHN[2], MENGEN[1]) was born WFT Est. 1816-1838, and died WFT Est. 1855-1921. He married SARA WOLFE WFT Est. 1831-1874. She was born WFT Est. 1809-1832, and died WFT Est. 1854-1920.

More About J. TRITT and SARA WOLFE:
Marriage: WFT Est. 1831-1874

Child of J. TRITT and SARA WOLFE is:

107.   i.   MARY JANE[12] TRITT, b. 02 Oct 1851; d. 06 Sep 1912.

89. PETER[11] TRITT (CHRISTIAN[10], ELIZABETH[9] LeFEVRE, GEORGE[8], PHILIP G[7], ISAAC[6], ABRAHAM[5], ANDREW[4], PHILIP[3], JOHN[2], MENGEN[1]) was born 24 Jun 1821 in Huntsdale, Pa., and died 16 Mar 1887 in Huntsdale, Pa. buried Pa. German Baptist Church, Huntsdale,Pa.. He married NANCY NICKEY 10 Jun 1845, daughter of SAMUEL NICKEY. She was born 02 Feb 1819 in Perry County, Pa., and died 28 Mar 1891 in Huntsdale, Pa. buried Pa. German Baptist Church, Huntsdale, Pa..

More About PETER TRITT and NANCY NICKEY:
Marriage: 10 Jun 1845

Children of PETER TRITT and NANCY NICKEY are:

	i.	CHRISTIAN[12] TRITT, b. 08 Jul 1846; d. 12 Jul 1846, buried Centerville, Pa..
108.	ii.	JOHN A. TRITT, b. 23 Sep 1847; d. 18 Sep 1929, Buried Centerville, Pa..
109.	iii.	SAMUEL JOHN TRITT, b. 1849; d. 1917.
110.	iv.	LYDIA JANE TRITT, b. 10 Aug 1851, Huntsdale, Pa; d. 25 Apr 1900, Greason, Pa. buried Presbyterian Churchyard Dickesen, Pa..
111.	v.	ELIZABETH TRITT, b. 23 Oct 1854; d. WFT Est. 1872-1948.
	vi.	MAGGIE T. TRITT, b. 1857; d. 09 Nov 1864, buried Centerville, Pa..
112.	vii.	PETER STOUGH TRITT, b. 08 Mar 1860; d. 03 Jun 1896, (of Pnuemonia) buried Huntsdale, Pa..

90. DR. ISSAC[11] LeFEVRE *(JACOB[10], LAWRENCE[9], GEORGE[8], PHILIP G[7], ISAAC[6], ABRAHAM[5], ANDREW[4], PHILIP[3], JOHN[2], MENGEN[1])* was born 15 Jun 1820 in Adams County, PA, and died 25 Oct 1893 in 411 Cumberland St, Harrisburg, PA. He married NANCY MULLET 11 Aug 1842. She was born 02 Sep 1821 in Gettysburg, Adams County, PA, and died 02 Jul 1900 in 411 Cumberland St, Harrisburg, PA.

Notes for DR. ISSAC LeFEVRE:
According to Perry County death records, Isaac was a doctor in New Bloomfield, Perry County. He died of 'interminting' fever at age 74.

More About ISSAC LeFEVRE and NANCY MULLET:
Marriage: 11 Aug 1842

Children of ISSAC LeFEVRE and NANCY MULLET are:

	i.	MARY ELIZABETH[12] LeFEVRE, b. 10 Aug 1844; d. 22 Nov 1887; m. MANOAH MERCER, 11 Nov 1866; b. 23 May 1844; d. Jan 1895.

More About MANOAH MERCER and MARY LeFEVRE:
Marriage: 11 Nov 1866

113.	ii.	DAVID GILBERT LeFEVRE, b. 08 Jan 1847; d. 01 Apr 1886.
	iii.	SARAH ANNE LeFEVRE, b. 26 Jul 1849; d. 07 Aug 1849.
	iv.	CHARLES LEINBACH LeFEVRE, b. 15 Jul 1851; d. 07 Aug 1915; m. MALINDA GRAFF, Dec 1880; b. 16 May 1849; d. 06 Jan 1944.

More About CHARLES LeFEVRE and MALINDA GRAFF:
Marriage: Dec 1880

	v.	EMMA REBECCA LeFEVRE, b. 02 May 1854; d. 31 May 1909.
	vi.	FANNY HALLETT LeFEVRE, b. 01 Aug 1857; d. 29 Jan 1885.
114.	vii.	DR. JOHN RUSSELL LeFEVRE, b. Oct 1860; d. 28 Jan 1935, Glen Ellyn, Illinois.

91. DAVID[11] LEFEVRE *(JOHN B.[10], LAWRENCE[9], GEORGE[8], PHILIP G[7], ISAAC[6], ABRAHAM[5], ANDREW[4], PHILIP[3], JOHN[2], MENGEN[1])* was born 05 Mar 1823, and died 1904. He married (1) MATILDA CUNNINGHAM 29 Dec 1847. She was born 19 Feb 1822, and died 08 Jan 1885. He married (2) MARGARET HOOVER 12 Oct 1886. She was born 14 Sep 1838.

More About MATILDA CUNNINGHAM:
Fact 1: Niece of Governor Ritner

More About DAVID LEFEVRE and MATILDA CUNNINGHAM:
Marriage: 29 Dec 1847

More About DAVID LEFEVRE and MARGARET HOOVER:
Marriage: 12 Oct 1886

Children of DAVID LEFEVRE and MATILDA CUNNINGHAM are:

	i.	JOHN[12] LEFEVRE, b. 02 Feb 1849; d. 18 Aug 1850.
	ii.	MARGARET LEFEVRE, b. 08 Sep 1850; d. 11 May 1942; m. CHARLES SMITH; b. 08 Aug 1847; d. 22 Aug 1924.
115.	iii.	HENRY RINE LEFEVRE, b. 20 Nov 1852; d. 14 Jun 1935, Cummingstown, Pennsylvania.
116.	iv.	DAVID LANDIS LEFEVRE, b. 11 Mar 1855; d. 22 May 1923.
	v.	JOSEPH CUNNINGHAM LEFEVRE, b. 18 Jan 1857; d. 25 Mar 1897; m. ELIZA TRITT, Jun 1886; b. 18 Jan 1856; d. 06 Nov 1922.

More About JOSEPH LEFEVRE and ELIZA TRITT:
Marriage: Jun 1886

	vi.	MATILDA LEFEVRE, b. 27 Apr 1859; d. 25 Jun 1921.
	vii.	BENJAMIN LEFEVRE, b. 06 Feb 1861; d. 26 Nov 1861.
	viii.	CLARINDA LEFEVRE, b. 10 Oct 1862; d. 01 Jul 1933; m. WILLIAM L. EYSTER, Oct 1882; b. 06 May 1860; d. 23 Jan 1926.

More About WILLIAM EYSTER and CLARINDA LEFEVRE:
Marriage: Oct 1882

	ix.	FANNY LEFEVRE, b. 28 Mar 1865; m. (1) ADAM STOUT, 20 Feb 1890; b. 15 Nov 1866; d. 26 Jun 1891; m. (2) BEVERIDGE LEECH, Dec 1893; b. 28 Dec 1871; d. Jun 1946.

More About ADAM STOUT and FANNY LEFEVRE:
Marriage: 20 Feb 1890

More About BEVERIDGE LEECH and FANNY LEFEVRE:
Marriage: Dec 1893

92. HENRY[11] LEFEVRE *(JOHN B.[10], LAWRENCE[9], GEORGE[8], PHILIP G[7], ISAAC[6], ABRAHAM[5], ANDREW[4], PHILIP[3], JOHN[2], MENGEN[1])* was born 02 Jan 1833 in Cumberland County, and died 15 Jul 1868. He married RACHEL BAER.

Child of HENRY LEFEVRE and RACHEL BAER is:

     i.   REBECCA[12] LEFEVRE, b. 16 Apr 1858; m. JOHN W. MCBRIDE, 03 Sep 1885.

        More About JOHN MCBRIDE and REBECCA LEFEVRE:
        Marriage: 03 Sep 1885

93. ISSAC LAWRENCE[11] LEFEVRE *(DAVID ALTER[10], LAWRENCE[9], GEORGE[8], PHILIP G[7], ISAAC[6], ABRAHAM[5], ANDREW[4], PHILIP[3], JOHN[2], MENGEN[1])* was born 08 Sep 1832 in Cumberland County, Pennsylvania, and died 07 Jan 1905. He married (1) ANNE PECK 05 Sep 1861. She was born 20 Sep 1841, and died 13 Jun 1889. He married (2) CATHERINE DUELL May 1890. She was born 05 Feb 1855, and died 11 Jul 1924.

More About ISSAC LAWRENCE LEFEVRE:
Fact 1: 1835, Moved to Indiana

More About ISSAC LEFEVRE and ANNE PECK:
Marriage: 05 Sep 1861

More About ISSAC LEFEVRE and CATHERINE DUELL:
Marriage: May 1890

Children of ISSAC LEFEVRE and ANNE PECK are:

117.   i.   WILLIAM UNION[12] LEFEVRE, b. 19 Feb 1863; d. 23 Mar 1928.
       ii.   MARY FRANCES LEFEVRE, b. 10 Aug 1864, Plymouth, Illinois; m. JESSE BIEBINGER, Feb 1890; b. 23 Sep 1863; d. 20 Jan 1940.

        More About JESSE BIEBINGER and MARY LEFEVRE:
        Marriage: Feb 1890

      iii.   ADA MAY LEFEVRE, b. 15 Oct 1867; d. 20 Sep 1896; m. WALLACE W. CROOK, 09 Nov 1887; b. 30 Nov 1861; d. 10 Jan 1948.

        More About WALLACE CROOK and ADA LEFEVRE:
        Marriage: 09 Nov 1887

118.   iv.   FRANK ORAN LEFEVRE, b. 24 Oct 1869, Milmine, Illinois.
       v.   ERVILLA BELLE LEFEVRE, b. 16 Feb 1872; d. 18 Feb 1949; m. ALVIN BEAL, 31 Dec 1899; b. 30 Nov 1872; d. 06 May 1929.

        More About ALVIN BEAL and ERVILLA LEFEVRE:
        Marriage: 31 Dec 1899

94. JOHN ALTER[11] LEFEVRE *(DAVID ALTER[10], LAWRENCE[9], GEORGE[8], PHILIP G[7], ISAAC[6], ABRAHAM[5], ANDREW[4], PHILIP[3], JOHN[2], MENGEN[1])* was born 28 Mar 1837, and died 30 Nov 1915. He married (1) ISABELLE MOYER 08 Oct 1860. She was born 08 Oct 1845, and died 1871. He married (2) SARAH MCMILLEN Feb 1876. She was born 18 Jun 1851, and died 13 Jan 1893.

More About JOHN LEFEVRE and ISABELLE MOYER:
Marriage: 08 Oct 1860

More About JOHN LEFEVRE and SARAH MCMILLEN:
Marriage: Feb 1876

Child of JOHN LEFEVRE and ISABELLE MOYER is:
      i. EDWARD FRANKLIN[12] LEFEVRE, b. 21 Apr 1867; d. 30 Nov 1926; m. BERTHA LEWIS, Mar 1901; b. 04 Jun 1878; d. 14 Aug 1940.

         More About EDWARD LEFEVRE and BERTHA LEWIS:
         Marriage: Mar 1901

Children of JOHN LEFEVRE and SARAH MCMILLEN are:
     ii. DAVID ROY[12] LEFEVRE, b. 15 Mar 1877; m. (1) HETTIE HOOVER, 30 Sep 1903; b. 1885; m. (2) CLAUDIA BURNS, 25 Mar 1912; b. 1889.

         More About DAVID LEFEVRE and HETTIE HOOVER:
         Marriage: 30 Sep 1903

         More About DAVID LEFEVRE and CLAUDIA BURNS:
         Marriage: 25 Mar 1912

    iii. ALICE WILT LEFEVRE, b. 22 Apr 1880; d. 14 May 1910; m. FRANK ROBINSON, 22 Jan 1905.

         More About FRANK ROBINSON and ALICE LEFEVRE:
         Marriage: 22 Jan 1905

119.   iv. PEARLY EMMET LEFEVRE, b. 19 Aug 1883, Nevada, Missouri.
      v. EMMA HOUSTIN LEFEVRE, b. 15 Apr 1885, Decatur, Illinois; d. 17 Jan 1925; m. GEORGE KLUMP; b. 04 Jul 1888.
     vi. BERNICE E. LEFEVRE, b. 03 Mar 1888, Greenfield, Ohio; m. J. FINAY LAVERY, 01 Nov 1917; b. 25 Aug 1878.

         More About J. LAVERY and BERNICE LEFEVRE:
         Marriage: 01 Nov 1917

    vii. LUCY RIDER LEFEVRE, b. 30 May 1890, Salem, Oregon; d. Oct

1968; m. JOHN BUCHANAN, 21 Dec 1912; b. 10 Jan 1887; d. Sep 1978.

More About LUCY RIDER LeFEVRE:
Fact 1: Social Security #: 544-20-6480
Fact 2: Last residence: OR 97361
Fact 3: State of issue: OR

More About JOHN BUCHANAN:
Fact 1: Social Security #: 526-07-5046
Fact 2: Last residence: OR 97367
Fact 3: State of issue: AZ

More About JOHN BUCHANAN and LUCY LeFEVRE:
Marriage: 21 Dec 1912

95. DAVID SLAYMAKER[11] LeFEVRE (*DAVID ALTER*[10], *LAWRENCE*[9], *GEORGE*[8], *PHILIP G*[7], *ISAAC*[6], *ABRAHAM*[5], *ANDREW*[4], *PHILIP*[3], *JOHN*[2], *MENGEN*[1]) was born 05 Sep 1841, and died 02 May 1911 in Lafayette, Indiana. He married ANNE WHITEMAN Aug 1864. She was born 23 Dec 1851, and died Dec 1903.

More About DAVID SLAYMAKER LeFEVRE:
Fact 1: Served in Union Army

More About DAVID LeFEVRE and ANNE WHITEMAN:
Marriage: Aug 1864

Children of DAVID LeFEVRE and ANNE WHITEMAN are:
      i.   JUSTIN FORREST[12] LeFEVRE, b. Abt. 1866.
      ii. OTHEL OLSEN LeFEVRE, b. Oct 1868; d. Oct 1888.
120. iii. ELLERY ELSTON LeFEVRE, b. 06 Mar 1870; d. 16 Dec 1943.
      iv. SYBIL LeFEVRE, b. 01 Jan 1879, Jonesboro, Arkansas; m. JOHN CASSELL, Sep 1899; b. 20 Apr 1878; d. 24 Apr 1950.

          More About JOHN CASSELL and SYBIL LeFEVRE:
          Marriage: Sep 1899

      v.   CECILE LeFEVRE, b. 14 Jan 1881, Lafayette, Indiana; m. JOSEPH JOHNSON.

96. JOHN A.[11] LINE (*GEORGE L.*[10], *ANNA BARBARA*[9] *LeFEVRE*, *GEORGE*[8], *PHILIP G*[7], *ISAAC*[6], *ABRAHAM*[5], *ANDREW*[4], *PHILIP*[3], *JOHN*[2], *MENGEN*[1]) was born 09 Apr 1834, and died WFT Est. 1870-1925. He married MARY B. BROWN 29 Dec 1865. She was born WFT Est. 1826-1848, and died WFT Est. 1870-1937.

More About JOHN LINE and MARY BROWN:
Marriage: 29 Dec 1865

Children of JOHN LINE and MARY BROWN are:

    i.   MIRIAM[12] LINE, b. WFT Est. 1855-1884; d. WFT Est. 1860-1966.
    ii. HERMAN BOWMAN LINE, b. WFT Est. 1855-1884; d. WFT Est. 1861-1963.
    iii. CHARLES EUGENE LINE, b. WFT Est. 1855-1884; d. WFT Est. 1861-1963.
    iv. JOHN RAYMOND LINE, b. WFT Est. 1855-1884; d. WFT Est. 1861-1963.

97. ABRAM L.[11] LINE *(GEORGE L.[10], ANNA BARBARA[9] LeFEVRE, GEORGE[8], PHILIP G[7], ISAAC[6], ABRAHAM[5], ANDREW[4], PHILIP[3], JOHN[2], MENGEN[1])* was born 02 Mar 1841, and died WFT Est. 1869-1932. He married SARAH H. MCMATH 21 Oct 1863. She was born WFT Est. 1825-1849, and died WFT Est. 1868-1938.

Notes for ABRAM L. LINE:
[Brøderbund WFT Vol. 3, Ed. 1, Tree #2268, Date of Import: Nov 9, 1996]

    Abram Line was a Civil War Soldier who enlisted July 2, 1862 Co. A. one hundred and thirtieth Reg. Pa. Vol. Inf. He was assigned to the Army of the Potomac and served in campaigns in Virginia and Maryland. He took part in the hard fought battles of South Mountain, Antietem, Fredericksburg, and Chancellorsville. He receiveda slight woulnd at Antietam and was honorably discharged in May 1963

More About ABRAM LINE and SARAH MCMATH:
Marriage: 21 Oct 1863

Children of ABRAM LINE and SARAH MCMATH are:

    i.   GEORGE E.[12] LINE, b. WFT Est. 1862-1891; d. WFT Est. 1868-1970.
    ii. LAURA AUGUST LINE, b. WFT Est. 1862-1891; d. WFT Est. 1867-1973.

98. DANIEL LEFEVRE[11] WOLF *(LYDIA[10] LEFEVRE, PETER[9], ADAM[8], PHILIP G[7], ISAAC[6], ABRAHAM[5], ANDREW[4], PHILIP[3], JOHN[2], MENGEN[1])* was born 22 Oct 1842 in York, PA, and died 30 Dec 1882 in Highspire, PA. He married ANNIE J HAIN. She was born 14 Feb 1844, and died 30 Apr 1907 in Highspire, PA.

Notes for DANIEL LEFEVRE WOLF:
1850 census lists Daniel Wolf as a son of George S - along w/ Franklin. Both ages are off by a year or two - OK if census was done a bit late. Daniel L Wolf - interred in Highspire near Franklin - could be the same person.

Children of DANIEL WOLF and ANNIE HAIN are:

      i.   FOREST R[12] WOLF, b. 16 Mar 1875, Highspire, PA; d. 27 Apr 1907, Highspire, PA.

121.   ii. FRANK JACOB WOLF, b. 1881, Highspire, PA; d. 1958, Highspire, PA.

99. FRANKLIN LEFEVERE[11] WOLF (*LYDIA[10] LEFEVRE, PETER[9], ADAM[8], PHILIP G[7], ISAAC[6], ABRAHAM[5], ANDREW[4], PHILIP[3], JOHN[2], MENGEN[1]*) was born 29 Dec 1849 in York County, PA, and died 02 Mar 1933 in Highspire, PA. He married (1) ELIZABETH HOKE 1869. She was born 07 Nov 1848, and died 12 Dec 1884 in Highspire, PA. He married (2) CATHERINE REBECCA OBER 1884, daughter of DAVID OBER and ANNA BRENNER. She was born 29 Apr 1857, and died 09 Feb 1943 in Highspire, PA.

Notes for FRANKLIN LEFEVERE WOLF:
From the "Commemorative Biographical Encyclopedia of Dauphin County, PA - 1896 (JM Runk & Co):

Pg 815 -816 (Portrait on 773)

Wolf, Franklin, farmer, Highspire PO, was born in York county, PA, December 29, 1849. He was the son of George W and Lydia (LeFevre) Wolf, natives of York county, PA. His father was a farmer and tobacco raiser. He was an active member of the Lutheran church. He was Republican in politics. He died in 1868, his wife in 1852. They had nine children, two of whom are now living; Annie, wife of Peter Shingle, or Goldsboro, York county, and Franklin.

Franklin was reared in York county and educated in the public schools till he was sixteen years old, when he became a worker for wages, hiring out as a farm laborer. In 1865 he came to Dauphin county, and lived with the Honorable Isaac Mumma (former judge and sheriff of Dauphin county - LBK) for 13 years. For the last eighteen years of this period he rented his farm and conducted the business for himself. In 1878 he engaged with Colonel John Motter (adjacent to the Mumma farm was the home of the famous Revolutionary soldier Colonel Edward Crouch, now owned by Colonel John Motter - and known as "Walnut Hill" - pg 433 - Star Barn? - LBK), and has since had charge of his farming interests. He is an active Republican. He has served as school director, treasurer and assessor of Lower Swatara Township. He is a member of Prince Edwin Lodge, No 486, F&AM, of Middletown (masons - LBK); of the Order of United American Mechanics, and of Harrisburg Lodge, No 68, and Encampment No. 10, IOOF, of Harrisburg. He was married in 1869 to Miss Elizabeth, daughter of Jacob Hoke, of Lower Swatara township. She died Dec 12, 1883, leaving four children: Harry E, married Elizabeth, daughter of David Smith, and has one child, Walter S.; Emma, wife of David Smith, of Lower Swatara township, and has two children, Annie and Harry; John Motter, and Harvey J. He was married again in 1884 to Miss Kate R Duncan, daughter of David Ober, of Swatara township, by whom he has four children; Clarence, Annie, Ober, and Mary.

Mr. Wolf and his family attend the Lutheran church.

Note: 2 years later, in 1898, Catherine Ruth Wolf was born - possibly at "Walnut Hill". Franklin built the home at High and Wolf streets in Highspire about 1900 - after this entry.

Franklin was a Civil War Veteran - according to a grave marker. Did Franklin follow in the footsteps of his older brother Daniel - leaving York Co for Highspire?

1910 Census
Franklin L Wolf
  Age: 60 State: PA
  Color: W Enumeration District: 0100
  Birth Place: Pennsylvania Visit: 0268
  County: Dauphin
  Relation: Head of Household
  Other Residents: Wife Catarine R 53, Pennsylvania
Son Jno M 29, Pennsylvania
Son Cl&rence R 23, Pennsylvania
Daughter Anni& B 21, Pennsylvania
Son David Obe- 19, Pennsylvania
Daughter Mary E 16, Pennsylvania
Son George E 13, Pennsylvania
Son Frank E 13, Pennsylvania
Daughter Atharine R 11, Pennsylvania

More About FRANKLIN LeFEVERE WOLF:
Burial: 04 Mar 1933, Highspire Cemetery

More About FRANKLIN WOLF and ELIZABETH HOKE:
Marriage: 1869

More About CATHERINE REBECCA OBER:
Burial: Highspire Cemetery

More About FRANKLIN WOLF and CATHERINE OBER:
Marriage: 1884

Children of FRANKLIN WOLF and ELIZABETH HOKE are:
       i. LEVI F[12] WOLF, b. 1869, Highspire, PA; d. 1870, Highspire, PA.
122.   ii. HARRY E WOLF, b. 1870, Highspire, PA; d. 1929, Highspire, PA.
     iii. MABEL E WOLF, b. 1879, Highspire, PA; d. 1879, Highspire, PA.
     iv. JOHN MOTTER WOLF, b. 1880; d. Aft. 1958, Harrisburg, PA.

      Notes for JOHN MOTTER WOLF:
      Lived with Franklin for 1910 census

123. v. HARVEY J WOLF, b. 1883, Highspire, PA; d. 1937, Highspire, PA.
124. vi. EMMA WOLF, b. Bef. 1885.

Children of FRANKLIN WOLF and CATHERINE OBER are:
125. vii. CLARENCE R[12] WOLF, b. 1886, Highspire, PA; d. Abt. 1970, Millville, NJ.
      viii. ANNA B WOLF, b. 1888; d. Hummelstown, PA; m. JOSEPH B HERSHEY; b. 09 Jul 1884; d. 28 Sep 1966, Hummelstown, PA.

      Notes for ANNA B WOLF:
      Hummelstown Cemetary

      Notes for JOSEPH B HERSHEY:
      Hershey, Joseph B   View Image Online
        Age: 37 Year: 1920
        Birthplace: Pennsylvania Roll: T625_1557
        Race: White Page: 14B

        State: Pennsylvania ED: 112

        County: Dauphin Image: 944

        Township: Hummelstown

      ----

126. ix. DAVID OBER WOLF, b. 1890, Highspire, PA; d. 09 Oct 1975, Highspire, PA.
       x. NELLIE I WOLF, b. 1891; d. Bef. 1910.
127. xi. MARY ESTELLE WOLF, b. 1893, Highspire, PA; d. 1930, Highspire, PA.
128. xii. FRANKLIN EARL WOLF, b. 15 Jan 1897, Highspire, PA; d. 07 Dec 1958, Highspire, PA.
129. xiii. GEORGE EDGAR WOLF, b. 15 Jan 1897; d. May 1977, Hannibal, MO.
130. xiv. CATHERINE REBECCA WOLF, b. 30 Apr 1898, Highspire, PA; d. 10 Jun 1986, Highspire, PA.

100. ELIZABETH[11] MOORE (REBECCA[10] LEFEVRE, JACOB[9], JACOB[8], PHILIP G[7], ISAAC[6], ABRAHAM[5], ANDREW[4], PHILIP[3], JOHN[2], MENGEN[1]) was born 19 Apr 1850. She married NATHANIEL P BROWN 29 Feb 1872 in Clay County, Indiana.

More About NATHANIEL BROWN and ELIZABETH MOORE:
Marriage: 29 Feb 1872, Clay County, Indiana

Children of ELIZABETH MOORE and NATHANIEL BROWN are:

131. i. FRANK A.[12] BROWN, b. 17 Oct.
132. ii. HARRY D. BROWN, b. 04 Mar 1873, Terre Haute, Indiana; d. Jun 1931, Terre Haute, Indiana.

101. JOHN MASON[11] REYNOLDS *(WILLIAM[10], JOHN[9], CATHERINE FERREE[8] LEFEVRE, SAMUEL[7], ISAAC[6], ABRAHAM[5], ANDREW[4], PHILIP[3], JOHN[2], MENGEN[1])* was born Abt. 1845.

Child of JOHN MASON REYNOLDS is:

133. i. ALAN DEFOREST[12] REYNOLDS, b. Abt. 1871; d. Aft. 1944.

102. MARY[11] EVANS *(LYDIA MOORE[10] REYNOLDS, JOHN[9], CATHERINE FERREE[8] LEFEVRE, SAMUEL[7], ISAAC[6], ABRAHAM[5], ANDREW[4], PHILIP[3], JOHN[2], MENGEN[1])* was born 1847. She married WILLIAM H HOFFMAN 1874.

More About WILLIAM HOFFMAN and MARY EVANS:
Marriage: 1874

Children of MARY EVANS and WILLIAM HOFFMAN are:

       i. FREDERICK E[12] HOFFMAN.
134. ii. KATHERINE HOFFMAN, b. 1876; d. 1959.
      iii. EMILY R HOFFMAN, b. 1878; d. 1959; m. HOFFMAN.

103. JOHN FULTON REYNOLDS[11] EVANS *(LYDIA MOORE[10] REYNOLDS, JOHN[9], CATHERINE FERREE[8] LEFEVRE, SAMUEL[7], ISAAC[6], ABRAHAM[5], ANDREW[4], PHILIP[3], JOHN[2], MENGEN[1])* was born 11 Aug 1851 in Lancaster, PA, and died 27 Aug 1882 in Lancaster, PA. He married MARGARETTA RUTHENAUFF 1876. She was born WFT Est. 1832-1859, and died WFT Est. 1881-1949.

More About JOHN EVANS and MARGARETTA RUTHENAUFF:
Marriage: 1876

Children of JOHN EVANS and MARGARETTA RUTHENAUFF are:

       i. KATE E.[12] EVANS, b. WFT Est. 1861-1899; d. WFT Est. 1872-1981.
      ii. WILLIAM R. EVANS, b. WFT Est. 1861-1899; d. WFT Est. 1872-1981.

104. HARRY L[11] EVANS *(LYDIA MOORE[10] REYNOLDS, JOHN[9], CATHERINE FERREE[8] LEFEVRE, SAMUEL[7], ISAAC[6], ABRAHAM[5], ANDREW[4], PHILIP[3], JOHN[2], MENGEN[1])* was born 1860. He married FANNY PALLOCK.

Children of HARRY EVANS and FANNY PALLOCK are:
  i.   ROSSWELL[12] EVANS.
  ii. CHARLES P EVANS.

105. MARY L[11] LANDIS *(CATHERINE FERREE[10] REYNOLDS, JOHN[9], CATHERINE FERREE[8] LEFEVRE, SAMUEL[7], ISAAC[6], ABRAHAM[5], ANDREW[4], PHILIP[3], JOHN[2], MENGEN[1])* was born Abt. 1850. She married JOHN SCOTTY.

Child of MARY LANDIS and JOHN SCOTTY is:
  i.   JOHN F B[12] SCOTTY.

106. EDWARD KNEASS[11] LANDIS *(CATHERINE FERREE[10] REYNOLDS, JOHN[9], CATHERINE FERREE[8] LEFEVRE, SAMUEL[7], ISAAC[6], ABRAHAM[5], ANDREW[4], PHILIP[3], JOHN[2], MENGEN[1])* was born 06 Feb 1859, and died 15 Jan 1904. He married EMILY F POTTS.

Child of EDWARD LANDIS and EMILY POTTS is:
  i.   ISABELLE POTTS[12] LANDIS, m. BARON OTTO VON BORCKE, 22 Jun 1912.

       Notes for BARON OTTO VON BORCKE:
       Lieutenant in the German Navy

       More About OTTO VON BORCKE and ISABELLE LANDIS:
       Marriage: 22 Jun 1912

Generation No. 12

107. MARY JANE[12] TRITT *(J. MILLER[11], CHRISTIAN[10], ELIZABETH[9] LEFEVRE, GEORGE[8], PHILIP G[7], ISAAC[6], ABRAHAM[5], ANDREW[4], PHILIP[3], JOHN[2], MENGEN[1])* was born 02 Oct 1851, and died 06 Sep 1912. She married DAVID SHEAFFER 1873. He was born 05 Feb 1836, and died 30 Jul 1919 in buried Pa. German Baptist Churchyard, Huntsdale, Pa..

More About DAVID SHEAFFER and MARY TRITT:
Marriage: 1873

Child of MARY TRITT and DAVID SHEAFFER is:
  i.   JACOB[13] SHEAFFER, b. WFT Est. 1863-1891; d. WFT Est. 1869-1971.

108. JOHN A.[12] TRITT *(PETER[11], CHRISTIAN[10], ELIZABETH[9] LEFEVRE, GEORGE[8],*

PHILIP G[7], ISAAC[6], ABRAHAM[5], ANDREW[4], PHILIP[3], JOHN[2], MENGEN[1]*) was born 23 Sep 1847, and died 18 Sep 1929 in Buried Centerville, Pa.. He married JENNIE E. TOBIAS WFT Est. 1862-1894. She was born 25 Jul 1845, and died 17 Oct 1920 in Buried Centerville, Pa..

More About JOHN TRITT and JENNIE TOBIAS:
Marriage: WFT Est. 1862-1894

Children of JOHN TRITT and JENNIE TOBIAS are:
     i. ALICE E.[13] TRITT, b. WFT Est. 1864-1893; d. WFT Est. 1870-1975.
    ii. EDGAR P. TRITT, b. WFT Est. 1864-1893; d. WFT Est. 1871-1972.
   iii. FLORENCE E. TRITT, b. WFT Est. 1864-1893; d. WFT Est. 1870-1975.
   iv. MAUD T. TRITT, b. WFT Est. 1864-1893; d. WFT Est. 1870-1975.
    v. MELVIN J. TRITT, b. WFT Est. 1864-1893; d. WFT Est. 1871-1972.
   vi. CLARENCE E. TRITT, b. WFT Est. 1864-1893; d. WFT Est. 1871-1972.

109. SAMUEL JOHN[12] TRITT (*PETER[11], CHRISTIAN[10], ELIZABETH[9] LeFEVRE, GEORGE[8], PHILIP G[7], ISAAC[6], ABRAHAM[5], ANDREW[4], PHILIP[3], JOHN[2], MENGEN[1]*) was born 1849, and died 1917. He married MARY LACEY WFT Est. 1868-1891. She was born 1852, and died 1901.

More About SAMUEL TRITT and MARY LACEY:
Marriage: WFT Est. 1868-1891

Child of SAMUEL TRITT and MARY LACEY is:
     i. CLARENCE ZIEGLER[13] TRITT, b. 30 Apr 1884; d. 1891, Huntsdale, Pa..

110. LYDIA JANE[12] TRITT (*PETER[11], CHRISTIAN[10], ELIZABETH[9] LeFEVRE, GEORGE[8], PHILIP G[7], ISAAC[6], ABRAHAM[5], ANDREW[4], PHILIP[3], JOHN[2], MENGEN[1]*) was born 10 Aug 1851 in Huntsdale, Pa, and died 25 Apr 1900 in Greason, Pa. buried Presbyterian Churchyard Dickesen, Pa.. She married J. MARION SHEAFFER WFT Est. 1864-1889. He was born 15 May 1843 in Huntsdale, Pa., and died 24 Nov 1927 in Carlisle, buried Westminster Cem..

More About J. SHEAFFER and LYDIA TRITT:
Marriage: WFT Est. 1864-1889

Children of LYDIA TRITT and J. SHEAFFER are:
     i. BERTIE F.[13] SHEAFFER, b. 03 Jan 1867; d. 07 Feb 1862, buried Pa. German Baptist Churchyard, Huntsdale, Pa..
135.   ii. ALICE MARGARET SHEAFFER, b. 26 Oct 1869, Craighead,

Cumberlan Co, Pa.; d. 07 Sep 1930, Dickesen, Pa..

136. iii. CHARLES M. SHEAFFER, b. 14 Jan 1874, Huntsdale, Pa.; d. 02 Oct 1965, Utica, New York buried St. Agnes Cem, Utica, NY.

111. ELIZABETH[12] TRITT *(PETER[11], CHRISTIAN[10], ELIZABETH[9] LeFEVRE, GEORGE[8], PHILIP G[7], ISAAC[6], ABRAHAM[5], ANDREW[4], PHILIP[3], JOHN[2], MENGEN[1])* was born 23 Oct 1854, and died WFT Est. 1872-1948. She married THOMAS FERREE WFT Est. 1870-1900. He was born 28 Dec 1852, and died WFT Est. 1872-1943.

More About THOMAS FERREE and ELIZABETH TRITT:
Marriage: WFT Est. 1870-1900

Child of ELIZABETH TRITT and THOMAS FERREE is:
i. ALICE[13] FERREE, b. WFT Est. 1872-1899; d. WFT Est. 1878-1982; m. MR. BOWMAN.

112. PETER STOUGH[12] TRITT *(PETER[11], CHRISTIAN[10], ELIZABETH[9] LeFEVRE, GEORGE[8], PHILIP G[7], ISAAC[6], ABRAHAM[5], ANDREW[4], PHILIP[3], JOHN[2], MENGEN[1])* was born 08 Mar 1860, and died 03 Jun 1896 in (of Pnuemonia) buried Huntsdale, Pa.. He married ANNIE MCMONUS WFT Est. 1877-1893. She was born 1861, and died 1953.

More About PETER TRITT and ANNIE MCMONUS:
Marriage: WFT Est. 1877-1893

Child of PETER TRITT and ANNIE MCMONUS is:
i. ALICE BELL[13] TRITT, b. 20 Sep 1881; d. 1883, buried Huntsdale, Pa.

113. DAVID GILBERT[12] LeFEVRE *(ISSAC[11], JACOB[10], LAWRENCE[9], GEORGE[8], PHILIP G[7], ISAAC[6], ABRAHAM[5], ANDREW[4], PHILIP[3], JOHN[2], MENGEN[1])* was born 08 Jan 1847, and died 01 Apr 1886. He married EMILY GRAFF Feb 1874. She was born 10 Mar 1848, and died 17 Feb 1933.

More About DAVID LeFEVRE and EMILY GRAFF:
Marriage: Feb 1874

Children of DAVID LeFEVRE and EMILY GRAFF are:
i. ISSAC GRAFF[13] LeFEVRE, b. 02 Nov 1875; d. 15 Oct 1876.
137. ii. CHARLES W. LeFEVRE, b. 09 Jan 1878; d. 16 Mar 1941, Drexel Hill, Pennsylvania.
iii. JOHN YEWELL LeFEVRE, b. 08 Jul 1879; d. 29 Jan 1946.
iv. ANNE MARY LeFEVRE, b. 25 Dec 1880.
v. EMMA JESSIE LeFEVRE, b. 19 Apr 1883, Philadelphia, Pennsylvania.

vi. FANNY MALINDA LEFEVRE, b. 22 May 1885; d. Apr 1976.

More About FANNY MALINDA LEFEVRE:
Fact 1: Social Security #: 178-18-0047
Fact 2: Last residence: DE 19807
Fact 3: State of issue: PA

114. DR. JOHN RUSSELL[12] LEFEVRE *(ISSAC[11], JACOB[10], LAWRENCE[9], GEORGE[8], PHILIP G[7], ISAAC[6], ABRAHAM[5], ANDREW[4], PHILIP[3], JOHN[2], MENGEN[1])* was born Oct 1860, and died 28 Jan 1935 in Glen Ellyn, Illinois. He married MYRA BELLE EBERSOLE 24 Aug 1886. She was born 16 Oct 1865.

More About JOHN LEFEVRE and MYRA EBERSOLE:
Marriage: 24 Aug 1886

Children of JOHN LEFEVRE and MYRA EBERSOLE are:
138.   i.   HALLETT RUDOLPH[13] LEFEVRE, b. 09 Oct 1887, Chicago, Illinois.
139.   ii. RUSSELL MOORE LEFEVRE, b. 15 Dec 1892.
       iii. LILLIAN EMMA LEFEVRE, b. 17 Oct 1894.
       iv. LOIS MARION LEFEVRE, b. 17 Jan 1897; m. GORDON S. MORGAN, 08 Mar 1919; b. 30 Apr 1892.

       More About GORDON MORGAN and LOIS LEFEVRE:
       Marriage: 08 Mar 1919

115. HENRY RINE[12] LEFEVRE *(DAVID[11], JOHN B.[10], LAWRENCE[9], GEORGE[8], PHILIP G[7], ISAAC[6], ABRAHAM[5], ANDREW[4], PHILIP[3], JOHN[2], MENGEN[1])* was born 20 Nov 1852, and died 14 Jun 1935 in Cummingstown, Pennsylvania. He married NANCY KELSO Nov 1876. She was born 12 Dec 1851, and died 01 Jul 1928 in Cummingstown, Pennsylvania.

More About HENRY LEFEVRE and NANCY KELSO:
Marriage: Nov 1876

Children of HENRY LEFEVRE and NANCY KELSO are:
       i.   MATILDA C.[13] LEFEVRE, b. 12 Aug 1877; m. JOHN BENTZ, 11 Jun 1925; b. 27 Jun 1866.

       More About JOHN BENTZ and MATILDA LEFEVRE:
       Marriage: 11 Jun 1925

       ii. JOHN K. LEFEVRE, b. 28 Nov 1878, Carlisle, Pennsylvania.
       iii. FRANCIS D. LEFEVRE, b. 12 May 1880; d. May 1892.
       iv. MARY BLANCHE LEFEVRE, b. 13 Dec 1881, Carlisle, Pennsylvania.
140.   v.   FLORENCE GRACE LEFEVRE, b. 25 Nov 1883, Carlisle, Pennsylvania; d. 12 Jan 1973, Park Haven Nursing Home,

Maryland.

vi. FANNY ISABELLE LEFEVRE, b. 09 Sep 1885, Philadelphia,
Pennsylvania.

vii. ADDA JUNE LEFEVRE, b. 22 Jun 1888, Carlisle, Pennsylvania; m.
HERMAN LAUFELD, 04 Oct 1917; b. 21 Mar 1874; d. 08 May
1934.

More About HERMAN LAUFELD and ADDA LEFEVRE:
Marriage: 04 Oct 1917

viii. PEARL IRENE LEFEVRE, b. 10 Sep 1890, Newville, Pennsylvania;
m. WALTER KELSO, 17 Dec 1914; b. 10 Aug 1888; d. May 1984.

More About WALTER KELSO:
Fact 1: Social Security #: 195-16-2793
Fact 2: Last residence: PA 18330

More About WALTER KELSO and PEARL LEFEVRE:
Marriage: 17 Dec 1914

ix. MARGARET J. LEFEVRE, b. 04 May 1892, Shippensburg,
Pennsylvania; m. WILLIAM SKELLY; b. 30 Oct 1891.

x. HELEN VIOLA LEFEVRE, b. 03 Jun 1895, Carlisle, Pennsylvania;
m. JESSE KURTZ; b. 17 Jun 1898; d. Nov 1984.

More About JESSE KURTZ:
Fact 1: Social Security #: 204-30-6037
Fact 2: Last residence: PA 17019

116. DAVID LANDIS[12] LEFEVRE *(DAVID[11], JOHN B.[10], LAWRENCE[9], GEORGE[8],
PHILIP G[7], ISAAC[6], ABRAHAM[5], ANDREW[4], PHILIP[3], JOHN[2], MENGEN[1])* was born 11
Mar 1855, and died 22 May 1923. He married MARGARET SEAVER Nov 1876.
She was born 09 Apr 1854, and died 06 Dec 1942.

More About DAVID LEFEVRE and MARGARET SEAVER:
Marriage: Nov 1876

Child of DAVID LEFEVRE and MARGARET SEAVER is:
i. ELIZABETH C.[13] LEFEVRE, b. 21 Jul 1879, Shippensburg,
Pennsylvania; m. JOSEPH MILLER; b. 08 Aug 1873; d. 14 Aug
1945.

117. WILLIAM UNION[12] LEFEVRE *(ISSAC LAWRENCE[11], DAVID ALTER[10],
LAWRENCE[9], GEORGE[8], PHILIP G[7], ISAAC[6], ABRAHAM[5], ANDREW[4], PHILIP[3], JOHN[2],
MENGEN[1])* was born 19 Feb 1863, and died 23 Mar 1928. He married
ELIZABETH ARMSWORTH 1889. She was born 22 Sep 1867, and died 04 Aug

1947.

More About WILLIAM LeFevre and ELIZABETH ARMSWORTH:
Marriage: 1889

Child of WILLIAM LeFevre and ELIZABETH ARMSWORTH is:
     i. CLARA FRANCES[13] LeFevre, b. 15 Oct 1890, Bement, Illinois; m. FREDERICK LUX, 24 Dec 1917; b. 15 Oct 1890.

       More About FREDERICK LUX and CLARA LeFevre:
       Marriage: 24 Dec 1917

118. FRANK ORAN[12] LeFevre *(ISSAC LAWRENCE[11], DAVID ALTER[10], LAWRENCE[9], GEORGE[8], PHILIP G[7], ISAAC[6], ABRAHAM[5], ANDREW[4], PHILIP[3], JOHN[2], MENGEN[1])* was born 24 Oct 1869 in Milmine, Illinois. He married (1) JOSEPHINE ARMSWORTH 10 Sep 1893. She was born 16 Nov 1872, and died 23 May 1916. He married (2) GERTRUDE LUCILE CARTER 20 Aug 1917. She was born 18 Sep 1895.

More About FRANK LeFevre and JOSEPHINE ARMSWORTH:
Marriage: 10 Sep 1893

More About FRANK LeFevre and GERTRUDE CARTER:
Marriage: 20 Aug 1917

Child of FRANK LeFevre and JOSEPHINE ARMSWORTH is:
141.   i. CLARENCE[13] LeFevre, b. 07 Aug 1894; d. Nov 1970.

Children of FRANK LeFevre and GERTRUDE CARTER are:
     ii. FRANCES ELIZABETH[13] LeFevre, b. 05 Oct 1918, Milmine, Illinois; m. DAVID MEDARIS, 26 Dec 1939; b. 23 Dec 1918.

       More About DAVID MEDARIS and FRANCES LeFevre:
       Marriage: 26 Dec 1939

     iii. MARY BELLE LeFevre, b. 28 Feb 1922; d. May 1985; m. JAMES WOMER, 16 Aug 1942; b. 23 Jul 1923.

       More About MARY BELLE LeFevre:
       Fact 1: Social Security #: 359-12-8701
       Fact 3: State of issue: IL

       More About JAMES WOMER and MARY LeFevre:
       Marriage: 16 Aug 1942

     iv. ERVILLE MAE LeFevre, b. 13 Apr 1930.

119. PEARLY EMMET[12] LEFEVRE *(JOHN ALTER[11], DAVID ALTER[10], LAWRENCE[9], GEORGE[8], PHILIP G[7], ISAAC[6], ABRAHAM[5], ANDREW[4], PHILIP[3], JOHN[2], MENGEN[1])* was born 19 Aug 1883 in Nevada, Missouri. He married FRANCES WRIGHT. She was born 09 Dec 1888.

Children of PEARLY LEFEVRE and FRANCES WRIGHT are:

    i.   AGNES LOIS[13] LEFEVRE, b. 30 Jul 1906; d. 18 Jun 1928; m. WAYNE BROOK; b. 29 Sep 1901.

    ii. GRACE PEARL LEFEVRE, b. 19 Jun 1911, Greeley, Colorado; m. EVERETT LEWIS; b. 19 Dec 1908.

120. ELLERY ELSTON[12] LEFEVRE *(DAVID SLAYMAKER[11], DAVID ALTER[10], LAWRENCE[9], GEORGE[8], PHILIP G[7], ISAAC[6], ABRAHAM[5], ANDREW[4], PHILIP[3], JOHN[2], MENGEN[1])* was born 06 Mar 1870, and died 16 Dec 1943. He married FRANCES POYNTER 02 Nov 1898. She was born 30 Sep 1879.

More About ELLERY LEFEVRE and FRANCES POYNTER:
Marriage: 02 Nov 1898

Children of ELLERY LEFEVRE and FRANCES POYNTER are:

    i.   GLADYS RUTH[13] LEFEVRE, b. 08 May 1900; d. 14 Oct 1929; m. DAVID ROSS, 06 Jul 1919; b. 20 Nov 1898; d. 12 Jul 1944.

       More About DAVID ROSS and GLADYS LEFEVRE:
       Marriage: 06 Jul 1919

142. ii. JACK LEFEVRE, b. 11 Oct 1902; d. Apr 1983.

    iii. ADALE FRANCES LEFEVRE, b. 01 Mar 1905, Alexandria, Virginia; m. HOBART CRONE, 02 Feb 1921; b. 30 Dec 1897; d. May 1964.

       More About HOBART CRONE:
       Fact 1: Social Security #: 400-03-4736
       Fact 2: Last residence: FL
       Fact 3: State of issue: KY

       More About HOBART CRONE and ADALE LEFEVRE:
       Marriage: 02 Feb 1921

    iv. EARL ELSTON LEFEVRE, b. 19 Nov 1907, Lafayette, Indiana; m. EVELYN ANTRIM; b. 31 Aug 1910; d. 23 Aug 1939.

121. FRANK JACOB[12] WOLF *(DANIEL LEFEVRE[11], LYDIA[10] LEFEVRE, PETER[9], ADAM[8], PHILIP G[7], ISAAC[6], ABRAHAM[5], ANDREW[4], PHILIP[3], JOHN[2], MENGEN[1])* was born 1881 in Highspire, PA, and died 1958 in Highspire, PA. He married ELLEN M UNKNOWN. She was born 1879 in Highspire, PA, and died 1967 in

Highspire, PA.

Notes for FRANK JACOB WOLF:
1910 Census in Highspire with wife at 168 Lumber St.
1920 Census has him on Penn St.

Child of FRANK WOLF and ELLEN UNKNOWN is:
     i. HELEN P[13] WOLF, b. 1915.

122. HARRY E[12] WOLF (*FRANKLIN LeFEVERE*[11], *LYDIA*[10] *LeFEVRE, PETER*[9], *ADAM*[8], *PHILIP G*[7], *ISAAC*[6], *ABRAHAM*[5], *ANDREW*[4], *PHILIP*[3], *JOHN*[2], *MENGEN*[1]) was born 1870 in Highspire, PA, and died 1929 in Highspire, PA. He married ELIZABETH J SMITH. She was born 1873, and died 1954 in Highspire, PA.

Children of HARRY WOLF and ELIZABETH SMITH are:
     i. NORA[13] WOLF, b. 1898, Highspire, PA; d. 1991, Highspire, PA;
       m. MR MCALPIN.
    ii. WALTER S WOLF.

123. HARVEY J[12] WOLF (*FRANKLIN LeFEVERE*[11], *LYDIA*[10] *LeFEVRE, PETER*[9], *ADAM*[8], *PHILIP G*[7], *ISAAC*[6], *ABRAHAM*[5], *ANDREW*[4], *PHILIP*[3], *JOHN*[2], *MENGEN*[1]) was born 1883 in Highspire, PA, and died 1937 in Highspire, PA. He married SARA M UNKNOWN. She was born 1885, and died 1977 in Highspire, PA.

Child of HARVEY WOLF and SARA UNKNOWN is:
     i. HAROLD C[13] WOLF, b. 1907; d. 1997, Highspire, PA.

124. EMMA[12] WOLF (*FRANKLIN LeFEVERE*[11], *LYDIA*[10] *LeFEVRE, PETER*[9], *ADAM*[8], *PHILIP G*[7], *ISAAC*[6], *ABRAHAM*[5], *ANDREW*[4], *PHILIP*[3], *JOHN*[2], *MENGEN*[1]) was born Bef. 1885. She married DAVID SMITH. He died in Lower Swatara Twp, Dauphin Co, PA.

Children of EMMA WOLF and DAVID SMITH are:
     i. ANNIE[13] SMITH.
    ii. HARRY SMITH.

125. CLARENCE R[12] WOLF (*FRANKLIN LeFEVERE*[11], *LYDIA*[10] *LeFEVRE, PETER*[9], *ADAM*[8], *PHILIP G*[7], *ISAAC*[6], *ABRAHAM*[5], *ANDREW*[4], *PHILIP*[3], *JOHN*[2], *MENGEN*[1]) was born 1886 in Highspire, PA, and died Abt. 1970 in Millville, NJ. He married MARY M MILLER. She was born 1893.

Notes for CLARENCE R WOLF:
Wolf, Clarence R   View Image Online
  Age: 43 Year: 1930

Birthplace: Pennsylvania Roll: T626_1327
Race: White Page: 1A

State: New Jersey ED: 52

County: Cumberland Image: 0266

Township: Millville

Children of CLARENCE WOLF and MARY MILLER are:
143.   i.   CLARENCE FRANKLIN[13] WOLF, b. 1912.
       ii.   MARY E WOLF, b. 1917; m. MARVIN L HOWARD; b. Abt. 1910.
      iii.   DAVID O WOLF, b. 1919; d. Abt. 1960.
      iv.   ALICE K WOLF, b. 1924; d. Abt. 1960.
144.   v.   JOHN S WOLF, b. 1926.
      vi.   BARBARA ANN WOLF, b. 1928; m. KRENAR SHAPLLO, 14 Jun 1952, Millville, NJ; b. Abt. 1910.

More About KRENAR SHAPLLO and BARBARA WOLF:
Marriage: 14 Jun 1952, Millville, NJ

126. DAVID OBER[12] WOLF *(FRANKLIN LeFEVERE[11], LYDIA[10] LeFEVRE, PETER[9], ADAM[8], PHILIP G[7], ISAAC[6], ABRAHAM[5], ANDREW[4], PHILIP[3], JOHN[2], MENGEN[1])* was born 1890 in Highspire, PA, and died 09 Oct 1975 in Highspire, PA. He married MARIAN TAYLOR STEELE 07 Apr 1923 in Pittsburgh, PA. She was born Abt. 1890, and died 28 Dec 1950.

Notes for DAVID OBER WOLF:
David was a WW I veteran Cpl US Army

More About DAVID WOLF and MARIAN STEELE:
Marriage: 07 Apr 1923, Pittsburgh, PA

Children of DAVID WOLF and MARIAN STEELE are:
      i.   MARIAN ELIZABETH[13] WOLF, b. Aft. 1923; d. Storrs, CT; m. CARL WILLIAM RETTENMEYER, 26 Jun, Ann Arbor, MI.

More About CARL RETTENMEYER and MARIAN WOLF:
Marriage: 26 Jun, Ann Arbor, MI

145.   ii.   MARJORIE ANN WOLF, b. Abt. 1928, Pittsburgh, PA; d. 30 Sep 1970, Glastonbury, CT.

127. MARY ESTELLE[12] WOLF *(FRANKLIN LeFEVERE[11], LYDIA[10] LeFEVRE, PETER[9], ADAM[8], PHILIP G[7], ISAAC[6], ABRAHAM[5], ANDREW[4], PHILIP[3], JOHN[2], MENGEN[1])* was born 1893 in Highspire, PA, and died 1930 in Highspire, PA. She married HOWARD JONES WILLIAMS 09 Dec 1922 in Pittsburgh, PA. He was born 16 Jun 1893 in Plymouth, PA, and died 1958 in Millville, NJ.

More About HOWARD WILLIAMS and MARY WOLF:
Marriage: 09 Dec 1922, Pittsburgh, PA

Children of MARY WOLF and HOWARD WILLIAMS are:

    i.   HOWARD JONES[13] WILLIAMS, b. 1924; d. Macon, GA; m. MARY DORRIS TIDWELL, 28 Dec, Douglassville, GA.

         More About HOWARD WILLIAMS and MARY TIDWELL:
         Marriage: 28 Dec, Douglassville, GA

    ii. RUTH L WILLIAMS, b. 1927; d. Union, NJ; m. HOWARD FORREST; b. Aft. 1900.
    iii. OBER WOLF WILLIAMS, b. 1929; d. Cincinnati, OH; m. MARCELINE ELODIA COLLE, 18 Aug 1956, Rochester, NY.

         More About OBER WILLIAMS and MARCELINE COLLE:
         Marriage: 18 Aug 1956, Rochester, NY

128. FRANKLIN EARL[12] WOLF (*FRANKLIN LEFEVERE[11], LYDIA[10] LEFEVRE, PETER[9], ADAM[8], PHILIP G[7], ISAAC[6], ABRAHAM[5], ANDREW[4], PHILIP[3], JOHN[2], MENGEN[1]*) was born 15 Jan 1897 in Highspire, PA, and died 07 Dec 1958 in Highspire, PA. He married HELEN GENE LANCASTER 01 Aug 1924 in West Chester, PA. She was born Abt. 1900.

Notes for FRANKLIN EARL WOLF:
Franklin E Wolf, 61, of 360 High St, Highspire, PA, died Sunday morning at his home.

He was a member of St Peterr's Lutheran Church of Highspire and was a retired employee of the Middletown Air Depot where he had served for 32 years. He was a veteran of WWI and was a member of Prince Edwin Lodge 486 of the Masons, Middletown, and the Harrisburg Consistory.

Mr Wolf is survived by his wife Mrs Helen G Wolf, a son, Franklin E, , New York City; four brothers, Clarence R., Millville, NJ, David O., Pittsburgh, George E., Hannibal, MO, and John M., Harrisburg; two sisters, Mrs. Joseph Hershey, Hummelstown, and Mrs. William White of Highspire, and one granddaughter.

Funeral services will be held at 2PM Wednesday from the funeral home, 31 2nd St, Highspire. The Rev William M Slee, his pastor, will officiate. Burial will be in Highspire Cemetary. Friends may call after 7pm Tuesday at the funeral home.

More About FRANKLIN WOLF and HELEN LANCASTER:
Marriage: 01 Aug 1924, West Chester, PA

Child of FRANKLIN WOLF and HELEN LANCASTER is:
146.   i.   FRANKLIN EARL[13] WOLF, b. Abt. 1930.

129.   GEORGE EDGAR[12] WOLF *(FRANKLIN LEFEVERE[11], LYDIA[10] LEFEVRE, PETER[9], ADAM[8], PHILIP G[7], ISAAC[6], ABRAHAM[5], ANDREW[4], PHILIP[3], JOHN[2], MENGEN[1])* was born 15 Jan 1897, and died May 1977 in Hannibal, MO. He married LELA BERNEICE BURNHAM 17 Apr 1926 in Springfield, IL. She was born Abt. 1880.

Notes for GEORGE EDGAR WOLF:
GEORGE WOLF Request Information (SS-5)
   SSN 492-36-7650 Residence: 63401 Hannibal, Marion, MO
   Born 15 Jan 1897 Last Benefit:
   Died May 1977 Issued: MO (1951)

More About GEORGE WOLF and LELA BURNHAM:
Marriage: 17 Apr 1926, Springfield, IL

Children of GEORGE WOLF and LELA BURNHAM are:
147.   i.   BARBARA J[13] WOLF, b. Aft. 1900.
148.   ii.   MARY L WOLF, b. Aft. 1900.
         iii.   EDGAR WOLF, b. Aft. 1900.

130.   CATHERINE REBECCA[12] WOLF *(FRANKLIN LEFEVERE[11], LYDIA[10] LEFEVRE, PETER[9], ADAM[8], PHILIP G[7], ISAAC[6], ABRAHAM[5], ANDREW[4], PHILIP[3], JOHN[2], MENGEN[1])* was born 30 Apr 1898 in Highspire, PA, and died 10 Jun 1986 in Highspire, PA. She married WILLIAM WALTER WHITE 05 Jul 1920 in Highspire, PA, son of JOHN WHITE and AMANDA BOYER. He was born 05 Mar 1895 in Highspire, PA, and died 23 Oct 1974 in Highspire, PA.

More About CATHERINE REBECCA WOLF:
Burial: Highspire Cemetery

Notes for WILLIAM WALTER WHITE:
According to Jason White:

William I met Catherine Wolfe as neighbors. Bill would be seen talking to her at the fence surrounding her house.

Bill had a great singing voice, and was in the choir a the Harrisburg Reformed Church. Later, he was a choir leader in Highspire.

Bill started his career working Bethlehem Steel in Steelton. After moving to Akron, Ohio for awhile, he and Catherine returned to Highspire, living in the Wolfe family home at High & Wolfe Streets. He then worked for the Reading Railroad in Harrisburg & Rutherford.

More About WILLIAM WALTER WHITE:
Burial: Highspire Cemetery

More About WILLIAM WHITE and CATHERINE WOLF:
Marriage: 05 Jul 1920, Highspire, PA

Child of CATHERINE WOLF and WILLIAM WHITE is:
149.   i.   WILLIAM WALTER[13] WHITE, b. 31 May 1923, Highspire, PA; d. 31 Aug 1998, Highspire, PA.

131. FRANK A.[12] BROWN *(ELIZABETH[11] MOORE, REBECCA[10] LEFEVRE, JACOB[9], JACOB[8], PHILIP G[7], ISAAC[6], ABRAHAM[5], ANDREW[4], PHILIP[3], JOHN[2], MENGEN[1])* was born 17 Oct. He married LULA STUCKWISH.

Children of FRANK BROWN and LULA STUCKWISH are:
     i.   LIVING[13] BROWN.
    ii.   LIVING BROWN.
   iii.   LIVING BROWN.

132. HARRY D.[12] BROWN *(ELIZABETH[11] MOORE, REBECCA[10] LEFEVRE, JACOB[9], JACOB[8], PHILIP G[7], ISAAC[6], ABRAHAM[5], ANDREW[4], PHILIP[3], JOHN[2], MENGEN[1])* was born 04 Mar 1873 in Terre Haute, Indiana, and died Jun 1931 in Terre Haute, Indiana. He married MAEBELL DINKEL 15 Oct 1897 in Terre Haute, Indiana. She was born 09 Nov 1875 in Brazil, Indiana, and died 1960 in Terre Haute, Indiana.

Notes for HARRY D. BROWN:
[rebeclefevre.FTW]

1. Married 10-15-1897

More About HARRY BROWN and MAEBELL DINKEL:
Marriage: 15 Oct 1897, Terre Haute, Indiana

Children of HARRY BROWN and MAEBELL DINKEL are:
     i.   LIVING[13] BROWN.
150.   ii.   HAROLD DINKEL, SR BROWN, b. 26 Dec 1898; d. 1980.

133. ALAN DEFOREST[12] REYNOLDS *(JOHN MASON[11], WILLIAM[10], JOHN[9], CATHERINE FERREE[8] LEFEVRE, SAMUEL[7], ISAAC[6], ABRAHAM[5], ANDREW[4], PHILIP[3],*

JOHN², MENGEN¹) was born Abt. 1871, and died Aft. 1944. He married MARGARET DAY. She died 1941.

Children of ALAN REYNOLDS and MARGARET DAY are:
  i. ALAN DEFOREST¹³ REYNOLDS.
  ii. JOHN MASON REYNOLDS.

134. KATHERINE¹² HOFFMAN *(MARY¹¹ EVANS, LYDIA MOORE¹⁰ REYNOLDS, JOHN⁹, CATHERINE FERREE⁸ LEFEVRE, SAMUEL⁷, ISAAC⁶, ABRAHAM⁵, ANDREW⁴, PHILIP³, JOHN², MENGEN¹)* was born 1876, and died 1959. She married KLINE.

Child of KATHERINE HOFFMAN and KLINE is:
  i. DAUGHTER¹³ KLINE, b. Abt. 1900; m. H K SHANNAHAN; b. Abt. 1900.

Generation No. 13

135. ALICE MARGARET¹³ SHEAFFER *(LYDIA JANE¹² TRITT, PETER¹¹, CHRISTIAN¹⁰, ELIZABETH⁹ LEFEVRE, GEORGE⁸, PHILIP G⁷, ISAAC⁶, ABRAHAM⁵, ANDREW⁴, PHILIP³, JOHN², MENGEN¹)* was born 26 Oct 1869 in Craighead, Cumberlan Co, Pa., and died 07 Sep 1930 in Dickesen, Pa.. She married THEODORE GOODHART 14 Nov 1889 in Mechanicsburg, Pa., son of LEWIS GOODHART and CHARLOTTE FARNER. He was born 24 Apr 1858 in Penn Twp, Cumberland Co, and died 26 Dec 1945 in buried Dickeson, Pa..

More About THEODORE GOODHART and ALICE SHEAFFER:
Marriage: 14 Nov 1889, Mechanicsburg, Pa.

Children of ALICE SHEAFFER and THEODORE GOODHART are:
151. i. PEARLE VIOLA¹⁴ GOODHART, b. 31 Jan 1891, Greason, Pa.; d. 30 Jul 1972, Carlisle, Pa. Buried Ashland Cem, Carlisle, Pa..
  ii. MARIAN ESTHER GOODHART, b. 25 Apr 1893, Greason, Pa.; d. 12 Mar 1896, Greason, Pa. of Diptheria buried Pres. Churchyard, Dickesen, Pa..
  iii. CHARLES FLOYD GOODHART, b. 28 Mar 1897, Greason, Pa.; d. 26 Jun 1974, buried in Upper Cem, Newville, Pa.; m. MARY GRACE WEAVER, 19 Jul 1932; b. 12 Oct 1901; d. 19 Mar 1974, Carlisle, Pa. Buried Upper Cem, Newville, Pa..

    More About CHARLES GOODHART and MARY WEAVER:
    Marriage: 19 Jul 1932

152. iv. MARGARET ELIZABETH ALICE GOODHART, b. 27 Jun 1899, Greason, Pa; d. 28 Jun 1994, Union Twp, Leb. Co, buried Ft.Indiantown Gap National Cem.
153. v. THEODORE RILEY GOODHART, b. 12 May 1902, Kerrsville, Pa.; d.

17 Dec 1936, Carlisle, Pa. buried Westminster Cem, near Carlisle, Pa..

vi. FLORA PAULINE GOODHART, b. 14 Dec 1904, Kerrsville, Pa.; d. 27 Nov 1976, Plainfield, Pa. buried Westminster Cem, near Carlisle, Pa.; m. LAWRENCE DELMAR CALAMAN, 21 Feb 1931, Greason, Pa.; b. 07 Oct 1899, Boiling Springs, Pa; d. 20 Jan 1965, Carlisle, Pa. buried Westminster Cem, near Carlisle.

More About FLORA GOODHART and LAWRENCE CALAMAN:
Marriage: 21 Feb 1931, Greason, Pa.

154. vii. CLARENCE EUGENE GOODHART, b. Private.
155. viii. LESTER SHEAFFER GOODHART, b. Private.

136. CHARLES M.[13] SHEAFFER *(LYDIA JANE[12] TRITT, PETER[11], CHRISTIAN[10], ELIZABETH[9] LEFEVRE, GEORGE[8], PHILIP G[7], ISAAC[6], ABRAHAM[5], ANDREW[4], PHILIP[3], JOHN[2], MENGEN[1])* was born 14 Jan 1874 in Huntsdale, Pa., and died 02 Oct 1965 in Utica, New York buried St. Agnes Cem, Utica, NY. He married ROSE FRANCES KANE 07 Sep 1912 in St.Frances De Sales Church, Utica, New York. She was born 03 Apr 1885 in Utica New York, and died 11 Feb 1947 in Yonkers, New York buried St. Agnes Cem, Utica, NY.

More About CHARLES SHEAFFER and ROSE KANE:
Marriage: 07 Sep 1912, St.Frances De Sales Church, Utica, New York

Child of CHARLES SHEAFFER and ROSE KANE is:
156. i. DORIS MADELINE[14] SHEAFFER, b. 08 Nov 1913; d. 25 Jan 1980, Utica, N.Y..

137. CHARLES W.[13] LEFEVRE *(DAVID GILBERT[12], ISSAC[11], JACOB[10], LAWRENCE[9], GEORGE[8], PHILIP G[7], ISAAC[6], ABRAHAM[5], ANDREW[4], PHILIP[3], JOHN[2], MENGEN[1])* was born 09 Jan 1878, and died 16 Mar 1941 in Drexel Hill, Pennsylvania. He married DORCAS W. MERCER 30 Jun 1902. She was born 10 Apr 1880.

More About CHARLES LEFEVRE and DORCAS MERCER:
Marriage: 30 Jun 1902

Children of CHARLES LEFEVRE and DORCAS MERCER are:
i. DORTHY W.[14] LEFEVRE, b. 12 Apr 1903; m. ELLWOOD ALTMAIER, 06 Nov 1928; b. 30 Jul 1904; d. Jun 1980.

More About ELLWOOD ALTMAIER:
Fact 1: Social Security #: 061-07-5063
Fact 2: Last residence: NJ 08247
Fact 3: State of issue: NY

More About ELLWOOD ALTMAIER and DORTHY LEFEVRE:
Marriage: 06 Nov 1928

    ii.   RUTH GRAFF LEFEVRE, b. 09 Jul 1906; m. HENRY J. PRESTON, 20 Jul 1932; b. 21 Nov 1909.

        More About HENRY PRESTON and RUTH LEFEVRE:
        Marriage: 20 Jul 1932

    iii. CHARLES H. LEFEVRE, b. 01 Jan 1916; m. LOUISE ECKER, 19 Jan 1943.

        More About CHARLES LEFEVRE and LOUISE ECKER:
        Marriage: 19 Jan 1943

138. HALLETT RUDOLPH[13] LEFEVRE (*JOHN RUSSELL[12], ISSAC[11], JACOB[10], LAWRENCE[9], GEORGE[8], PHILIP G[7], ISAAC[6], ABRAHAM[5], ANDREW[4], PHILIP[3], JOHN[2], MENGEN[1]*) was born 09 Oct 1887 in Chicago, Illinois. He married ETHEL INGRAM 24 Jun 1912. She was born 13 Jun 1889.

More About HALLETT LEFEVRE and ETHEL INGRAM:
Marriage: 24 Jun 1912

Children of HALLETT LEFEVRE and ETHEL INGRAM are:
    i.   LAWRENCE INGRAM[14] LEFEVRE, b. 01 Apr 1913; m. IDA CHAFFIN, 11 Jan 1948; b. 17 May 1920.

        More About LAWRENCE LEFEVRE and IDA CHAFFIN:
        Marriage: 11 Jan 1948

    ii. RICHARD HALLETT LEFEVRE, b. 12 Feb 1916; m. RUTH CLAUSEN, 03 Sep 1949; b. 26 Mar 1920.

        More About RICHARD LEFEVRE and RUTH CLAUSEN:
        Marriage: 03 Sep 1949

    iii. JOHN WILLIAM LEFEVRE, b. 17 Jan 1920; m. GLORIA SWANSON, 01 Jun 1946; b. 01 Mar 1921.

        More About JOHN LEFEVRE and GLORIA SWANSON:
        Marriage: 01 Jun 1946

139. RUSSELL MOORE[13] LEFEVRE (*JOHN RUSSELL[12], ISSAC[11], JACOB[10], LAWRENCE[9], GEORGE[8], PHILIP G[7], ISAAC[6], ABRAHAM[5], ANDREW[4], PHILIP[3], JOHN[2], MENGEN[1]*) was born 15 Dec 1892. He married KATHERINE FRAZER Aug 1920. She was born 24 Oct 1894, and died 08 Jun 1950.

More About RUSSELL LeFEVRE and KATHERINE FRAZER:
Marriage: Aug 1920

Child of RUSSELL LeFEVRE and KATHERINE FRAZER is:
    i. MARY ELIZABETH[14] LeFEVRE, b. 20 Oct 1921.

140. FLORENCE GRACE[13] LeFEVRE (*HENRY RINE[12], DAVID[11], JOHN B.[10], LAWRENCE[9], GEORGE[8], PHILIP G[7], ISAAC[6], ABRAHAM[5], ANDREW[4], PHILIP[3], JOHN[2], MENGEN[1]*) was born 25 Nov 1883 in Carlisle, Pennsylvania, and died 12 Jan 1973 in Park Haven Nursing Home, Maryland. She married WILLIAM SCOTT 30 Nov 1909 in Cummingstown, Pennsylvania. He was born 14 Feb 1886 in Pennsylvania, and died 13 Sep 1926 in Chandler, Arizona.

More About FLORENCE GRACE LeFEVRE:
Fact 1: Social Security #: 195-32-0579
Fact 2: Last residence: MD 20901

More About WILLIAM SCOTT and FLORENCE LeFEVRE:
Marriage: 30 Nov 1909, Cummingstown, Pennsylvania

Children of FLORENCE LeFEVRE and WILLIAM SCOTT are:
157.   i. MARGARETA JUNE[14] SCOTT, b. 07 Oct 1910, Weldona, Colorado.
158.   ii. WILLIAM RINE SCOTT, b. 03 Mar 1914, Los Angeles, California.
       iii. JOHN LeFEVRE SCOTT, b. 16 Aug 1916, Cummingstown, Pennsylvania; m. JEAN FISHER.
159.   iv. ROBERT EDWARD SCOTT, b. 23 Sep 1925.

141. CLARENCE[13] LEFEVRE (*FRANK ORAN[12], ISSAC LAWRENCE[11], DAVID ALTER[10], LAWRENCE[9], GEORGE[8], PHILIP G[7], ISAAC[6], ABRAHAM[5], ANDREW[4], PHILIP[3], JOHN[2], MENGEN[1]*) was born 07 Aug 1894, and died Nov 1970. He married GRACE BAUMANN. She was born 04 Apr 1895, and died 02 Jun 1989.

More About CLARENCE LEFEVRE:
Fact 1: Social Security #: 351-32-4417
Fact 2: Last residence: IL 61855
Fact 3: State of issue: IL

More About GRACE BAUMANN:
Fact 1: Social Security #: 338-40-5810
Fact 2: Last residence: 61855
Fact 3: State of issue: IL

Children of CLARENCE LEFEVRE and GRACE BAUMANN are:
    i. JOSEPHINE BAUMANN[14] LEFEVRE, b. 19 May 1919; m. CLARENCE BASTERT, 26 Aug 1947; b. 27 Jul 1910.

More About CLARENCE BASTERT and JOSEPHINE LEFEVRE:
Marriage: 26 Aug 1947

    ii.   CHARLOTTE BIRDELIA LEFEVRE, b. 11 Oct 1921.
    iii. ELEANOR ANN LEFEVRE, b. 03 Dec 1924; m. RICHARD
           SKAGENBERG, 25 Aug 1946; b. 19 Mar 1924.

More About RICHARD SKAGENBERG and ELEANOR LEFEVRE:
Marriage: 25 Aug 1946

142. JACK[13] LEFEVRE *(ELLERY ELSTON[12], DAVID SLAYMAKER[11], DAVID ALTER[10], LAWRENCE[9], GEORGE[8], PHILIP G[7], ISAAC[6], ABRAHAM[5], ANDREW[4], PHILIP[3], JOHN[2], MENGEN[1])* was born 11 Oct 1902, and died Apr 1983. He married IRENE SMITH 01 May 1931. She was born 28 Apr 1906.

More About JACK LEFEVRE:
Fact 1: Social Security #: 311-30-1294
Fact 2: Last residence: IN 47905
Fact 3: State of issue: IN

More About JACK LEFEVRE and IRENE SMITH:
Marriage: 01 May 1931

Child of JACK LEFEVRE and IRENE SMITH is:
    i.   DAVID LYNN[14] LEFEVRE, b. 02 May 1940.

143. CLARENCE FRANKLIN[13] WOLF *(CLARENCE R[12], FRANKLIN LEFEVERE[11], LYDIA[10] LEFEVRE, PETER[9], ADAM[8], PHILIP G[7], ISAAC[6], ABRAHAM[5], ANDREW[4], PHILIP[3], JOHN[2], MENGEN[1])* was born 1912. He married VERNA DILKS. She was born Abt. 1910.

Children of CLARENCE WOLF and VERNA DILKS are:
    i.   RAY[14] WOLF, b. Abt. 1930.
    ii.   ALICE K WOLF, b. Abt. 1930.
    iii. MARGARET M WOLF, b. Abt. 1930.

144. JOHN S[13] WOLF *(CLARENCE R[12], FRANKLIN LEFEVERE[11], LYDIA[10] LEFEVRE, PETER[9], ADAM[8], PHILIP G[7], ISAAC[6], ABRAHAM[5], ANDREW[4], PHILIP[3], JOHN[2], MENGEN[1])* was born 1926. He married DOROTHY KASPER. She was born Abt. 1910.

Children of JOHN WOLF and DOROTHY KASPER are:
    i.   HOLLY ANN[14] WOLF, b. Aft. 1930.
    ii.   MARY E WOLF, b. Aft. 1930.

145. MARJORIE ANN[13] WOLF (*DAVID OBER*[12], *FRANKLIN LEFEVERE*[11], *LYDIA*[10] *LEFEVRE, PETER*[9], *ADAM*[8], *PHILIP G*[7], *ISAAC*[6], *ABRAHAM*[5], *ANDREW*[4], *PHILIP*[3], *JOHN*[2], *MENGEN*[1]*)* was born Abt. 1928 in Pittsburgh, PA, and died 30 Sep 1970 in Glastonbury, CT. She married ALLAN BAKER PARTRIDGE 25 Jun 1955 in Durham, NH.

More About ALLAN PARTRIDGE and MARJORIE WOLF:
Marriage: 25 Jun 1955, Durham, NH

Children of MARJORIE WOLF and ALLAN PARTRIDGE are:
  i.   CHARLES ALLAN[14] PARTRIDGE.
  ii. DIANE LOUISE PARTRIDGE.

146. FRANKLIN EARL[13] WOLF (*FRANKLIN EARL*[12], *FRANKLIN LEFEVERE*[11], *LYDIA*[10] *LEFEVRE, PETER*[9], *ADAM*[8], *PHILIP G*[7], *ISAAC*[6], *ABRAHAM*[5], *ANDREW*[4], *PHILIP*[3], *JOHN*[2], *MENGEN*[1]*)* was born Abt. 1930. He married HILDA GONZALEZ. She was born Abt. 1930.

Child of FRANKLIN WOLF and HILDA GONZALEZ is:
  i.   MARIA[14] WOLF, b. 1963.

147. BARBARA J[13] WOLF (*GEORGE EDGAR*[12], *FRANKLIN LEFEVERE*[11], *LYDIA*[10] *LEFEVRE, PETER*[9], *ADAM*[8], *PHILIP G*[7], *ISAAC*[6], *ABRAHAM*[5], *ANDREW*[4], *PHILIP*[3], *JOHN*[2], *MENGEN*[1]*)* was born Aft. 1900. She married RICHARD WILSON. He was born Abt. 1900.

Children of BARBARA WOLF and RICHARD WILSON are:
  i.   PATRICIA A[14] WILSON, b. Abt. 1925.
  ii. RICHARD WILSON, JR, b. Abt. 1925.

148. MARY L[13] WOLF (*GEORGE EDGAR*[12], *FRANKLIN LEFEVERE*[11], *LYDIA*[10] *LEFEVRE, PETER*[9], *ADAM*[8], *PHILIP G*[7], *ISAAC*[6], *ABRAHAM*[5], *ANDREW*[4], *PHILIP*[3], *JOHN*[2], *MENGEN*[1]*)* was born Aft. 1900. She married WILLIAM T HASSLER. He was born Aft. 1900.

Child of MARY WOLF and WILLIAM HASSLER is:
  i.   MICHAEL[14] HASSLER, b. Abt. 1930.

149. WILLIAM WALTER[13] WHITE (*CATHERINE REBECCA*[12] *WOLF, FRANKLIN LEFEVERE*[11], *LYDIA*[10] *LEFEVRE, PETER*[9], *ADAM*[8], *PHILIP G*[7], *ISAAC*[6], *ABRAHAM*[5], *ANDREW*[4], *PHILIP*[3], *JOHN*[2], *MENGEN*[1]*)* was born 31 May 1923 in Highspire, PA, and died 31 Aug 1998 in Highspire, PA. He married (1) EMMA AMELIA HACKMAN 07 Aug 1942 in St. Peter's Lutheran Church, Highspire, PA, daughter of WILLIS HACKMAN and EMMA GEIB. She was born 28 May 1921 in Millport, Warwick Township, Lancaster County, PA, and died 03 Nov 1994 in Elizabethtown, PA. He married (2) CHRISTABEL J DEIMLER Oct 1994. She was born Abt. 1945 in Perry County.

Notes for WILLIAM WALTER WHITE:
Former chauffeur for John Vartan of Harrisburg.

Former owner of the White Cab Company

Former trumpet player in Les Brown's Band

More About WILLIAM WALTER WHITE:
Burial: Highspire Cemetery - in an unmarked grave at the foot of his mother's

Notes for EMMA AMELIA HACKMAN:
First female cab driver in Pennsylvania

More About EMMA AMELIA HACKMAN:
Burial: Ashes spread near Millport farm

More About WILLIAM WHITE and EMMA HACKMAN:
Marriage: 07 Aug 1942, St. Peter's Lutheran Church, Highspire, PA
Other-Ending: 1971

More About WILLIAM WHITE and CHRISTABEL DEIMLER:
Marriage: Oct 1994

Children of WILLIAM WHITE and EMMA HACKMAN are:
160.   i.   EMILY FALINE[14] WHITE, b. 16 Feb 1943, Lititz, PA.
161.   ii. WILLIAM WALTER WHITE, b. 12 Dec 1944.

150. HAROLD[13] DINKEL, SR BROWN *(HARRY D.[12] BROWN, ELIZABETH[11] MOORE, REBECCA[10] LEFEVRE, JACOB[9], JACOB[8], PHILIP G[7], ISAAC[6], ABRAHAM[5], ANDREW[4], PHILIP[3], JOHN[2], MENGEN[1])* was born 26 Dec 1898, and died 1980. He married (1) MAUDE MULVIHILL. She was born 15 Nov 1907, and died 1948. He married (2) LIVING LADD.

Child of HAROLD DINKEL and MAUDE MULVIHILL is:
162.   i.   LIVING[14] BROWN.

Children of HAROLD DINKEL and LIVING LADD are:
        ii. LIVING[14] BROWN.

iii. LIVING BROWN.
iv. LIVING BROWN.
v. LIVING BROWN.

Generation No. 14

151. PEARLE VIOLA[14] GOODHART *(ALICE MARGARET[13] SHEAFFER, LYDIA JANE[12] TRITT, PETER[11], CHRISTIAN[10], ELIZABETH[9] LEFEVRE, GEORGE[8], PHILIP G[7], ISAAC[6], ABRAHAM[5], ANDREW[4], PHILIP[3], JOHN[2], MENGEN[1])* was born 31 Jan 1891 in Greason, Pa., and died 30 Jul 1972 in Carlisle, Pa. Buried Ashland Cem, Carlisle, Pa.. She married WILLIAM SHIVELY WEAVER 03 Oct 1928 in Cadiz, Ohio. He was born 18 Feb 1899, and died 15 Mar 1978 in Carlisle, Pa. Buried Ashland Cem, Carlisle, Pa..

More About WILLIAM WEAVER and PEARLE GOODHART:
Marriage: 03 Oct 1928, Cadiz, Ohio

Child of PEARLE GOODHART and WILLIAM WEAVER is:
        i. THEODORE FLOYD[15] WEAVER, b. Private.

152. MARGARET ELIZABETH ALICE[14] GOODHART *(ALICE MARGARET[13] SHEAFFER, LYDIA JANE[12] TRITT, PETER[11], CHRISTIAN[10], ELIZABETH[9] LEFEVRE, GEORGE[8], PHILIP G[7], ISAAC[6], ABRAHAM[5], ANDREW[4], PHILIP[3], JOHN[2], MENGEN[1])* was born 27 Jun 1899 in Greason, Pa, and died 28 Jun 1994 in Union Twp, Leb. Co, buried Ft.Indiantown Gap National Cem. She married ROBERT WILLIAM HIPPENSTEEL 26 Mar 1920 in Harrisburg, Pa.. He was born 28 Sep 1896 in Mt. Rock, Cumberland Co, Pa., and died 03 Nov 1990 in Union Twp, Leb. Co, buried Ft. Indiantown Gap National Cem..

More About ROBERT HIPPENSTEEL and MARGARET GOODHART:
Marriage: 26 Mar 1920, Harrisburg, Pa.

Children of MARGARET GOODHART and ROBERT HIPPENSTEEL are:
163.   i. ROBERT GOODHART[15] HIPPENSTEEL, b. Private.
164.   ii. DOROTHY JEAN HIPPENSTEEL, b. Private.
165. iii. DORIS MADELINE HIPPENSTEEL, b. Private.
166.   iv. MARGARET JOANNE HIPPENSTEEL, b. Private.

153. THEODORE RILEY[14] GOODHART *(ALICE MARGARET[13] SHEAFFER, LYDIA JANE[12] TRITT, PETER[11], CHRISTIAN[10], ELIZABETH[9] LEFEVRE, GEORGE[8], PHILIP G[7], ISAAC[6], ABRAHAM[5], ANDREW[4], PHILIP[3], JOHN[2], MENGEN[1])* was born 12 May 1902 in Kerrsville, Pa., and died 17 Dec 1936 in Carlisle, Pa. buried Westminster Cem, near Carlisle, Pa.. He married ANNA MABEL RICE 16 Jun 1927 in Phoenixville, Pa.. She was born 10 Aug 1902, and died 1994 in buried Westminster Cem, near Carlisle, Pa..

More About THEODORE GOODHART and ANNA RICE:
Marriage: 16 Jun 1927, Phoenixville, Pa.

Child of THEODORE GOODHART and ANNA RICE is:
      i. THEODORE RICE[15] GOODHART, b. 15 Jan 1935; d. 03 Oct 1987.

154. CLARENCE EUGENE[14] GOODHART (*ALICE MARGARET*[13] *SHEAFFER, LYDIA JANE*[12] *TRITT, PETER*[11]*, CHRISTIAN*[10]*, ELIZABETH*[9] *LEFEVRE, GEORGE*[8]*, PHILIP G*[7]*, ISAAC*[6]*, ABRAHAM*[5]*, ANDREW*[4]*, PHILIP*[3]*, JOHN*[2]*, MENGEN*[1]) was born Private. He married MARY MILDRED PIPER Private. She was born 07 Sep 1907, and died 1994.

More About CLARENCE GOODHART and MARY PIPER:
Marriage date: Private
Private-Begin: Private

Children of CLARENCE GOODHART and MARY PIPER are:
167.   i. CHARLES DALE[15] GOODHART, b. Private.
168.   ii. LEE PIPER GOODHART, b. Private.

155. LESTER SHEAFFER[14] GOODHART (*ALICE MARGARET*[13] *SHEAFFER, LYDIA JANE*[12] *TRITT, PETER*[11]*, CHRISTIAN*[10]*, ELIZABETH*[9] *LEFEVRE, GEORGE*[8]*, PHILIP G*[7]*, ISAAC*[6]*, ABRAHAM*[5]*, ANDREW*[4]*, PHILIP*[3]*, JOHN*[2]*, MENGEN*[1]) was born Private. He married BLANCHE SHOTZER Private. She was born Private.

More About LESTER GOODHART and BLANCHE SHOTZER:
Marriage date: Private
Private-Begin: Private

Children of LESTER GOODHART and BLANCHE SHOTZER are:
      i. EDWARD SHEAFFER[15] GOODHART, b. Private; m. MARY JANE RAMSIES, Private; b. Private.

        More About EDWARD GOODHART and MARY RAMSIES:
        Marriage date: Private
        Private-Begin: Private

169.   ii. ROBERT MICHAEL GOODHART, b. Private.
      iii. ANN BETTA GOODHART, b. Private.

156. DORIS MADELINE[14] SHEAFFER (*CHARLES M.*[13]*, LYDIA JANE*[12] *TRITT, PETER*[11]*, CHRISTIAN*[10]*, ELIZABETH*[9] *LEFEVRE, GEORGE*[8]*, PHILIP G*[7]*, ISAAC*[6]*, ABRAHAM*[5]*, ANDREW*[4]*, PHILIP*[3]*, JOHN*[2]*, MENGEN*[1]) was born 08 Nov 1913, and died 25 Jan 1980 in Utica, N.Y.. She married CARMEN JOSEPH LUCENTI WFT

Est. 1934-1965. He was born 18 Feb 1922, and died 27 Aug 1986 in Utica, N.Y,.

More About CARMEN LUCENTI and DORIS SHEAFFER:
Marriage: WFT Est. 1934-1965

Children of DORIS SHEAFFER and CARMEN LUCENTI are:
170.   i.   TERESA ROSE CHARLENE[15] LUCENTI, b. Private.
171.   ii. SANDRA MARIE LUCENTI, b. Private.

157. MARGARETA JUNE[14] SCOTT *(FLORENCE GRACE[13] LeFEVRE, HENRY RINE[12], DAVID[11], JOHN B.[10], LAWRENCE[9], GEORGE[8], PHILIP G[7], ISAAC[6], ABRAHAM[5], ANDREW[4], PHILIP[3], JOHN[2], MENGEN[1])* was born 07 Oct 1910 in Weldona, Colorado. She married REV. JAMES GOODHART GLENN. He was born 17 Apr 1909 in Cummingstown, Pennsylvania.

Notes for REV. JAMES GOODHART GLENN:
[BKGlenn.FTW]

From the autobiography of James Johnston Glenn ...

    James Goodhart Glenn, our first child was born at the Manse of the Dickinson Presbyterian Church, April 17th, 1909. The birth was difficult for both mother and child. Instruments were used -- resulting in tears for the mother and many bruises for the child. Many years later when listening to his sermon out in the Southwest my thoughts went back to that tiny, much scarred baby boy wrapped in swaddling clothes, and lying in the arms of his nurse -- good old Grandma Fickes.
    The doctor and others did not seem to give much encouragement that the babe would keep on breathing, it was so irregular. I don't think I ever prayed more earnestly. At times breathing would stop, but his father never lost hope that he would live. He knew how great sorrow would come to the mother, if that child stopped breathing. So, by the Grace of God, he did keep on breathing. Today 38 years after, he is breathing still and is pastor of the first Presbyterian Church of Borger, Texas.
    James, I think joined the church when eight years of age. He first went to school at Cummingstown, in the building that is now the Parish House. He later took the classical course in Carlisle High School, graduating in the Class of 1928. Then he entered Dickinson College, graduating A.B. Class of 1932. He entered Princeton Seminary in the fall of the same year. During vacation he did missionary work i the mountains of Tennessee. He graduated from the seminary in 1935. He was married to Margaretta June Scott, daughter of William Alexander Scott and Grace LeFevre Scott, May 17th, 1935, in Dickinson Presbyterian Church.
    June was a graduate of Carlisle High School in 1928, and had attended Shippensburg Teachers College and taught in the public school five years. James served National Missions Board from 1935 - 1940, at Payson, Clifton, and Morenci, Arizona. He received a call to the First Presbyterian Church of

Borger, Texas in 1940. There with a capable helpmate, a growing church, he carries on his chosen profession. They have three children -- James Scott born April 14, 1937, at Payson, Arizona. John Edward born March 19, 1941 at Borger, Texas. Joyce Carol born December 5, 1943 at Borger, Texas.

At this time James is busy helping to plan the erection of a new church. This is much needed as the town is growing and with it the congregation. Borger is a comparatively new town. Yet has a present population of 20,000 people. The chief industry is the manufacture of carbon black. Forty percent of our auto tires is carbon black and one fourth of this material is made in Borger and vicinity.

A year ago, I visited my son and family. As his father, and having spent my life in the ministry, I write with all a loving father's joy that I am convinced my son is doing a good work in the church of the living Christ. I was pleased with his preaching. His sermon as well as his teaching showed thought and preparation. I also felt that he stood in well with his people. Also, and not least, the home life was contented and happy.

Children of MARGARETA SCOTT and JAMES GLENN are:
       i.   JAMES SCOTT[15] GLENN, b. 14 Apr 1937.
172. ii. JOHN EDWARD GLENN, b. 19 Mar 1941, Borger, texas.
173. iii. JOYCE CAROL GLENN, b. 05 Dec 1943.

158. WILLIAM RINE[14] SCOTT (*FLORENCE GRACE[13] LeFEVRE, HENRY RINE[12], DAVID[11], JOHN B.[10], LAWRENCE[9], GEORGE[8], PHILIP G[7], ISAAC[6], ABRAHAM[5], ANDREW[4], PHILIP[3], JOHN[2], MENGEN[1]*) was born 03 Mar 1914 in Los Angeles, California. He married PAULINE KITZMILLER.

Children of WILLIAM SCOTT and PAULINE KITZMILLER are:
       i.   ANN[15] SCOTT.
      ii. MARY SCOTT, b. 1943.

159. ROBERT EDWARD[14] SCOTT (*FLORENCE GRACE[13] LeFEVRE, HENRY RINE[12], DAVID[11], JOHN B.[10], LAWRENCE[9], GEORGE[8], PHILIP G[7], ISAAC[6], ABRAHAM[5], ANDREW[4], PHILIP[3], JOHN[2], MENGEN[1]*) was born 23 Sep 1925. He married (1) VIRGINIA HIGGINBOTHAM. He married (2) POLLY.

Children of ROBERT SCOTT and VIRGINIA HIGGINBOTHAM are:
       i.   VIRGINIA ANN[15] SCOTT.
      ii. LEONA GRACE SCOTT.

160. EMILY FALINE[14] WHITE (*WILLIAM WALTER[13], CATHERINE REBECCA[12] WOLF, FRANKLIN LeFEVERE[11], LYDIA[10] LeFEVRE, PETER[9], ADAM[8], PHILIP G[7], ISAAC[6], ABRAHAM[5], ANDREW[4], PHILIP[3], JOHN[2], MENGEN[1]*) was born 16 Feb 1943 in Lititz, PA. She married LAWRENCE DAVID KNORR 03 Aug 1963 in Church of

the Brethern, Elizabethtown, PA, son of GEORGE KNORR and ALICE BURNISH.
He was born 04 May 1943 in Reading, PA.

Notes for EMILY FALINE WHITE:

Emily was born in Lititz, Lancaster County, PA. She also lived briefly in Miami, FL - but mainly in Elizabethtown, PA. As a young girl, she spent a lot of time with her White grandparents in Highspire. In 1961, Emily was the first female student at Penn State Berks - where she met husband Larry.

For most of her adult life, Emily has been a homemaker - an excellent cook, decorator and seamstress. She has worked various jobs - mostly retail in the apparel or fabric industries.

Notes for LAWRENCE DAVID KNORR:

Larry is a mechanical engineer, specializing in heavy equipment design. He works for the DeShazo Crane Company in Alabaster, AL.

According to Gerald Knorr (brother):

When Larry was in high school (Reading) - he lived on 10th St. He would attend church at 10th and Green while dating Barbara. During a program at church on Sunday evening, he was to play (guitar) and sing. His parents attended - Grandma was very nervous. When Dad played and sung 'Grandma got goose bumps.'

According to Jack Knorr (brother):

When Larry was on work program at Birdsboro Steel (Penn St) - both he and Jack worked there. Both did drafting with pencils and boards. When Jack got up from his seat and went somewhere, Larry and a co-worker emptied a pencil sharpener on Jack's seat. Jack had been proud of a new pair of slacks he was wearing When he sat down on the pencil shavings - he became furious. He grabbed Larry's drawing and crumbled it into a ball. When the boss came in, Larry got in trouble - and had to finish the drawing.

When Larry was little - on the 2nd farm in Jacksonwald - he stepped in front of a game of quaits and was struck on top of the head.

According to Larry (himself):

As a young boy, he was very accurate with a sling shot. One day, to get back at his older brothers (Jack & Marty) - while they stood by a bee hive - he pegged the hive with a rock and sent them running from a swarm of bees.

More About LAWRENCE KNORR and EMILY WHITE:
Marriage: 03 Aug 1963, Church of the Brethern, Elizabethtown, PA

Children of EMILY WHITE and LAWRENCE KNORR are:

174.   i.   LAWRENCE KEVIN[15] KNORR, b. 05 May 1964, Reading Hospital, Reading, PA.

175.   ii. ALICE KATHLEEN KNORR, b. 11 Aug 1965, Reading, PA.

       iii. DAVID BRIAN KNORR, b. 07 Apr 1968, Reading, PA; m. TARA

PHILLIPS, 19 May 1995, Gulfport, MS; b. Abt. 1972.

Notes for DAVID BRIAN KNORR:
David is a very talented guitarist. He started a guitar instruction business, and is the busiest teacher on the Gulf Coast. David composes his own music, dabbling in all forms. David also plays the piano, violin & synthesizer. Presently, he is in a band with his wife (the lead singer).

More About DAVID KNORR and TARA PHILLIPS:
Marriage: 19 May 1995, Gulfport, MS

161. WILLIAM WALTER[14] WHITE *(WILLIAM WALTER[13], CATHERINE REBECCA[12] WOLF, FRANKLIN LEFEVERE[11], LYDIA[10] LEFEVRE, PETER[9], ADAM[8], PHILIP G[7], ISAAC[6], ABRAHAM[5], ANDREW[4], PHILIP[3], JOHN[2], MENGEN[1])* was born 12 Dec 1944. He married DOROTHY KRAFFT. She was born 1955.

Children of WILLIAM WHITE and DOROTHY KRAFFT are:
     i.   SHELBY[15] WHITE, b. 19 Feb 1986.
    ii.   MCKENZIE WHITE, b. 09 Mar 1988.

162. LIVING[14] BROWN *(HAROLD[13] DINKEL, SR BROWN, HARRY D.[12] BROWN, ELIZABETH[11] MOORE, REBECCA[10] LEFEVRE, JACOB[9], JACOB[8], PHILIP G[7], ISAAC[6], ABRAHAM[5], ANDREW[4], PHILIP[3], JOHN[2], MENGEN[1])* He married LIVING THORNTON.

Children of LIVING BROWN and LIVING THORNTON are:
176.   i.   LIVING[15] BROWN.
177.   ii.   LIVING BROWN.
178.   iii.   LIVING BROWN.

Generation No. 15

163. ROBERT GOODHART[15] HIPPENSTEEL *(MARGARET ELIZABETH ALICE[14] GOODHART, ALICE MARGARET[13] SHEAFFER, LYDIA JANE[12] TRITT, PETER[11], CHRISTIAN[10], ELIZABETH[9] LEFEVRE, GEORGE[8], PHILIP G[7], ISAAC[6], ABRAHAM[5], ANDREW[4], PHILIP[3], JOHN[2], MENGEN[1])* was born Private. He married CAROLYN ANN WEIGLE Private. She was born 03 Oct 1926, and died 02 Dec 1988.

More About ROBERT HIPPENSTEEL and CAROLYN WEIGLE:
Marriage date: Private
Private-Begin: Private

Children of ROBERT HIPPENSTEEL and CAROLYN WEIGLE are:
     i.   SANDRA LEE[16] HIPPENSTEEL, b. Private; m. ROBERT TOMILSON, Private; b. Private.

More About ROBERT TOMILSON and SANDRA HIPPENSTEEL:
Marriage date: Private
Private-Begin: Private

    ii.   JUDY ANN HIPPENSTEEL, b. Private; m. (1) JAMES COPLEY, Private; b. Private; m. (2) ROBERT ROURKE, Private; b. Private.

More About JAMES COPLEY and JUDY HIPPENSTEEL:
Marriage date: Private
Private-Begin: Private

More About ROBERT ROURKE and JUDY HIPPENSTEEL:
Marriage date: Private
Private-Begin: Private

    iii.   INFANT SON HIPPENSTEEL, b. Private.

164. DOROTHY JEAN[15] HIPPENSTEEL *(MARGARET ELIZABETH ALICE[14] GOODHART, ALICE MARGARET[13] SHEAFFER, LYDIA JANE[12] TRITT, PETER[11], CHRISTIAN[10], ELIZABETH[9] LeFEVRE, GEORGE[8], PHILIP G[7], ISAAC[6], ABRAHAM[5], ANDREW[4], PHILIP[3], JOHN[2], MENGEN[1])* was born Private. She married RALPH E. MOHLER Private. He was born Private.

More About RALPH MOHLER and DOROTHY HIPPENSTEEL:
Marriage date: Private
Private-Begin: Private

Children of DOROTHY HIPPENSTEEL and RALPH MOHLER are:
179.   i.   KATHRYN ANN[16] MOHLER, b. Private.
180.   ii.   JOHN ROBERT MOHLER, b. Private.
       iii.   DAVID RALPH MOHLER, b. Private; m. (1) CAROLYN ROGERS, Private; b. Private; m. (2) SUSAN WAKELY, Private; b. Private.

More About DAVID MOHLER and CAROLYN ROGERS:
Marriage date: Private
Private-Begin: Private

More About DAVID MOHLER and SUSAN WAKELY:
Marriage date: Private
Private-Begin: Private

165. DORIS MADELINE[15] HIPPENSTEEL *(MARGARET ELIZABETH ALICE[14] GOODHART, ALICE MARGARET[13] SHEAFFER, LYDIA JANE[12] TRITT, PETER[11], CHRISTIAN[10], ELIZABETH[9] LeFEVRE, GEORGE[8], PHILIP G[7], ISAAC[6], ABRAHAM[5], ANDREW[4], PHILIP[3], JOHN[2], MENGEN[1])* was born Private. She married ADAM

LEROY WEST Private. He was born 11 Jun 1924 in Fayetteville, Franklin County, Pa., and died 18 Mar 1987 in Clarksville, Tennesee.

More About ADAM WEST and DORIS HIPPENSTEEL:
Marriage date: Private
Private-Begin: Private

Children of DORIS HIPPENSTEEL and ADAM WEST are:
181.   i.   DIANE ELIZABETH[16] WEST, b. Private.
182.   ii. BARBARA ELAINE WEST, b. Private.

166. MARGARET JOANNE[15] HIPPENSTEEL (*MARGARET ELIZABETH ALICE[14] GOODHART, ALICE MARGARET[13] SHEAFFER, LYDIA JANE[12] TRITT, PETER[11], CHRISTIAN[10], ELIZABETH[9] LEFEVRE, GEORGE[8], PHILIP G[7], ISAAC[6], ABRAHAM[5], ANDREW[4], PHILIP[3], JOHN[2], MENGEN[1]*) was born Private. She married (1) WALTER J. BERNHEISEL Private. He was born Private. She married (2) O. P. STANCER Private. He was born Private.

More About WALTER BERNHEISEL and MARGARET HIPPENSTEEL:
Marriage date: Private
Private-Begin: Private

More About O. STANCER and MARGARET HIPPENSTEEL:
Marriage date: Private
Private-Begin: Private

Children of MARGARET HIPPENSTEEL and WALTER BERNHEISEL are:
        i.   MICHAEL SCOTT[16] BERNHEISEL, b. Private.
        ii. PATRICK ALAN BERNHEISEL, b. Private.
        iii. TONI KAREN BERNHEISEL, b. Private.

167. CHARLES DALE[15] GOODHART (*CLARENCE EUGENE[14], ALICE MARGARET[13] SHEAFFER, LYDIA JANE[12] TRITT, PETER[11], CHRISTIAN[10], ELIZABETH[9] LEFEVRE, GEORGE[8], PHILIP G[7], ISAAC[6], ABRAHAM[5], ANDREW[4], PHILIP[3], JOHN[2], MENGEN[1]*) was born Private. He married BETTY JANE CAHILL Private. She was born Private.

More About CHARLES GOODHART and BETTY CAHILL:
Marriage date: Private
Private-Begin: Private

Children of CHARLES GOODHART and BETTY CAHILL are:
        i.   JAMES LEE[16] GOODHART, b. Private; m. GLENDA VOGELSONG, Private; b. Private.

        More About JAMES GOODHART and GLENDA VOGELSONG:

Marriage date: Private
Private-Begin: Private

183.　　ii.　JOHN CHARLES GOODHART, b. Private.

168. LEE PIPER[15] GOODHART (*CLARENCE EUGENE*[14], *ALICE MARGARET*[13] *SHEAFFER, LYDIA JANE*[12] *TRITT, PETER*[11], *CHRISTIAN*[10], *ELIZABETH*[9] *LEFEVRE, GEORGE*[8], *PHILIP G*[7], *ISAAC*[6], *ABRAHAM*[5], *ANDREW*[4], *PHILIP*[3], *JOHN*[2], *MENGEN*[1]) was born Private. He married (1) ISABELLE LINE Private. She was born Private. He married (2) SANDRA RISSINGER Private. She was born Private. He married (3) IRENE FLICKINGER Private. She was born Private. He married (4) HELEN JULIA JACKSON Private. She was born Private.

More About LEE GOODHART and ISABELLE LINE:
Marriage date: Private
Private-Begin: Private

More About LEE GOODHART and SANDRA RISSINGER:
Marriage date: Private
Private-Begin: Private

More About LEE GOODHART and IRENE FLICKINGER:
Marriage date: Private
Private-Begin: Private

More About LEE GOODHART and HELEN JACKSON:
Marriage date: Private
Private-Begin: Private

Children of LEE GOODHART and SANDRA RISSINGER are:
　　i.　WINIFRED SUE[16] GOODHART, b. Private; m. HOCKLEY.
　　ii.　SHARON AGNES GOODHART, b. Private; m. RAKESTRON.

169. ROBERT MICHAEL[15] GOODHART (*LESTER SHEAFFER*[14], *ALICE MARGARET*[13] *SHEAFFER, LYDIA JANE*[12] *TRITT, PETER*[11], *CHRISTIAN*[10], *ELIZABETH*[9] *LEFEVRE, GEORGE*[8], *PHILIP G*[7], *ISAAC*[6], *ABRAHAM*[5], *ANDREW*[4], *PHILIP*[3], *JOHN*[2], *MENGEN*[1]) was born Private. He married DIANE WENGERT Private. She was born Private.

More About ROBERT GOODHART and DIANE WENGERT:
Marriage date: Private
Private-Begin: Private

Children of ROBERT GOODHART and DIANE WENGERT are:
　　i.　TRACI DIANE[16] GOODHART, b. Private.
　　ii.　ERIK MICHAEL GOODHART, b. Private.

170. TERESA ROSE CHARLENE[15] LUCENTI *(DORIS MADELINE[14] SHEAFFER, CHARLES M.[13], LYDIA JANE[12] TRITT, PETER[11], CHRISTIAN[10], ELIZABETH[9] LEFEVRE, GEORGE[8], PHILIP G[7], ISAAC[6], ABRAHAM[5], ANDREW[4], PHILIP[3], JOHN[2], MENGEN[1])* was born Private. She married LAWRENCE R. TAYLOR Private. He was born Private.

More About LAWRENCE TAYLOR and TERESA LUCENTI:
Marriage date: Private
Private-Begin: Private

Child of TERESA LUCENTI and LAWRENCE TAYLOR is:
      i.   TRACI ANN[16] TAYLOR, b. Private.

171. SANDRA MARIE[15] LUCENTI *(DORIS MADELINE[14] SHEAFFER, CHARLES M.[13], LYDIA JANE[12] TRITT, PETER[11], CHRISTIAN[10], ELIZABETH[9] LEFEVRE, GEORGE[8], PHILIP G[7], ISAAC[6], ABRAHAM[5], ANDREW[4], PHILIP[3], JOHN[2], MENGEN[1])* was born Private. She married TEVAS KAHLANCE Private. He was born Private.

More About TEVAS KAHLANCE and SANDRA LUCENTI:
Marriage date: Private
Private-Begin: Private

Child of SANDRA LUCENTI and TEVAS KAHLANCE is:
      i.   TARA ROSE[16] KAHLANCE, b. Private.

172. JOHN EDWARD[15] GLENN *(MARGARETA JUNE[14] SCOTT, FLORENCE GRACE[13] LEFEVRE, HENRY RINE[12], DAVID[11], JOHN B.[10], LAWRENCE[9], GEORGE[8], PHILIP G[7], ISAAC[6], ABRAHAM[5], ANDREW[4], PHILIP[3], JOHN[2], MENGEN[1])* was born 19 Mar 1941 in Borger, texas. He married ANJIA RUTH DOUWSMA 15 Aug 1964 in Metuchen , New Jersey. She was born 22 Jul 1941 in Canal Zone, Panama CA.

More About JOHN GLENN and ANJIA DOUWSMA:
Marriage: 15 Aug 1964, Metuchen , New Jersey

Children of JOHN GLENN and ANJIA DOUWSMA are:
      i.   ARTHUR LLEWELLYN[16] GLENN, b. 09 Jan 1967, Pittsburgh, Pennsylvania.
     ii.   LAURA WENDOLYN GLENN, b. 11 Apr 1971, Findlay, Ohio.

173. JOYCE CAROL[15] GLENN *(MARGARETA JUNE[14] SCOTT, FLORENCE GRACE[13] LEFEVRE, HENRY RINE[12], DAVID[11], JOHN B.[10], LAWRENCE[9], GEORGE[8], PHILIP G[7], ISAAC[6], ABRAHAM[5], ANDREW[4], PHILIP[3], JOHN[2], MENGEN[1])* was born 05 Dec 1943. She married COY HUNT.

Child of JOYCE GLENN and COY HUNT is:

    i.   AMANDA[16] HUNT, b. Nov 1971, Texas; m. STEPHEN MILLS, 24 Aug 1996.

        More About STEPHEN MILLS and AMANDA HUNT:
        Marriage: 24 Aug 1996

174. LAWRENCE KEVIN[15] KNORR *(EMILY FALINE[14] WHITE, WILLIAM WALTER[13], CATHERINE REBECCA[12] WOLF, FRANKLIN LeFEVERE[11], LYDIA[10] LeFEVRE, PETER[9], ADAM[8], PHILIP G[7], ISAAC[6], ABRAHAM[5], ANDREW[4], PHILIP[3], JOHN[2], MENGEN[1])* was born 05 May 1964 in Reading Hospital, Reading, PA. He married (1) SHELLY JEAN HARRIS 18 May 1985 in Sheraton, Wyomissing, PA, daughter of ROBERT HARRIS and PATRICIA MANN. She was born 23 Jul 1965 in Reading, PA. He married (2) DR ANN LOUISE BERGER 05 Nov 1994 in Palm Island Resort, Englewood, Florida, daughter of ROBERT BERGER and MILDRED ROESCHER. She was born 25 Jul 1965 in Reading Hostpital, Reading, PA. He married (3) TAMMI KAY McCOY 14 May 2010 in Bathkeeper's Cottage, Berkeley Springs, WV, daughter of JOHN McCOY and LORRAINE COOPER. She was born 20 Mar 1969 in Harrisburg, PA.

Notes for LAWRENCE KEVIN KNORR:
The author

More About LAWRENCE KNORR and SHELLY HARRIS:
Divorce: Dec 1988, Reading, PA
Marriage: 18 May 1985, Sheraton, Wyomissing, PA

Notes for DR ANN LOUISE BERGER:
Ann is a professor at the Pennsylvania State University in the Teacher Education field. She received her Ph.D. in Curriculum and Instruction in 1997 from Penn State.

More About LAWRENCE KNORR and ANN BERGER:
Divorce: 06 May 2010, Carlisle, PA
Marriage: 05 Nov 1994, Palm Island Resort, Englewood, Florida

Notes for TAMMI KAY McCOY:
Tammi is retired from a 20 year career in information systems. She is an artist, photographer and author, having published numerous books on art for Sunbury Press.

More About LAWRENCE KNORR and TAMMI McCOY:
Marriage: 14 May 2010, Bathkeeper's Cottage, Berkeley Springs, WV

Children of LAWRENCE KNORR and ANN BERGER are:

    i.   TAYLOR[16] BERGER-KNORR, b. 22 Jun 1998, Reading Hospital, Reading, PA.

Notes for TAYLOR BERGER-KNORR:
Taylor was born Father's Day night via cesarean section. Her mother's water broke during the movie "JackPot" (Jimmy Stewart). After rushing from Carlisle to Reading - arriving at midnight - we prepared for the operation. Taylor was born three or four weeks premature. Dad & Mommom watched the whole thing. She was 5 lbs 6 oz and 19". By eight weeks, she was over 11 lbs.

More About TAYLOR BERGER-KNORR:
Baptism: 06 Jun 1999, 8 Appaloosa Way   Carlisle, PA

    ii. ABBEY BERGER-KNORR, b. 04 May 2002, Reading Hostpital, Reading, PA.

Notes for ABBEY BERGER-KNORR:
Abbey was born via c-section at 10:48 AM on her grandpa's birthday - one hour and twelve minutes short of her father's birthday. The odds of such an event is over 65,000 to 1! She was 7 pounds, 3 ounces - with jet black hair - and 20 inches long. She came out screaming!

175. ALICE KATHLEEN[15] KNORR *(EMILY FALINE[14] WHITE, WILLIAM WALTER[13], CATHERINE REBECCA[12] WOLF, FRANKLIN LEFEVERE[11], LYDIA[10] LEFEVRE, PETER[9], ADAM[8], PHILIP G[7], ISAAC[6], ABRAHAM[5], ANDREW[4], PHILIP[3], JOHN[2], MENGEN[1])* was born 11 Aug 1965 in Reading, PA. She met (1) GARY FIDLER in Pennside, PA. He was born Abt. 1955 in Reading, PA. She married (2) GLENN BUCHMAN 23 Jun 1990 in Reading, PA. He was born Abt. 1953 in Kutztown, PA.

Notes for ALICE KATHLEEN KNORR:
Alice & Glenn are printers.

More About GARY FIDLER and ALICE KNORR:
Friends: Pennside, PA

More About GLENN BUCHMAN and ALICE KNORR:
Marriage: 23 Jun 1990, Reading, PA

Child of ALICE KNORR and GARY FIDLER is:
    i. GARY KYLE[16] BUCHMAN, b. 30 Apr 1983.

176. LIVING[15] BROWN *(LIVING[14], HAROLD[13] DINKEL, SR BROWN, HARRY D.[12] BROWN, ELIZABETH[11] MOORE, REBECCA[10] LEFEVRE, JACOB[9], JACOB[8], PHILIP G[7], ISAAC[6], ABRAHAM[5], ANDREW[4], PHILIP[3], JOHN[2], MENGEN[1])* She married LIVING REID.

Child of LIVING BROWN and LIVING REID is:
    i.   LIVING[16] REID.

177. LIVING[15] BROWN (*LIVING[14], HAROLD[13] DINKEL, SR BROWN, HARRY D.[12] BROWN, ELIZABETH[11] MOORE, REBECCA[10] LEFEVRE, JACOB[9], JACOB[8], PHILIP G[7], ISAAC[6], ABRAHAM[5], ANDREW[4], PHILIP[3], JOHN[2], MENGEN[1]*) She married LIVING ROBERTSON.

Child of LIVING BROWN and LIVING ROBERTSON is:
    i.   LIVING[16] ROBERTSON.

178. LIVING[15] BROWN (*LIVING[14], HAROLD[13] DINKEL, SR BROWN, HARRY D.[12] BROWN, ELIZABETH[11] MOORE, REBECCA[10] LEFEVRE, JACOB[9], JACOB[8], PHILIP G[7], ISAAC[6], ABRAHAM[5], ANDREW[4], PHILIP[3], JOHN[2], MENGEN[1]*) She married LIVING ROACH.

Children of LIVING BROWN and LIVING ROACH are:
    i.   LIVING[16] ROACH.
    ii.   LIVING ROACH.
    iii.   LIVING ROACH.
    iv.   LIVING ROACH.
    v.   LIVING ROACH.
    vi.   LIVING ROACH.

Generation No. 16

179. KATHRYN ANN[16] MOHLER (*DOROTHY JEAN[15] HIPPENSTEEL, MARGARET ELIZABETH ALICE[14] GOODHART, ALICE MARGARET[13] SHEAFFER, LYDIA JANE[12] TRITT, PETER[11], CHRISTIAN[10], ELIZABETH[9] LEFEVRE, GEORGE[8], PHILIP G[7], ISAAC[6], ABRAHAM[5], ANDREW[4], PHILIP[3], JOHN[2], MENGEN[1]*) was born Private. She married (1) COLIN CROUSE Private. He was born Private. She married (2) JOHN DANIELS Private. He was born Private.

More About COLIN CROUSE and KATHRYN MOHLER:
Marriage date: Private
Private-Begin: Private

More About JOHN DANIELS and KATHRYN MOHLER:
Marriage date: Private
Private-Begin: Private

Child of KATHRYN MOHLER and COLIN CROUSE is:
184.   i.   ANGELA DAWN[17] CROUSE, b. Private.

180. JOHN ROBERT[16] MOHLER *(DOROTHY JEAN[15] HIPPENSTEEL, MARGARET ELIZABETH ALICE[14] GOODHART, ALICE MARGARET[13] SHEAFFER, LYDIA JANE[12] TRITT, PETER[11], CHRISTIAN[10], ELIZABETH[9] LEFEVRE, GEORGE[8], PHILIP G[7], ISAAC[6], ABRAHAM[5], ANDREW[4], PHILIP[3], JOHN[2], MENGEN[1])* was born Private. He married CINDY JOAN BLOOM Private. She was born Private.

More About JOHN MOHLER and CINDY BLOOM:
Marriage date: Private
Private-Begin: Private

Children of JOHN MOHLER and CINDY BLOOM are:
      i. MATTHEW ROBERT[17] MOHLER, b. Private.
     ii. MARK ANDREW MOHLER, b. Private.

181. DIANE ELIZABETH[16] WEST *(DORIS MADELINE[15] HIPPENSTEEL, MARGARET ELIZABETH ALICE[14] GOODHART, ALICE MARGARET[13] SHEAFFER, LYDIA JANE[12] TRITT, PETER[11], CHRISTIAN[10], ELIZABETH[9] LEFEVRE, GEORGE[8], PHILIP G[7], ISAAC[6], ABRAHAM[5], ANDREW[4], PHILIP[3], JOHN[2], MENGEN[1])* was born Private. She married LYNN RICHARD WENGER Private. He was born Private.

More About LYNN WENGER and DIANE WEST:
Marriage date: Private
Private-Begin: Private

Children of DIANE WEST and LYNN WENGER are:
      i. ETHAN RICHARD[17] WENGER, b. Private.
     ii. SETH JONATHAN WENGER, b. Private.
    iii. LAURA BETH WENGER, b. Private.

182. BARBARA ELAINE[16] WEST *(DORIS MADELINE[15] HIPPENSTEEL, MARGARET ELIZABETH ALICE[14] GOODHART, ALICE MARGARET[13] SHEAFFER, LYDIA JANE[12] TRITT, PETER[11], CHRISTIAN[10], ELIZABETH[9] LEFEVRE, GEORGE[8], PHILIP G[7], ISAAC[6], ABRAHAM[5], ANDREW[4], PHILIP[3], JOHN[2], MENGEN[1])* was born Private. She married BARRY LEE BATZ Private. He was born Private.

More About BARRY BATZ and BARBARA WEST:
Marriage date: Private
Private-Begin: Private

Children of BARBARA WEST and BARRY BATZ are:
      i. JASON BARRY[17] BATZ, b. Private.
     ii. CHRISTY AMANDA BATZ, b. Private.

183. JOHN CHARLES[16] GOODHART *(CHARLES DALE[15], CLARENCE EUGENE[14], ALICE MARGARET[13] SHEAFFER, LYDIA JANE[12] TRITT, PETER[11], CHRISTIAN[10], ELIZABETH[9] LEFEVRE, GEORGE[8], PHILIP G[7], ISAAC[6], ABRAHAM[5], ANDREW[4], PHILIP[3], JOHN[2], MENGEN[1])* was born Private. He married JOY COMMITTUS Private. She was born Private.

More About JOHN GOODHART and JOY COMMITTUS:
Marriage date: Private
Private-Begin: Private

Children of JOHN GOODHART and JOY COMMITTUS are:
    i.   DOMINIC CHARLES[17] GOODHART, b. Private.
   ii.   BENJAMIN SCOTT GOODHART, b. Private.

Generation No. 17

184. ANGELA DAWN[17] CROUSE *(KATHRYN ANN[16] MOHLER, DOROTHY JEAN[15] HIPPENSTEEL, MARGARET ELIZABETH ALICE[14] GOODHART, ALICE MARGARET[13] SHEAFFER, LYDIA JANE[12] TRITT, PETER[11], CHRISTIAN[10], ELIZABETH[9] LEFEVRE, GEORGE[8], PHILIP G[7], ISAAC[6], ABRAHAM[5], ANDREW[4], PHILIP[3], JOHN[2], MENGEN[1])* was born Private. She married GORDON WOGLEMUTH Private. He was born Private.

More About GORDON WOGLEMUTH and ANGELA CROUSE:
Marriage date: Private
Private-Begin: Private

Child of ANGELA CROUSE and GORDON WOGLEMUTH is:
    i.   SEAN[18] WOGLEMUTH, b. Private.

William Reynolds, brother of John

Sister Lydia Reynolds (1818 - 1896)

Name	Relationship with John Reynolds	Civil	Canon
?, Eleanor	Wife of the uncle		
	Wife of the 3rd cousin once removed		
Adams, Charles Frazier	Husband of the 3rd cousin		
	Husband of the 4th cousin		
Adams, Eleanor	Wife of the 3rd cousin		
	Wife of the 4th cousin		
Adams, Eliza	Wife of the 3rd cousin once removed		
	Wife of the 4th cousin once removed		
Algeo, Thomas	Husband of the grandaunt		
	Husband of the 2nd cousin twice removed		
Alter, Veronica	Wife of the 2nd cousin once removed		
	Wife of the 3rd cousin once removed		
Altmaier, Ellwood	Husband of the 3rd cousin 4 times removed		
	Husband of the 4th cousin 4 times removed		
Angeny, Sarah	Wife of the nephew		
	Wife of the 4th cousin once removed		
Annie	3rd cousin once removed	IX	5
	4th cousin once removed	XI	6
Antrim, Evelyn	Wife of the 3rd cousin 3 times removed		
	Wife of the 4th cousin 3 times removed		
Armsworth, Elizabeth	Wife of the 3rd cousin twice removed		
	Wife of the 4th cousin twice removed		
Armsworth, Josephine	Wife of the 3rd cousin twice removed		
	Wife of the 4th cousin twice removed		
Arnold, Nancy	Wife of the 3rd cousin		
	Wife of the 4th cousin		
Babb, Caroline	Wife of the 3rd cousin		
	Wife of the 4th cousin		
Babb, Minerva	Wife of the 3rd cousin		
	Wife of the 4th cousin		
Baer, Henry	Husband of the 3rd cousin once removed		
	Husband of the 4th cousin once removed		
Baer, Rachel	Wife of the 3rd cousin once removed		
	Wife of the 4th cousin once removed		
Bair, Elizabeth	Wife of the 2nd cousin		
	Wife of the 4th cousin		
Barnum, Thomas B.	Husband of the 3rd cousin		
	Husband of the 4th cousin		
Barton, Gilbert	Husband of the 3rd cousin		
	Husband of the 4th cousin		
Bastert, Clarence	Husband of the 3rd cousin 4 times removed		
	Husband of the 4th cousin 4 times removed		
Batz, Barry Lee	Husband of the 3rd cousin 6 times removed		
	Husband of the 4th cousin 6 times removed		
Batz, Christy Amanda	3rd cousin 7 times removed	XV	11
	4th cousin 7 times removed	XVII	12
Batz, Jason Barry	3rd cousin 7 times removed	XV	11
	4th cousin 7 times removed	XVII	12
Baughman, Hannah	Wife of the 3rd cousin		
	Wife of the 4th cousin		
Baumann, Grace	Wife of the 3rd cousin 3 times removed		
	Wife of the 4th cousin 3 times removed		
Baxter, James	Husband of the 3rd cousin		
	Husband of the 4th cousin		
Beal, Alvin	Husband of the 3rd cousin twice removed		
	Husband of the 4th cousin twice removed		
Belch, Elizabeth	Wife of the 3rd cousin		
	Wife of the 4th cousin		
Bentz, John	Husband of the 3rd cousin 3 times removed		
	Husband of the 4th cousin 3 times removed		
Berger, Ann Louise	Ex-wife of the 3rd cousin 5 times removed		
	Ex-wife of the 4th cousin 5 times removed		
Berger-Knorr, Abbey	3rd cousin 6 times removed	XIV	10

Name	Relationship with John Reynolds	Civil	Canon
Berger-Knorr, Ann Louise	4th cousin 6 times removed	XVI	11
	Ex-wife of the 3rd cousin 5 times removed		
Berger-Knorr, Taylor	Ex-wife of the 4th cousin 5 times removed		
	3rd cousin 6 times removed	XIV	10
Bernheisel, Michael Scott	4th cousin 6 times removed	XVI	11
	3rd cousin 6 times removed	XIV	10
Bernheisel, Patrick Alan	4th cousin 6 times removed	XVI	11
	3rd cousin 6 times removed	XIV	10
Bernheisel, Toni Karen	4th cousin 6 times removed	XVI	11
	3rd cousin 6 times removed	XIV	10
Bernheisel, Walter J.	4th cousin 6 times removed	XVI	11
	Husband of the 3rd cousin 5 times removed		
Biebinger, Jesse	Husband of the 4th cousin 5 times removed		
	Husband of the 3rd cousin twice removed		
Bigger	Husband of the 4th cousin twice removed		
	Husband of the 2nd cousin once removed		
Black, Samuel	Husband of the 3rd cousin once removed		
	Husband of the 3rd cousin once removed		
Block, Catherine	Husband of the 4th cousin once removed		
	Wife of the 3rd cousin		
Bloom, Cindy Joan	Wife of the 4th cousin		
	Wife of the 3rd cousin 6 times removed		
Blosser, Benjamin	Wife of the 4th cousin 6 times removed		
	Husband of the 3rd cousin once removed		
Boggs, Elizabeth	Husband of the 4th cousin once removed		
	Wife of the 3rd cousin once removed		
Bowerman, Michael	Wife of the 4th cousin once removed		
	Husband of the 3rd cousin		
Bowman, Mr.	Husband of the 4th cousin		
	Husband of the 3rd cousin 3 times removed		
Bowman, Susanna	Husband of the 4th cousin 3 times removed		
	Wife of the 2nd cousin once removed		
Boyer, Samuel S	Wife of the 3rd cousin once removed		
	Husband of the 2nd cousin once removed		
Braden, Adaline	Husband of the 3rd cousin once removed		
	Wife of the 3rd cousin		
Brook, Wayne	Wife of the 4th cousin		
	Husband of the 3rd cousin 3 times removed		
Brown, Catherine	Husband of the 4th cousin 3 times removed		
	Wife of the 2nd cousin once removed		
Brown, Frank A.	Wife of the 3rd cousin once removed		
	3rd cousin twice removed	X	6
Brown, Harry D.	4th cousin twice removed	XII	7
	3rd cousin twice removed	X	6
Brown, Living	4th cousin twice removed	XII	7
	3rd cousin 4 times removed	XII	8
Brown, Living	4th cousin 4 times removed	XIV	9
	3rd cousin 5 times removed	XIII	9
Brown, Living	4th cousin 5 times removed	XV	10
	3rd cousin 5 times removed	XIII	9
Brown, Living	4th cousin 5 times removed	XV	10
	3rd cousin 5 times removed	XIII	9
Brown, Living	4th cousin 5 times removed	XV	10
	3rd cousin 3 times removed	XI	7
Brown, Living	4th cousin 3 times removed	XIII	8
	3rd cousin 4 times removed	XII	8
Brown, Living	4th cousin 4 times removed	XIV	9
	3rd cousin 4 times removed	XII	8
Brown, Living	4th cousin 4 times removed	XIV	9
	3rd cousin 4 times removed	XII	8
Brown, Living	4th cousin 4 times removed	XIV	9
	3rd cousin 4 times removed	XII	8
Brown, Living	4th cousin 4 times removed	XIV	9
	3rd cousin 3 times removed	XI	7

Name	Relationship with John Reynolds	Civil	Canon
	4th cousin 3 times removed	XIII	8
Brown, Living	3rd cousin 3 times removed	XI	7
	4th cousin 3 times removed	XIII	8
Brown, Living	3rd cousin 3 times removed	XI	7
	4th cousin 3 times removed	XIII	8
Brown, Mary B.	Wife of the 3rd cousin once removed		
	Wife of the 4th cousin once removed		
Brown, Nathan	Husband of the 3rd cousin		
	Husband of the 4th cousin		
Brown, Nathaniel P	Husband of the 3rd cousin once removed		
	Husband of the 4th cousin once removed		
Brua, Susan	Wife of the 3rd cousin		
	Wife of the 4th cousin		
Brubaker, Susan	Wife of the 3rd cousin		
	Wife of the 3rd cousin once removed		
	Wife of the 4th cousin		
	Wife of the 4th cousin once removed		
Buchanan, John	Husband of the 3rd cousin twice removed		
	Husband of the 4th cousin twice removed		
Buchman, Gary Kyle	3rd cousin 6 times removed	XIV	10
	4th cousin 6 times removed	XVI	11
Buchman, Glenn	Husband of the 3rd cousin 5 times removed		
	Husband of the 4th cousin 5 times removed		
Buckwalter, Martin	Husband of the 3rd cousin		
	Husband of the 4th cousin		
Buffington, Ruth	Wife of the 2nd great-granduncle		
Burnham, Lela Berneice	Wife of the 3rd cousin twice removed		
	Wife of the 4th cousin twice removed		
Burns, Claudia	Wife of the 3rd cousin twice removed		
	Wife of the 4th cousin twice removed		
Byers, Joseph	Husband of the 3rd cousin		
	Husband of the 4th cousin		
Cahill, Betty Jane	Wife of the 3rd cousin 5 times removed		
	Wife of the 4th cousin 5 times removed		
Calaman, Lawrence Delmar	Wife of the 3rd cousin 4 times removed		
	Wife of the 4th cousin 4 times removed		
Calvert, Peter	Husband of the 3rd cousin once removed		
	Husband of the 4th cousin once removed		
Camp, Mary Ann	Wife of the 2nd cousin once removed		
	Wife of the 3rd cousin once removed		
Camp, Polly	Wife of the 3rd cousin		
	Wife of the 4th cousin		
Carpenter, Salome	Wife of the granduncle		
	Wife of the 2nd cousin twice removed		
Carter, Gertrude Lucile	Wife of the 3rd cousin twice removed		
	Wife of the 4th cousin twice removed		
Cassell, John	Husband of the 3rd cousin twice removed		
	Husband of the 4th cousin twice removed		
Cease, Margaret	Wife of the 3rd cousin		
	Wife of the 4th cousin		
Cecil, Nancy	Wife of the 3rd cousin		
	Wife of the 4th cousin		
Chaffin, Ida	Wife of the 3rd cousin 4 times removed		
	Wife of the 4th cousin 4 times removed		
Christy, Henry	Husband of the 1st cousin twice removed		
	Husband of the 2nd cousin twice removed		
Clack, Elizabeth	Wife of the 2nd cousin once removed		
	Wife of the 3rd cousin once removed		
Clark, Augustus	Husband of the 3rd cousin once removed		
	Husband of the 4th cousin once removed		
Clausen, Ruth	Wife of the 3rd cousin 4 times removed		
	Wife of the 4th cousin 4 times removed		
Cole, Miriam	Wife of the 3rd cousin		
	Wife of the 4th cousin		

Name	Relationship with John Reynolds	Civil	Canon
Colle, Marceline Elodia	Wife of the 3rd cousin 3 times removed		
	Wife of the 4th cousin 3 times removed		
Committus, Joy	Wife of the 3rd cousin 6 times removed		
	Wife of the 4th cousin 6 times removed		
Copley, James	Husband of the 3rd cousin 6 times removed		
	Husband of the 4th cousin 6 times removed		
Cornell, Aaron	Husband of the 3rd cousin		
	Husband of the 4th cousin		
Cough, Samuel	Husband of the 3rd cousin		
	Husband of the 4th cousin		
Coulson, Milton	Husband of the 3rd cousin		
	Husband of the 4th cousin		
Cox, Sarah	Wife of the 3rd cousin		
	Wife of the 4th cousin		
Crone, Hobart	Husband of the 3rd cousin 3 times removed		
	Husband of the 4th cousin 3 times removed		
Crook, Wallace W.	Husband of the 3rd cousin twice removed		
	Husband of the 4th cousin twice removed		
Crouse, Angela Dawn	3rd cousin 7 times removed	XV	11
	4th cousin 7 times removed	XVII	12
Crouse, Colin	Husband of the 3rd cousin 6 times removed		
	Husband of the 4th cousin 6 times removed		
Crowe, Benjamin	Husband of the 3rd cousin		
	Husband of the 4th cousin		
Cryder, George	Husband of the 1st cousin 3 times removed		
Cunkle, Mary	Wife of the 1st cousin twice removed		
	Wife of the 2nd cousin twice removed		
Cunningham, Matilda	Wife of the 3rd cousin once removed		
	Wife of the 4th cousin once removed		
Curry, Agnes	Wife of the 2nd cousin once removed		
	Wife of the 3rd cousin once removed		
Dan, Chatham Tanner	3rd cousin	VIII	4
	4th cousin	X	5
Dan, Paradise Tanner	2nd cousin once removed	VII	4
	3rd cousin once removed	IX	5
Daniels, John	Husband of the 3rd cousin 6 times removed		
	Husband of the 4th cousin 6 times removed		
Dauchey, Hawley	Husband of the 3rd cousin		
	Husband of the 4th cousin		
David, Mary Lydia	Wife of the 3rd cousin		
	Wife of the 4th cousin		
Davis, Lucy	Wife of the 3rd cousin		
	Wife of the 4th cousin		
Davis, Mary	Wife of the 3rd cousin		
	Wife of the 4th cousin		
Davis, Richard	Husband of the 2nd great-grandaunt		
Day, Margaret	Wife of the grandnephew		
	Wife of the 4th cousin twice removed		
Deimler, Christabel J	Wife of the 3rd cousin 3 times removed		
	Wife of the 4th cousin 3 times removed		
DeLawter, Lewis	Husband of the 3rd cousin		
	Husband of the 4th cousin		
Dellinger, John F	Husband of the 3rd cousin		
	Husband of the 4th cousin		
Dellinger, William	Husband of the 3rd cousin		
	Husband of the 4th cousin		
Denlinger, Barbara	Wife of the 3rd cousin		
	Wife of the 4th cousin		
Denlinger, Christian	Husband of the 2nd cousin once removed		
	Husband of the 3rd cousin once removed		
Denny, Mary	Wife of the 2nd cousin once removed		
	Wife of the 3rd cousin once removed		
Derr, Christina	Wife of the 3rd cousin		
	Wife of the 4th cousin		

Name	Relationship with John Reynolds	Civil	Canon
Derr, George	Husband of the 2nd cousin once removed		
	Husband of the 3rd cousin once removed		
Deshler, David	Husband of the great-grandaunt		
	Husband of the 1st cousin 3 times removed		
Deyo, Elizabeth	Wife of the 3rd great-granduncle		
Dilks, Verna	Wife of the 3rd cousin 3 times removed		
	Wife of the 4th cousin 3 times removed		
Dinkel, Harold, Sr Brown	3rd cousin 3 times removed	XI	7
	4th cousin 3 times removed	XIII	8
Dinkel, Maebell	Ex-wife of the 3rd cousin twice removed		
	Ex-wife of the 4th cousin twice removed		
Dodds, Josephus	Husband of the 3rd cousin		
	Husband of the 4th cousin		
Douglas, Elizabeth	3rd cousin once removed	IX	5
	4th cousin once removed	XI	6
Douglas, John	Husband of the 3rd cousin		
	Husband of the 4th cousin		
Douglas, John	3rd cousin once removed	IX	5
	4th cousin once removed	XI	6
Douwsma, Anjia Ruth	Wife of the 3rd cousin 5 times removed		
	Wife of the 4th cousin 5 times removed		
Dram, Elizabeth	Wife of the 3rd cousin		
	Wife of the 4th cousin		
Duell, Catherine	Wife of the 3rd cousin once removed		
	Wife of the 4th cousin once removed		
DuVall, Nimrod	Husband of the 3rd cousin		
	Husband of the 4th cousin		
Dye, Fielding	Husband of the 3rd cousin		
	Husband of the 4th cousin		
Ebersole, Myra Belle	Wife of the 3rd cousin twice removed		
	Wife of the 4th cousin twice removed		
Ecker, Louise	Wife of the 3rd cousin 4 times removed		
	Wife of the 4th cousin 4 times removed		
Eckert, George	Husband of the 2nd cousin		
	Husband of the 4th cousin		
Eckman, Catherine Messenkop	Wife of the granduncle		
	Wife of the 2nd cousin twice removed		
Eckman, Henry	Husband of the 1st cousin twice removed		
	Husband of the 2nd cousin twice removed		
Eckman, Peter	Husband of the 2nd cousin once removed		
	Husband of the 3rd cousin once removed		
Erb, Catherine	Wife of the 2nd cousin once removed		
	Wife of the 3rd cousin once removed		
Esbenshade, Daniel	Husband of the 2nd cousin once removed		
	Husband of the 3rd cousin once removed		
Esbenshade, Mary	Wife of the 3rd cousin		
	Wife of the 4th cousin		
Eshleman, Martha	Wife of the 3rd cousin		
	Wife of the 4th cousin		
Evans, Catharine	Niece	III	2
	4th cousin once removed	XI	6
Evans, Charles P	Grandnephew	IV	3
	4th cousin twice removed	XII	7
Evans, Hale	Nephew	III	2
	4th cousin once removed	XI	6
Evans, Harry L	Nephew	III	2
	4th cousin once removed	XI	6
Evans, John Fulton Reynolds	Nephew	III	2
	4th cousin once removed	XI	6
Evans, Kate E.	Grandniece	IV	3
	4th cousin twice removed	XII	7
Evans, Mary	Niece	III	2
	4th cousin once removed	XI	6
Evans, Nathaniel	Brother-in-law		

Name	Relationship with John Reynolds	Civil	Canon
	Husband of the 4th cousin		
Evans, Rosswell	Grandnephew	IV	3
	4th cousin twice removed	XII	7
Evans, William R.	Grandniece	IV	3
	4th cousin twice removed	XII	7
Eyster, William L.	Husband of the 3rd cousin twice removed		
	Husband of the 4th cousin twice removed		
Falck, Elizabeth	Wife of the 3rd cousin		
	Wife of the 4th cousin		
Faulkner, Thomas	Husband of the 2nd great-grandaunt		
Felty, John	Husband of the 3rd cousin		
	Husband of the 4th cousin		
Ferguson, Elizabeth	Wife of the 3rd cousin		
	Wife of the 4th cousin		
Ferree, Abraham	Husband of the 2nd cousin once removed		
	Husband of the 3rd cousin once removed		
Ferree, Alice	3rd cousin 3 times removed	XI	7
	4th cousin 3 times removed	XIII	8
Ferree, Anne	Wife of the 1st cousin twice removed		
	Wife of the 2nd cousin twice removed		
Ferree, Catherine	2nd great-grandmother	IV	4
	2nd great-grandaunt	VI	5
Ferree, Conrad	1st cousin 3 times removed	VII	5
Ferree, Daniel	3rd great-grandfather	V	5
Ferree, Daniel	2nd great-grandfather	IV	4
	2nd great-granduncle	VI	5
Ferree, David	Husband of the great-grandaunt		
	Husband of the 1st cousin twice removed		
	Husband of the 1st cousin 3 times removed		
	Husband of the 2nd cousin twice removed		
Ferree, Elizabeth	Great-grandaunt	V	4
	1st cousin 3 times removed	VII	5
	Wife of the great-granduncle		
	Wife of the 1st cousin 3 times removed		
Ferree, Jacob	Husband of the 2nd cousin once removed		
	Husband of the 3rd cousin once removed		
Ferree, James	Husband of the 2nd cousin once removed		
	Husband of the 3rd cousin once removed		
Ferree, Jane	2nd great-grandaunt	VI	5
Ferree, John	2nd great-granduncle	VI	5
Ferree, Lydia	Great-grandmother	III	3
	1st cousin 3 times removed	VII	5
	Wife of the 1st cousin 3 times removed		
Ferree, Lydia	2nd cousin once removed	VII	4
	3rd cousin once removed	IX	5
	Wife of the granduncle		
	Wife of the 2nd cousin twice removed		
Ferree, Mary	2nd great-grandaunt	VI	5
Ferree, Philip	2nd great-granduncle	VI	5
Ferree, Susanna	1st cousin 3 times removed	VII	5
Ferree, Thomas	Husband of the 3rd cousin twice removed		
	Husband of the 4th cousin twice removed		
Fidler, Gary	Friend of the 3rd cousin 5 times removed		
	Friend of the 4th cousin 5 times removed		
Fishburn, Anthony	Husband of the 3rd cousin		
	Husband of the 3rd cousin once removed		
	Husband of the 4th cousin		
	Husband of the 4th cousin once removed		
Fisher, Jean	Wife of the 3rd cousin 4 times removed		
	Wife of the 4th cousin 4 times removed		
Flickinger, Irene	Wife of the 3rd cousin 5 times removed		
	Wife of the 4th cousin 5 times removed		
Foreman, Christiana	Wife of the 3rd cousin		
	Wife of the 4th cousin		

Name	Relationship with John Reynolds	Civil	Canon
Forrer, Anne	Wife of the 3rd cousin		
	Wife of the 4th cousin		
Forrer, Christiana	Wife of the 3rd cousin		
	Wife of the 4th cousin		
Forrest, Howard	Husband of the 3rd cousin 3 times removed		
	Husband of the 4th cousin 3 times removed		
Fortney, Jacob	Husband of the 3rd cousin		
	Husband of the 4th cousin		
Foster, Christiana	Wife of the 2nd cousin		
	Wife of the 4th cousin		
Foster, Rachel	Wife of the 1st cousin once removed		
	Wife of the 3rd cousin once removed		
Frazer, Katherine	Wife of the 3rd cousin 3 times removed		
	Wife of the 4th cousin 3 times removed		
Freeland, John C	Husband of the 2nd cousin		
	Husband of the 4th cousin		
French, Henry	Husband of the 2nd cousin once removed		
	Husband of the 3rd cousin once removed		
French, Jacob	Husband of the 3rd cousin		
	Husband of the 4th cousin		
French, Permelia	Wife of the 3rd cousin		
	Wife of the 4th cousin		
Fritz, Anne	Wife of the 3rd cousin		
	Wife of the 4th cousin		
Fritz, Susan	Wife of the 3rd cousin		
	Wife of the 4th cousin		
Fulton, Jane	Grandmother	II	2
Fulton, John	Great-grandfather	III	3
Fulweiler, Mary A.	Wife of the 2nd cousin once removed		
	Wife of the 3rd cousin once removed		
Gall, Elizabeth Smeltz	Wife of the 2nd cousin once removed		
	Wife of the 3rd cousin once removed		
Gaul, Jacob	Husband of the 3rd cousin		
	Husband of the 4th cousin		
Gildersleeve, George	Brother-in-law		
	Husband of the 4th cousin		
Gildersleeve, William Reynolds	Nephew	III	2
	4th cousin once removed	XI	6
Glatfelter, Elijah	Husband of the 3rd cousin		
	Husband of the 4th cousin		
Glenn, Arthur Llewellyn	3rd cousin 6 times removed	XIV	10
	4th cousin 6 times removed	XVI	11
Glenn, James Goodhart	Husband of the 3rd cousin 4 times removed		
	Husband of the 4th cousin 4 times removed		
Glenn, James Scott	3rd cousin 5 times removed	XIII	9
	4th cousin 5 times removed	XV	10
Glenn, John Edward	3rd cousin 5 times removed	XIII	9
	4th cousin 5 times removed	XV	10
Glenn, Joyce Carol	3rd cousin 5 times removed	XIII	9
	4th cousin 5 times removed	XV	10
Glenn, Laura Wendolyn	3rd cousin 6 times removed	XIV	10
	4th cousin 6 times removed	XVI	11
Gonzalez, Hilda	Wife of the 3rd cousin 3 times removed		
	Wife of the 4th cousin 3 times removed		
Goodhart, Ann Betta	3rd cousin 5 times removed	XIII	9
	4th cousin 5 times removed	XV	10
Goodhart, Benjamin Scott	3rd cousin 7 times removed	XV	11
	4th cousin 7 times removed	XVII	12
Goodhart, Charles Dale	3rd cousin 5 times removed	XIII	9
	4th cousin 5 times removed	XV	10
Goodhart, Charles Floyd	3rd cousin 4 times removed	XII	8
	4th cousin 4 times removed	XIV	9
Goodhart, Clarence Eugene	3rd cousin 4 times removed	XII	8
	4th cousin 4 times removed	XIV	9

Name	Relationship with John Reynolds	Civil	Canon
Goodhart, Dominic Charles	3rd cousin 7 times removed	XV	11
	4th cousin 7 times removed	XVII	12
Goodhart, Edward Sheaffer	3rd cousin 5 times removed	XIII	9
	4th cousin 5 times removed	XV	10
Goodhart, Erik Michael	3rd cousin 6 times removed	XIV	10
	4th cousin 6 times removed	XVI	11
Goodhart, Flora Pauline	3rd cousin 4 times removed	XII	8
	4th cousin 4 times removed	XIV	9
Goodhart, James Lee	3rd cousin 6 times removed	XIV	10
	4th cousin 6 times removed	XVI	11
Goodhart, John Charles	3rd cousin 6 times removed	XIV	10
	4th cousin 6 times removed	XVI	11
Goodhart, Lee Piper	3rd cousin 5 times removed	XIII	9
	4th cousin 5 times removed	XV	10
Goodhart, Lester Sheaffer	3rd cousin 4 times removed	XII	8
	4th cousin 4 times removed	XIV	9
Goodhart, Margaret Elizabeth Alice	3rd cousin 4 times removed	XII	8
	4th cousin 4 times removed	XIV	9
Goodhart, Marian Esther	3rd cousin 4 times removed	XII	8
	4th cousin 4 times removed	XIV	9
Goodhart, Pearle Viola	3rd cousin 4 times removed	XII	8
	4th cousin 4 times removed	XIV	9
Goodhart, Robert Michael	3rd cousin 5 times removed	XIII	9
	4th cousin 5 times removed	XV	10
Goodhart, Sharon Agnes	3rd cousin 6 times removed	XIV	10
	4th cousin 6 times removed	XVI	11
Goodhart, Theodore	Husband of the 3rd cousin 3 times removed		
	Husband of the 4th cousin 3 times removed		
Goodhart, Theodore Rice	3rd cousin 5 times removed	XIII	9
	4th cousin 5 times removed	XV	10
Goodhart, Theodore Riley	3rd cousin 4 times removed	XII	8
	4th cousin 4 times removed	XIV	9
Goodhart, Traci Diane	3rd cousin 6 times removed	XIV	10
	4th cousin 6 times removed	XVI	11
Goodhart, Winifred Sue	3rd cousin 6 times removed	XIV	10
	4th cousin 6 times removed	XVI	11
Graff, Emily	Wife of the 3rd cousin twice removed		
	Wife of the 4th cousin twice removed		
Graff, Malinda	Wife of the 3rd cousin twice removed		
	Wife of the 4th cousin twice removed		
Grissinger, Samuel Z	Husband of the 3rd cousin		
	Husband of the 4th cousin		
Groff, Benjamin	Husband of the 3rd cousin		
	Husband of the 3rd cousin once removed		
	Husband of the 4th cousin		
	Husband of the 4th cousin once removed		
Groff, Susan	Wife of the 3rd cousin		
	Wife of the 3rd cousin once removed		
	Wife of the 4th cousin		
	Wife of the 4th cousin once removed		
Gryder, Mary	Wife of the 3rd cousin		
	Wife of the 4th cousin		
Hackman, Emma Amelia	Wife of the 3rd cousin 3 times removed		
	Wife of the 4th cousin 3 times removed		
Hain, Annie J	Wife of the 3rd cousin once removed		
	Wife of the 4th cousin once removed		
Hamm, John	Husband of the 3rd cousin		
	Husband of the 4th cousin		
Hammer, Catherine	Wife of the 2nd cousin once removed		
	Wife of the 3rd cousin once removed		
Harmon, Daniel	Husband of the great-grandaunt		
	Husband of the 1st cousin 3 times removed		
Harmon, John	1st cousin twice removed	VI	4
	2nd cousin twice removed	VIII	5

Name	Relationship with John Reynolds	Civil	Canon
Harmon, Samuel	Husband of the 3rd cousin		
	Husband of the 4th cousin		
Harper, David	Husband of the 3rd cousin		
	Husband of the 4th cousin		
Harper, Delilah	Wife of the 3rd cousin		
	Wife of the 4th cousin		
Harris, Elizabeth	Great-grandmother	III	3
Harris, Nancy Anne	Wife of the 2nd cousin once removed		
	Wife of the 3rd cousin once removed		
Harris, Shelly Jean	Ex-wife of the 3rd cousin 5 times removed		
	Ex-wife of the 4th cousin 5 times removed		
Hartman, Jacob	Husband of the 2nd cousin once removed		
	Husband of the 3rd cousin once removed		
Hartman, Sussana	Wife of the 2nd cousin once removed		
	Wife of the 3rd cousin once removed		
Hassler, Michael	3rd cousin 4 times removed	XII	8
	4th cousin 4 times removed	XIV	9
Hassler, William T	Husband of the 3rd cousin 3 times removed		
	Husband of the 4th cousin 3 times removed		
Hatfield, Elizabeth	Wife of the 3rd cousin		
	Wife of the 4th cousin		
Haup, Rudolph	Husband of the 1st cousin twice removed		
	Husband of the 2nd cousin twice removed		
Heller, Christian	Husband of the 3rd cousin		
	Husband of the 4th cousin		
Henning, Margaret	Wife of the 1st cousin twice removed		
	Wife of the 2nd cousin twice removed		
Herr, Anne	Wife of the 3rd cousin		
	Wife of the 4th cousin		
Herr, Anne W	Wife of the 3rd cousin		
	Wife of the 4th cousin		
Herr, Elizabeth	Wife of the 3rd cousin		
	Wife of the 4th cousin		
Herr, Maria Catherine	Wife of the great-granduncle		
	Wife of the 1st cousin 3 times removed		
Herrick, Anne E.	Wife of the 3rd cousin		
	Wife of the 4th cousin		
Hershey, Joseph B	Husband of the 3rd cousin twice removed		
	Husband of the 4th cousin twice removed		
Hess, Elizabeth	Wife of the 2nd cousin once removed		
	Wife of the 3rd cousin once removed		
Hess, Rachel	Wife of the 3rd cousin		
	Wife of the 4th cousin		
Hickey, Mary	Wife of the 3rd cousin		
	Wife of the 4th cousin		
Higginbotham, Virginia	Wife of the 3rd cousin 4 times removed		
	Wife of the 4th cousin 4 times removed		
Hill, Nancy C	Wife of the 3rd cousin		
	Wife of the 4th cousin		
Himminger	Husband of the 3rd cousin once removed		
	Husband of the 4th cousin once removed		
Hippensteel, Doris Madeline	3rd cousin 5 times removed	XIII	9
	4th cousin 5 times removed	XV	10
Hippensteel, Dorothy Jean	3rd cousin 5 times removed	XIII	9
	4th cousin 5 times removed	XV	10
Hippensteel, Infant Son	3rd cousin 6 times removed	XIV	10
	4th cousin 6 times removed	XVI	11
Hippensteel, Judy Ann	3rd cousin 6 times removed	XIV	10
	4th cousin 6 times removed	XVI	11
Hippensteel, Margaret Joanne	3rd cousin 5 times removed	XIII	9
	4th cousin 5 times removed	XV	10
Hippensteel, Robert Goodhart	3rd cousin 5 times removed	XIII	9
	4th cousin 5 times removed	XV	10
Hippensteel, Robert William	Husband of the 3rd cousin 4 times removed		

Name	Relationship with John Reynolds	Civil	Canon
Hippensteel, Sandra Lee	Husband of the 4th cousin 4 times removed		
	3rd cousin 6 times removed	XIV	10
Hitchman, William H	4th cousin 6 times removed	XVI	11
	Husband of the 2nd cousin		
Hockley	Husband of the 4th cousin		
	Husband of the 3rd cousin 6 times removed		
Hoffman	Husband of the 4th cousin 6 times removed		
	Husband of the grandniece		
Hoffman, Emily R	Husband of the 4th cousin twice removed		
	Grandniece	IV	3
Hoffman, Frederick E	4th cousin twice removed	XII	7
	Grandnephew	IV	3
Hoffman, Katherine	4th cousin twice removed	XII	7
	Grandniece	IV	3
Hoffman, William H	4th cousin twice removed	XII	7
	Husband of the niece		
Hoffstott, Catherine	Husband of the 4th cousin once removed		
	Wife of the 3rd cousin		
Hoke, Elizabeth	Wife of the 4th cousin		
	Wife of the 3rd cousin once removed		
Holtzapfel, Henry	Wife of the 4th cousin once removed		
	Husband of the 2nd cousin once removed		
Hoover, Hettie	Husband of the 3rd cousin once removed		
	Wife of the 3rd cousin twice removed		
Hoover, Margaret	Wife of the 4th cousin twice removed		
	Wife of the 3rd cousin once removed		
Hopkins, David W.	Wife of the 4th cousin once removed		
	Husband of the 3rd cousin		
Hostetter, Mary	Husband of the 4th cousin		
	Wife of the 3rd cousin		
Householder, Christianna	Wife of the 4th cousin		
	Wife of the 2nd cousin once removed		
Householder, Frederick	Wife of the 3rd cousin once removed		
	Husband of the 2nd cousin once removed		
Houser, Anne	Husband of the 3rd cousin once removed		
	Wife of the 3rd cousin		
Houser, John	Wife of the 4th cousin		
	Husband of the 3rd cousin		
Howard, Marvin L	Husband of the 4th cousin		
	Husband of the 3rd cousin 3 times removed		
Howery, Elizabeth	Husband of the 4th cousin 3 times removed		
	Wife of the 2nd cousin once removed		
Huber, Rebecca	Wife of the 3rd cousin once removed		
	Wife of the 3rd cousin		
Hunt, Amanda	Wife of the 4th cousin		
	3rd cousin 6 times removed	XIV	10
Hunt, Coy	4th cousin 6 times removed	XVI	11
	Husband of the 3rd cousin 5 times removed		
Iddings, Henry	Husband of the 4th cousin 5 times removed		
	Husband of the 3rd cousin		
Ingersol, Henrietta	Husband of the 4th cousin		
	Wife of the 3rd cousin		
Ingram, Ethel	Wife of the 4th cousin		
	Wife of the 3rd cousin 3 times removed		
Iorns, Martha Routh	Wife of the 4th cousin 3 times removed		
	Wife of the 3rd cousin		
Iorns, Rebecca	Wife of the 4th cousin		
	Wife of the 3rd cousin		
Irvin, Susanna	Wife of the 4th cousin		
	Wife of the 3rd cousin		
Jackson, Helen Julia	Wife of the 4th cousin		
	Wife of the 3rd cousin 5 times removed		
Jackson, Mary	Wife of the 4th cousin 5 times removed		
	Wife of the 2nd cousin once removed		

Name	Relationship with John Reynolds	Civil	Canon
	Wife of the 3rd cousin once removed		
Jewett, Martha	Wife of the 3rd cousin		
	Wife of the 4th cousin		
Johnson, John	Husband of the 3rd cousin		
	Husband of the 4th cousin		
Johnson, Joseph	Husband of the 3rd cousin twice removed		
	Husband of the 4th cousin twice removed		
Johnston, James	Husband of the 3rd cousin		
	Husband of the 4th cousin		
Kahlance, Tara Rose	3rd cousin 6 times removed	XIV	10
	4th cousin 6 times removed	XVI	11
Kahlance, Tevas	Husband of the 3rd cousin 5 times removed		
	Husband of the 4th cousin 5 times removed		
Kane, Rose Frances	Wife of the 3rd cousin 3 times removed		
	Wife of the 4th cousin 3 times removed		
Kasper, Dorothy	Wife of the 3rd cousin 3 times removed		
	Wife of the 4th cousin 3 times removed		
Keeports, Daniel	Husband of the 2nd cousin once removed		
	Husband of the 3rd cousin once removed		
Keeports, Elizabeth	3rd cousin	VIII	4
	4th cousin	X	5
	Wife of the 2nd cousin once removed		
	Wife of the 3rd cousin once removed		
Keeports, John	Husband of the 3rd cousin		
	Husband of the 4th cousin		
Kelsey, Rebecca	Wife of the 3rd cousin		
	Wife of the 4th cousin		
Kelsey, William	Husband of the 3rd cousin		
	Husband of the 4th cousin		
Kelso, Nancy	Wife of the 3rd cousin twice removed		
	Wife of the 4th cousin twice removed		
Kelso, Walter	Husband of the 3rd cousin 3 times removed		
	Husband of the 4th cousin 3 times removed		
Kemp, Catherine Hite	Wife of the 3rd cousin		
	Wife of the 4th cousin		
Kendig, Catherine	Wife of the 3rd cousin		
	Wife of the 4th cousin		
Kepler, George	Husband of the 3rd cousin		
	Husband of the 4th cousin		
Kerns, Maris	Husband of the 3rd cousin		
	Husband of the 4th cousin		
Kerr, Mary Catherine	Wife of the great-granduncle		
	Wife of the 1st cousin 3 times removed		
King, Johann Philip	Husband of the 2nd cousin once removed		
	Husband of the 3rd cousin once removed		
King, Pardon	Husband of the 3rd cousin		
	Husband of the 4th cousin		
King, Phiip	Husband of the 2nd cousin once removed		
	Husband of the 3rd cousin once removed		
Kitzmiller, Pauline	Wife of the 3rd cousin 4 times removed		
	Wife of the 4th cousin 4 times removed		
Kline	Husband of the grandniece		
	Husband of the 4th cousin twice removed		
Kline, Daughter	Great-grandniece	V	4
	4th cousin 3 times removed	XIII	8
Klump, George	Husband of the 3rd cousin twice removed		
	Husband of the 4th cousin twice removed		
Knapp, Grata	Wife of the 3rd cousin		
	Wife of the 4th cousin		
Knorr, Alice Kathleen	3rd cousin 5 times removed	XIII	9
	4th cousin 5 times removed	XV	10
Knorr, David Brian	3rd cousin 5 times removed	XIII	9
	4th cousin 5 times removed	XV	10
Knorr, Lawrence David	Husband of the 3rd cousin 4 times removed		

Name	Relationship with John Reynolds	Civil	Canon
Knorr, Lawrence Kevin	Husband of the 4th cousin 4 times removed		
	3rd cousin 5 times removed	XIII	9
Koch, Catherine	4th cousin 5 times removed	XV	10
	Wife of the 3rd cousin		
Krafft, Dorothy	Wife of the 4th cousin		
	Wife of the 3rd cousin 4 times removed		
Kreider, John	Wife of the 4th cousin 4 times removed		
	Husband of the 3rd cousin		
Krug, Rebecca	Husband of the 4th cousin		
	Sister-in-law		
Kuhn, Mary Ann	Wife of the 4th cousin		
	Wife of the 3rd cousin		
Kuhns, Leah	Wife of the 4th cousin		
	Wife of the 3rd cousin once removed		
Kunkle, John	Wife of the 4th cousin once removed		
	Husband of the 3rd cousin		
Kurtz, Jesse	Husband of the 4th cousin		
	Husband of the 3rd cousin 3 times removed		
	Husband of the 4th cousin 3 times removed		
La Verree, Jean	4th great-grandfather	VI	6
la Warembur, Marie de	3rd great-grandmother	V	5
Lacey, Mary	Wife of the 3rd cousin twice removed		
	Wife of the 4th cousin twice removed		
Ladd, Living	Wife of the 3rd cousin 3 times removed		
	Wife of the 4th cousin 3 times removed		
Lafever, Harrison	3rd cousin once removed	IX	5
	4th cousin once removed	XI	6
Lafever, Susan	3rd cousin once removed	IX	5
	4th cousin once removed	XI	6
Lafever, WIlliam F	3rd cousin once removed	IX	5
	4th cousin once removed	XI	6
Lancaster, Helen Gene	Wife of the 3rd cousin twice removed		
	Wife of the 4th cousin twice removed		
Landis, Bertha Lefevre	Niece	III	2
	4th cousin once removed	XI	6
Landis, Edward Kneass	Nephew	III	2
	4th cousin once removed	XI	6
Landis, Henry D	Brother-in-law		
	Husband of the 4th cousin		
Landis, Henry G	Nephew	III	2
	4th cousin once removed	XI	6
Landis, Isabelle Potts	Grandniece	IV	3
	4th cousin twice removed	XII	7
Landis, John Fulton Reynolds	Nephew	III	2
	4th cousin once removed	XI	6
Landis, Kate Ferree	Niece	III	2
	4th cousin once removed	XI	6
Landis, Mary L	Niece	III	2
	4th cousin once removed	XI	6
Landis, William Reynolds	Nephew	III	2
	4th cousin once removed	XI	6
Lane, Jacob	Husband of the 3rd cousin		
	Husband of the 4th cousin		
Lantz, George	Husband of the 2nd cousin once removed		
	Husband of the 3rd cousin once removed		
Laufeld, Herman	Husband of the 3rd cousin 3 times removed		
	Husband of the 4th cousin 3 times removed		
Lavery, J. Finay	Husband of the 3rd cousin twice removed		
	Husband of the 4th cousin twice removed		
Leaman, George	Husband of the 3rd cousin		
	Husband of the 4th cousin		
Leaman, Joseph	Husband of the 2nd cousin once removed		
	Husband of the 3rd cousin once removed		
Leaman, Susanna	Wife of the granduncle		

Name	Relationship with John Reynolds	Civil	Canon
	Wife of the 2nd cousin twice removed		
Leech, Beveridge	Husband of the 3rd cousin twice removed		
	Husband of the 4th cousin twice removed		
Lefevre, Abraham	3rd great-grandfather	V	5
LeFevre, Abraham	Great-granduncle	V	4
	1st cousin 3 times removed	VII	5
	Husband of the great-grandaunt		
	Husband of the 1st cousin 3 times removed		
LeFevre, Abraham	2nd cousin once removed	VII	4
	3rd cousin once removed	IX	5
LeFevre, Abraham	3rd cousin	VIII	4
	4th cousin	X	5
LeFevre, Abraham	3rd cousin	VIII	4
	4th cousin	X	5
LeFevre, Ada May	3rd cousin twice removed	X	6
	4th cousin twice removed	XII	7
LeFevre, Adale Frances	3rd cousin 3 times removed	XI	7
	4th cousin 3 times removed	XIII	8
LeFevre, Adam	1st cousin twice removed	VI	4
	2nd cousin twice removed	VIII	5
LeFevre, Adam	2nd cousin once removed	VII	4
	3rd cousin once removed	IX	5
LeFevre, Adam	2nd cousin once removed	VII	4
	3rd cousin once removed	IX	5
LeFevre, Adam	3rd cousin	VIII	4
	4th cousin	X	5
Lefevre, Adam	3rd cousin	VIII	4
	4th cousin	X	5
LeFevre, Adam	3rd cousin	VIII	4
	4th cousin	X	5
LeFevre, Adda June	3rd cousin 3 times removed	XI	7
	4th cousin 3 times removed	XIII	8
LeFevre, Agnes J.	3rd cousin	VIII	4
	4th cousin	X	5
LeFevre, Agnes Lois	3rd cousin 3 times removed	XI	7
	4th cousin 3 times removed	XIII	8
LeFevre, Albert T	2nd cousin	VI	3
	4th cousin	X	5
LeFevre, Alfred	3rd cousin	VIII	4
	4th cousin	X	5
LeFevre, Alice Wilt	3rd cousin twice removed	X	6
	4th cousin twice removed	XII	7
Lefevre, Amasa	3rd cousin	VIII	4
	4th cousin	X	5
Lefevre, Amelia	3rd cousin	VIII	4
	4th cousin	X	5
LeFevre, Amos	3rd cousin	VIII	4
	4th cousin	X	5
LeFevre, Amy H	3rd cousin	VIII	4
	4th cousin	X	5
Lefevre, Andrew	1st cousin 4 times removed	VIII	6
Lefevre, Andrew	4th great-grandfather	VI	6
Lefevre, Andrew	3rd great-granduncle	VII	6
Lefevre, Andrew	Granduncle	IV	3
	2nd cousin twice removed	VIII	5
LeFevre, Anna	1st cousin twice removed	VI	4
	2nd cousin twice removed	VIII	5
LeFevre, Anna Barbara	2nd cousin once removed	VII	4
	3rd cousin once removed	IX	5
Lefevre, Anna Maria	2nd cousin once removed	VII	4
	3rd cousin once removed	IX	5
LeFevre, Anne	2nd cousin once removed	VII	4
	3rd cousin once removed	IX	5
LeFevre, Anne	3rd cousin	VIII	4

Name	Relationship with John Reynolds	Civil	Canon
LeFevre, Anne	4th cousin	X	5
	3rd cousin	VIII	4
LeFevre, Anne	4th cousin	X	5
	3rd cousin	VIII	4
LeFevre, Anne B.	4th cousin	X	5
	3rd cousin once removed	IX	5
	4th cousin once removed	XI	6
LeFevre, Anne Barbara	3rd cousin	VIII	4
	4th cousin	X	5
LeFevre, Anne Mary	3rd cousin 3 times removed	XI	7
	4th cousin 3 times removed	XIII	8
LeFevre, Barabara	3rd cousin	VIII	4
	3rd cousin once removed	IX	5
	4th cousin	X	5
	4th cousin once removed	XI	6
LeFevre, Barbara Line	3rd cousin	VIII	4
	4th cousin	X	5
LeFevre, Benjamin	3rd cousin	VIII	4
	4th cousin	X	5
LeFevre, Benjamin	3rd cousin	VIII	4
	3rd cousin once removed	IX	5
	4th cousin	X	5
	4th cousin once removed	XI	6
LeFevre, Benjamin	3rd cousin twice removed	X	6
	4th cousin twice removed	XII	7
LeFevre, Bernice E.	3rd cousin twice removed	X	6
	4th cousin twice removed	XII	7
LeFevre, Bertha	Wife of the nephew		
	Wife of the 4th cousin once removed		
LeFevre, Caroline E	3rd cousin	VIII	4
	4th cousin	X	5
LeFevre, Caroline E.	3rd cousin once removed	IX	5
	4th cousin once removed	XI	6
LeFevre, Catherine	1st cousin twice removed	VI	4
	2nd cousin twice removed	VIII	5
Lefevre, Catherine	1st cousin twice removed	VI	4
	2nd cousin twice removed	VIII	5
	Wife of the 1st cousin twice removed		
	Wife of the 2nd cousin twice removed		
LeFevre, Catherine	2nd cousin once removed	VII	4
	3rd cousin once removed	IX	5
LeFevre, Catherine	2nd cousin once removed	VII	4
	3rd cousin once removed	IX	5
LeFevre, Catherine	2nd cousin once removed	VII	4
	3rd cousin once removed	IX	5
LeFevre, Catherine	2nd cousin once removed	VII	4
	3rd cousin once removed	IX	5
LeFevre, Catherine	2nd cousin once removed	VII	4
	3rd cousin once removed	IX	5
LeFevre, Catherine	2nd cousin once removed	VII	4
	3rd cousin once removed	IX	5
Lefevre, Catherine	2nd cousin once removed	VII	4
	3rd cousin once removed	IX	5
LeFevre, Catherine	3rd cousin	VIII	4
	4th cousin	X	5
LeFevre, Catherine	3rd cousin	VIII	4
	4th cousin	X	5
LeFevre, Catherine	3rd cousin	VIII	4
	4th cousin	X	5
LeFevre, Catherine	3rd cousin	VIII	4
	4th cousin	X	5
LeFevre, Catherine	3rd cousin	VIII	4
	4th cousin	X	5
	Wife of the 3rd cousin		

Name	Relationship with John Reynolds	Civil	Canon
	Wife of the 4th cousin		
LeFevre, Catherine	3rd cousin	VIII	4
	3rd cousin once removed	IX	5
	4th cousin	X	5
	4th cousin once removed	XI	6
Lefevre, Catherine	3rd cousin	VIII	4
	4th cousin	X	5
LeFevre, Catherine	3rd cousin	VIII	4
	4th cousin	X	5
LeFevre, Catherine	3rd cousin	VIII	4
	3rd cousin once removed	IX	5
	4th cousin	X	5
	4th cousin once removed	XI	6
LeFevre, Catherine A.	3rd cousin once removed	IX	5
	4th cousin once removed	XI	6
LeFevre, Catherine Ferree	Grandmother	II	2
	2nd cousin twice removed	VIII	5
LeFevre, Cecile	3rd cousin twice removed	X	6
	4th cousin twice removed	XII	7
Lefevre, Charles	2nd great-granduncle	VI	5
LeFevre, Charles H.	3rd cousin 4 times removed	XII	8
	4th cousin 4 times removed	XIV	9
LeFevre, Charles Leinbach	3rd cousin twice removed	X	6
	4th cousin twice removed	XII	7
LeFevre, Charles McClung	2nd cousin	VI	3
	4th cousin	X	5
LeFevre, Charles W.	3rd cousin 3 times removed	XI	7
	4th cousin 3 times removed	XIII	8
LeFevre, Charlotte Birdelia	3rd cousin 4 times removed	XII	8
	4th cousin 4 times removed	XIV	9
LeFevre, Christian	1st cousin twice removed	VI	4
	2nd cousin twice removed	VIII	5
LeFevre, Christian	2nd cousin once removed	VII	4
	3rd cousin once removed	IX	5
LeFevre, Christian	3rd cousin	VIII	4
	4th cousin	X	5
LeFevre, Christian	3rd cousin	VIII	4
	3rd cousin once removed	IX	5
	4th cousin	X	5
	4th cousin once removed	XI	6
LeFevre, Christian	3rd cousin	VIII	4
	4th cousin	X	5
LeFevre, Christian	3rd cousin	VIII	4
	4th cousin	X	5
LeFevre, Christian Herr	3rd cousin	VIII	4
	4th cousin	X	5
LeFevre, Clara Frances	3rd cousin 3 times removed	XI	7
	4th cousin 3 times removed	XIII	8
Lefevre, Clarence	3rd cousin 3 times removed	XI	7
	4th cousin 3 times removed	XIII	8
LeFevre, Clarinda	3rd cousin twice removed	X	6
	4th cousin twice removed	XII	7
LeFevre, Cyrus H	3rd cousin	VIII	4
	4th cousin	X	5
LeFevre, Daniel	Great-granduncle	V	4
	1st cousin 3 times removed	VII	5
Lefevre, Daniel	1st cousin twice removed	VI	4
	2nd cousin twice removed	VIII	5
LeFevre, Daniel	2nd cousin once removed	VII	4
	3rd cousin once removed	IX	5
LeFevre, Daniel	2nd cousin once removed	VII	4
	3rd cousin once removed	IX	5
LeFevre, Daniel	2nd cousin once removed	VII	4
	3rd cousin once removed	IX	5

Name	Relationship with John Reynolds	Civil	Canon
LeFevre, Daniel	2nd cousin once removed	VII	4
	3rd cousin once removed	IX	5
LeFevre, Daniel	3rd cousin	VIII	4
	4th cousin	X	5
LeFevre, Daniel	3rd cousin	VIII	4
	4th cousin	X	5
LeFevre, Daniel	3rd cousin	VIII	4
	3rd cousin once removed	IX	5
	4th cousin	X	5
	4th cousin once removed	XI	6
	Husband of the 3rd cousin		
	Husband of the 4th cousin		
LeFevre, Daniel	3rd cousin	VIII	4
	4th cousin	X	5
LeFevre, Daniel	3rd cousin	VIII	4
	4th cousin	X	5
LeFevre, Daniel	3rd cousin	VIII	4
	4th cousin	X	5
LeFevre, Daniel	3rd cousin	VIII	4
	4th cousin	X	5
LeFevre, Daniel	3rd cousin	VIII	4
	4th cousin	X	5
Lefevre, Daniel	3rd cousin	VIII	4
	4th cousin	X	5
LeFevre, Daniel	3rd cousin	VIII	4
	4th cousin	X	5
LeFevre, Daniel L	3rd cousin	VIII	4
	4th cousin	X	5
LeFevre, Daniel Line	3rd cousin	VIII	4
	4th cousin	X	5
Lefevre, David	1st cousin twice removed	VI	4
	2nd cousin twice removed	VIII	5
LeFevre, David	3rd cousin	VIII	4
	4th cousin	X	5
LeFevre, David	3rd cousin	VIII	4
	4th cousin	X	5
LeFevre, David	3rd cousin	VIII	4
	4th cousin	X	5
LeFevre, David	3rd cousin	VIII	4
	4th cousin	X	5
LeFevre, David	3rd cousin	VIII	4
	4th cousin	X	5
LeFevre, David	3rd cousin once removed	IX	5
	4th cousin once removed	XI	6
LeFevre, David	3rd cousin	VIII	4
	4th cousin	X	5
LeFevre, David Alter	3rd cousin	VIII	4
	4th cousin	X	5
LeFevre, David Gilbert	3rd cousin twice removed	X	6
	4th cousin twice removed	XII	7
LeFevre, David Landis	3rd cousin twice removed	X	6
	4th cousin twice removed	XII	7
LeFevre, David Lynn	3rd cousin 4 times removed	XII	8
	4th cousin 4 times removed	XIV	9
LeFevre, David Porter	3rd cousin once removed	IX	5
	4th cousin once removed	XI	6
LeFevre, David Roy	3rd cousin twice removed	X	6
	4th cousin twice removed	XII	7
LeFevre, David Slaymaker	3rd cousin once removed	IX	5
	4th cousin once removed	XI	6
LeFevre, David W	3rd cousin	VIII	4
	4th cousin	X	5
LeFevre, Dorthy W.	3rd cousin 4 times removed	XII	8
	4th cousin 4 times removed	XIV	9

Name	Relationship with John Reynolds	Civil	Canon
LeFevre, Earl Elston	3rd cousin 3 times removed	XI	7
	4th cousin 3 times removed	XIII	8
LeFevre, Edith Viola	3rd cousin twice removed	X	6
	4th cousin twice removed	XII	7
Lefevre, Edmund	3rd cousin	VIII	4
	4th cousin	X	5
LeFevre, Edward Franklin	3rd cousin twice removed	X	6
	4th cousin twice removed	XII	7
LeFevre, Eleanor Ann	3rd cousin 4 times removed	XII	8
	4th cousin 4 times removed	XIV	9
LeFevre, Eli	3rd cousin	VIII	4
	4th cousin	X	5
LeFevre, Eli McCalley	2nd cousin	VI	3
	4th cousin	X	5
Lefevre, Elias	1st cousin twice removed	VI	4
	2nd cousin twice removed	VIII	5
LeFevre, Elias	2nd cousin once removed	VII	4
	3rd cousin once removed	IX	5
Lefevre, Elias	3rd cousin	VIII	4
	4th cousin	X	5
LeFevre, Elias	3rd cousin	VIII	4
	4th cousin	X	5
LeFevre, Elizabeth	1st cousin twice removed	VI	4
	2nd cousin twice removed	VIII	5
LeFevre, Elizabeth	Grandaunt	IV	3
	2nd cousin twice removed	VIII	5
LeFevre, Elizabeth	2nd cousin once removed	VII	4
	3rd cousin once removed	IX	5
LeFevre, Elizabeth	2nd cousin once removed	VII	4
	3rd cousin once removed	IX	5
LeFevre, Elizabeth	2nd cousin once removed	VII	4
	3rd cousin once removed	IX	5
LeFevre, Elizabeth	2nd cousin once removed	VII	4
	3rd cousin once removed	IX	5
LeFevre, Elizabeth	2nd cousin once removed	VII	4
	3rd cousin once removed	IX	5
LeFevre, Elizabeth	2nd cousin once removed	VII	4
	3rd cousin once removed	IX	5
LeFevre, Elizabeth	2nd cousin once removed	VII	4
	3rd cousin once removed	IX	5
Lefevre, Elizabeth	2nd cousin once removed	VII	4
	3rd cousin once removed	IX	5
LeFevre, Elizabeth	3rd cousin	VIII	4
	4th cousin	X	5
LeFevre, Elizabeth	3rd cousin	VIII	4
	4th cousin	X	5
LeFevre, Elizabeth	3rd cousin	VIII	4
	4th cousin	X	5
LeFevre, Elizabeth	3rd cousin	VIII	4
	4th cousin	X	5
LeFevre, Elizabeth	3rd cousin	VIII	4
	4th cousin	X	5
LeFevre, Elizabeth	3rd cousin	VIII	4
	4th cousin	X	5
	Wife of the 3rd cousin		
	Wife of the 3rd cousin once removed		
	Wife of the 4th cousin		
	Wife of the 4th cousin once removed		
Lefevre, Elizabeth	3rd cousin	VIII	4
	4th cousin	X	5
LeFevre, Elizabeth	3rd cousin	VIII	4
	4th cousin	X	5
LeFevre, Elizabeth	3rd cousin	VIII	4
	4th cousin	X	5

Name	Relationship with John Reynolds	Civil	Canon
LeFevre, Elizabeth	3rd cousin	VIII	4
	4th cousin	X	5
LeFevre, Elizabeth	3rd cousin	VIII	4
	4th cousin	X	5
LeFevre, Elizabeth	3rd cousin	VIII	4
	4th cousin	X	5
LeFevre, Elizabeth	3rd cousin	VIII	4
	4th cousin	X	5
LeFevre, Elizabeth	3rd cousin	VIII	4
	4th cousin	X	5
Lefevre, Elizabeth	3rd cousin	VIII	4
	4th cousin	X	5
LeFevre, Elizabeth	3rd cousin	VIII	4
	4th cousin	X	5
LeFevre, Elizabeth	3rd cousin	VIII	4
	4th cousin	X	5
LeFevre, Elizabeth	3rd cousin	VIII	4
	3rd cousin once removed	IX	5
	4th cousin	X	5
	4th cousin once removed	XI	6
LeFevre, Elizabeth C.	3rd cousin 3 times removed	XI	7
	4th cousin 3 times removed	XIII	8
LeFevre, Elizabeth W.	3rd cousin	VIII	4
	4th cousin	X	5
LeFevre, Ellery Elston	3rd cousin twice removed	X	6
	4th cousin twice removed	XII	7
LeFevre, Emma Houstin	3rd cousin twice removed	X	6
	4th cousin twice removed	XII	7
Lefevre, Emma Jane	3rd cousin	VIII	4
	4th cousin	X	5
LeFevre, Emma Jane	3rd cousin	VIII	4
	4th cousin	X	5
LeFevre, Emma Jessie	3rd cousin 3 times removed	XI	7
	4th cousin 3 times removed	XIII	8
LeFevre, Emma Rebecca	3rd cousin twice removed	X	6
	4th cousin twice removed	XII	7
LeFevre, Enoch	3rd cousin	VIII	4
	4th cousin	X	5
LeFevre, Enos	3rd cousin	VIII	4
	4th cousin	X	5
LeFevre, Ervilla Belle	3rd cousin twice removed	X	6
	4th cousin twice removed	XII	7
LeFevre, Erville Mae	3rd cousin 3 times removed	XI	7
	4th cousin 3 times removed	XIII	8
LeFevre, Esther	Great-grandaunt	V	4
	1st cousin 3 times removed	VII	5
LeFevre, Esther	1st cousin twice removed	VI	4
	2nd cousin twice removed	VIII	5
Lefevre, Esther	1st cousin twice removed	VI	4
	2nd cousin twice removed	VIII	5
Lefevre, Esther	2nd cousin once removed	VII	4
	3rd cousin once removed	IX	5
LeFevre, Esther	2nd cousin once removed	VII	4
	3rd cousin once removed	IX	5
Lefevre, Esther	3rd cousin	VIII	4
	4th cousin	X	5
Lefevre, Esther	3rd cousin	VIII	4
	4th cousin	X	5
LeFevre, Esther	3rd cousin once removed	IX	5
	4th cousin once removed	XI	6
LeFevre, Evaline	3rd cousin	VIII	4
	4th cousin	X	5

Name	Relationship with John Reynolds	Civil	Canon
LeFevre, Eve	1st cousin twice removed	VI	4
	2nd cousin twice removed	VIII	5
LeFevre, Fanny	3rd cousin	VIII	4
	4th cousin	X	5
LeFevre, Fanny	3rd cousin once removed	IX	5
	4th cousin once removed	XI	6
LeFevre, Fanny	3rd cousin twice removed	X	6
	4th cousin twice removed	XII	7
LeFevre, Fanny Hallett	3rd cousin twice removed	X	6
	4th cousin twice removed	XII	7
LeFevre, Fanny Isabelle	3rd cousin 3 times removed	XI	7
	4th cousin 3 times removed	XIII	8
LeFevre, Fanny Malinda	3rd cousin 3 times removed	XI	7
	4th cousin 3 times removed	XIII	8
LeFevre, Florence Grace	3rd cousin 3 times removed	XI	7
	4th cousin 3 times removed	XIII	8
LeFevre, Frances Elizabeth	3rd cousin 3 times removed	XI	7
	4th cousin 3 times removed	XIII	8
LeFevre, Francis D.	3rd cousin 3 times removed	XI	7
	4th cousin 3 times removed	XIII	8
LeFevre, Frank Oran	3rd cousin twice removed	X	6
	4th cousin twice removed	XII	7
LeFevre, George	1st cousin twice removed	VI	4
	2nd cousin twice removed	VIII	5
LeFevre, George	2nd cousin once removed	VII	4
	3rd cousin once removed	IX	5
LeFevre, George	2nd cousin once removed	VII	4
	3rd cousin once removed	IX	5
LeFevre, George	2nd cousin once removed	VII	4
	3rd cousin once removed	IX	5
LeFevre, George	2nd cousin once removed	VII	4
	3rd cousin once removed	IX	5
LeFevre, George	2nd cousin once removed	VII	4
	3rd cousin once removed	IX	5
LeFevre, George	2nd cousin once removed	VII	4
	3rd cousin once removed	IX	5
LeFevre, George	3rd cousin	VIII	4
	4th cousin	X	5
LeFevre, George	3rd cousin	VIII	4
	4th cousin	X	5
LeFevre, George	3rd cousin	VIII	4
	4th cousin	X	5
LeFevre, George	3rd cousin	VIII	4
	4th cousin	X	5
LeFevre, George	3rd cousin	VIII	4
	4th cousin	X	5
LeFevre, George	3rd cousin	VIII	4
	4th cousin	X	5
LeFevre, George	3rd cousin	VIII	4
	4th cousin	X	5
LeFevre, George	3rd cousin	VIII	4
	4th cousin	X	5
LeFevre, George	3rd cousin	VIII	4
	4th cousin	X	5
Lefevre, George	3rd cousin	VIII	4
	4th cousin	X	5
LeFevre, George	3rd cousin once removed	IX	5
	4th cousin once removed	XI	6
LeFevre, George Line	3rd cousin	VIII	4
	4th cousin	X	5
LeFevre, George Newton	3rd cousin once removed	IX	5
	4th cousin once removed	XI	6

Name	Relationship with John Reynolds	Civil	Canon
Lefevre, George W	3rd cousin	VIII	4
	4th cousin	X	5
LeFevre, George W.	3rd cousin	VIII	4
	4th cousin	X	5
LeFevre, Gladys Ruth	3rd cousin 3 times removed	XI	7
	4th cousin 3 times removed	XIII	8
LeFevre, Grace Pearl	3rd cousin 3 times removed	XI	7
	4th cousin 3 times removed	XIII	8
LeFevre, Hallett Rudolph	3rd cousin 3 times removed	XI	7
	4th cousin 3 times removed	XIII	8
LeFevre, Hannah	1st cousin once removed	V	3
	3rd cousin once removed	IX	5
LeFevre, Hannah Matilda	3rd cousin	VIII	4
	4th cousin	X	5
LeFevre, Harriet Sue	3rd cousin once removed	IX	5
	4th cousin once removed	XI	6
LeFevre, Helen Viola	3rd cousin 3 times removed	XI	7
	4th cousin 3 times removed	XIII	8
LeFevre, Henry	2nd cousin once removed	VII	4
	3rd cousin once removed	IX	5
LeFevre, Henry	2nd cousin once removed	VII	4
	3rd cousin once removed	IX	5
LeFevre, Henry	3rd cousin	VIII	4
	4th cousin	X	5
LeFevre, Henry	3rd cousin	VIII	4
	4th cousin	X	5
Lefevre, Henry	3rd cousin	VIII	4
	4th cousin	X	5
LeFevre, Henry	3rd cousin once removed	IX	5
	4th cousin once removed	XI	6
LeFevre, Henry B	2nd cousin once removed	VII	4
	3rd cousin once removed	IX	5
Lefevre, Henry J	3rd cousin	VIII	4
	4th cousin	X	5
LeFevre, Henry Rine	3rd cousin twice removed	X	6
	4th cousin twice removed	XII	7
LeFevre, Henry W	3rd cousin	VIII	4
	4th cousin	X	5
LeFevre, Hester	2nd cousin once removed	VII	4
	3rd cousin once removed	IX	5
LeFevre, Hester	3rd cousin	VIII	4
	4th cousin	X	5
LeFevre, Hester	3rd cousin	VIII	4
	4th cousin	X	5
LeFevre, Hettie Veronica	3rd cousin once removed	IX	5
	4th cousin once removed	XI	6
LeFevre, Hiram	3rd cousin	VIII	4
	4th cousin	X	5
Lefevre, Isaac	1st cousin 4 times removed	VIII	6
Lefevre, Isaac	3rd great-granduncle	VII	6
Lefevre, Isaac	2nd great-grandfather	IV	4
LeFevre, Isaac	Husband of the 2nd great-grandaunt		
	1st cousin twice removed	VI	4
	2nd cousin twice removed	VIII	5
LeFevre, Isaac	2nd cousin once removed	VII	4
	3rd cousin once removed	IX	5
LeFevre, Isaac	2nd cousin once removed	VII	4
	3rd cousin once removed	IX	5
LeFevre, Isaac	3rd cousin	VIII	4
	4th cousin	X	5
LeFevre, Isaac	3rd cousin	VIII	4
	4th cousin	X	5
LeFevre, Isaac	3rd cousin	VIII	4
	4th cousin	X	5

Name	Relationship with John Reynolds	Civil	Canon
LeFevre, Isaac	3rd cousin	VIII	4
	4th cousin	X	5
LeFevre, Isaac	3rd cousin	VIII	4
	4th cousin	X	5
LeFevre, Isaac	3rd cousin	VIII	4
	4th cousin	X	5
LeFevre, Issac	3rd great-granduncle	VII	6
LeFevre, Issac	3rd cousin once removed	IX	5
	4th cousin once removed	XI	6
LeFevre, Issac Graff	3rd cousin 3 times removed	XI	7
	4th cousin 3 times removed	XIII	8
LeFevre, Issac Lawrence	3rd cousin once removed	IX	5
	4th cousin once removed	XI	6
LeFevre, Jack	3rd cousin 3 times removed	XI	7
	4th cousin 3 times removed	XIII	8
Lefevre, Jacob	2nd great-granduncle	VI	5
Lefevre, Jacob	1st cousin twice removed	VI	4
	2nd cousin twice removed	VIII	5
LeFevre, Jacob	2nd cousin once removed	VII	4
	3rd cousin once removed	IX	5
LeFevre, Jacob	2nd cousin once removed	VII	4
	3rd cousin once removed	IX	5
LeFevre, Jacob	2nd cousin once removed	VII	4
	3rd cousin once removed	IX	5
Lefevre, Jacob	2nd cousin once removed	VII	4
	3rd cousin once removed	IX	5
LeFevre, Jacob	3rd cousin	VIII	4
	4th cousin	X	5
LeFevre, Jacob	3rd cousin	VIII	4
	4th cousin	X	5
LeFevre, Jacob	3rd cousin	VIII	4
	4th cousin	X	5
LeFevre, Jacob	3rd cousin	VIII	4
	4th cousin	X	5
LeFevre, Jacob	3rd cousin	VIII	4
	4th cousin	X	5
Lefevre, Jacob	3rd cousin	VIII	4
	4th cousin	X	5
LeFevre, Jacob	3rd cousin	VIII	4
	4th cousin	X	5
Lefevre, Jacob	3rd cousin	VIII	4
	4th cousin	X	5
LeFevre, Jacob B	3rd cousin	VIII	4
	4th cousin	X	5
LeFevre, Jacob Camp	3rd cousin	VIII	4
	4th cousin	X	5
LeFevre, Jacob F.	3rd cousin once removed	IX	5
	4th cousin once removed	XI	6
LeFevre, Jacob L	3rd cousin	VIII	4
	4th cousin	X	5
LeFevre, Jacob Sailer	3rd cousin once removed	IX	5
	4th cousin once removed	XI	6
LeFevre, James V	3rd cousin	VIII	4
	4th cousin	X	5
LeFevre, Jesse	3rd cousin	VIII	4
	4th cousin	X	5
LeFevre, Jesse	3rd cousin	VIII	4
	4th cousin	X	5
LeFevre, Joel Lightner	2nd cousin	VI	3
	4th cousin	X	5
Lefevre, John	1st cousin 4 times removed	VIII	6
Lefevre, John	6th great-grandfather	VIII	8
Lefevre, John	1st cousin twice removed	VI	4
	2nd cousin twice removed	VIII	5

Name	Relationship with John Reynolds	Civil	Canon
LeFevre, John	2nd cousin once removed	VII	4
	3rd cousin once removed	IX	5
LeFevre, John	2nd cousin once removed	VII	4
	3rd cousin once removed	IX	5
LeFevre, John	2nd cousin once removed	VII	4
	3rd cousin once removed	IX	5
LeFevre, John	2nd cousin once removed	VII	4
	3rd cousin once removed	IX	5
	Husband of the 3rd cousin		
	Husband of the 4th cousin		
LeFevre, John	2nd cousin once removed	VII	4
	3rd cousin once removed	IX	5
LeFevre, John	3rd cousin	VIII	4
	4th cousin	X	5
LeFevre, John	3rd cousin	VIII	4
	4th cousin	X	5
LeFevre, John	3rd cousin	VIII	4
	3rd cousin once removed	IX	5
	4th cousin	X	5
	4th cousin once removed	XI	6
LeFevre, John	3rd cousin	VIII	4
	4th cousin	X	5
LeFevre, John	3rd cousin	VIII	4
	4th cousin	X	5
LeFevre, John	3rd cousin	VIII	4
	4th cousin	X	5
Lefevre, John	3rd cousin	VIII	4
	4th cousin	X	5
LeFevre, John	3rd cousin	VIII	4
	4th cousin	X	5
LeFevre, John	3rd cousin once removed	IX	5
	4th cousin once removed	XI	6
LeFevre, John	3rd cousin twice removed	X	6
	4th cousin twice removed	XII	7
LeFevre, John Alter	3rd cousin once removed	IX	5
	4th cousin once removed	XI	6
LeFevre, John B.	3rd cousin	VIII	4
	4th cousin	X	5
LeFevre, John Carpenter	1st cousin once removed	V	3
	3rd cousin once removed	IX	5
LeFevre, John Curry	3rd cousin	VIII	4
	4th cousin	X	5
Lefevre, John Erb	3rd cousin	VIII	4
	4th cousin	X	5
LeFevre, John F	2nd cousin	VI	3
	4th cousin	X	5
LeFevre, John K.	3rd cousin 3 times removed	XI	7
	4th cousin 3 times removed	XIII	8
LeFevre, John L.	2nd cousin once removed	VII	4
	3rd cousin once removed	IX	5
LeFevre, John Porter	3rd cousin	VIII	4
	4th cousin	X	5
LeFevre, John Russell	3rd cousin twice removed	X	6
	4th cousin twice removed	XII	7
LeFevre, John T	3rd cousin	VIII	4
	4th cousin	X	5
LeFevre, John Wesley	3rd cousin	VIII	4
	4th cousin	X	5
LeFevre, John Wiegner	3rd cousin	VIII	4
	4th cousin	X	5
LeFevre, John William	3rd cousin 4 times removed	XII	8
	4th cousin 4 times removed	XIV	9
LeFevre, John Yewell	3rd cousin 3 times removed	XI	7
	4th cousin 3 times removed	XIII	8

Name	Relationship with John Reynolds	Civil	Canon
LeFevre, Joseph	Granduncle	IV	3
	2nd cousin twice removed	VIII	5
	Husband of the 2nd cousin once removed		
	Husband of the 3rd cousin once removed		
LeFevre, Joseph	2nd cousin once removed	VII	4
	3rd cousin once removed	IX	5
LeFevre, Joseph	3rd cousin	VIII	4
	4th cousin	X	5
LeFevre, Joseph	3rd cousin	VIII	4
	4th cousin	X	5
LeFevre, Joseph	3rd cousin	VIII	4
	4th cousin	X	5
LeFevre, Joseph Cunningham	3rd cousin twice removed	X	6
	4th cousin twice removed	XII	7
LeFevre, Joseph Henry	2nd cousin	VI	3
	4th cousin	X	5
LeFevre, Joseph Lines	3rd cousin once removed	IX	5
	4th cousin once removed	XI	6
LeFevre, Joseph Ritner	3rd cousin	VIII	4
	4th cousin	X	5
LeFevre, Joseph Ritner	3rd cousin	VIII	4
	4th cousin	X	5
LeFevre, Joseph Smith	1st cousin once removed	V	3
	3rd cousin once removed	IX	5
LeFevre, Josephine	2nd cousin	VI	3
	4th cousin	X	5
LeFevre, Josephine Baumann	3rd cousin 4 times removed	XII	8
	4th cousin 4 times removed	XIV	9
LeFevre, Josiah W.	3rd cousin	VIII	4
	4th cousin	X	5
Lefevre, Judith	3rd great-grandaunt	VII	6
Lefevre, Judith	2nd great-grandaunt	VI	5
LeFevre, Justin Forrest	3rd cousin twice removed	X	6
	4th cousin twice removed	XII	7
LeFevre, Lawrence	2nd cousin once removed	VII	4
	3rd cousin once removed	IX	5
	Husband of the 3rd cousin		
	Husband of the 4th cousin		
LeFevre, Lawrence	3rd cousin once removed	IX	5
	4th cousin once removed	XI	6
LeFevre, Lawrence Ingram	3rd cousin 4 times removed	XII	8
	4th cousin 4 times removed	XIV	9
LeFevre, Leah	2nd cousin once removed	VII	4
	3rd cousin once removed	IX	5
Lefevre, Leah	3rd cousin	VIII	4
	4th cousin	X	5
LeFevre, Leander Fleming	3rd cousin	VIII	4
	4th cousin	X	5
LeFevre, Levi	3rd cousin	VIII	4
	4th cousin	X	5
LeFevre, Lillian Emma	3rd cousin 3 times removed	XI	7
	4th cousin 3 times removed	XIII	8
LeFevre, Lincoln L	3rd cousin twice removed	X	6
	4th cousin twice removed	XII	7
LeFevre, Lois Marion	3rd cousin 3 times removed	XI	7
	4th cousin 3 times removed	XIII	8
LeFevre, Lucy Rider	3rd cousin twice removed	X	6
	4th cousin twice removed	XII	7
LeFevre, Ludwig	1st cousin twice removed	VI	4
	2nd cousin twice removed	VIII	5
LeFevre, Lydia	Grandaunt	IV	3
	2nd cousin twice removed	VIII	5
LeFevre, Lydia	2nd cousin once removed	VII	4
	3rd cousin once removed	IX	5

Name	Relationship with John Reynolds	Civil	Canon
LeFevre, Lydia	1st cousin once removed	V	3
	3rd cousin once removed	IX	5
LeFevre, Lydia	1st cousin once removed	V	3
	3rd cousin once removed	IX	5
Lefevre, Lydia	2nd cousin once removed	VII	4
	3rd cousin once removed	IX	5
LeFevre, Lydia	3rd cousin	VIII	4
	4th cousin	X	5
LeFevre, Lydia	3rd cousin	VIII	4
	4th cousin	X	5
LeFevre, Lydia	3rd cousin	VIII	4
	4th cousin	X	5
LeFevre, Lydia	3rd cousin	VIII	4
	4th cousin	X	5
LeFevre, Lydia	3rd cousin	VIII	4
	4th cousin	X	5
LeFevre, Lydia Ferree	1st cousin once removed	V	3
	3rd cousin	VIII	4
	3rd cousin once removed	IX	5
	4th cousin	X	5
LeFevre, Magdalena	2nd cousin once removed	VII	4
	3rd cousin once removed	IX	5
LeFevre, Margaret	3rd cousin	VIII	4
	4th cousin	X	5
LeFevre, Margaret	3rd cousin	VIII	4
	4th cousin	X	5
LeFevre, Margaret	3rd cousin	VIII	4
	4th cousin	X	5
LeFevre, Margaret	3rd cousin once removed	IX	5
	4th cousin once removed	XI	6
LeFevre, Margaret	2nd cousin	VI	3
	4th cousin	X	5
LeFevre, Margaret	3rd cousin twice removed	X	6
	4th cousin twice removed	XII	7
LeFevre, Margaret J.	3rd cousin 3 times removed	XI	7
	4th cousin 3 times removed	XIII	8
LeFevre, Maria	3rd cousin	VIII	4
	4th cousin	X	5
LeFevre, Maria	3rd cousin	VIII	4
	4th cousin	X	5
LeFevre, Maria	3rd cousin once removed	IX	5
	4th cousin once removed	XI	6
Lefevre, Maria Barbara	2nd cousin once removed	VII	4
	3rd cousin once removed	IX	5
	Wife of the 2nd cousin once removed		
	Wife of the 3rd cousin once removed		
Lefevre, Mary	1st cousin 4 times removed	VIII	6
Lefevre, Mary	2nd great-grandaunt	VI	5
Lefevre, Mary	2nd great-grandaunt	VI	5
Lefevre, Mary	Great-grandaunt	V	4
	1st cousin 3 times removed	VII	5
LeFevre, Mary	1st cousin twice removed	VI	4
	2nd cousin twice removed	VIII	5
LeFevre, Mary	2nd cousin once removed	VII	4
	3rd cousin once removed	IX	5
LeFevre, Mary	2nd cousin once removed	VII	4
	3rd cousin once removed	IX	5
LeFevre, Mary	2nd cousin once removed	VII	4
	3rd cousin once removed	IX	5
Lefevre, Mary	2nd cousin once removed	VII	4
	3rd cousin once removed	IX	5
	Wife of the 2nd cousin once removed		
	Wife of the 3rd cousin once removed		
LeFevre, Mary	2nd cousin once removed	VII	4

Name	Relationship with John Reynolds	Civil	Canon
	3rd cousin once removed	IX	5
LeFevre, Mary	Grandaunt	IV	3
	2nd cousin twice removed	VIII	5
LeFevre, Mary	2nd cousin once removed	VII	4
	3rd cousin once removed	IX	5
LeFevre, Mary	2nd cousin once removed	VII	4
	3rd cousin once removed	IX	5
LeFevre, Mary	3rd cousin	VIII	4
	4th cousin	X	5
LeFevre, Mary	3rd cousin	VIII	4
	4th cousin	X	5
Lefevre, Mary	3rd cousin	VIII	4
	4th cousin	X	5
LeFevre, Mary	3rd cousin	VIII	4
	4th cousin	X	5
Lefevre, Mary	3rd cousin	VIII	4
	4th cousin	X	5
	Wife of the 3rd cousin		
	Wife of the 4th cousin		
LeFevre, Mary	3rd cousin	VIII	4
	4th cousin	X	5
LeFevre, Mary	3rd cousin	VIII	4
	3rd cousin once removed	IX	5
	4th cousin	X	5
	4th cousin once removed	XI	6
Lefevre, Mary	3rd cousin	VIII	4
	4th cousin	X	5
LeFevre, Mary	3rd cousin	VIII	4
	4th cousin	X	5
LeFevre, Mary A.	3rd cousin	VIII	4
	4th cousin	X	5
LeFevre, Mary Ann	1st cousin once removed	V	3
	3rd cousin	VIII	4
	3rd cousin once removed	IX	5
	4th cousin	X	5
LeFevre, Mary Ann	3rd cousin	VIII	4
	4th cousin	X	5
LeFevre, Mary Ann	3rd cousin	VIII	4
	4th cousin	X	5
LeFevre, Mary Belle	3rd cousin 3 times removed	XI	7
	4th cousin 3 times removed	XIII	8
LeFevre, Mary Blanche	3rd cousin 3 times removed	XI	7
	4th cousin 3 times removed	XIII	8
LeFevre, Mary Elizabeth	3rd cousin twice removed	X	6
	4th cousin twice removed	XII	7
LeFevre, Mary Elizabeth	3rd cousin 4 times removed	XII	8
	4th cousin 4 times removed	XIV	9
LeFevre, Mary Ellen	3rd cousin once removed	IX	5
	4th cousin once removed	XI	6
LeFevre, Mary Frances	3rd cousin twice removed	X	6
	4th cousin twice removed	XII	7
LeFevre, Mary Matilda	3rd cousin	VIII	4
	4th cousin	X	5
LeFevre, Mary Page	3rd cousin	VIII	4
	4th cousin	X	5
Lefevre, Matilda	3rd cousin	VIII	4
	4th cousin	X	5
LeFevre, Matilda	3rd cousin twice removed	X	6
	4th cousin twice removed	XII	7
LeFevre, Matilda C.	3rd cousin 3 times removed	XI	7
	4th cousin 3 times removed	XIII	8
Lefevre, Mengen	7th great-grandfather	IX	9
Lefevre, Meshach	3rd cousin	VIII	4
	4th cousin	X	5

Name	Relationship with John Reynolds	Civil	Canon
Lefevre, Nancy	3rd cousin	VIII	4
	4th cousin	X	5
LeFevre, Nancy	3rd cousin	VIII	4
	4th cousin	X	5
LeFevre, Naomi	3rd cousin	VIII	4
	4th cousin	X	5
LeFevre, Nathaniel	2nd cousin	VI	3
	4th cousin	X	5
Lefevre, Nimrod D	3rd cousin	VIII	4
	4th cousin	X	5
LeFevre, Othel Olsen	3rd cousin twice removed	X	6
	4th cousin twice removed	XII	7
LeFevre, Owen E	3rd cousin once removed	IX	5
	4th cousin once removed	XI	6
LeFevre, Pearl Irene	3rd cousin 3 times removed	XI	7
	4th cousin 3 times removed	XIII	8
LeFevre, Pearly Emmet	3rd cousin twice removed	X	6
	4th cousin twice removed	XII	7
LeFevre, Peter	1st cousin twice removed	VI	4
	2nd cousin twice removed	VIII	5
	Husband of the 1st cousin twice removed		
	Husband of the 2nd cousin twice removed		
LeFevre, Peter	2nd cousin once removed	VII	4
	3rd cousin once removed	IX	5
	Husband of the 2nd cousin once removed		
	Husband of the 3rd cousin once removed		
LeFevre, Peter	2nd cousin once removed	VII	4
	3rd cousin once removed	IX	5
LeFevre, Peter	2nd cousin once removed	VII	4
	3rd cousin once removed	IX	5
	Husband of the 2nd cousin once removed		
	Husband of the 3rd cousin once removed		
LeFevre, Peter	3rd cousin	VIII	4
	4th cousin	X	5
LeFevre, Peter	3rd cousin	VIII	4
	4th cousin	X	5
Lefevre, Peter	3rd cousin	VIII	4
	4th cousin	X	5
LeFevre, Peter	3rd cousin	VIII	4
	4th cousin	X	5
LeFevre, Peter Perry	3rd cousin	VIII	4
	4th cousin	X	5
LeFevre, Peter Wilt	3rd cousin once removed	IX	5
	4th cousin once removed	XI	6
Lefevre, Philip	5th great-grandfather	VII	7
Lefevre, Philip	2nd great-granduncle	VI	5
Lefevre, Philip	2nd cousin once removed	VII	4
	3rd cousin once removed	IX	5
LeFevre, Philip	3rd cousin	VIII	4
	4th cousin	X	5
	Husband of the 3rd cousin		
	Husband of the 4th cousin		
LeFevre, Philip	3rd cousin	VIII	4
	4th cousin	X	5
LeFevre, Philip G	Great-granduncle	V	4
	1st cousin 3 times removed	VII	5
LeFevre, Phillip	3rd cousin once removed	IX	5
	4th cousin once removed	XI	6
LeFevre, Polly	3rd cousin	VIII	4
	4th cousin	X	5
LeFevre, Rachel	2nd cousin once removed	VII	4
	3rd cousin once removed	IX	5
Lefevre, Rachel	3rd cousin	VIII	4
	4th cousin	X	5

Name	Relationship with John Reynolds	Civil	Canon
LeFevre, Rachel	3rd cousin	VIII	4
	4th cousin	X	5
LeFevre, Rebecca	3rd cousin	VIII	4
	4th cousin	X	5
Lefevre, Rebecca	3rd cousin	VIII	4
	4th cousin	X	5
LeFevre, Rebecca	3rd cousin once removed	IX	5
	4th cousin once removed	XI	6
LeFevre, Rebecca	3rd cousin	VIII	4
	4th cousin	X	5
LeFevre, Rebecca	3rd cousin twice removed	X	6
	4th cousin twice removed	XII	7
LeFevre, Rezon	3rd cousin	VIII	4
	4th cousin	X	5
LeFevre, Rhuhana C.	3rd cousin	VIII	4
	4th cousin	X	5
LeFevre, Richard Hallett	3rd cousin 4 times removed	XII	8
	4th cousin 4 times removed	XIV	9
Lefevre, Rudolph	3rd cousin	VIII	4
	4th cousin	X	5
LeFevre, Russell Moore	3rd cousin 3 times removed	XI	7
	4th cousin 3 times removed	XIII	8
LeFevre, Ruth Graff	3rd cousin 4 times removed	XII	8
	4th cousin 4 times removed	XIV	9
LeFevre, Salome	1st cousin once removed	V	3
	3rd cousin once removed	IX	5
LeFevre, Salome	2nd cousin	VI	3
	4th cousin	X	5
LeFevre, Salome	2nd cousin	VI	3
	4th cousin	X	5
LeFevre, Salome Ann	3rd cousin	VIII	4
	3rd cousin once removed	IX	5
	4th cousin	X	5
	4th cousin once removed	XI	6
LeFevre, Samuel	Great-grandfather	III	3
	1st cousin 3 times removed	VII	5
	Husband of the 1st cousin 3 times removed		
LeFevre, Samuel	Granduncle	IV	3
	2nd cousin twice removed	VIII	5
LeFevre, Samuel	2nd cousin once removed	VII	4
	3rd cousin once removed	IX	5
LeFevre, Samuel	2nd cousin once removed	VII	4
	3rd cousin once removed	IX	5
LeFevre, Samuel	2nd cousin once removed	VII	4
	3rd cousin once removed	IX	5
LeFevre, Samuel	3rd cousin	VIII	4
	4th cousin	X	5
LeFevre, Samuel	3rd cousin	VIII	4
	4th cousin	X	5
Lefevre, Samuel	3rd cousin	VIII	4
	4th cousin	X	5
LeFevre, Samuel	3rd cousin	VIII	4
	4th cousin	X	5
Lefevre, Samuel	3rd cousin	VIII	4
	4th cousin	X	5
LeFevre, Samuel	3rd cousin	VIII	4
	4th cousin	X	5
LeFevre, Samuel	3rd cousin	VIII	4
	4th cousin	X	5
LeFevre, Samuel	3rd cousin	VIII	4
	3rd cousin once removed	IX	5
	4th cousin	X	5
	4th cousin once removed	XI	6
LeFevre, Samuel A	3rd cousin	VIII	4

Name	Relationship with John Reynolds	Civil	Canon
LeFevre, Samuel S	4th cousin	X	5
	2nd cousin	VI	3
LeFevre, Samuel Slaymaker	4th cousin	X	5
	3rd cousin	VIII	4
LeFevre, Sarah	4th cousin	X	5
	Grandaunt	IV	3
LeFevre, Sarah	2nd cousin twice removed	VIII	5
	2nd cousin once removed	VII	4
LeFevre, Sarah	3rd cousin once removed	IX	5
	1st cousin once removed	V	3
LeFevre, Sarah	3rd cousin once removed	IX	5
	2nd cousin once removed	VII	4
Lefevre, Sarah	3rd cousin once removed	IX	5
	2nd cousin once removed	VII	4
LeFevre, Sarah	3rd cousin once removed	IX	5
	3rd cousin	VIII	4
LeFevre, Sarah	4th cousin	X	5
	3rd cousin	VIII	4
LeFevre, Sarah	4th cousin	X	5
	3rd cousin	VIII	4
LeFevre, Sarah	4th cousin	X	5
	3rd cousin	VIII	4
LeFevre, Sarah	4th cousin	X	5
	3rd cousin	VIII	4
LeFevre, Sarah	4th cousin	X	5
	3rd cousin	VIII	4
LeFevre, Sarah	4th cousin	X	5
	3rd cousin	VIII	4
Lefevre, Sarah	4th cousin	X	5
	3rd cousin	VIII	4
LeFevre, Sarah	4th cousin	X	5
	3rd cousin	VIII	4
LeFevre, Sarah Ann	4th cousin	X	5
	3rd cousin	VIII	4
LeFevre, Sarah Anne	4th cousin	X	5
	3rd cousin twice removed	X	6
LeFevre, Sarah M.	4th cousin twice removed	XII	7
	3rd cousin	VIII	4
Lefevre, Simon	4th cousin	X	5
Lefevre, Solomon	3rd great-granduncle	VII	6
	1st cousin twice removed	VI	4
LeFevre, Solomon	2nd cousin twice removed	VIII	5
	3rd cousin	VIII	4
LeFevre, Susan	4th cousin	X	5
	3rd cousin	VIII	4
LeFevre, Susan A	4th cousin	X	5
	2nd cousin	VI	3
LeFevre, Susan Fowkes	4th cousin	X	5
	3rd cousin	VIII	4
LeFevre, Susan Salome	4th cousin	X	5
	3rd cousin once removed	IX	5
LeFevre, Susan W	4th cousin once removed	XI	6
	3rd cousin once removed	IX	5
Lefevre, Susanna	4th cousin once removed	XI	6
	2nd great-grandaunt	VI	5
Lefevre, Susanna	2nd cousin once removed	VII	4
	3rd cousin once removed	IX	5
Lefevre, Susanna	2nd cousin once removed	VII	4
	3rd cousin once removed	IX	5
Lefevre, Susanna	1st cousin once removed	V	3
	3rd cousin once removed	IX	5
LeFevre, Susanna	3rd cousin	VIII	4

Name	Relationship with John Reynolds	Civil	Canon
	4th cousin	X	5
LeFevre, Susanna	3rd cousin	VIII	4
	4th cousin	X	5
LeFevre, Susanna Elizabeth	2nd cousin	VI	3
	4th cousin	X	5
LeFevre, Sybil	3rd cousin twice removed	X	6
	4th cousin twice removed	XII	7
LeFevre, Walter D.	3rd cousin	VIII	4
	4th cousin	X	5
LeFevre, Washington	3rd cousin	VIII	4
	4th cousin	X	5
LeFevre, William	3rd cousin	VIII	4
	4th cousin	X	5
LeFevre, William Alter	3rd cousin	VIII	4
	4th cousin	X	5
LeFevre, William C Minor	3rd cousin	VIII	4
	4th cousin	X	5
LeFevre, William Denny	3rd cousin	VIII	4
	4th cousin	X	5
LeFevre, William Henry	3rd cousin	VIII	4
	4th cousin	X	5
LeFevre, William Union	3rd cousin twice removed	X	6
	4th cousin twice removed	XII	7
Leninger, Maria	2nd great-grandmother	IV	4
	Wife of the 2nd great-granduncle		
Leonard, Sarah	Wife of the 3rd cousin		
	Wife of the 4th cousin		
Lewis, Bertha	Wife of the 3rd cousin twice removed		
	Wife of the 4th cousin twice removed		
Lewis, Everett	Husband of the 3rd cousin 3 times removed		
	Husband of the 4th cousin 3 times removed		
Lightner, Joel	Husband of the 1st cousin once removed		
	Husband of the 3rd cousin once removed		
Line, Abram L.	3rd cousin once removed	IX	5
	4th cousin once removed	XI	6
Line, Catherina	3rd cousin	VIII	4
	4th cousin	X	5
	Wife of the 3rd cousin		
	Wife of the 4th cousin		
Line, Charles Eugene	3rd cousin twice removed	X	6
	4th cousin twice removed	XII	7
Line, David	3rd cousin	VIII	4
	4th cousin	X	5
Line, Elizabeth	Wife of the 2nd cousin once removed		
	Wife of the 3rd cousin once removed		
Line, Elizabeth M.	3rd cousin once removed	IX	5
	4th cousin once removed	XI	6
Line, Emmanuel C.	3rd cousin once removed	IX	5
	4th cousin once removed	XI	6
Line, George E.	3rd cousin twice removed	X	6
	4th cousin twice removed	XII	7
Line, George L.	3rd cousin	VIII	4
	4th cousin	X	5
Line, Herman Bowman	3rd cousin twice removed	X	6
	4th cousin twice removed	XII	7
Line, Isabelle	Wife of the 3rd cousin 5 times removed		
	Wife of the 4th cousin 5 times removed		
Line, John A	Husband of the 2nd cousin once removed		
	Husband of the 3rd cousin once removed		
Line, John A.	3rd cousin once removed	IX	5
	4th cousin once removed	XI	6
Line, John Raymond	3rd cousin twice removed	X	6
	4th cousin twice removed	XII	7
Line, Laura August	3rd cousin twice removed	X	6

Name	Relationship with John Reynolds	Civil	Canon
Line, Maria	4th cousin twice removed	XII	7
	Wife of the 3rd cousin		
Line, Mary Ann Coulter	Wife of the 4th cousin		
	3rd cousin	VIII	4
Line, Miriam	4th cousin	X	5
	3rd cousin twice removed	X	6
Line, Salome	4th cousin twice removed	XII	7
	3rd cousin	VIII	4
	4th cousin	X	5
	Wife of the 2nd cousin once removed		
Line, Sarah	Wife of the 3rd cousin once removed		
	Wife of the 3rd cousin		
Line, Sarah	Wife of the 4th cousin		
	Wife of the 3rd cousin		
Lingenfelter, Elizabeth	Wife of the 4th cousin		
	Wife of the 2nd cousin once removed		
Lingenfelter, Eve Margaret	Wife of the 3rd cousin once removed		
	Wife of the 2nd cousin once removed		
Long, Laura	Wife of the 3rd cousin once removed		
	Wife of the 3rd cousin once removed		
Long, Wesley	Wife of the 4th cousin once removed		
	Husband of the 3rd cousin		
Lowman, Elizabeth C	Husband of the 4th cousin		
	Wife of the 3rd cousin		
Lucenti, Carmen Joseph	Wife of the 4th cousin		
	Husband of the 3rd cousin 4 times removed		
Lucenti, Sandra Marie	Husband of the 4th cousin 4 times removed		
	3rd cousin 5 times removed	XIII	9
Lucenti, Teresa Rose Charlene	4th cousin 5 times removed	XV	10
	3rd cousin 5 times removed	XIII	9
Luttman, Jacob	4th cousin 5 times removed	XV	10
	Husband of the 1st cousin twice removed		
Lutz, Christopher	Husband of the 2nd cousin twice removed		
	Husband of the 3rd cousin		
Lux, Frederick	Husband of the 4th cousin		
	Husband of the 3rd cousin 3 times removed		
Mace	Husband of the 4th cousin 3 times removed		
	3rd cousin	VIII	4
Maish, David	4th cousin	X	5
	Husband of the 2nd cousin once removed		
Manderbaugh, Henry	Husband of the 3rd cousin once removed		
	Husband of the 2nd cousin once removed		
Martin, Anne	Husband of the 3rd cousin once removed		
	Wife of the 3rd cousin		
Martin, Elizabeth	Wife of the 4th cousin		
	Wife of the 3rd cousin		
Martin, George W	Wife of the 4th cousin		
	Husband of the 3rd cousin		
Martin, Jaruncia	Husband of the 4th cousin		
	Wife of the 1st cousin twice removed		
Marvel, Paul M	Wife of the 2nd cousin twice removed		
	Husband of the 3rd cousin twice removed		
Mathiot, Catherine	Husband of the 4th cousin twice removed		
	Wife of the 2nd cousin once removed		
McAllister, R B	Wife of the 3rd cousin once removed		
	Husband of the 3rd cousin		
	Husband of the 3rd cousin once removed		
	Husband of the 4th cousin		
McAlpin, Mr	Husband of the 4th cousin once removed		
	Husband of the 3rd cousin 3 times removed		
McBride, John W.	Husband of the 4th cousin 3 times removed		
	Husband of the 3rd cousin twice removed		
McBride, Samuel F	Husband of the 4th cousin twice removed		
	Husband of the 2nd cousin		

Name	Relationship with John Reynolds	Civil	Canon
	Husband of the 4th cousin		
McCalley, Hugh	Husband of the grandaunt		
	Husband of the 2nd cousin twice removed		
McClung, Elizabeth	Wife of the 1st cousin once removed		
	Wife of the 3rd cousin once removed		
McCoy, Tammi Kay	Wife of the 3rd cousin 5 times removed		
	Wife of the 4th cousin 5 times removed		
McCullough, Florence Charlotte	Wife of the 3rd cousin		
	Wife of the 4th cousin		
McGahan, Nancy	Wife of the 2nd cousin once removed		
	Wife of the 3rd cousin once removed		
McKee, Mary Ann	Wife of the 3rd cousin		
	Wife of the 4th cousin		
McMath, Sarah H.	Wife of the 3rd cousin once removed		
	Wife of the 4th cousin once removed		
McMillen, Sarah	Wife of the 3rd cousin once removed		
	Wife of the 4th cousin once removed		
McMonus, Annie	Wife of the 3rd cousin twice removed		
	Wife of the 4th cousin twice removed		
Meck, Nicholas	Husband of the 1st cousin twice removed		
	Husband of the 2nd cousin twice removed		
Medaris, David	Husband of the 3rd cousin 3 times removed		
	Husband of the 4th cousin 3 times removed		
Meek, Catherine	Wife of the 2nd cousin once removed		
	Wife of the 3rd cousin once removed		
Meloy, Jely	Wife of the 2nd cousin once removed		
	Wife of the 3rd cousin once removed		
Mercer, Dorcas W.	Wife of the 3rd cousin 3 times removed		
	Wife of the 4th cousin 3 times removed		
Mercer, Manoah	Husband of the 3rd cousin twice removed		
	Husband of the 4th cousin twice removed		
Messenkop, Catherine	Wife of the granduncle		
	Wife of the 2nd cousin twice removed		
Miller, Catherine	Wife of the 3rd cousin		
	Wife of the 4th cousin		
Miller, Joseph	Husband of the 3rd cousin 3 times removed		
	Husband of the 4th cousin 3 times removed		
Miller, Mary M	Wife of the 3rd cousin twice removed		
	Wife of the 4th cousin twice removed		
Mills, Stephen	Husband of the 3rd cousin 6 times removed		
	Husband of the 4th cousin 6 times removed		
Mohler, David Ralph	3rd cousin 6 times removed	XIV	10
	4th cousin 6 times removed	XVI	11
Mohler, John Robert	3rd cousin 6 times removed	XIV	10
	4th cousin 6 times removed	XVI	11
Mohler, Kathryn Ann	3rd cousin 6 times removed	XIV	10
	4th cousin 6 times removed	XVI	11
Mohler, Mark Andrew	3rd cousin 7 times removed	XV	11
	4th cousin 7 times removed	XVII	12
Mohler, Matthew Robert	3rd cousin 7 times removed	XV	11
	4th cousin 7 times removed	XVII	12
Mohler, Ralph E.	Husband of the 3rd cousin 5 times removed		
	Husband of the 4th cousin 5 times removed		
Moiser, Louisa	Wife of the 3rd cousin		
	Wife of the 4th cousin		
Moore, Elizabeth	3rd cousin once removed	IX	5
	4th cousin once removed	XI	6
Moore, John	Husband of the 3rd cousin once removed		
	Husband of the 4th cousin once removed		
Moore, Lydia	Mother	I	1
	Wife of the 3rd cousin once removed		
Moore, Samuel	Grandfather	II	2
Moore, Thomas	Husband of the 3rd cousin		
	Husband of the 4th cousin		

Name	Relationship with John Reynolds	Civil	Canon
Morgan, Eleanor	Wife of the 3rd cousin		
	Wife of the 4th cousin		
Morgan, Gordon S.	Husband of the 3rd cousin 3 times removed		
	Husband of the 4th cousin 3 times removed		
Morris	Husband of the 3rd cousin		
	Husband of the 4th cousin		
Moyer, Isabelle	Wife of the 3rd cousin once removed		
	Wife of the 4th cousin once removed		
Mullet, Nancy	Wife of the 3rd cousin once removed		
	Wife of the 4th cousin once removed		
Mulvihill, Maude	Wife of the 3rd cousin 3 times removed		
	Wife of the 4th cousin 3 times removed		
Murray, Elizabeth Van Horn	Sister-in-law		
Musgrave, Mary	Wife of the 4th cousin		
Musser, George	Wife of the 2nd great-granduncle		
	Husband of the 2nd cousin once removed		
	Husband of the 3rd cousin once removed		
Myers, John	Husband of the 3rd cousin once removed		
	Husband of the 4th cousin once removed		
Naylor, John	Husband of the 3rd cousin		
	Husband of the 4th cousin		
Neff, Barbara	Wife of the 3rd cousin		
	Wife of the 4th cousin		
Neff, Jacob	Husband of the 2nd cousin once removed		
	Husband of the 3rd cousin once removed		
Neff, Magdalene	Wife of the 3rd cousin		
	Wife of the 4th cousin		
Nickey, Nancy	Wife of the 3rd cousin once removed		
	Wife of the 4th cousin once removed		
Oatman, Andrew	Husband of the 2nd cousin once removed		
	Husband of the 3rd cousin once removed		
Ober, Catherine Rebecca	Wife of the 3rd cousin once removed		
	Wife of the 4th cousin once removed		
Pachtel, Rebecca	Wife of the 2nd cousin once removed		
	Wife of the 3rd cousin once removed		
Pallock, Fanny	Wife of the nephew		
	Wife of the 4th cousin once removed		
Palm, David	Husband of the 3rd cousin		
	Husband of the 4th cousin		
Parks, Sidney	Wife of the 3rd cousin		
	Wife of the 4th cousin		
Partridge, Allan Baker	Husband of the 3rd cousin 3 times removed		
	Husband of the 4th cousin 3 times removed		
Partridge, Charles Allan	3rd cousin 4 times removed	XII	8
	4th cousin 4 times removed	XIV	9
Partridge, Diane Louise	3rd cousin 4 times removed	XII	8
	4th cousin 4 times removed	XIV	9
Paules, Elizabeth	Wife of the 1st cousin twice removed		
	Wife of the 2nd cousin twice removed		
Peck, Anne	Wife of the 3rd cousin once removed		
	Wife of the 4th cousin once removed		
Peck, Elizabeth	Wife of the 1st cousin twice removed		
	Wife of the 2nd cousin twice removed		
Persinger	Husband of the 3rd cousin		
	Husband of the 4th cousin		
Peterman, Catherine	Wife of the 1st cousin twice removed		
	Wife of the 2nd cousin twice removed		
Phelps	Wife of the 3rd cousin		
	Wife of the 4th cousin		
Phillips, Tara	Wife of the 3rd cousin 5 times removed		
	Wife of the 4th cousin 5 times removed		
Piper, Mary Mildred	Wife of the 3rd cousin 4 times removed		
	Wife of the 4th cousin 4 times removed		
Polly	Wife of the 3rd cousin 4 times removed		

Name	Relationship with John Reynolds	Civil	Canon
	Wife of the 4th cousin 4 times removed		
Pond, Pamila	Wife of the 3rd cousin		
	Wife of the 4th cousin		
Porter, Mary Jane	Wife of the 2nd cousin once removed		
	Wife of the 3rd cousin once removed		
Potts, Emily F	Wife of the nephew		
	Wife of the 4th cousin once removed		
Powers, William	Husband of the 3rd cousin		
	Husband of the 4th cousin		
Poynter, Frances	Wife of the 3rd cousin twice removed		
	Wife of the 4th cousin twice removed		
Preston, Henry J.	Husband of the 3rd cousin 4 times removed		
	Husband of the 4th cousin 4 times removed		
Price, George	Husband of the 2nd cousin once removed		
	Husband of the 3rd cousin once removed		
Rakestron	Husband of the 3rd cousin 6 times removed		
	Husband of the 4th cousin 6 times removed		
Ramsies, Mary Jane	Wife of the 3rd cousin 5 times removed		
	Wife of the 4th cousin 5 times removed		
Rankin, Daniel	Husband of the 3rd cousin		
	Husband of the 4th cousin		
Rathfon, Jacob	Husband of the 2nd cousin once removed		
	Husband of the 3rd cousin once removed		
Reed, Elizabeth Malzena	Wife of the 3rd cousin		
	Wife of the 4th cousin		
Reed, Elvira	Wife of the 3rd cousin		
	Wife of the 4th cousin		
Reed, George B	Husband of the 3rd cousin		
	Husband of the 4th cousin		
Reese, Peter	Husband of the 2nd cousin once removed		
	Husband of the 3rd cousin once removed		
Reid, Living	Husband of the 3rd cousin 5 times removed		
	Husband of the 4th cousin 5 times removed		
Reid, Living	3rd cousin 6 times removed	XIV	10
	4th cousin 6 times removed	XVI	11
Reinhart, Catherine	Wife of the 3rd cousin		
	Wife of the 4th cousin		
Rettenmeyer, Carl William	Husband of the 3rd cousin 3 times removed		
	Husband of the 4th cousin 3 times removed		
Reynolds, Alan DeForest	Great-grandnephew	V	4
	4th cousin 3 times removed	XIII	8
Reynolds, Alan DeForest	Grandnephew	IV	3
	4th cousin twice removed	XII	7
Reynolds, Anne Elizabeth	Sister	II	1
	4th cousin	X	5
Reynolds, Catherine Ferree	Sister	II	1
	4th cousin	X	5
Reynolds, Edward B	Brother	II	1
	4th cousin	X	5
Reynolds, Edward Coleman	Brother	II	1
	4th cousin	X	5
Reynolds, Eleanor	Sister	II	1
	4th cousin	X	5
Reynolds, Harriet Sumner	Sister	II	1
	4th cousin	X	5
Reynolds, James Lefevre	Brother	II	1
	4th cousin	X	5
Reynolds, Jane Moore	Sister	II	1
	4th cousin	X	5
Reynolds, John	Father	I	1
	3rd cousin once removed	IX	5
Reynolds, John Fulton	Self		0
	4th cousin	X	5
Reynolds, John Mason	Great-grandnephew	V	4

Name	Relationship with John Reynolds	Civil	Canon
	4th cousin 3 times removed	XIII	8
Reynolds, John Mason	Nephew	III	2
	4th cousin once removed	XI	6
Reynolds, Lydia	Aunt	III	2
	3rd cousin once removed	IX	5
Reynolds, Lydia Moore	Sister	II	1
	4th cousin	X	5
Reynolds, Mary Jane	Sister	II	1
	4th cousin	X	5
Reynolds, Samuel Lefevre	Uncle	III	2
	3rd cousin once removed	IX	5
Reynolds, Samuel Moore	Brother	II	1
	4th cousin	X	5
Reynolds, Sarah McCoy	Niece	III	2
	4th cousin once removed	XI	6
Reynolds, William	Great-grandfather	III	3
Reynolds, William	Grandfather	II	2
	Husband of the 2nd cousin twice removed		
Reynolds, William	Uncle	III	2
	3rd cousin once removed	IX	5
Reynolds, William	Brother	II	1
	4th cousin	X	5
Rice, Anna Mabel	Wife of the 3rd cousin 4 times removed		
	Wife of the 4th cousin 4 times removed		
Richmond, Rebecca T	Wife of the 3rd cousin		
	Wife of the 4th cousin		
Rine, Elizabeth	Wife of the 3rd cousin		
	Wife of the 4th cousin		
Rine, Rebecca	Wife of the 3rd cousin		
	Wife of the 4th cousin		
Ripley, Christiana	Wife of the 3rd cousin		
	Wife of the 4th cousin		
Rissinger, Sandra	Wife of the 3rd cousin 5 times removed		
	Wife of the 4th cousin 5 times removed		
Roach, Living	Husband of the 3rd cousin 5 times removed		
	Husband of the 4th cousin 5 times removed		
Roach, Living	3rd cousin 6 times removed	XIV	10
	4th cousin 6 times removed	XVI	11
Roach, Living	3rd cousin 6 times removed	XIV	10
	4th cousin 6 times removed	XVI	11
Roach, Living	3rd cousin 6 times removed	XIV	10
	4th cousin 6 times removed	XVI	11
Roach, Living	3rd cousin 6 times removed	XIV	10
	4th cousin 6 times removed	XVI	11
Roach, Living	3rd cousin 6 times removed	XIV	10
	4th cousin 6 times removed	XVI	11
Roach, Living	3rd cousin 6 times removed	XIV	10
	4th cousin 6 times removed	XVI	11
Robertson, Living	Husband of the 3rd cousin 5 times removed		
	Husband of the 4th cousin 5 times removed		
Robertson, Living	3rd cousin 6 times removed	XIV	10
	4th cousin 6 times removed	XVI	11
Robinson, Frank	Husband of the 3rd cousin twice removed		
	Husband of the 4th cousin twice removed		
Rockhill, Mr.	Husband of the 3rd cousin		
	Husband of the 4th cousin		
Rogers, Carolyn	Wife of the 3rd cousin 6 times removed		
	Wife of the 4th cousin 6 times removed		
Rogers, Phoebe	Wife of the 3rd cousin		
	Wife of the 4th cousin		
Ross, David	Husband of the 3rd cousin 3 times removed		
	Husband of the 4th cousin 3 times removed		
Ross, Issac D.	Husband of the 3rd cousin		
	Husband of the 4th cousin		

Name	Relationship with John Reynolds	Civil	Canon
Rourke, Robert	Husband of the 3rd cousin 6 times removed		
	Husband of the 4th cousin 6 times removed		
Ruch, John	Husband of the 3rd cousin		
	Husband of the 4th cousin		
Ruthenauff, Margaretta	Wife of the nephew		
	Wife of the 4th cousin once removed		
Saylor, E Cory	Husband of the 3rd cousin		
	Husband of the 4th cousin		
Schaeffer, Michael	Husband of the 2nd cousin once removed		
	Husband of the 3rd cousin once removed		
Schenk, Elizabeth	Wife of the 3rd cousin		
	Wife of the 4th cousin		
Schmid, Henrich	Husband of the 2nd cousin once removed		
	Husband of the 3rd cousin once removed		
Schofstall, Elizabeth	Wife of the granduncle		
	Wife of the 2nd cousin twice removed		
Scott, Ann	3rd cousin 5 times removed	XIII	9
	4th cousin 5 times removed	XV	10
Scott, John LeFevre	3rd cousin 4 times removed	XII	8
	4th cousin 4 times removed	XIV	9
Scott, Leona Grace	3rd cousin 5 times removed	XIII	9
	4th cousin 5 times removed	XV	10
Scott, Margareta June	3rd cousin 4 times removed	XII	8
	4th cousin 4 times removed	XIV	9
Scott, Mary	3rd cousin 5 times removed	XIII	9
	4th cousin 5 times removed	XV	10
Scott, Robert Edward	3rd cousin 4 times removed	XII	8
	4th cousin 4 times removed	XIV	9
Scott, Virginia Ann	3rd cousin 5 times removed	XIII	9
	4th cousin 5 times removed	XV	10
Scott, William	Husband of the 3rd cousin 3 times removed		
	Husband of the 4th cousin 3 times removed		
Scott, William Rine	3rd cousin 4 times removed	XII	8
	4th cousin 4 times removed	XIV	9
Scotty, John	Husband of the niece		
	Husband of the 4th cousin once removed		
Scotty, John F B	Grandnephew	IV	3
	4th cousin twice removed	XII	7
Seaver, Margaret	Wife of the 3rd cousin twice removed		
	Wife of the 4th cousin twice removed		
Seitz, John	Husband of the 2nd cousin once removed		
	Husband of the 3rd cousin once removed		
Seitz, John	Husband of the 2nd cousin once removed		
	Husband of the 3rd cousin once removed		
Shaefer, Magdelena	Wife of the 2nd cousin once removed		
	Wife of the 3rd cousin once removed		
Shank, Martha	Wife of the 3rd cousin		
	Wife of the 4th cousin		
Shannahan, H K	Husband of the great-grandniece		
	Husband of the 4th cousin 3 times removed		
Shapllo, Krenar	Husband of the 3rd cousin 3 times removed		
	Husband of the 4th cousin 3 times removed		
Sheaffer, Alice Margaret	3rd cousin 3 times removed	XI	7
	4th cousin 3 times removed	XIII	8
Sheaffer, Bertie F.	3rd cousin 3 times removed	XI	7
	4th cousin 3 times removed	XIII	8
Sheaffer, Charles M.	3rd cousin 3 times removed	XI	7
	4th cousin 3 times removed	XIII	8
Sheaffer, David	Husband of the 3rd cousin twice removed		
	Husband of the 4th cousin twice removed		
Sheaffer, Doris Madeline	3rd cousin 4 times removed	XII	8
	4th cousin 4 times removed	XIV	9
Sheaffer, J. Marion	Husband of the 3rd cousin twice removed		
	Husband of the 4th cousin twice removed		

Name	Relationship with John Reynolds	Civil	Canon
Sheaffer, Jacob	3rd cousin 3 times removed	XI	7
	4th cousin 3 times removed	XIII	8
Shearer, John	Husband of the 3rd cousin once removed		
	Husband of the 4th cousin once removed		
Shindle, Peter	Husband of the 3rd cousin once removed		
	Husband of the 4th cousin once removed		
Shinn, Elisha	Husband of the 3rd cousin		
	Husband of the 4th cousin		
Shotzer, Blanche	Wife of the 3rd cousin 4 times removed		
	Wife of the 4th cousin 4 times removed		
Shriver, Catherine	Wife of the 3rd cousin		
	Wife of the 4th cousin		
Shroder, Catherine	Wife of the 3rd cousin		
	Wife of the 4th cousin		
Shultz, John	Husband of the 2nd cousin once removed		
	Husband of the 3rd cousin once removed		
Sims, William	Husband of the 3rd cousin once removed		
	Husband of the 4th cousin once removed		
Skagenberg, Richard	Husband of the 3rd cousin 4 times removed		
	Husband of the 4th cousin 4 times removed		
Skelly, William	Husband of the 3rd cousin 3 times removed		
	Husband of the 4th cousin 3 times removed		
Slaymaker, Anna Barbara	Wife of the 1st cousin twice removed		
	Wife of the 2nd cousin twice removed		
Smith, Alexander H.	Husband of the 3rd cousin		
	Husband of the 4th cousin		
Smith, Annie	3rd cousin 3 times removed	XI	7
	4th cousin 3 times removed	XIII	8
Smith, Charles	Husband of the 3rd cousin twice removed		
	Husband of the 4th cousin twice removed		
Smith, David	Husband of the 3rd cousin twice removed		
	Husband of the 4th cousin twice removed		
Smith, Elizabeth J	Wife of the 3rd cousin twice removed		
	Wife of the 4th cousin twice removed		
Smith, Harry	3rd cousin 3 times removed	XI	7
	4th cousin 3 times removed	XIII	8
Smith, Henry	Husband of the 2nd cousin once removed		
	Husband of the 3rd cousin once removed		
Smith, Irene	Wife of the 3rd cousin 3 times removed		
	Wife of the 4th cousin 3 times removed		
Smith, Lorenzo	Husband of the 3rd cousin		
	Husband of the 4th cousin		
Smith, Priscilla	Wife of the 3rd cousin		
	Wife of the 4th cousin		
Snyder, Elizabeth	Wife of the 3rd cousin		
	Wife of the 4th cousin		
Somers, Anne E	Wife of the 3rd cousin		
	Wife of the 4th cousin		
Souder, Samuel	Husband of the 3rd cousin once removed		
	Husband of the 4th cousin once removed		
Speck, Margaret	Wife of the 3rd cousin		
	Wife of the 4th cousin		
Speer, Robert	Husband of the 3rd cousin		
	Husband of the 4th cousin		
Speers, Margaret	Wife of the 3rd cousin		
	Wife of the 4th cousin		
Sperow, Maria	Wife of the 3rd cousin		
	Wife of the 4th cousin		
Stancer, O. P.	Husband of the 3rd cousin 5 times removed		
	Husband of the 4th cousin 5 times removed		
Stanton, John	Husband of the 3rd cousin		
	Husband of the 3rd cousin once removed		
	Husband of the 4th cousin		
	Husband of the 4th cousin once removed		

Name	Relationship with John Reynolds	Civil	Canon
Stark, John	Husband of the 3rd cousin		
	Husband of the 4th cousin		
Statler, Elizabeth	Wife of the 3rd cousin		
	Wife of the 4th cousin		
Steele, Marian Taylor	Wife of the 3rd cousin twice removed		
	Wife of the 4th cousin twice removed		
Stephens, Henry	Husband of the 3rd cousin		
	Husband of the 4th cousin		
Sterling, Catherine	Wife of the 3rd cousin		
	Wife of the 4th cousin		
Stough, Lydia Jane	Wife of the 3rd cousin		
	Wife of the 4th cousin		
Stout, Adam	Husband of the 3rd cousin twice removed		
	Husband of the 4th cousin twice removed		
Strickler, Mary	Wife of the 3rd cousin		
	Wife of the 4th cousin		
Strohm, Henry	Husband of the 2nd cousin once removed		
	Husband of the 3rd cousin once removed		
Stuckwish, Lula	Wife of the 3rd cousin twice removed		
	Wife of the 4th cousin twice removed		
Sulser, Anne Margaret	Wife of the 2nd cousin once removed		
	Wife of the 3rd cousin once removed		
Sultzaberger, Eliza	Wife of the 3rd cousin		
	Wife of the 4th cousin		
Swanson, Gloria	Wife of the 3rd cousin 4 times removed		
	Wife of the 4th cousin 4 times removed		
Sweinhart, Susan E	Wife of the 3rd cousin		
	Wife of the 3rd cousin once removed		
	Wife of the 4th cousin		
	Wife of the 4th cousin once removed		
Swope, Ephraim	Husband of the 3rd cousin		
	Husband of the 4th cousin		
Swope, Rachel	Wife of the 3rd cousin		
	Wife of the 4th cousin		
Swope, Thomas	Husband of the 3rd cousin		
	Husband of the 4th cousin		
Syster, Rebecca	Wife of the 3rd cousin		
	Wife of the 4th cousin		
Taylor, Lawrence R.	Husband of the 3rd cousin 5 times removed		
	Husband of the 4th cousin 5 times removed		
Taylor, Traci Ann	3rd cousin 6 times removed	XIV	10
	4th cousin 6 times removed	XVI	11
Teneycke, Henry	Husband of the 3rd cousin		
	Husband of the 4th cousin		
Thatcher, Joseph	Husband of the 3rd cousin		
	Husband of the 4th cousin		
Thornberg, Robert	Husband of the 3rd cousin		
	Husband of the 4th cousin		
Thornton, Living	Wife of the 3rd cousin 4 times removed		
	Wife of the 4th cousin 4 times removed		
Tidwell, Mary Dorris	Wife of the 3rd cousin 3 times removed		
	Wife of the 4th cousin 3 times removed		
Tobias, Jennie E.	Wife of the 3rd cousin twice removed		
	Wife of the 4th cousin twice removed		
Tobias, Rebecca	Wife of the 3rd cousin		
	Wife of the 4th cousin		
Tomilson, Robert	Husband of the 3rd cousin 6 times removed		
	Husband of the 4th cousin 6 times removed		
Tritt, Alice Bell	3rd cousin 3 times removed	XI	7
	4th cousin 3 times removed	XIII	8
Tritt, Alice E.	3rd cousin 3 times removed	XI	7
	4th cousin 3 times removed	XIII	8
Tritt, Anne	3rd cousin	VIII	4
	4th cousin	X	5

Name	Relationship with John Reynolds	Civil	Canon
Tritt, Barbara	3rd cousin	VIII	4
	4th cousin	X	5
Tritt, Barbara	3rd cousin	VIII	4
	4th cousin	X	5
Tritt, Catherine	3rd cousin	VIII	4
	4th cousin	X	5
Tritt, Christian	3rd cousin	VIII	4
	4th cousin	X	5
Tritt, Christian	3rd cousin twice removed	X	6
	4th cousin twice removed	XII	7
Tritt, Clarence E.	3rd cousin 3 times removed	XI	7
	4th cousin 3 times removed	XIII	8
Tritt, Clarence Ziegler	3rd cousin 3 times removed	XI	7
	4th cousin 3 times removed	XIII	8
Tritt, Edgar P.	3rd cousin 3 times removed	XI	7
	4th cousin 3 times removed	XIII	8
Tritt, Eliza	Wife of the 3rd cousin twice removed		
	Wife of the 4th cousin twice removed		
Tritt, Elizabeth	3rd cousin	VIII	4
	4th cousin	X	5
Tritt, Elizabeth	3rd cousin twice removed	X	6
	4th cousin twice removed	XII	7
Tritt, Florence E.	3rd cousin 3 times removed	XI	7
	4th cousin 3 times removed	XIII	8
Tritt, George	3rd cousin	VIII	4
	4th cousin	X	5
Tritt, J. Miller	3rd cousin once removed	IX	5
	4th cousin once removed	XI	6
Tritt, Jacob	3rd cousin	VIII	4
	4th cousin	X	5
Tritt, John	3rd cousin	VIII	4
	4th cousin	X	5
	Husband of the 3rd cousin		
	Husband of the 4th cousin		
Tritt, John A.	3rd cousin twice removed	X	6
	4th cousin twice removed	XII	7
Tritt, Joseph	3rd cousin	VIII	4
	4th cousin	X	5
Tritt, Lydia Jane	3rd cousin twice removed	X	6
	4th cousin twice removed	XII	7
Tritt, Maggie T.	3rd cousin twice removed	X	6
	4th cousin twice removed	XII	7
Tritt, Mary Jane	3rd cousin twice removed	X	6
	4th cousin twice removed	XII	7
Tritt, Maud T.	3rd cousin 3 times removed	XI	7
	4th cousin 3 times removed	XIII	8
Tritt, Melvin J.	3rd cousin 3 times removed	XI	7
	4th cousin 3 times removed	XIII	8
Tritt, Peter	Husband of the 2nd cousin once removed		
	Husband of the 3rd cousin once removed		
Tritt, Peter	3rd cousin	VIII	4
	4th cousin	X	5
Tritt, Peter	3rd cousin once removed	IX	5
	4th cousin once removed	XI	6
Tritt, Peter Stough	3rd cousin twice removed	X	6
	4th cousin twice removed	XII	7
Tritt, Samuel	3rd cousin	VIII	4
	4th cousin	X	5
Tritt, Samuel John	3rd cousin twice removed	X	6
	4th cousin twice removed	XII	7
Tritt, William K.	3rd cousin	VIII	4
	4th cousin	X	5
Trout, Adam	Husband of the 2nd cousin		
	Husband of the 4th cousin		

Name	Relationship with John Reynolds	Civil	Canon
Trout, Hannah	Wife of the 2nd cousin		
	Wife of the 4th cousin		
Tullis, Malissa	Wife of the 3rd cousin		
	Wife of the 4th cousin		
Twigg, Naomi	Wife of the 3rd cousin		
	Wife of the 4th cousin		
Unknown, Ellen M	Wife of the 3rd cousin twice removed		
	Wife of the 4th cousin twice removed		
Unknown, Eve	Wife of the 1st cousin twice removed		
	Wife of the 2nd cousin twice removed		
Unknown, Mary	Wife of the 2nd great-granduncle		
Unknown, Sara M	Wife of the 3rd cousin twice removed		
	Wife of the 4th cousin twice removed		
Unknown, Susanna	Wife of the 1st cousin twice removed		
	Wife of the 2nd cousin twice removed		
Vogelsong, Glenda	Wife of the 3rd cousin 6 times removed		
	Wife of the 4th cousin 6 times removed		
von Borcke, Otto	Husband of the grandniece		
	Husband of the 4th cousin twice removed		
Von Colson, Henrietta Louisa	Wife of the 2nd cousin once removed		
	Wife of the 3rd cousin once removed		
Vondersmith, John Valentine	Husband of the 2nd cousin once removed		
	Husband of the 3rd cousin once removed		
Wakely, Susan	Wife of the 3rd cousin 6 times removed		
	Wife of the 4th cousin 6 times removed		
Wambaugh, Julia	Wife of the 3rd cousin		
	Wife of the 4th cousin		
Warrenbuer, Mary	3rd great-grandmother	V	5
Watson, Mary	Wife of the 3rd cousin		
	Wife of the 4th cousin		
Weaver, Barbara	Wife of the 3rd cousin		
	Wife of the 4th cousin		
Weaver, Johnathan	Husband of the 3rd cousin		
	Husband of the 4th cousin		
Weaver, Mary Grace	Wife of the 3rd cousin 4 times removed		
	Wife of the 4th cousin 4 times removed		
Weaver, Theodore Floyd	3rd cousin 5 times removed	XIII	9
	4th cousin 5 times removed	XV	10
Weaver, William Shively	Husband of the 3rd cousin 4 times removed		
	Husband of the 4th cousin 4 times removed		
Weber, Jonathan	Husband of the 1st cousin twice removed		
	Husband of the 2nd cousin twice removed		
Weigle, Carolyn Ann	Wife of the 3rd cousin 5 times removed		
	Wife of the 4th cousin 5 times removed		
Wenger, Ethan Richard	3rd cousin 7 times removed	XV	11
	4th cousin 7 times removed	XVII	12
Wenger, Laura Beth	3rd cousin 7 times removed	XV	11
	4th cousin 7 times removed	XVII	12
Wenger, Lynn Richard	Husband of the 3rd cousin 6 times removed		
	Husband of the 4th cousin 6 times removed		
Wenger, Seth Jonathan	3rd cousin 7 times removed	XV	11
	4th cousin 7 times removed	XVII	12
Wengert, Diane	Wife of the 3rd cousin 5 times removed		
	Wife of the 4th cousin 5 times removed		
Wertz, Julia C	Wife of the 3rd cousin		
	Wife of the 4th cousin		
West, Adam Leroy	Husband of the 3rd cousin 5 times removed		
	Husband of the 4th cousin 5 times removed		
West, Barbara Elaine	3rd cousin 6 times removed	XIV	10
	4th cousin 6 times removed	XVI	11
West, Diane Elizabeth	3rd cousin 6 times removed	XIV	10
	4th cousin 6 times removed	XVI	11
Wheeler, Amasa	Husband of the 3rd cousin		
	Husband of the 4th cousin		

Name	Relationship with John Reynolds	Civil	Canon
White, Emily Faline	3rd cousin 4 times removed	XII	8
	4th cousin 4 times removed	XIV	9
White, Henry	Husband of the 3rd cousin once removed		
	Husband of the 4th cousin once removed		
White, McKenzie	3rd cousin 5 times removed	XIII	9
	4th cousin 5 times removed	XV	10
White, Shelby	3rd cousin 5 times removed	XIII	9
	4th cousin 5 times removed	XV	10
White, William Walter	Husband of the 3rd cousin twice removed		
	Husband of the 4th cousin twice removed		
White, William Walter	3rd cousin 3 times removed	XI	7
	4th cousin 3 times removed	XIII	8
White, William Walter	3rd cousin 4 times removed	XII	8
	4th cousin 4 times removed	XIV	9
Whiteman, Anne	Wife of the 3rd cousin once removed		
	Wife of the 4th cousin once removed		
Whiting, Judith	Wife of the 3rd cousin		
	Wife of the 4th cousin		
Whitmyer, George	Husband of the 3rd cousin		
	Husband of the 4th cousin		
Wiegner, Hannah	Wife of the 2nd cousin once removed		
	Wife of the 3rd cousin once removed		
Wilhelm, Lavina	Wife of the 3rd cousin		
	Wife of the 4th cousin		
Williams, Howard Jones	Husband of the 3rd cousin twice removed		
	Husband of the 4th cousin twice removed		
Williams, Howard Jones	3rd cousin 3 times removed	XI	7
	4th cousin 3 times removed	XIII	8
Williams, Ober Wolf	3rd cousin 3 times removed	XI	7
	4th cousin 3 times removed	XIII	8
Williams, Ruth L	3rd cousin 3 times removed	XI	7
	4th cousin 3 times removed	XIII	8
Wills	Wife of the 3rd cousin		
	Wife of the 4th cousin		
Wills, Robert	Husband of the 3rd cousin		
	Husband of the 4th cousin		
Wilson, Patricia A	3rd cousin 4 times removed	XII	8
	4th cousin 4 times removed	XIV	9
Wilson, Richard	Husband of the 3rd cousin 3 times removed		
	Husband of the 4th cousin 3 times removed		
Wilson, Richard, Jr	3rd cousin 4 times removed	XII	8
	4th cousin 4 times removed	XIV	9
Wilt, Harriet	Wife of the 3rd cousin		
	Wife of the 4th cousin		
Witmer, Esther	Wife of the 2nd cousin once removed		
	Wife of the 3rd cousin once removed		
Witmer, Jacob	Husband of the 1st cousin once removed		
	Husband of the 3rd cousin once removed		
Witmer, Jacob	Husband of the 3rd cousin		
	Husband of the 4th cousin		
Witmer, John	Husband of the 3rd cousin		
	Husband of the 4th cousin		
Woglemuth, Gordon	Husband of the 3rd cousin 7 times removed		
	Husband of the 4th cousin 7 times removed		
Woglemuth, Sean	3rd cousin 8 times removed	XVI	12
	4th cousin 8 times removed	XVIII	13
Wolf, Alice K	3rd cousin 3 times removed	XI	7
	4th cousin 3 times removed	XIII	8
Wolf, Alice K	3rd cousin 4 times removed	XII	8
	4th cousin 4 times removed	XIV	9
Wolf, Anna B	3rd cousin twice removed	X	6
	4th cousin twice removed	XII	7
Wolf, Barbara	3rd cousin once removed	IX	5
	4th cousin once removed	XI	6

Name	Relationship with John Reynolds	Civil	Canon
Wolf, Barbara Ann	3rd cousin 3 times removed	XI	7
	4th cousin 3 times removed	XIII	8
Wolf, Barbara J	3rd cousin 3 times removed	XI	7
	4th cousin 3 times removed	XIII	8
Wolf, Catherine Rebecca	3rd cousin twice removed	X	6
	4th cousin twice removed	XII	7
Wolf, Clarence Franklin	3rd cousin 3 times removed	XI	7
	4th cousin 3 times removed	XIII	8
Wolf, Clarence R	3rd cousin twice removed	X	6
	4th cousin twice removed	XII	7
Wolf, Daniel Lefevre	3rd cousin once removed	IX	5
	4th cousin once removed	XI	6
Wolf, David	3rd cousin once removed	IX	5
	4th cousin once removed	XI	6
Wolf, David O	3rd cousin 3 times removed	XI	7
	4th cousin 3 times removed	XIII	8
Wolf, David Ober	3rd cousin twice removed	X	6
	4th cousin twice removed	XII	7
Wolf, Edgar	3rd cousin 3 times removed	XI	7
	4th cousin 3 times removed	XIII	8
Wolf, Emma	3rd cousin twice removed	X	6
	4th cousin twice removed	XII	7
Wolf, Forest R	3rd cousin twice removed	X	6
	4th cousin twice removed	XII	7
Wolf, Frank Jacob	3rd cousin twice removed	X	6
	4th cousin twice removed	XII	7
Wolf, Franklin Earl	3rd cousin twice removed	X	6
	4th cousin twice removed	XII	7
Wolf, Franklin Earl	3rd cousin 3 times removed	XI	7
	4th cousin 3 times removed	XIII	8
Wolf, Franklin LeFevere	3rd cousin once removed	IX	5
	4th cousin once removed	XI	6
Wolf, George Edgar	3rd cousin twice removed	X	6
	4th cousin twice removed	XII	7
Wolf, George W	Husband of the 3rd cousin		
	Husband of the 4th cousin		
Wolf, Harold C	3rd cousin 3 times removed	XI	7
	4th cousin 3 times removed	XIII	8
Wolf, Harry E	3rd cousin twice removed	X	6
	4th cousin twice removed	XII	7
Wolf, Harvey J	3rd cousin twice removed	X	6
	4th cousin twice removed	XII	7
Wolf, Helen P	3rd cousin 3 times removed	XI	7
	4th cousin 3 times removed	XIII	8
Wolf, Holly Ann	3rd cousin 4 times removed	XII	8
	4th cousin 4 times removed	XIV	9
Wolf, John Motter	3rd cousin twice removed	X	6
	4th cousin twice removed	XII	7
Wolf, John S	3rd cousin 3 times removed	XI	7
	4th cousin 3 times removed	XIII	8
Wolf, Levi F	3rd cousin twice removed	X	6
	4th cousin twice removed	XII	7
Wolf, Lydia Ann	3rd cousin once removed	IX	5
	4th cousin once removed	XI	6
Wolf, Mabel E	3rd cousin twice removed	X	6
	4th cousin twice removed	XII	7
Wolf, Margaret	Wife of the 3rd cousin		
	Wife of the 4th cousin		
Wolf, Margaret M	3rd cousin 4 times removed	XII	8
	4th cousin 4 times removed	XIV	9
Wolf, Maria	3rd cousin 4 times removed	XII	8
	4th cousin 4 times removed	XIV	9
Wolf, Marian Elizabeth	3rd cousin 3 times removed	XI	7
	4th cousin 3 times removed	XIII	8

Name	Relationship with John Reynolds	Civil	Canon
Wolf, Marjorie Ann	3rd cousin 3 times removed	XI	7
	4th cousin 3 times removed	XIII	8
Wolf, Mary E	3rd cousin 3 times removed	XI	7
	4th cousin 3 times removed	XIII	8
Wolf, Mary E	3rd cousin 4 times removed	XII	8
	4th cousin 4 times removed	XIV	9
Wolf, Mary Estelle	3rd cousin twice removed	X	6
	4th cousin twice removed	XII	7
Wolf, Mary L	3rd cousin 3 times removed	XI	7
	4th cousin 3 times removed	XIII	8
Wolf, Nellie I	3rd cousin twice removed	X	6
	4th cousin twice removed	XII	7
Wolf, Nora	3rd cousin 3 times removed	XI	7
	4th cousin 3 times removed	XIII	8
Wolf, Ray	3rd cousin 4 times removed	XII	8
	4th cousin 4 times removed	XIV	9
Wolf, Sarah	3rd cousin once removed	IX	5
	4th cousin once removed	XI	6
Wolf, Walter S	3rd cousin 3 times removed	XI	7
	4th cousin 3 times removed	XIII	8
Wolfe, Sara	Wife of the 3rd cousin once removed		
	Wife of the 4th cousin once removed		
Womer, James	Husband of the 3rd cousin 3 times removed		
	Husband of the 4th cousin 3 times removed		
Wood, Robert W.	Husband of the 3rd cousin		
	Husband of the 4th cousin		
Wright, Frances	Wife of the 3rd cousin twice removed		
	Wife of the 4th cousin twice removed		
Zeller, Mary	Wife of the 1st cousin twice removed		
	Wife of the 2nd cousin twice removed		
Zook, David	Husband of the 3rd cousin		
	Husband of the 4th cousin		
Zuk, David	Husband of the 2nd cousin once removed		
	Husband of the 3rd cousin once removed		

Index of Individuals

Susanna: 153, 251
Boyer -
   Amanda M: 224
   Samuel S: 143, 251
Braden -
   Adaline: 167, 251
Brenner -
   Anna Barabara: 210
Brook -
   Wayne: 220, 251
Brown -
   Catherine: 177, 251
   Frank A.: 213, 225, 251
   Harry D.: 213, 225, 232, 238,
      244, 245, 251
   Living: 232, 238, 244, 245, 251
   Living: 238, 244, 245, 251
   Living: 238, 245, 251
   Living: 238, 245, 251
   Living: 225, 251
   Living: 232, 251
   Living: 233, 251
   Living: 233, 251
   Living: 233, 251
   Living: 225, 251, 252
   Living: 225, 252
   Living: 225, 252
   Mary B.: 208, 209, 252
   Nathan: 163, 252
   Nathaniel P: 212, 213, 252
Brua -
   Susan: 170, 252
Brubaker -
   Susan: 166, 252
Buchanan -
   John: 208, 252
Buchman -
   Gary Kyle: 244, 252
   Glenn: 244, 252
Buckwalter -
   Martin: 152, 252
Buffington -
   Ruth: 109, 252
Burnham -
   Lela Berneice: 224, 252

Burnish -
   Alice Rebecca: 237
Burns -
   Claudia: 207, 252
Byers -
   Joseph: 180, 252
Cahill -
   Betty Jane: 240, 252
Calaman -
   Lawrence Delmar: 227, 252
Calvert -
   Peter: 186, 252
Camp -
   Mary Ann: 161, 162, 252
   Polly: 161, 252
Carpenter -
   Salome: 106, 148, 149, 252
Carter -
   Gertrude Lucile: 219, 252
Cassell -
   John: 208, 252
Cease -
   Margaret: 162, 252
Cecil -
   Nancy: 176, 252
Chaffin -
   Ida: 228, 252
Christy -
   Henry: 135, 252
Clack -
   Elizabeth: 166, 252
Clark -
   Augustus: 188, 252
Clausen -
   Ruth: 228, 252
Cole -
   Miriam: 159, 252
Colle -
   Marceline Elodia: 223, 253
Committus -
   Joy: 247, 253
Cooper -
   Lorraine Marie: 243
Copley -
   James: 239, 253